COSMIC THEOGONY

Other Books by Ashish Dalela:

The Science of God
Time and Consciousness
Conceiving the Inconceivable
The Balanced Organization
The Yellow Pill
Emotion
Mystic Universe
Moral Materialism
Signs of Life
Uncommon Wisdom
Gödel's Mistake
Quantum Meaning
Sāṅkhya and Science
Is the Apple Really Red?
Six Causes

COSMIC THEOGONY

The Personalization of Nature

Ashish Dalela

Cosmic Theogony—The Personalization of Nature
by Ashish Dalela
www.shabda.co

Interior Design: Ciprian Begu
Cover Design: SN

Published by Shabda Press
www.press.shabda.co
ISBN 978-93-85384-11-0
v1.5(03/2021)

SHABDA
PRESS

Dedicated to Sri Chaitanya Mahaprabhu, who envisioned the ecumenical unity of world religions based on the chanting of the Holy Names of God—regardless of the different names envisioned in those religions—dialoguing with the members of other religions and emphasizing that in this age of quarrels there is only one way to find peace and happiness: the chanting of the Holy Names of God.

But it is not proper to constantly propagate the controversial superiority of the teachers of one's own country over those of another country although one may, nay one should, cherish such a belief in order to acquire steadiness in a faith of your own. But no good can be affected to the world by such quarrels.

—Srila Bhaktivinode Thakur

Another important point mentioned in this connection is anindaya [avoiding blasphemy]—we should not criticise others' methods of religion. A devotee, instead of criticising such systems, will encourage the followers to stick to their principles.

—Srila A. C. Bhaktivedānta Swami Prabhupāda

Contents

List of Figures

List of Tables

Preface

It is possible to see history through the eyes of religious change. But I'm not going to do that. The description of history is fraught with problems, and religious history has even more. It is nearly impossible to decipher the exact events of most religions by taking into account their literal records because every new religion has to contend with the problem of accumulating followers who do not adhere to the same set of beliefs. To gain new followers, the new religion must (1) delineate problems in the previous religions, (2) without antagonizing their current followers. This is a very difficult issue. On the one hand there is a push toward a new belief system which motivates the new followers. On the other hand, there are the followers who want to retain many of the older ideas. This creates inherent contradictions in the religion, which must be resolved through ideological compromises. But once a compromise is made, the reasons for which it was made must be obfuscated to avoid the impression that the ideology was altered to suit a particular group of followers. Revealing such compromises makes the religion tenuous and uncertain about its principles and encourages others to demand similar concessions in the future.

Most modern religions have made such concessions over the ages because the religious establishment was compelled to increase its followers for monetary, social, political, and cultural gains. The reasons for such changes were often obfuscated to prevent the demand for more changes, and hence the self-authored history of such religions is sometimes not a reliable source of information about the real causes of change, as their records had to be modified multiple times to gain a new set of followers, strengthen the establishment, or gain entrance into a new society and culture. The stated history can be trusted only when the religion doesn't have an establishment obliged to grow its following or strengthen its social, political, or cultural position. To achieve that status, the spiritual beliefs of the religion must be disconnected from the cultural and political aims of the practitioners. Whenever religion has been mixed with politics and culture, it has been owned by an establishment that has diluted its purpose through compromises to further its own position.

You can have a political system subordinated to religious edicts, if the religion has no political ambitions—e.g., power, wealth, or followers. But you cannot have a religious system subordinated to the political ends of its followers, because the religious principles are then compromised by politics. In that sense, the preceptors of religion—the priestly class of people—must be separate from politics (the separation of politics and religion in modern times) but the political system must be subordinated to the religious one. For most of the recent past, two alternatives have been followed. First, the religious institutions had political ambitions and the religious leader desired to control the population. Second, when religion and politics were separated, the political system became independent of the moral values espoused by religion. At this juncture, the history was written by the political system, not the religious one. Specifically, the political system had to deemphasize the importance of religion in day-to-day life, and its influence on the citizens' thought process.

Neither of these alternatives bodes well for an accurate historical depiction of the religion and how it evolved from its predecessors because when religion is enmeshed with politics then it rewrites its own history after modifying its principles, and when religion and politics are totally separated, then politics continually undermines the role of religion, creating a schism in which either religion must lose out to politics (e.g., communism) or religion must gain control over the political system (e.g., theocracy). In either case, the written records have either been tampered with by religious institutions themselves or partly obliterated by the political class as part of persecuting religion.

Therefore, I consider seeing world history through the lenses of religions too imprecise to have a constructive impact on our religious life. I find that a more reliable approach to studying the evolution of modern religions is to break away from records and look at cultures and religions that might seem superficially different from each other, but share numerous ideological, symbolical, cultural, or social similarities. The stated differences between the histories in such cases are not as useful as the cultural and ideological similarities. The similarities between religions give us clues about continuity and how one religion shared the ideas from others and imbibed its culture, symbolism, ideology, and imagery, in order to gain followers from their predecessors.

This is then what this book will try to do. It will show similarities across cultures in terms of their religious practices but refrain from interpreting that similarity into an *evolution.* People often write history in order to feel good about themselves, and the historians are compelled to tell a story that takes the reader thousands of years in the past in terms of their antecedents. Such projects of painting a great past have been tried and continue to be written. But beyond the feel-good factor, they present little religious value.

My approach differs in this respect. My goal is to focus on the religion, not the history and politics of it. I don't want to paint a picture of how one religion evolved from another over time, but the fact that a religion with a certain type of worship and gods existed. How it changed, why it changed, and who thought who was better than whom is not primarily of concern to me. In other words, I just want to *collect* the dots over the ages and aggregate them into unique classes, see how the classes themselves are related or different, without trying to *connect* the dots in terms of how one thing evolved from another. The reader is free to fill in the blanks on their own—if they so wish—and I do anticipate that similarities prompt people to speculate on the actual evolution.

For example, when Darwin saw a similarity between apes and humans, he speculated that humans came from apes. I have never understood why the reverse could not be said—e.g., that some humans left civilization and started living in forests and thereby developed a body or lifestyle suited to jungle life. Instead of considering men as advanced apes, we could think of apes as uncivilized men. What drives one toward one type of interpretation over another? Was there a need in Darwin—and Europeans in general—to paint themselves as the pinnacle of the human evolution, implying in the process that everyone else was inferior by contrast? My point is that evolutionary history has many problems. It can never find enough evidence to substantiate its evolutionary claims, but in the process, it diverts our attention from the main point, namely, that there are numerous similarities which can assist a *classification.*

Inferring classification into evolution is what historians and evolutionists like to do, but I will not be so audacious. I will stick to classification because I think inferring evolution—through assessment of historical events—is a very hard problem. In the case of living species, for example, it is relatively easy to draw a tree of life forms but claiming that one species evolved from another is much harder: We were never there to know if it actually happened. Of course, drawing the tree itself is not trivial. Have we considered all the different forms? Should we attach one life form to one branch of the tree vs. another? Above all, what is the trunk of the tree from which the branches have emanated?

Drawing out that tree of classification among religious ideas is what this book will try to do. In other words, which theology is more primordial, which other theology details the idea in the primordial ideology, and can lead to other kinds of theologies? If we draw such a tree of ideological and theological diversification, and if that tree of diversification proves robust in the sense of being able to depict highly diverse forms of religions into a consistent picture—at least as a way of classifying the religions—then it is possible to talk about the evolution of one religion from another, not purely in the sense that one religion *became* another, but in the sense that ideas of one are logically related to the other and to the preexisting ideas native to the culture that adopted the new religion. Such idea exchanges don't have definite historical records in all cases. In many cases, as we noted above, the history is itself rewritten to prove its novelty and departure from the past, in order to mark a new beginning.

Human ideological evolution follows a gradual change over long periods of time, followed by sudden upheavals in thinking. Thomas Kuhn[1] identified this pattern in the case of scientific revolutions where an ideological change is resisted for long periods of time until the evidence against it becomes overwhelming. Biologists have similarly found ages where a sudden burst of new species is found, that did not emerge through a gradual step-by-step change[2]. Technological change also follows a similar kind of pattern in which old and established technologies—that were previously developed and improved over long periods of time—are rapidly replaced by new ones[3]. The economic cycles of boom and bust are too well known to be ignored[4]. Social cycle theorists[5] have similarly argued for the cycles in civilizational evolution[6]. There is no reason why religious and theological change must follow a different pattern. In general, tracing the exact historical events which sow the seeds of such eventual disruption is very hard, because until the time when the disruption occurs, the agents of such change remain subterranean and tend to be disregarded. It is only much later that one can see the seed of the future in the past, but why suddenly that seed germinates into a full-blown tree remains a mystery. Often the seeds that bring the winds of change remain unknown. Therefore, it is difficult to objectively trace the histories based on current records. It is easier to simply draw a tree of theologies based on the ideas themselves.

Drawing such a tree of theologies requires a *theory* of religion in which we distinguish between primary and secondary concepts and show how the secondary concepts can—or could—be derived from the primary ones. Like we draw trees of various species of life, of scientific theories and philosophical claims, similarly it is possible to draw a tree of theologies through the study of similarities and differences between the different religions. In the interest of full disclosure, I will use Vedic philosophy to delineate this tree for three main reasons. First, the Vedic system of religion is highly diverse; even within the surviving traditions there are *Shaiva*, *Shakta*, and *Vaishnava* traditions with their own literature. Second, these systems of religion have many tiers in which the primary principle is expanded into secondary principles. Third, and this is most important, there is a way to understand their unity. In short, we have a *template* of enormous diversity from a singular unity. The Vedic texts describe religion as diverse roads that lead to the same destination. These roads are the leaves and branches that terminate into the same root.

Most modern commentators on Vedic philosophy do not understand this tree, because they don't even consider the possibility that these constitute a single system. They see different texts and find new and disparate ideas. Then, in order to describe the system as a whole, they postulate an *evolution* of ideas—positing that one text is prior and the other text is subsequent—when according to the texts themselves, they existed in oral form much before they were written down. The date of writing them down isn't important; of course, they were written in order, but more important is the fact that they existed in parallel before. The Vedic system did not encourage textual recording of knowledge; the system encouraged the passing of knowledge from teacher to disciple. The recorded history of the Vedic system through books is therefore recent, and just because you can date a book to a time doesn't mean that date actually constitutes the origin of the ideas recorded in the book itself.

In the same vein, the ideas in other religious texts—e.g., the Genesis story in the Bible—should be presumed to have existed in the culture before they were written down. They may have been borrowed from other cultures, or they were revealed by enlightened teachers at some point but recorded much later. The New Testament is itself a text that was recorded many years after Jesus, so the pattern of an oral tradition getting formalized into books is quite common. The origin of what exists in a religious text cannot be traced simply to the date at which the text was authored. This pattern is seen repeatedly in Vedic texts when they record the exposition on a topic as a conversation between a teacher and a disciple. Clearly, the teacher is not saying things to the student that he hasn't himself heard or understood in the past from others. Similarly, it is not necessary that the conversation was recorded exactly when it was spoken, and this is particularly true of the Vedic records. A reliable way of understanding the ideas in religious texts is to relate the ideas to each other and provide a systematic and complete picture of their interrelations.

In other words, we don't dwell on who said to whom and when, but what was actually said, and how it relates to the sayings from other conversations. The *content* is of greater importance than the vehicles of its presentation. The vehicles may be numerous and diverse, and the quoted vehicle may come earlier or later in time, but that doesn't indicate the age of the idea itself. In that specific sense, the histories of ideological presentation are completely irrelevant to the content itself—presuming that the ideas are true. Of course, if the ideas aren't true, because they were modified to fit a particular ideology, then history becomes relevant to understand if these things were modified and when and for what purpose. Given that we cannot accurately trace these events in all cases, I will not suppose that the ideas were modified—although we do know that in several cases modifications were likely made. I will instead restrict myself to what we know and avoid conspiracy theories.

There is a particular kind of picture I expect to assemble through such an analysis, which is not unique to religion or theology, but applies to any grouping of ideas. The picture I have in mind is that of a *tree*, and I will explain here why this picture should be expected. When any kind of ideological system is analyzed, we often find the use of circular logic or the existence of contradictions. Circular logic involves justifying an idea based on itself—e.g., the *Ontological Argument* for the existence of God[7]. Similarly, contradictions within a system—e.g., free will combined with eternal hell or heaven, which deny a continued role for free will—lead to internal inconsistencies. A picture that explains theologies must avoid these two problems, and that entails the picture of ideas must be *loop-free*. A loop can exist in two ways. First, it can exist as a circle—where an argument is used to justify itself. Second, it can exist as a *Möbius strip*[8] where the claims result in a self-contradiction. For a system to be consistent and not employ circular logic, it should be depicted as a tree because a tree is a loop-free structure, free of self-contradictions. This structure follows simply from the need for self-consistency and clarity within the system of ideas, and is not particularly dependent on religion or theology per se.

The systems of religion—if there is indeed truth in religion—must be depicted through a tree; they must originate in a root and branch out into many leaves. The diversity of ideas is a problem if each idea claims to be the root—this is a common fact about all religions as they claim to be the absolute root. But this problem doesn't necessarily entail that one religion is true while the others are false simply because they are different or inconsistent. It is also possible that the unity between them is not perceived because they are not the roots, but actually branches of a tree whose root has been neglected.

The tree of ideological diversification presents us with the process by which we can understand different religions in which a single God—i.e., monotheism—would constitute the root, but as this root diversifies into other branches other forms of God—i.e., polytheism—would also manifest. The diverse branches can be understood as different *paths* to the final destination or the root, meant for different types of people based on their ideological and theological proclivities. For instance, if someone wants to worship God through nature, there can be an understanding in which a form of God is perceived in nature. Likewise, if one wants to worship God through their work, another form of God that appears in our activities—if those activities are performed properly—can be understood. Some people might want to understand God through knowledge, others might like to perform meditation, and yet others believe in the performance of specific rituals. Finally, some people might consider themselves eternal and hence god-like, because God manifests in each individual person through His qualities. Each method appears to describe a different process and understanding of God, which leads to an unnecessary conflict if the diverse paths are not connected toward a single goal.

In Vedic philosophy, the many 'gods' of polytheism are subordinate to the single root of monotheism. Vedic texts describe how God expands into many forms—like a whole has many parts, like a concept has diverse instantiations, and like a long-term goal manifests into many short-term goals. The existence of smaller parts, individual instances, or short-term goals doesn't deny the reality of the bigger picture, unless, of course, we ignore the fact that these are branches of the tree, not its root. God—as the root of this tree—can be seen as the principle of unity in diversity, whereas the soul is the principle of diversity who desires different things which are in turn parts, instances, and shorter-term goals of the whole. The tree structure helps us reconcile the diversity into a unity, solves the problem of their apparent contradiction, and helps us see how different paths are useful for different people to help them progress toward a single destination. Religion is then viewed as a *path* whereas God is understood as the final goal, complete truth, and the original person.

Vedic philosophy describes both material and transcendental worlds as trees diversifying from a root. The diversity is the *energy* of God, and the unity is God. The diversifying energy has both material and spiritual forms, which means that both material and spiritual worlds are trees, with their origin in God. The soul is the choice of being at one of the many locations on the tree. Through its choices, the soul moves on the tree, adopts different positions and different religious ideologies are included in the position on the tree. There are innumerable branches of the tree, which means that there are innumerable true religions, which lead to the same destination. However, there are also false ideas on the same tree which cause the soul to go around in circles.

The truth is loop-free, and the lies are loopy. Therefore, if we focus on the tree, we will find all that is true. Once we understand that truth, we can also see how some ideas are loopy, which are also inconsistent or circular. Finally, we can see that on the tree some places are closer to the root while others are farther from it. Therefore, even if some ideas are true (because they are loop-free) they are not as complete a truth as the ones closer to the root. Hence, using the tree we can not only separate the truth from the lies, but also organize the truth using a hierarchy from less complete to more complete.

An example of incomplete truth is the reality of the self regardless of other souls and God. Vedic texts describe that in between the material and the spiritual diversities lies a realm called *Brahman* in which the soul sees his own reality but remains unaware of any other diversity. Self-existence is certainly a truth, but it is an *incomplete* truth, because other things exist as well. This, in particular, includes the existence of other souls, and material reality. The soul presents the unity in the diversity of its own experiences. However, God represents the unity in the diversity of different souls. He is called the Supreme Soul because all other souls are parts of God. Therefore, when the diversity between the souls and the unity of these souls in God is not understood then the eternity of the self is only realized as a partial truth. In the material world, the souls are distinguished based on their material roles, bodies, and personalities. If these roles, bodies, and personalities are discarded, then the distinction between the souls disappears in a *material* sense. We are then unable to distinguish between the souls, and this *indistinguishability* presents a form of ignorance which can also be conceived as a *unity* although it is not truly a unity. This region of reality is called *Brahman* and it constitutes the realm of souls that are unable to distinguish between the different souls because they haven't yet realized that this unity is God. If we disregard the diversity of souls, then each individual soul becomes the unity of the diversified material experiences. One has to transcend this material unity to see the diversity of souls and then another kind of unity which God is, then one has to transcend the *Brahman* realization.

Every dominant religious tradition—monotheism, polytheism, and impersonalism—exists within the Vedic tradition. Accompanying these philosophies there are also different methods of religious practice ranging from purely philosophical, to purely ritualistic, to purely mystical, to purely mundane. Accordingly, religious practice is defined in *jnana-yoga* as the pursuit of higher truth, in *karma-kānda* as the performance of rituals, in *aśtānga-yoga* as mystical practices, in *karma-yoga* as the execution of one's prescribed duties, and in *bhakti-yoga* as devotion to God in paternal, fraternal, conjugal, or servitor relations. Over the ages, people have used one or more of these paths, and indeed all the paths are complementary and yield different benefits.

Just as God manifests into many forms as His parts, functions, and goals, similarly, in the material world, God delegates the parts, functions, and goals to other living beings who are not God—they are called *demigods*. Like an ambassador represents the ruler but is actually not the ruler, similarly, the demigods have the delegated and representative power of

God, but they are not God. Celestial bodies such as the sun, the moon, planets, and stars are agents of delegated power, through which they control the parts, functions, and goals of our life. The demigods[9] (*polytheism*) are different from the many forms of God (*monotheism*)—because the demigod is a *role* occupied by a person for a fixed duration of time. Unlike God, Whose person is the role—i.e., He never relinquishes the role—the demigods are powerful positions occupied by living beings only temporarily. Polytheism is true, but it is subordinate to monotheism. When someone worships a demigod, and the person occupying that role changes, the new person in the role is responsible for the rewards.

The existence of diverse theological positions, combined with the diverse paths on which these goals can be achieved, followed by the inclusion of demigods as powerful delegates of God, makes the Vedic system extremely diverse, and hence a good *template* for understanding both religious diversity and its unification. I will therefore spend considerable effort in describing this diversity and how it is unified, in order to construct a tree of diversification. The tree involves not just personalities and individuals, but a considerable amount of philosophy that deals with the nature of the soul, and how the soul has three aspects which manifest into parts, functions, and goals, which divide into smaller parts, limited functions, and short-term goals. This philosophy of diversification is the *theory* using which the tree can be constructed, and the tree is naturally understood only when the underlying philosophy is grasped.

Once we draw the tree using the philosophy, then we can see the synergies and similarities with diverse other religious ideologies and practices. Indeed, we can now *place* the many religions and sects at *locations* on this tree as different trunks, branches, and leaves. We can also see philosophical similarities between the different systems, and common patterns of difference across different religions. One could argue that if this tree of diversification is true, then the leaves must have grown from the trunks, which emanated from the root. At least we can see how all the religious systems embody parts, functions, and goals of the whole truth, and how they take us toward the whole truth, although some might be closer to the destination than others.

This is a type of 'comparative religion' where the comparison helps us construct the tree, helps us see the diverse religions as part of a single whole, and illustrates how many paths can lead to a destination, provided one follows the ascending path from leaves to branches to trunks and finally to the root. Instead of perceiving the differences between religions as mutual contradictions, we can see these differences as distinct branches coming from the same root. This approach to 'comparative religion' can be fruitful in (a) advancing our understanding of religions, (b) giving each religion a place in the world as a different path to the same goal, and (c) resolving their mutual conflicts.

The diversity of Vedic thought—and the underlying unity which is often not understood—can be employed to understand the diversity and unity of other religions. The Vedic system is today globally recognized as the oldest surviving religion and practice. This doesn't necessarily mean that Vedic thought *contains* all other religions because the theology tree can grow new branches or shed older leaves. Some newer branches or leaves have not been anticipated in the Vedic texts, and many things described in these texts don't exist in any meaningful form in modern times. In that sense, new branches and leaves constitute new religions that did not exist in Vedic times, and many of the branches and leaves that previously existed are now extinct.

However, that doesn't entail a complete novelty in the new religion forbidding us to place the new religion on the tree of theological diversification. Certainly, the Vedic system emphasized and grew some branches, but given the diversity of paths enunciated in different Vedic texts, there was certainly no claim of a single path being the only feasible path to the truth. For instance, in the *Bhagavad-Gita* at least four different paths—*karma-yoga*, *aśtānga-yoga*, *jnana-yoga*, and *bhakti-yoga* are clearly mentioned; they are described successively as the listener (*Arjuna*) expresses his inability to practice them. Inherent in this description is the recognition that there are many paths leading to a single destination. Religion is the path, and God is the destination. That leaves the door open for other paths, suitable to the practitioner's ability.

I don't want to imply that every kind of religious doctrine ever conceived will fit into this tree as a part, function, or goal of a whole. There are certainly some problematic doctrines—e.g., eternal hell and eternal heaven, or the non-existence of individual souls—which are outside this tree. I will discuss the reasons why they lie outside, and what problems their existence causes to the religion that adopts them. But this commentary should not be construed as an indirect criticism of that religion or the doctrine itself. Each doctrine has certain benefits, even the above noted ones, although in the longer run, their problems might outstrip their benefits. Certainly, there is a perspective from which the doctrine can seem very useful and powerful, but another perspective from which it can seem implausible and difficult. Discussing such pros and cons of these doctrines helps us put them into perspective; it by no means implies that the religion that uses the doctrine should extend or abort the doctrine.

The topics on religion have been the subject of historical conflict and continue to be sensitive emotional topics. What new things can be said that are both constructive and useful, to all the parties involved? This is the question that has bothered me prior to and during the course of writing this book.

I'm intimately aware that any work that places a religious ideology at a certain 'place' (higher or lower) relative to other ideologies may not be appreciated—not because it is false, but because it makes others uncomfortable. Tracing an ideological continuity without outlining the historical events is itself likely to lead to questions of how one idea could have evolved from others except through cultural contact. But in the end, I felt that there is enough value in drawing such ideological trees and tracing philosophical continuities even if the empirical evidence for the events that back them is not provided—and in many cases could not be provided because the historical records have either disappeared or were deliberately doctored. And while giving positions to ideologies may mean that some religion is not the ultimate truth, it may be—for some people—a relatively small price to pay in order to understand why the contrasting ideas also carry much truth, although by treating each of these conflicting ideologies as roots—rather than as different branches—we create irreconcilable conflicts, which then preempt a superior understanding.

With that worth in mind, I think this book might be valuable to many readers. It does require one to have an open mind to other religions, and is certainly not meant as a drumbeat for 'Hinduism'—because what is 'Hinduism' if not the collection of many diverse and often contradictory philosophies, claims, deities, and practices? The 'Hindus' could view these diversities themselves as the problem within 'Hinduism' that needs to be solved by employing the tree of ideologies where different paths can help us progress toward the same goal. Others, who haven't encountered such problems before within a single religion would still be aware of the problem between many religions. My contention is that these are not different issues; they are rather begging a common answer: (a) understanding the diversity, and (b) unifying the understanding.

A few words might be said about different paths to a destination. If you have walked in a city then traveling to a destination involves a single path, which is comprised of many individual roads and streets, called by different names. A particular street has a beginning and an end, which means that the road takes us to a particular destination where another road begins. In that sense, all roads don't directly lead to the same destination; however, they lead to a destination from where another road can take you further. Each node on this tree joins many branches; only one branch goes closer to the root; others go farther away from the root. In that sense, too, every road doesn't take one to the destination: you could move closer to the root by completing one road and then move away from the root by taking another path away from it.

Unless we know the root, simply by traversing the roads we don't know if we are getting closer or farther. Therefore, even to know that we are getting closer to the root, we must know what the destination is, how far the present road will take us, and what the next road must be. Religious doctrines can thus be viewed as roads; some roads less traveled can take us to the destination faster than other roads frequented more often. This is then the goal of 'comparative religion' in my view: it is meant to help us find the shortest route that we are *comfortable* taking. What would be the point of a road that is very short, but we don't like walking on it? And what would be the use of a road that we like traveling on, but is so long that the process seems endless?

Comparative religion was called *Mimāṃsa*, and is one of the six schools of Vedic philosophy, following directly after *Vedanta*. The purpose of *Vedanta* is to explain the nature of the final destination, while the purpose of *Mimāṃsa* is to identify the best path to reach that destination—after analyzing many diverse paths. They have thus also been called *Uttara-Mimāṃsa* and *Pūrva-Mimāṃsa*, respectively—dealing with the destination and the path to it. Clearly, the first step in determining the goodness of a path is to find the destination itself. In that sense, the primary purpose of religion is to first delineate the nature of God, and then to describe how that God creates many branches, twigs, and leaves, which appear diversified but are actually unified. This book can be viewed primarily as a type of path analysis—i.e., *Pūrva-Mimāṃsa*—after a brief discussion of the nature of the goal itself. Now, you might disagree with the goal, in which case the discussion of the paths remains moot. However, I will spend enough time describing a philosophy by which you can assess the nature of the goal before we discuss the differences in the paths themselves.

If the mind has thus been opened to interesting possibilities, and the general outline of the approach adopted in the book makes sense to you, then the rest of the book will prove to be a new way of looking at religions.

1

Introductory Background

Any person who, with all the sincerity of heart, is in search for God, on land or in the sea, is worthy of respect.

— Riaz Ahmed Gohar Shahi

Personalism vs. Impersonalism

Nature is viewed at present, through the lens of modern science, *impersonally*. In the scientific picture, nature is comprised of particles and forces which cause the particles to move and change, governed by mathematical laws. This motion and aggregation of particles due to force supposedly creates life forms, and these then form ecosystems and societies, developing aspirations[1]. Modern science grew out of the need to remove mind and consciousness from the description of nature. It aspired to do two things— (1) replace contextualization with universalization, and (2) replace personality with objectivity. Once we remove personality from nature, my purpose—resulting in happiness or distress—becomes a subjective illusion and cannot have a fundamental causal role in nature. Once we remove contexts from nature, then the importance attached to a role and its responsibilities becomes a delusion because roles that we occupy in the world enunciate contextual responsibilities, which are called *dharma* in the Vedic system. The term 'dharma' is sometimes confused with 'religion' but they are different. *Dharma* represents contextual duties—for instance those performed by a father, a mother, a student, a citizen, etc. It is a social construct, which prescribes how to construct a society through roles and responsibilities. Religion, however, describes the nature of Absolute Truth, the ultimate reality, or the personality from which everything else springs. When science rejects contexts, it also rejects the existence of roles which are contextual. Out goes morality and duty from the scientific study. The 'impersonal' explanation of the world divorces choice and responsibility from the discourse about nature and replaces these with the universal laws of force acting on material particles. Several things follow from here. Most prominently, the sense of duty and responsibility is no longer scientific. And you also have no choice, because your personality is replaced by objectivity.

Of course, just because science ignores the observers (or reduces them to particles) doesn't mean it is successful. Its descriptions succeed in so far as the personalization of nature roughly approximates the persons but fails when it doesn't. You can measure the pressure to be applied on a trigger to fire a bullet, but it doesn't tell you whether the pressure must be applied at all. The impersonal description of nature is generally adequate as long as you leave choice and responsibility out the question of reality, but in so far as they are necessary to explain the most ordinary facts and problems of life, science is a failure. Its successes in explaining the world keeping choice and responsibility aside have numbed us into believing that it is the complete answer.

Prior to the dawn of modern science, nature was described *personally*. Not only did humans consider other humans and animals to have souls, but even inanimate objects like trees, rivers, mountains, and the earth itself were considered persons. The planets in the sky were persons. The star constellations were personalities, and time, space, wind, water, and fire, were characters in the cosmic drama. The primordial properties of nature were said to be the original persons, and when something had two or more such primordial properties, it was designated as a 'child' of the primordial, original persons.

Today we call the personal description of nature 'mythology'—the study of folklores and fabricated stories. It comprises descriptions of how nature was personalized through deities, and demigods, who are similar to us—e.g., they eat, have wives and children, and defend their positions aggressively. The difference is that they have superior powers, and vaster control over nature. Owing to their control, humankind is always at the 'mercy of nature's fury'. Indeed, some of our phraseology such as 'nature's fury' personalizes nature.

In the personalist view, nature is controlled by persons and under impersonalism by mathematical laws. Modern science presumes that the laws of nature never change in time, and they apply to all places in space.

To be very clear, these are *assumptions* about nature. These assumptions are, however, necessary for science to conclude that nature must not be controlled by persons, because the scope of ordinary persons is always limited. If something applies to all places and times, then it must be beyond a personal control. Similarly, under a personal control, the laws don't fully determine the outcomes, although they *restrict* the possibilities. The restriction is called *freedom* which we use through *free will.* The freedom is not the same in all the situations; some persons may have more or less freedom, which means that the outcomes under their control would seem to change with time. This too would be problematic for the universalization in science, because it *contextualizes* the laws. A single necessity—i.e., the need to universalize the same laws to all space and time—demarcates the impersonalist view from the personalist one.

If nature is governed by persons rather than impersonal laws, then we would explain its evolution as the behavior of personalities, and its origin as the creativity of an original person, who created other child persons. But if nature is governed by impersonal laws, then we would seek the beginning in logic, numbers, truth values, and counting. In either alternative, we require assumptions because the most fundamental ideas of each of the approaches cannot be confirmed empirically. Most of us are familiar with the issues in empirically confirming the existence of God. But not many people are aware of the issues in giving logic, numbers, and counting an empirical foundation.

The issue is that even if you can count with your fingers, you cannot reduce numbers to that counting. Why? Because to count till five, the concept of 'five' must exist before the counting begins in order to count the *fifth* entity. If you did not already know the number 'five' you could not count *fifth*. We can conclude that if 'five' did not exist prior, we could not have five fingers. As a result, numbers must precede our counting as pure ideas that we can observe in collections and count using fingers but cannot reduce to collections or the act of counting. In fact, now, the numbers exist *both* empirically and as pure ideas, and hence there are multiple ways to speak about numbers— (1) the property of a collection, (2) the act of counting, and (3) the pure idea.

The act of counting further involves a *method.* For instance, if you are sequencing the books in a library, you need a method. You can sequence the books by their height and weight, by the publishers' names, by the names of the authors who wrote the books, by the subjects they deal in, or by the year of publication, and many others. Given these diverse methods of sequencing a set of things into an order, which is then used to count, mathematicians now recognize that counting involves a *choice*. You must choose a method in order to sequence, and that method is choice.

We are now led to the problem that to complete even the theory of numbers, we need to acknowledge two additional things—(a) the primacy of the numeric ideas, which precede our use in counting, and (b) the use of choice in ordering things before they can be counted. The existence of ideas now leads to the judgments of truth, while the existence of choice leads to new kinds of judgments—of right and good. Choices can be right or wrong; for instance, if you started ordering the books in a library by their height and weight, it would be a wrong method of classification, even though theoretically possible. Your job as a librarian is to help people find the books in the best way possible and classifying them by their physical properties contradicts your role. Similarly, since you can choose more than one method of classification, you can ask: Which is the method I *like* most? For instance, books in libraries are classified in at least two ways—(a) by the author name, and (b) by subject. Some people like to search for books by authors—because they have previously heard of the author's reputation or might have read other books by the same author. Other people just like to search by subject, because they don't know the different authors. So, there are natural preferences by which you choose to classify and order.

The existence of ideas requires the judgment of true and false—i.e., is the idea true or false? The existence of choices requires the judgments of right and good. Mathematics at present is unprepared to deal with such questions, including judgments like 'right' and 'good'. The problem with these questions is that the world is no longer just the truth; even falsities can exist. Similarly, the world is no longer just the right and good; wrong and bad also exist. Therefore, you cannot resolve the question of 'reality' simply by testing what *exists*, since false, wrong, and bad also exist. You have to go beyond existence, and talk about judgments of truth, right, and good, and conclude that all that exists is not necessarily true, right, and good, although there is true, right, and good. The preponderance of choices makes these individual judgments. And once everyone can choose their *personal* truth, right, and good, you have a big problem of what is the Absolute Truth, Right, and Good. Given the existence of choice, we must naturally say that this Absolute Truth, Right, and Good is God, because we cannot rely on the absoluteness of individual judgments.

Similarly, the axiom of an 'idea' leads to a hierarchy of ideas—some ideas are abstract while others are detailed, and the abstract doesn't disappear when the detail exists. Indeed, the detailed ideas are derived from the abstract ideas, and therefore the abstract must be logically prior. The abstract, however, cannot be observed, and it must hence exist as a pure idea. The hierarchy of ideas entails a hierarchy of actions, and hence a hierarchy of choices, followed by a hierarchy of true, right, and good. This hierarchy entails a hierarchy of persons. Some of these persons will perceive abstract instead of detailed ideas, their actions will control other persons below them, and they will constitute a higher good than others. This is not a new magical idea; it is rather an idea necessitated in the attempts to fix the problems of impersonalism.

People falsely assume that impersonalism is consistent and complete and overlook its problems. If we examined those problems and tried to find a solution, we would realize why personalism is necessary. Due to profound ignorance about the problems in reasoning with numbers, and an oversimplified caricature of personalization as 'mythology', the modern education system propagates a biased viewpoint about nature, and most people have naively accepted that view in today's time. Therefore, it is essential to realize the kinds of problems that exist in the impersonal description of nature which can only be overcome in the personal description. This doesn't mean that every system of gods from the past is true. It does, however, mean that some form of personalization is absolutely necessary. The precise form that personalization must take now is contingent upon a further analysis of ideas and choices. For example, which are the most primordial ideas in nature? And what types of operations can be performed on these ideas? The system of gods as embodiments of these ideas and choices can be subject to the same rigor that is applied to the study of nature in modern science. Through that rigor and analysis, we hope to either confirm or deny—over time—the reality of different systems.

We have to examine the 'myths' scientifically—e.g., question why only certain gods are necessary rather than others? Why did a culture induct certain gods instead of others? Was it a shortfall in imagination? Or was something more profound involved in the idols? We seldom look cross-culturally to see the similarities between these myths across time and space, which might not only indicate a common conceptual origin, but also compel us to reconsider them as pure myths. We also suppose that humans have become smart only recently—after they adopted the impersonal viewpoint during the Western Renaissance and Enlightenment but were primitive fools in the ages gone by. This view is informed by the ignorance of the enormous times for which humanity has existed in far more sophisticated civilizations than today.

It is possible, for instance, that future generations might consider the present humanity a dismal catastrophe because it destroyed flora and fauna, concentrated population in polluted urban areas, leading to excessive competition for survival, resulting in the birth of new illnesses, compensated only by a medical system that hurts the immunity even while it tries to heal, making the body and mind further depleted and dependent on the drugs, while breaking the fabric of loving relationships to idolize individualism. There is simply no evidence that life today is much better than all the past. It might seem better than the past in a limited sense, when primitive people did not have the intellect to organize society and society was mired in tribalism and blind faith. But to extend that state of human existence to all time in history is preposterous. We should reconsider the idea of progress based on the recent changes.

Since the word 'mythology' has derogatory connotations, I will avoid the use of this term except when we have to deal with the question if these are ideas in our mind, stories that we fabricated in order to instill morals, or merely something that is the innate property of the many human minds.

I will base this book on the idea that there are two descriptions of nature—impersonal and personal—which are equally amenable to scientific inquiry under different assumptions. Just as we seek to know the number of fundamental particles and forces in particle physics for the theory of nature to be complete, we can also ask how many gods suffice for a complete description of all that we can observe. Just as we seek the origin and explanation of material particles based on a fundamental theory of nature, similarly, we could seek the genesis of the gods themselves, from some primordial God. The criterion for 'mythology' is therefore no different than currently employed in science: we are seeking a causal explanation and origin of all that we experience.

I'm quite certain that nobody at present views the descriptions of demigods as constituting a *personalized* alternative to the modern scientific *impersonalized* explanation of the world. For this reason alone, this book might be interesting, although I don't want to consider something interesting just because it is different from the mainstream. I also want to analyze the 'mythologies' with the aim of separating the wheat from the chaff. This means describing a system of gods that can constitute a consistent and complete theory of nature. The laws of nature, in this system, are still impersonal—quite like the governmental laws which entail a consequence—good or bad. Since they are impersonal, they can be documented for people to know in advance—i.e., before they are judged. However, the judgment—based on the law—is delivered by a person. There is hence an impersonal law and a person who judges based on that law. The personal and the impersonal are not contradictory: the laws are not personal whims and the consequence of the laws is not automatic.

Broadening the Material Ontology

The idea that nature's laws are created by a person seems unintuitive to the modern mind, but this can be understood if the material ontology was broadened to include *roles* and *goals*. The law of nature is that each person must fulfill their goals in accordance with the expected behaviors of their roles. As new roles are created in nature, new laws have to be created for those roles, which define the expected behaviors for the roles. Therefore, the law is identical to the expected behavior of the role, and there can be as many laws as there are unique roles. These laws would be applied to the *persons* who enter that role. A person plays many roles in a society, and the laws of different roles can seem to contradict each other in some situations. In such cases, we must understand the hierarchy of the roles, and the higher role takes precedence over the lower roles. The laws pertaining to a particular role are therefore not universal because they can be overridden by the laws of the higher roles.

A role affords us freedom of action and choices. To make that choice, we must have some goals, to select an alternative out of all possible alternatives. The role and the goal are thus complementary ideas; the role creates *freedom* and the goal constitutes *free will*. An event is their combination. When modern science impersonalizes the laws of nature, it discards roles and goals. As a result, the law is not unique to a person in a given time, place, and situation. Instead, since the laws are universalized, each person has the same role. As new roles are created, the laws remain unchanged, and the laws become universal. Similarly, because there is no role, there cannot be freedom associated with the role, and the goals used to make a selection are not required.

Thus, as science universalizes the natural laws, it discards both roles and goals, thereby impersonalizing the person into an object. However, when we remove roles and goals, then we also remove the judgments of right and good. The judgment or right and wrong exists only with a role—e.g., shooting itself is not bad, when performed by a soldier. Similarly, the judgment of good and bad depends on what one desires—e.g., some food is good if I enjoy its consumption without falling sick. If we remove the judgments of right and good from nature, there cannot be consequences of actions based on whether the action was right or wrong, and there cannot be reward or punishment based on a person's sense of happiness and distress. Now nature degenerates into a causal model that involves only causes and effects, without moral consequences.

We still have the judgment of true and false, but the judgment of truth also depends on the existence of meanings. If something is meaningless, we can talk about its *existence* but not its *truth*. Thus, for instance, I can think that the 'sky is green' and the thought may *exist,* but its truth cannot be decided. When the truth cannot be determined, the study of the mind also reduces to the existence of molecules, not whether these molecules represent truths or lies.

Since all meanings are hierarchical—i.e., there can be abstract and contingent meanings—if we reject meanings, then we must also *reduce* the abstractions to the contingent details. This now leads to *reductionism* in which meaning doesn't exist because only the smallest details of the world are real. For example, the concept 'mammal' exists as the refinement of the idea of 'animal'. If we only acknowledge the smallest details, then we must reduce 'animal' to 'mammal', then reduce 'mammal' to the individual species, which must then be reduced to the individual members of species, and each member must be reduced to their body parts, all the way to atoms which make up the body parts. As this reduction is carried to its logical limit, we lose all the *words* in language. We can no longer say that there is something called a giraffe because what is a giraffe if not the sum of the body parts and the collection of atoms?

Effectively, all sciences are ultimately reduced to the study of atoms, but now we find that the science of atomism is *incomplete* because nature exists as a possibility which has to be converted into a reality[2], but the mechanism of that conversion has to be something other than the matter we reduced.

One proposal to overcome this incompleteness is that we add choices or goals to the selection of possibilities. But nobody realizes that if you bring choices into science, then you must also bring the judgment of good and bad, which determines which choice is to be made (because it is good). Similarly, if you bring in choices, then there must be moral judgments too—i.e., to decide if the choice that I consider good is also the right choice based on the role. The removal of role and goal in science has been an utter failure. Similarly, the notion that we can completely know nature by deciding what exists is also a failure because this 'reality' exists as a possibility which cannot be known until a selection is made. But even if we granted the existence of role, goal, and choice, in order to solve the problem of incompleteness in physics, it would still be a *physical* theory in the sense that it could not study the mind—e.g., whether the molecule in the brain denotes the idea 'the sky is green', which is false. We could give the molecules a definite state, but we could not give them meaning or truth. Thus, even the answer to atomic indeterminism through the addition of choices turns out to be hopelessly incomplete in the truth judgment.

At the bare minimum, we have to think of matter as not just things that exist, but also the *meanings* and *truths* of those existents. In other words, we have to study these existents as *symbols* rather than *things.* These symbols will get their meaning by rejecting reduction, which means the meaning of the symbol is given in relation to a more abstract concept. All these concepts must exist materially, so they must be given a location in some new kind of space. This new kind of space, as it turns out, looks like a *tree* rather than a *box.* In the box view of space, there is no hierarchy because you can rotate the box in any direction and all directions and locations remain equivalent. To give objects in the box meaning, you must give the locations themselves meaning.

This kind of meaning is available in the everyday world—e.g., inside a house, which looks like a box, but its locations are given meanings such as bedroom, toilet, study room, dining room, children's room, guest room, kitchen, etc. When a table is placed inside the study, it becomes a *study table*; when the same table is placed inside the kitchen, it becomes a *kitchen* table. In other words, the *meaning* of the object is modified by its location in space, and therefore you could say that the meaning is the location itself, although the location is defined in a completely new way—the *origin* of the space is a box in relation to which all other locations are defined and thereby given a meaning.

The new problem now is—how can the origin be the box? Isn't the origin supposed to be a *point* and the box is an extended object with numerous points? Indeed, you break the box into its walls, bottom and cover, which means that the box is itself reducible to its parts. Therefore, in what sense can we talk about the box as the origin of a space in relation to which all the locations inside the box would be given a new type of *semantic* location?

This is when we have to replace the box with a tree. The box is like the root of the tree from which the many locations inside the box are created like branches from the root. The root is the *context* and each branch from the root is an *object*. The object is given a meaning in relation to the root, which means that if you define your location in relation to the origin of space, that location itself represents meaning, although this is not a location in a box, but on a tree. We have to now think of the box—i.e., the root—as the whole, and the objects inside the box as parts of the whole. However, the whole is logically prior to the parts because it is a higher node in the tree. Effectively, the whole and the part are separately real, and the whole cannot be reduced to its parts.

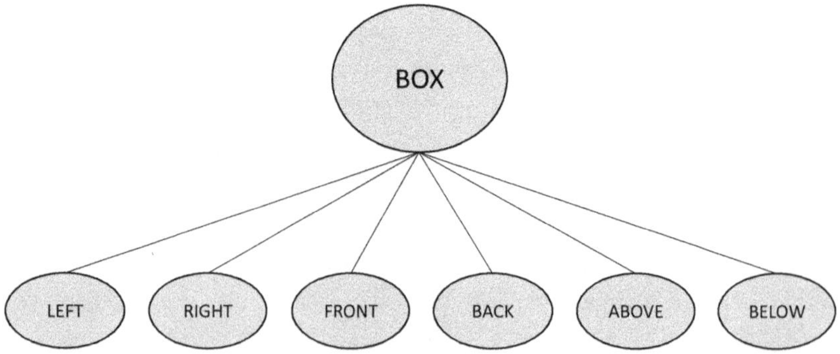

Figure-1 Conversion of a Box into a Tree

The six sides of the box are branches from the root—the whole box—and the objects inside the box must be further branches in relation to the six sides. An object closest to the left side of the box is a 'child' of the 'left' branch of the tree. If you move the object to the 'right' side, then it changes its 'parent' to the right branch. Due to the change in the parent-child relation between the parts and the whole, the different locations in the space are not equivalent. Rather, each location is identified by a different *hierarchy* from the object to the root of space. This hierarchy represents the complete meaning of the object, and this meaning can be used to judge the truth in relation to other truths.

Once we understand how the judgment of truth depends on a hierarchical structure, then we can also understand how one's role is defined in relation to a higher role, thus producing a hierarchy of roles—e.g., seen in government, businesses, or educational institutions, in which the junior role gets its duties defined by their senior, whose duties are in turn defined by their seniors. Finally, we can see that goals too are hierarchical because a longer-term goal is divided into shorter-term goals, which are further divided into even smaller goals. The action of an employee is thus judged by their supervisor, and the success of the action is determined relative to the goals. The decision whether the employee did their job is the judgment of *right*. But, whether the performance of the duty accomplished the goal is the judgment of *good*.

Now we can see how an object must be true, right, and good. That is, it must be meaningful in the context, and the meaning must be consistent with some standard of meaning—e.g., a company that is supposed to make nuts and bolts cannot produce scrap, and those nuts and bolts must adhere to the standards such as the specified sizes, the types of grooves, etc. The production of nuts and bolts instead of scrap is the meaning; and the conformance of these meanings to standards is the truth. Similarly, the things must be produced in the right way—e.g., following the necessary duties of each person doing their job, with no job being left out, and no job being performed unnecessarily. Such conformance to the rules of roles makes the actions right. Finally, the things produced by such meticulous working and conformance to standards must attain a goal—e.g., that they must be bought by customers for a payment. Clearly, the purpose of making nuts and bolts is to earn a profit. The profit, being the final goal, is broken into many smaller goals, roles, and standards.

The Process of Measurement

Each person has to produce the expected product, following the expected duties or processes, in order to attain the expected goals. The *measurement* is defined relative to the standards set for the product, process, and goal. Which means that there is an ideal product, an ideal process, and an ideal goal. If the product is less than ideal, produced through a less-than-ideal process, meeting less-than-ideal goals, then the outcomes of measurement are not true, right, or good. If they meet the standards then they are true, right, and good.

One cannot engage in a process-controlled activity without having some goal. And the process cannot be defined without knowing the product to be produced. If a bolt conforms to the standards, then it is true beyond the meaning. If following the processes produces the bolt conforming to the standard, then the processes are right. Finally, if the bolt is desired by customers and bought by them, then the product is good. Sometimes, you can create the true product, using the wrong processes, which may not be purchased by the customers. At other times, you may create the true product, following the right processes, and the product may still not be sold. At other times, customers may buy substandard products that don't conform to standards and were produced by wrong processes. There is hence one ideal state—when the bolt is true, right, and good—but seven non-ideal states in which bolt may not conform to the right standard, may not be created by the right process, and may not be bought by customers, or different combinations of these three possibilities.

The truth, right, and good may also vary from one person to another. For the worker producing the bolts, producing more bolts may be good if he is compensated by the number of bolts he produces, but other co-workers may have a problem with that if they are not able to match the productivity. For the supervisor, having more bolts produced may be good in some cases if that indicates a higher productivity of his operation and bad in some cases if he doesn't have enough space to hold an inventory because the bolts are not being sold as quickly. For the salesman, a larger number of bolts may be good if he is able to sell them as quickly but bad if the increased productivity is not matched by the increased sales. As a result, the same reality is interpreted differently based on a person's context and changing the context can change their judgment. The context also changes the meaning being judged. For example, a worker's process of producing a bolt is different from a supervisor's process for rewarding the different workers, and from the salesman's process of invoicing a customer. Both reality (meaning) and its judgment (truth, right, and good) are highly contextual, and the measurement is relative to the context.

Thus, each person has a product, process, and goal, but they are not the same for each person. Each person also has a judgment of the product, process, and goal, but they are not the same for each person. Clearly, all three have to be combined, but there is enormous variety in these combinations. Each of these three has its own hierarchy, so they are three separate trees which have to be combined. We will discuss the combination of three trees in the next chapter, but the basic idea is that an object can perform many functions (e.g., a knife can be used to cut and pierce), and a function can be used for many purposes (e.g., cutting vegetables to cook or cutting paper to make crafts).

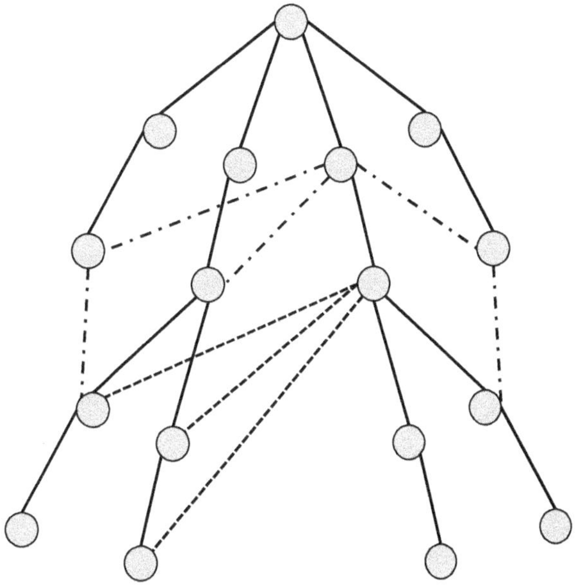

Figure-2 The Combination of Three Trees

In Figure-2 we denote this idea with three types of hierarchies; the solid line hierarchy denotes objects, the dashed line hierarchy functions, and the dotted-dashed line denotes purposes. There is a clear hierarchy among the objects, functions, and purposes, which make each of the three individual trees. However, when an object is used for a different function, and a function is performed for a different purpose, the hierarchy gets muddled. In fact, in such cases we begin to see the creation of loops from trees, and loop-free properties of the tree are lost. Now, because a knife is used to pierce, you could (erroneously) perceive it as a needle; similarly, because the knife was used to pierce, you could conclude that it cannot be used for the purposes of cooking.

Cross-connections in the tree thus create perceptual, functional, and intentional errors. The three trees must be conceived individually because objects, functions, and purposes are not identical. We have to combine the three trees because only the combination produces an outcome. However, there are ideal and non-ideal combinations. The ideal combination is one in which the part is perfectly designed for a function, and the function is perfectly performed for a purpose. The non-ideal combination is one in which a part is used for a function which it cannot perform perfectly, and the function is employed to achieve a purpose although that function is not ideally suited to achieve the purpose. The three trees are therefore ideal, but their *combination* into reality is non-ideal. God creates these three trees as the ideals, but the soul combines them into the ideal and non-ideal experiences. The fact that God has created the three trees perfectly doesn't take away the soul's free will of combination. Similarly, just because the soul combines the trees created by God doesn't make God responsible for the combination. God creates the ideal—the truth, right, and good. However, when we combine it in new ways, we often create the false, wrong, and bad. Therefore, the soul has the need to perceive the world and judge it in order to find the ideal—truth, right, and good.

As the whole divides into parts, it becomes less true, less right, and less good. The soul is situated on different parts of the tree, and accordingly his judgments of truth, right, and good are incomplete and often flawed. To judge the truth, right, and good correctly, one must view this not from their viewpoint but from the viewpoint of God—the root of the tree. If the soul doesn't know God, he must accept God's word in regard to the judgments of truth, right, and good. This acceptance generally comes through the words of an enlightened master who transmits the understanding of truth, right, and good to the soul. Based on the soul's individual situation on the tree there is a unique truth, right, and good judgment for other things perceived from that vantage point. Note that these judgments are *choices*; given the situation of the soul, there is always a best choice, which is what God would have chosen if He was in the situation. God here simply represents the *ideal* choice. To make the true, right, and good choices, therefore, one has to know God—the *ideal.* In different situations, there are different kinds of ideals. Accordingly, there are many forms of God, which constitute the true, right, and good choices. Just because the form of God changes doesn't mean that there are many 'gods'. It just means that the truth, right, and good has changed its form for the situation.

Modern science is a flawed ideology about nature for many reasons. First, it removes role and goal from the consideration of reality, and thereby the judgments or right and good. Second, it flattens the hierarchy thereby removing meanings and truths from our judgment. Third, it collapses the distinction between the soul and matter, thereby taking away the possibility of choice and interpretation. Fourth, it discards the idea of God Who constitutes the ideal standard for judging the nature of truth, right, and good. Only the material particles are left, and they are modeled according to physical forces; but even here, the conception of space and time is flattened rather than hierarchical.

Since the judgments of truth, right, and good have to be always combined in order to experience anything, the theory of truth alone can never be empirically confirmed. However, the theory of truth, right, and good can be *collectively* confirmed by experience because their combination produces an experience. In so far as modern science removes the questions of right and good from nature, it also creates problems of incompleteness: you can make observations, but you can never explain those observations just with truth. As a result, the observations are always complete, but the *theories* explaining those observations must always remain incomplete unless the material ontology is broadened to include role and goal, right and good, meaning and truth.

The personalization of nature can be a scientific theory that takes into account roles and goals along with the hierarchy and contextual judgments. The roles *contextualize* rather than universalize, the goals *personify* rather than objectify the individual, and the hierarchy creates *meanings* rather than things. Personalization also involves a shift in the causal model to include consequences, besides causes and effects: the consequence is based on the rightness of the action, and the reward is based on what one considers goodness. If the action was right, then the reward must be good. The rightness is relative to the role, and the goodness is relative to a goal. Thus, the reward can be experienced in many ways. Personalization is not a substitution of the impersonal model; it also expands the scientific causality from cause and effect to cause, effect, and consequence; the consequence is based on moral rightness, and the result must be delivered relative to how the receiver defines goodness.

For example, in modern society, valorous soldiers upon return from a successful war may be rewarded with a promotion in rank, but that promotion doesn't help the soldier if he wants to retire and lead a civilian life. The soldier may prefer to get a house and medical security, instead of a bigger badge of honor, and the promotion—if it only gives a bigger badge instead of a house and medical security—would seem an inadequate reward by the soldier. The consequence of valorous action by a soldier is a *reward* rather than a *punishment* (a civilian killing other people would be punished). However, the reward is meaningful only in relation to what the person wants or considers good.

In Vedic philosophy, the reward is called *karma* and the desire is called *guna*. *Karma* is created as the consequence of an action based on what was expected of the person from their given role (i.e., whether the role was fulfilled or unfulfilled), but the result is delivered relative to the person's desires or *guna*. Thus, by the law of nature, all soldiers who fought valorously must be rewarded, but only according to their desire: some soldier (who takes greater pride in a bigger badge of honor) will be awarded such a badge while another soldier (who finds greater happiness in a comfortable home and medical security) will receive such a life. Their reward is the same, but the observable is different. To understand such differences, we have to accommodate both roles and goals, as the mechanisms for explaining the observed outcomes.

The roles and laws cannot be seen by the senses because they only constitute what *should* happen, not what *actually* happens. When the actions are completed, the laws dictate the consequences of the actions, i.e.,, what *should* happen, but hasn't yet happened. The material objects also are not predetermined; they only constitute what *could* happen—i.e., the possibilities which can be enacted through an action. Finally, a person's desires constitute what *would* happen if only they desired it. The reality therefore comprises *could*, *should*, and *would*, but the senses cannot perceive any of this reality. What the senses perceive is a combination of could, would, and should, and when science models nature based on all that we can perceive, it makes a gross error of judgment in supposing that what we cannot see by the senses must not actually exist. The impersonal description of nature is such a mistake: it overemphasizes sense perception and overlooks could, would, and should causality.

It is in this broader context of explaining our observations that we must study nature's personalization: demigods control could, should, and would, which cannot be perceived by the senses, and hence their creators too cannot be perceived by the senses. The inability to apply sense perception in understanding nature shouldn't surprise us because even in modern science there is a very important role for imagination by which we create concepts, properties, and theories. None of these are ever perceived by the senses. However, their combination produces a sense observation, and the theory is confirmed or denied by that evidence. The criterion for empiricism is therefore not different. However, the ideology employed in theory formation must now be adjusted. In the new ideology, we see the world not as material objects governed by universal laws, but as persons whose bodies are abilities of what *could* happen, who are placed in roles that define what *should* be done, and their choices decide what *would* happen—i.e., if they will enjoy or suffer in life.

The world around us exists as a *possibility*. As these possibilities are combined, they are also *reduced*. For instance, what *should* happen will happen only if it *could* happen; we cannot expect a righteous action to occur if it were impossible. Similarly, what *would* happen would only happen if it *could* happen; we cannot expect a desire to be fulfilled if it were impossible. Finally, the things that *should* happen will happen only when someone *would* do it by desiring the alternative. The world of possibility is reduced to a definite perception through the overlap of different kinds of possibilities. We may say that an unmanifest world becomes manifest by the combinations in the unmanifest. When we take such a philosophical and theoretical view, then personalism is no longer an imaginary mythology; it is rather the basis of a science.

The Philosophy of Personalism

The personalist explanation seems to contravene the impersonalist viewpoint only because it is much *broader* and much *deeper*. It is broader because it includes roles and goals besides concepts of knowing and acting. It is deeper because the concepts, roles, and goals are hierarchical. This depth and breadth must be useful: it can be employed for explaining the phenomena that the narrower explanation fails to illuminate. The personalist explanation is not the worldview of the primitive minds who saw ghosts and goblins in natural processes. It is rather a worldview of one who can see beyond the senses.

It is noteworthy that the senses—produced of the concepts of knowing and acting—can only see the combination of could, should, and would, not any of them individually. Even if we see this combination, the senses only perceive what previously was 'could'—i.e., the abilities in the body. Even during sensation, we cannot perceive roles and goals[3]. Thus, sense perception is hopelessly incomplete for understanding nature. If, based on sense perception, we discard roles then we must also discard the idea of duties. If we discard the fundamentality of goals in life, then we must also reject the consequentiality of our actions due to choices. Without the morality emanating from responsibility and the purpose surcharging our lives with the search for happiness, why would anyone even aspire to explain the working of the world impersonally? After all, if there is no morality, then why *should* a scientist be truthful about his findings? And if the understanding of nature gives us happiness but happiness is not essential for survival, then why seek an understanding at all?

The quest for reality in science through reason and experience is not flawed. It is only that the reality, when envisioned so narrowly—by excluding roles and goals, and by flattening the conceptual hierarchy—denies the usefulness of scientific pursuits themselves, producing a self-contradiction. The personalist view, instead, populates the world with many *types* of living beings, but it has far more explanatory power, and it is at least self-consistent.

This clarification about the personalist system is essential at the start because without such a background 'mythology' may be culturally and historically significant, but it is of no innate value in today's world. At best, you learn something about history. At worst, you would believe the people formerly were probably foolish to have explained nature using a system of gods. But, in fact, their achievements in mathematics, architecture, medicine, economics, social organization, astronomy, metallurgy, and mastery over the body and mind, would seem paradoxical, given the contrast between their worldview and the one that we believe in today. The only way to reconcile their worldview with their achievements in material well-being is to see their worldview as constituting a radical and different *kind* of natural explanation.

We may have better magnifying glasses through which we can see deeper into nature, but that amplification of the properties for the senses makes all that can be seen by the mind as possibility seem insignificant. If we instead look deeper within ourselves, all that is obtained by looking into the magnifying glasses would seem irrelevant. Neither viewpoint is unempirical, although the one that looks outward fails to see what cannot be seen by the senses and concludes that it doesn't exist. The personalized worldview is obtained by seeing within, which doesn't remove what is visible to the external vision but opens additional realities. We realize that our desires to enjoy, by which we relate to specific parts of the world, are a fundamental feature of our existence. We also understand that our happiness results from the fulfilment of desires, but those desires must be subordinated to principles of morality, which cannot be defined without defining roles and responsibilities. The quest for happiness and its subordination to morality gives us a new type of picture of reality in which the world is a place for moral happiness and it reflects all the properties of the self in matter, far more than seen through the magnifying glass.

We do not seek to know the world in itself. We seek to know ourselves through the world. Therefore, we have to see the world not *through* a magnifying glass in which the observer is minimized and the objects are magnified. We have to rather see the world itself as a mirror in which the observer is reflected, and no matter where we look into nature, only the self is to be known. The personalist description of nature emerges from many onlookers peering into the same mirror. Some onlookers see the big picture and see themselves as owners of that big picture, because they see the mirror from a distance. Other onlookers see the detailed picture, and see themselves as that detailed picture, because they see the mirror closely. The picture being seen by various onlookers is therefore impersonal, as it is embodied in the mirror of nature, but the onlooker is personal: he chooses to see the mirror closely or distantly, he decides to identify with that picture, and he tries to modify and create the picture in his own image. This onlooker can be satisfied only if the picture is an accurate representation of the self, as one imagines the self to be, and the picture has to be personalized as a reflection of the person seeing it.

This personalization of the impersonal is in one sense an illusion, because the picture of the person is indeed impersonal. And yet, the picture would not exist without the person looking into the mirror to create a reflection. The picture is thus a *symbol* of the person, whereas the person is the meaning of that symbol. To detach the person from the picture, to view it as just another thing, would ultimately fail to explain the picture, besides failing to account for the fact that we are *interested* in this picture. We identify with our material reflection because through this reflection we can know ourselves. By the looking in the mirror of material nature, and seeing the reflected image, a personalization of the impersonal picture is created because we identify with the image. But the image is created only because there is a person who looks and identifies, while the picture is sufficiently satisfying for one to keep looking.

The World of Demigods

The demigods are those onlookers who create, control, and see the big picture, and themselves as that big picture. That big picture constitutes their body and mind—which are material—and yet the soul identifies with that reflection in the looking glass. The demigods have a 'higher' position—the vantage point from which they see the big picture—like a man sitting on top of a tall building can see the city landscape but cannot perceive the color of the tie worn by the street passerby. The activities of demigods change the big picture of the universe, and the macroscopic change influences the details.

The humans are onlookers in the same mirror, but we see the picture closely, and hence we only see the details. Our freedom, accordingly, is limited to defining the details, not the big picture. Our freedom is not lost just because the big picture is controlled by the demigods, although the scope of our influence is considerably limited. Changes to the big picture also change the details, but we are unaware of how we are thrown around by the winds of 'circumstances' beyond our control. That is because we have a 'lower' position in the universe—ours is a vantage point that allows us to see the tie of the passerby but not the entire city landscape. What we cannot see by the senses in a single perception, we try to aggregate through multiple repeated observations, and *theorize* and *speculate* using the mind after aggregating the data. The demigod is a person who can *see* what we can only theorize and speculate.

Abstract concepts—which we employ in scientific theories—are mental constructs for us, but they are sensually perceivable by the demigods. For instance, we see colors such as yellow and red, or tastes such as bitter and sweet, but we cannot see the ideas of 'color' or 'taste', which remain mental constructs. Similarly, modern science employs concepts such as 'energy' and 'momentum'; we can measure the values of these properties, but we cannot perceive 'energy' itself, or 'momentum' itself. What is abstract to us becomes sensually perceivable to the demigods. In that sense, we can say that there is a 'god' of vision, a 'god' of smell, or a 'god' of taste, because he sees vision, smell, or taste like we perceive sweet, yellow, or bitter. Similarly, mathematical theorems are sensations for the demigods because they *sensually* perceive the ideas and know their truth and reality, which we can only understand by proving the theorem step by step employing sensually perceivable symbols[4]. The symbols on paper are directly perceivable to us, while the theorem is indirectly understood by the mind. A demigod can, however, see the theorem sensually and doesn't need the proof. The reality that we call colors and sounds is too detailed for someone who sees the world from a different vantage point. And what we can only imagine by our minds is sensually real for them.

To understand this philosophy, we have to realize that both senses and the mind perceive concepts or *information*. The world is objectively comprised of 'bits' of information, but the *interpretation* of these bits is subjective. These bits are organized hierarchically in a tree—from root to leaf. Human perception is also hierarchical from sensations at the lowest level to concepts, beliefs, intentions, and morals at higher levels. The different souls are situated at different places on the tree. They consider their location on the tree as the 'root' of their subjective space, which means that the bits where they are situated are perceived as the morals (the highest-level reality), and the subsequent 'branches' are perceived as intentions, beliefs, concepts, and sensations. The soul doesn't see the successive expansions of the tree beyond the branch that they *subjectively* call 'sensations'. However, through experimental procedures, that which is smaller than the human perceptible sensations can be magnified. In such magnification we still perceive sensations, but those sensations are produced by making the very small sufficiently large for human perception. Indeed, this is how we know about the atomic reality at present: we do not see the atoms; we rather see moving needles and hear detector clicks.

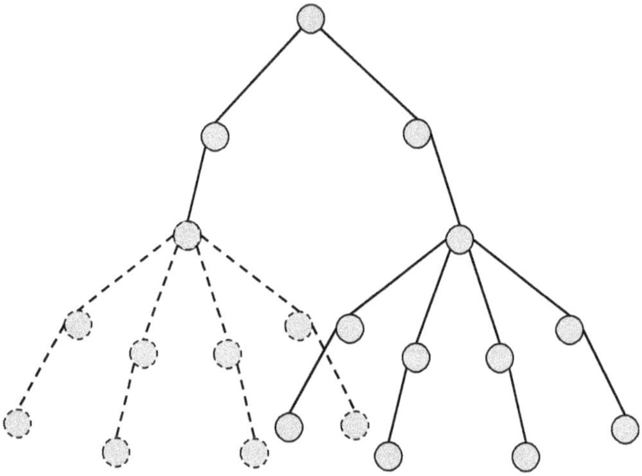

Figure-3 Absolute and Relative Spaces

The things that we don't perceive by our senses—e.g., the atoms and molecules—are perceived by other living entities such as the microorganisms. What we consider 'sensations' can be their morals, intentions, contexts, and concepts, and what we cannot perceive by our senses can be their sensations or thoughts. The microscope gives us a vision of reality that can be directly and sensually perceived by the virus or bacteria, and by such perception our consciousness is lowered in the tree. Perception is therefore *relative* to the soul's position on the universal tree (higher or lower) in two ways. First, different souls can perceive different realities by their senses. Second, the reality they perceive is *interpreted* differently as objects, sensations, concepts, beliefs, intentions, or morals. The demigods are situated higher up the tree than humans. As a result, what we perceive as sensations remains invisible to the demigods. However, what we consider concepts are sensations for the demigods.

The space of the universe constitutes a single *universal* tree. However, because the soul is placed at different branches of this tree, there is also a *relative* space unique to each observer—whose origin is the soul's location on the tree. The soul perceives this origin of the relative space as morals, and successive branches from that relative 'root' become goals, beliefs, concepts, sensations, and objects. Having attained the perception of objects, the relative space ends, but the absolute space doesn't. As a result, through scientific advancements, we can *convert* the things beyond our relative space into things within our relative space. The measurement of subatomic particles is an example of this magnification that converts atoms into sensations. These magnified sensations are the *symbols* of reality that we could not directly perceive by the senses. Therefore, detector clicks and pointer movements are no longer just *phenomena.* They are rather symbols for the existence of atoms and molecules. Effectively, we never see beyond our space, but we *infer* things that we perceive within our space to be *caused* by a reality that lies outside our space.

In modern science, the absolute space is discarded and only the relative space is admitted because science supposes that no observer is 'higher' or 'lower' (Einstein formulated relativity as the *equivalence* of coordinate reference frames pertaining to each observer). This equivalence is a problem; there can be relative space (a) without rejecting the universal space, and (b) without the equivalence of all observers. In Vedic philosophy, the universal tree is the *Universal Form* of God by which God becomes omniscient and omnipotent—i.e., He can control all parts of the universe and He knows everything in the universe. The souls are not omniscient or omnipotent because they are not the roots of the Universal Form. Being situated on different branches of this tree, the souls have different levels of knowledge and control. The demigods have higher control than humans, and the humans have greater control than bacteria. Hence, the humans are 'superior' to bacteria, and the demigods are 'superior' to humans. Since the soul can be situated on any branch of the tree (except the root), there is egalitarian but meritorious equivalence of all souls. But that doesn't mean that the *perspectives* of these souls are equivalent.

Relativity, when it rejects the universal space, creates the illusion of equivalence, which results in the idea that the *form* of the law is universal—i.e., that the same laws apply to all persons and roles, essentially discarding the role, thence the freedom associated with a role, and finally the choice and responsibility in that role. A single idea—the relativity of space—becomes the bedrock of impersonalism. Although Einstein is often regarded as the greatest scientist of the modern era, in time people will realize that he seeded the most materialistic and impersonalist ideas. His impersonalism became a hindrance to the comprehension of atomic theory in which ideas such as contextuality contradict universalism, and choice from a possibility opposed determinism. If we are committed to the universalism and determinism of classical physics, then the contextuality and choice are impossible to reconcile with classical physics. Since most modern scientists are already committed to the truth of classical physical ideas, the understanding of atomic theory has eluded scientists for more than a hundred years, and the conflict between atomic theory and relativity remains the greatest unsolved problem in science.

This contradiction can be solved if we view the universe as an inverted tree, because this reconciles universal and relative viewpoints: each view has an *observer* and God is the view of the observer situated at the root of the tree, while demigods and other beings are situated at different branches of the tree. The meaning of a branch is given in relation to the next higher branch, and not universally. There is hence contextuality embedded in the tree. There is also choice with regard to the specific branch of the tree on which we wish to be situated, and with that choice comes a responsibility: you are not expected to interact with some branches being situated on certain locations. Not obeying that expectation means losing the position to a different position.

The changes in positions on the tree now become the *law of motion*, which is called the *reincarnation* of the soul in Vedic philosophy by which the soul is moved to different positions on the tree, giving it different visions of the world, through different bodies and minds. The body and mind changes occur not just at the end of a lifetime; they are occurring at every moment in time. Hence, there is a continuous *change* in body, rather than the *same* body moving into a new location. Effectively, the continuity in motion (by which we think the same thing moved to a new position) is established by the soul, and hence the soul gives rise to the impression that the self is the same although the body has changed. We know this fact quite well: our bodies change dramatically from childhood, to youth, to old age, but we consider the *person* to be the same. The *person* is thus not the body; it is the soul which creates continuity in motion; however, the motion or change involves the discrete branches of the tree. In so far as science is the discovery of the law of motion, reincarnation is that law. But it is a moral law, based on perspective, choice, and responsibility.

The demigods have a different perspective, they make different choices, and they are bound by a different level of responsibility. The consequences of misusing their choices are that they will lose their privileged position. The demigods being aware of those consequences obey the expectations diligently. Due to their obedience to these expectations, nature appears orderly to us, which science models as the impersonal laws of nature devoid of personalities. The situation is similar to the predetermined schedule followed by trains. Just because the train arrives and departs at a fixed time doesn't mean there is no train driver. It rather means that the train driver runs the train in a punctual manner because breaking that schedule would mean the driver would lose his job. Similarly, the demigods are also afraid of breaking the laws, although the laws could, in principle, be broken at the risk of their own displacement from their professions. Impersonalism models that strict adherence to schedules and routines as the non-existence of a personal control of nature.

When the demigods modify the world using their senses, their control of the world becomes the 'conceptual law' which modern science impersonalizes through physical concepts and mathematical formulae. This impersonalization is false although there are concepts being manipulated by demigods, quite like we manipulate our sensations. The humans and the demigods are not in separate worlds. Rather, the world we live in is hierarchical—structured like a tree—and the higher levels of the tree automatically define the lower levels of the tree. The person more adept at manipulating the higher level automatically gains control over the lower-level reality. But the soul conditioned by impersonalism thinks that because the higher-level control is beyond its ability, so the things that it cannot control must be outside everyone else's control—i.e., that control must be the universal, unchanging, impersonal 'laws of nature'. What we consider 'science' at present becomes mythology when the above understanding of nature is incorporated. Conversely, what we consider 'mythology' at present becomes science using the same understanding.

Most people imagine that if nature were controlled by persons, then it would not have the regularity as evidenced by repeated observations.

They imagine that personal control would mean whimsical changes to nature: for example, the days and nights would vary irregularly if the motion of the sun varies with the whims of the sun god. This idea is true if there is no responsibility associated with whimsicality. If the penalties of whims are severe, you will see order in nature governed by persons. Therefore, order in nature is not contrary to personal control, because the order is accompanied by a responsibility and consequences. Just as an employee is liable to lose his or her job if they don't obey the rules of their employment, similarly, the demigods are also workers for hire in highly empowered positions. They can break the laws, but by doing so, they will lose their position. They comply because they are *attached* to their position, and fearful of a mistake resulting in a loss.

The Evolution of Ideas

Nevertheless, there is still continual modification in the ideas. For instance, motor cars, smart phones, toasters, and air conditioners are mathematical formulae, which evolve quite rapidly—you expect to see a new model of a car, a new smart phone, and advancements in technology every year. The old ideas still exist, but the new ideas are being created, and over time the old ideas become almost non-existent. For instance, with the advent of cars, horse carriages are considered quaint today. Nobody carries a large walkie-talkie because the smart phones fit into your pockets. It is therefore false to suppose that ideas remain fixed in time. What we call our 'creativity' is the new objects being created by the demigods, which appear as ideas in our minds.

Quite separately, we must note that the more widespread the law, the more abstract are the associated concepts, which entails a higher position on the tree, which then implies a slower rate of change. For example, the evolution of scientific theories—e.g., from Newton's physics to Maxwell's electrodynamics, to Schrödinger's Wave Mechanics, to the Standard Model of particle physics—are slower evolutions, relative to the technologies built using them. These laws are relatively more universal as compared to the formulae embodied in technology devices. They are *models* of behavior that are modified over time, but because they are very widespread, the modification is slower.

We cannot claim that the laws of nature discovered by science are universal if we keep changing the laws! We might, however, seek a meta-theory that explains the evolution of theories themselves. Thomas Kuhn formulated such a meta-theory in his book *The Structure of Scientific Revolutions*[5] where he argued that theories evolve after a considerable amount of contrary data has accumulated. As the contrary data accumulates, it simply cannot be fit into the older way of thinking. To accommodate the new and old data, a *paradigm shift* is needed. The widely accepted theories therefore cannot change quickly because (1) a lot more data has to be collected before a change will be allowed, and (2) the change will itself revolutionize and overturn the older thinking. Such changes are resisted unless the evidence is overwhelming, and when a large number of people are committed to overturn the older ideas.

The key point is that the deeper ideas evolve slowly as compared to the superficial ideas. The deeper ideas are also—by virtue of being situated higher up in the tree—applicable to more individual objects than the models of technology that apply to a much smaller number of devices. Thus, you can expect a new type of vacuum cleaner every few years, but you expect a lot of time to pass before a new widely applicable physical theory is accepted in science because the revision of fundamental theories implies bigger change. The longer life of deeper ideas and scientific theories corresponds to the longer lifespan of the demigods who control these ideas and theories. The acceptance of the new ideas depends on the demigods moving into new stages in their life. Indeed, the advent of new concepts, theories, models, and formulae, is itself the creativity of demigods: they *create,* and we *discover*. That is, what they produce as sensual products appears as ideas in our minds. Thus, if we create the ideas, but the demigods haven't yet moved to these new ideas, then the ideas would not be widely accepted by others. The inventions will lie in our minds and will not see any significant adoption. A widespread change in the world depends on higher control; that control also rests upon the evolution of the universe—but it is an *ideological* change. As time passes, it naturally brings new ideas, and many good ideas are subsequently called "ahead of their times".

The true laws of nature are based on the nature of the soul. But until this nature is realized, there are many temporary and fictitious laws, as the history of scientific evolution indicates. While we think that we discover the nature of reality, the demigod only creates a new object—like a new type of pottery, new dish of food, or a new type of clothing. In their world, too, different things are enjoyed at different times, and that change in 'fashion' appears to us as intellectual discovery. So, it is futile to say that the scientific theories we discover are constant, because the theories are changing continuously. However, there is indeed a universal theory based on the nature of the soul that never changes, because the soul's nature never changes. If we discovered that theory, it would remain constant, and applicable to all living experiences in the world.

Greek philosopher Plato postulated that ideas reside in a 'Platonic world', which is true in one sense as the demigods who perceive these ideas are also their controllers. We can mentally access the idea-world, but our pleasure experienced by such accesses is minimal. The demigods are in a 'Platonic world' quite like the ideas they perceive are in that world. In another sense, there is a single world because we can know those theorems too, although we cannot sensually perceive them. The Platonic world is mentally accessible to us, but it is sensually perceived only by the demigods. The sensual proofs of the ideas, however, are perceived by the human but disregarded by the demigods.

The pride that scientists take in discovering new theories, theorems, and conjectures—just one or two in their lifetimes—is somewhat misplaced because the ideas that scientists take pride in discovering are freely available to demigods like objects in our world. Discovering a new idea for them is like traveling on an idea-like land where you observe new and beautiful landscapes not seen before. But since they see that idea sensually, they also see how it is related to the other ideas—at their level of abstraction. They too don't see the 'big picture' from their standpoint, which means that there is something even higher than their vantage point. Just as we formulate scientific theories to explain our world, and thus try to rise beyond our current existence, similarly, the demigods too aspire to explain how their world of ideas appeared in the first place, and how it evolves over time. In their attempt to explain the ideological evolution, they mentally formulate higher level theories, and they may someday perceive those ideas sensually. There is hence a progression in knowledge, activity, relations, and pleasure, even among the demigods.

The Practice of Mantra Chanting

The Vedic practice of sacrifice or *yajña* was formerly used to satisfy the demigods, and this system has since existed all over the world as religious rituals. The primary technique in a *yajña* is the chanting of some *mantra*, which is a sound symbol whose meanings may not be apparent to the uninitiated. While humans can hear those sounds, and try to understand their meanings, the demigods don't hear the sounds, but the meanings in our mind become their sense objects. To create such sense objects for the demigods one must not only utter the sounds, but also have the mind concentrate on the meanings at the same time. Alternately, one might think of the meanings in the mind without even uttering the sound; but uttering the sound without the mental concentration would not produce the desired effect. If one only utters the *mantra* and the mind is not attentive—i.e., the mind is thinking something other than the *mantra*—then the chanting of these *mantra* becomes pointless as the objects in our mind are absent, and so the sensations for demigods are missing. Hence, merely uttering the sounds in a *mantra* is not sufficient, although just thinking about the meanings in the mind (without the sound utterance) is sufficient. However, because the mind is distracted, uttering the sound helps the mind's concentration, and hence verbal utterance is encouraged.

At present, the *mantras* have become mumbo-jumbo because the minds of the worshippers are wandering (even with verbal utterances). These utterances are akin to cycling or swimming, where the mind is not following the bodily activity and hence the mental meanings are not created. If these meanings are not produced in the mind, then they fail to satisfy the demigods because the demigods are not perceiving our sensual objects; they perceive our mental objects as their sensations. But the priest who concentrates his mind on the sound can offer great sense enjoyment to demigods. The demigods, if satisfied in this way, can provide the basic ingredients for human life—soil, water, light, minerals, rain, wind, besides healthy mind and body.

The worship of demigods is not useful at present because mind control is itself very hard for the priests. Mind control begins in character development, leading a regulated life, and restrained enjoyment. If the senses and the mind are not regulated, they remain distracted and even sensual activities are not performed perfectly. A person who lacks concentration may chant the *mantra,* but their utterance would vary each time because the senses are not controlled; their mind would therefore be producing different thoughts. Indeed, most chanters don't have a controlled mind. Anyone who has practiced *mantra* chanting attests to this problem: it is hard to perfect the chanting by concentration. It takes long practice to reduce the levels of sensual and mental distraction and being in that state requires lifestyle changes. Because such mind control and lifestyle is not mastered by everyone, only a person who can attain such advancement is qualified to be a 'scientist'. Formerly, the *Brahmana* led an austere and regulated life to master sense and mind control. By such control they perfected the chanting of *mantra* and therefore became the scientists to manipulate nature. Everyone else could understand the science theoretically but they could not practice it, and hence the *Brahmana* had a unique position in society due to their mastery of the self and the world around us.

The *Brahmana* could lead a simple and austere life because many of the day-to-day necessities of their living were provided by other sections of society, primarily the government or the ruler, who collected taxes from the businessmen and distributed it to the *Brahmana* so that they were not hassled by the things that disturb the mind and the senses. The problem of sense and mind control is not just an individual prerogative. Rather, quite like the government and the military today fund scientific research and development, similarly, in the past, the kings and queens funded the *Brahmana.* The ideology underlying the older science differed radically but the method of freeing up the *Brahmana* to pursue sense and mind control was beneficial to the society as a whole quite like new advancements in scientific knowledge today benefit society as a whole. Revival of that science requires a systemic change in society. We can understand theoretically how that science can work, and how it was practiced in the past, but we cannot practice it without a systemic change.

The Universal Administrative System

The demigods are roles in nature; since roles are natural constructs, and the roles are hierarchical, the demigods are higher roles. These roles can be occupied by persons. A higher role empowers the person to define and control the freedom of the other persons in the lower role. Due to this greater and lesser freedom, a person occupying a particular role enjoys or suffers—depending on what they desire to achieve through life. In the Vedic system, the demigod roles are permanent, but the demigods (persons) themselves are not permanently occupying those roles. Thus, even the souls occupying the human body can in the future become the demigods, and similarly, the persons in the demigod role will eventually fall down from their higher position into a lower position—unless they successfully end the entire journey of material existence. A demigod is therefore like the president or bureaucrat in a country: the person and the role are different; as long as the universe exists, the role will exist, but different persons will occupy these roles at different times.

The Vedic system also details the duration of time for which these occupations or jobs are held by a person—which are then called the lifetimes of demigods. Yes, the demigods are not eternally in that role. They certainly live longer than the human life duration, but they must leave their position eventually. In that sense, the system of demigods doesn't constitute the *polytheism* comprising many 'gods' who are all in that position eternally. The Vedic demigod system is like a system of administration in which the roles are permanent but the persons occupying the roles perform a job and eventually leave.

Modern science assumes that the laws of nature are universal. Indeed, one of the cornerstones of Einstein's theory of relativity is that the *form* of the law is unchanged across different observers. This *form* in Vedic philosophy, and all personalist ideologies, is a *role*, which, if occupied by a person, gives them power over the lower roles by which they can control the persons occupying the lower roles. Each role is therefore a law—a *normative* law—although not a *descriptive* law. That is, the law states what *should* happen, but doesn't describe what *would* happen. Ideally, a person is expected to live within the bounds of the normative law, which present themselves as 'freedom' afforded to a person in order to fulfill their desires within restrictions. If the normative law is broken (because it is only a possibility, not a reality), the law creates a consequence which is subsequently delivered by the demigod by changing a person's situation. Each situation is therefore a law—because it entails an expected behavior. And each situation is the consequence of a previous action. The laws of nature are not universal, because a person's role is the law that creates expectations, and the demigod's role is the law that delivers the consequences produced from exceeding or falling short of expectations.

The demigods are not free, because they too are judged by persons occupying higher roles and obliged to obey the higher laws regarding how they must apply their laws of judgment. The system of gods therefore operates like a bureaucracy in a government. The lowest level bureaucrats enforce the laws. The higher-level bureaucrats ensure that the lower-level bureaucrats are enforcing the laws correctly. Even higher-level ministers define the laws suitable to the time, place, and situation—i.e., as new types of situations arise, the laws have to be defined to deal with the new situations, subject to the overall intent and purpose of the administration being met. Finally, the top ruler can define the intent and purpose of the administrative system itself. The study of the 'mythology' is no different than the study of an administrative system.

In fact, such a study can tell us how a government within a country should be organized—i.e., how many tiers must exist, the functions and duties of each tier, the laws of the persons occupying the roles at different tiers of organization, and how each tier must work to fulfill the demands of the ruler. The ruler of the cosmos is represented in the earthly rulers if their rule is compatible with the intent of the supreme ruler in the cosmos. The king or queen is therefore not God, but a *representation* of the intent that underscores the rule, if indeed he or she follows the intent. If they disobey that intent, then the consequences for them—individually—are very severe because they hold a far more powerful position and neglecting its duties means a greater punishment. The roles of politicians, kings, and queens, are therefore not to be held whimsically. A person can obtain such a powerful position due to their *karma*. But neglecting its responsibilities also entails far greater suffering in the future. Therefore, the rulers must be educated in the laws of nature—i.e., the intent of God as it applies to the time, place, and situation that a ruler is governing.

Every person inhabits multiple roles. You might simultaneously be a parent, a child, a citizen, an employee, etc. The demands of these roles often conflict with each other, and you have to prioritize your duties. For instance, if your child falls sick, but you are expected to complete the duties of your employment, should you prioritize childcare or the duties of your occupation? In some situations, childcare is more important, but in others your occupation will take precedence. Therefore, even if the laws of a role are well-defined, the conflict between duties necessitates prioritization. The prioritization arises because there are higher and lower duties—ruled by higher and lower demigods—and in case of a conflict, the higher demigod's duty must be prioritized. In that sense, the understanding of the natural hierarchy is important for us to lead a dutiful life, because conflicts among duties are the norm rather than the exception. If we don't understand this hierarchy, we might fulfill the lower duty—and call it 'doing our jobs'—while a higher duty is neglected.

The laws of nature are not universal because the prioritization of duties is highly contextual. Such conflicts are apparent in every legal system of judgment. A judge has many laws to follow, and the laws are often contradictory. For example, does the basic right to defend oneself entail the empowerment to indiscriminately bear arms, which might be used offensively rather than defensively? Or, does the fundamental right to human expression and speech entail the needless use of speech to criticize and humiliate other people? The answer to these questions varies from situation to situation, and has to be determined contextually because every right, when demanded excessively becomes a disgrace, and every duty if applied mindlessly becomes an abomination. Nothing by itself is right or wrong; the context makes it so. The rules to be followed are subject to the situation and cannot be given universally.

As a result, the only guideline applicable universally is to satisfy the highest lawmaker—God—even if it means undermining all other duties. In case of other conflicts, the duties related to the higher demigods must be prioritized over the duties related to the lower demigods. The duty of an individual—and the judgment of right and wrong—called *dharma* is a complex topic, and its fulfillment depends on a science pertaining to the roles in the universe and the duties they entail in our lives. The *dharma*—often called 'religion'—is not to be manufactured whimsically by individuals, nor can a manufactured religion help a person free themselves from the consequences of neglected duties. These topics are not a matter of 'faith', nor are they 'myths' created by fertile minds. But when we take the understanding of natural laws as normative rather than descriptive laws, which allow a person freedom of action and the free will to prioritize their actions, religion naturally manifests as the performance of duties governed by a hierarchy of functions and their leaders.

The modern secular legal and administrative systems were preceded by religious systems that defined rules specific to that time, place, and situation, because they were suitable to achieve a specific intent at that time, place, and situation. The rules themselves can be changed if the intent is fulfilled. And the rules have no meaning without an intent. In that sense, the impersonal laws of nature are insufficient because just by reading the law you cannot understand the intent: the same law is compatible with multiple intents under different situations. If therefore we remove the intent, then we must also remove the contexts. And now the existence of laws themselves cannot be justified: Why only these laws and no others? Scientific laws in this sense are unjustifiable because we cannot seek their intent, and whether that intent is fulfilled differently in different contexts. We have to just take the laws for granted.

However, the governmental laws are created to fulfill a purpose, which explains why the laws change over time as the governments change: the new laws are better suited to fulfill a given intent in a new time, place, and situation. Intents explain why a particular law (as opposed to other laws) exists. And that question can only be answered by a *person* who creates the laws because the laws were chosen after rejecting alternatives based on an intent.

Myths and Psychoanalysis

Since the demigods can be understood by the mind, there is a close parallel between the 'mythologies' of the religions and facts about the human psyche. The reason for this parallel is that the sensual activities of the demigods correspond to the mental activities of the human beings, and psychologists such as Carl Jung[6] have sought the psychological foundations of these myths. The trouble with such a search is that it appears to undermine the reality of the demigods, because the activities of these demigods are explained as 'myths' of the human mind. The dominant explanation of such mythology is only elevated from complete concoction to a pervasive feature of every culture and era. However, it still doesn't answer some key questions: Why only these archetypes and none others? The existence of these universal archetypes begs an explanation, which Carl Jung avoided by postulating a "collective unconscious" as a repository for the universal myths. These postulates are emblematic of the modernist mindset that depersonalizes nature, and when it cannot be depersonalized—e.g., in psychology—then to approximate the personalism with impersonal idea repositories such as the "collective unconscious" rather than recognizing the reality of the depicted personalities themselves.

Nevertheless, just as a higher sensual reality can be accessed mentally, similarly, the study of the "collective unconscious" also presents us with the opportunity to investigate why certain archetypes and myths are universal. The commonalities among the system of gods across Greek, Roman, Egyptian, Mesopotamian, and Vedic cultures is not an accident. It is also not simply a reflection of a "collective unconscious" from which the numerous conscious minds draw inadvertently. These 'myths' are rather a new way of viewing nature, and explaining it using a worldview quite different from the one prevalent in the Western world in the last few centuries. The personalization of nature that prevailed two thousand years ago was rejected by modern religions in favor of a singular monotheistic God, before modern science further depersonalized nature by even rejecting that singular God while recognizing the reality of the mind, which too has now been—in the 20th century and later—been depersonalized as merely molecules. Therefore, to personalize nature, we have to retrace our steps to a time when depersonalization hadn't yet begun. It involves not just reexamining modern science, but even the religions that began the depersonalization by calling the erstwhile religions 'paganism'[7].

There are several tools that can aid in this quest. These include the analysis of commonalities in the system of gods across diverse ancient cultures, understanding these cultures as reflections of deep-seated archetypes in the human mind, a scientific analysis for why certain personality types constitute causal explanations of our experiences, and a theory of the soul that ties all this together. This is a broad set, and for this reason alone, the discussion of 'mythology' in this book is hardly going to be about the stories, which can be found elsewhere. We will rather take a scientific approach to understanding the nature of the soul, natural causality in matter, and how this causality has to be explained in a personalist manner based on the theory of the soul.

The comparative analysis of the different systems of gods that existed in diverse cultures and left its imprints on society that we can see today, is perhaps the only empirical material that we can reliably use, and all such materials are open to diverse interpretations. The main contentions of this book are not dependent as much on the empirical details as on the theoretical necessities that I mentioned above. Therefore, my focus will not be so much on delving into the details of each type of god and their associated narrations, but on what kind of role they were expected to play vis-à-vis people's lives and nature in general. Their associated stories may not be false, but to even understand what they mean, we have to first understand who the person is. This book is not long enough to capture all possible details. I would be satisfied if I have been successful in conveying the notion that mythology can be a science.

Book Overview

A natural tool in the early stages of any investigation is *classification* which emerges out of seeing similarities and dissimilarities. Once we identify classes, we can ask: Which of these classes might be more fundamental as compared to the others? And the criterion of distinguishing the fundamental from the superficial is that the fundamental is expected to explain the superficial. Through such explanations we construct a *tree* of diversification—the origin is unified, but it branches into numerous intermediate and superficial observables. The structure of knowledge and explanation is created by envisioning a tree of conceptual diversity produced from a conceptual unity. Classification is the reverse process of trying to see some level of unity in the diversity.

Searching for similarities in the different personalized explanations however has a shortcoming in that the process helps us initially with some obvious parallels and differences, but it doesn't help us achieve the level of unity that is needed for conceptual simplification. We can end up with more than one alternative explanation which needs to be confirmed or denied based on some facts, but it is not clear what those facts might be. This is typical of most systems of gods where similarities with other systems might be apparent, but the differences between them are unresolvable based on what we can perceive. Now, if you cannot perceive something, how do you resolve their differences? This is where a theoretical unification becomes important. The system of gods should be diversified (so that it can explain the diverse aspects of our existence) and unified (so we can provide a simple explanation of their origin). But the explanation alone doesn't entail the truth; it must also be grounded in facts that *we* can accept intuitively based on our individual experiences.

This is where the Vedic system of gods, as expanded from the nature of the soul, and then divided into types of cognition, relation, and emotion is important. Even though we cannot directly perceive the demigods, we can understand their existence based on the *theory* of the soul and its experiences. The demigods will thus necessarily remain theoretical entities which can be experimentally confirmed provided we can raise our perception to experience the form of these ideas. The second, third, and fourth chapters deal with the description of these types, based on the descriptions of Vedic cosmology.

The second chapter details some basic ideas about space and time, and how they are expanded from the three properties of the soul—*sat, chit,* and *ānanda*. The third chapter extends this understanding with regard to the cosmology of the sun, and the basis of the 12 signs of the zodiac. And the fourth chapter then describes the type-based theories regarding the moon and the stars. These types manifest as locations in space, sun signs, the sun's associates, the phases of the moon, and the different star signs. Everything has a philosophical basis, and if we grasp the philosophy, we can understand why nature is described in precisely these types, and why they are not arbitrary.

Once these types are understood, we can see the basis for so-called 'polytheism' where many gods are worshipped, but they are ultimately *expansions* from a single God. The theory underlying cosmology also becomes the theory of conscious experience, and that gives us the basis on which to speak about the unity in diversity of the diverse religions. Chapter five then deals with the questions of religious unification and how these religions are diversifications from a single root; each branch can lead us to the root, provided we stop treating ourselves as the root. These branches can thus be progressive paths to the ultimate realization of the scientific truth, but if we remain stuck with each branch as the ultimate truth, we will also be limited in our realizations.

The sixth chapter delves into several commonalities between different religions. As I have noted earlier, the differences are less important if we want to construct the tree of unification; at least, we must note the similarities to identify the ideological classes before we see the differences between them. Accordingly, this chapter delves into the similarities across diverse religions—e.g., the worship of the sun, the moon, and the stars, the idea of trinity, the use of male and female deities and their impact on human society, etc. Once we see these similarities, we can note the differences too, and the primary difference is that the problem of the soul's free will is incredibly complicated; free will never dies, which means that if the soul has been liberated, it can fall down again due to free will. Similarly, if the soul has fallen it can be resurrected in the future. The chapter discusses how this issue leads to *karma*, reincarnation, different places in the universe which are better or worse, and then to many forms of demigods who control the delivery of the consequences of previous actions. These might seem theological excesses to many people today, but they are a necessary outcome of the problem of free will. I will describe when religions did not want to deal with this problem in its full resplendence and decided to simplify the issue by instituting the ideas of eternal hell and heaven, rejecting reincarnation and *karma*, and eliminating the existence of demigods as 'pagan gods'. That flaw has subsequently come back to bite them. For example, a God that creates free will, but then sends a person to eternal hell upon misuse of that free will leads to the idea that God is not benevolent.

The seventh and final chapter deals with the role of psychology in the context of religion, especially with the question of whether the religious stories and moralizing ideals are widespread properties of the human mind or they are also real things outside the human mind. While many people reject scripture as fabricated stories that could never happen, a growing number of people have taken a stance between considering them to be literally true versus treating them to be outright false. This latter stance corresponds to the idea that religion is a fact of the human mind, not of a transcendent soul or God. This idea is justified based on the realization that the stories and morals religion institutes are seen recurring in diverse religions, cultures, civilizations, and ages. How do we *explain* this recurrence except by supposing that they are all products of the human mind, and that the mind has universal properties due to which it recreates the same 'myths' and 'stories' over and over?

The chapter discusses how ideas in our mind are sensations at a higher level; what appears in our mind is shared because there is indeed a higher reality which we can understand but cannot perceive. The use of metaphors in language is the means by which we know the use of sensual language in describing mental experiences, so the problem is not limited to religions. The discussion of metaphors in language—and how they are created—liberates the problem out of the religious context into a generic perceptual and linguistic context. We are then able to tackle it better and realize that our use of sensual metaphors to describe mental concepts indicates the existence of a reality that is sensual for demigods although it is only mental for us. As a result, we don't have to think that what I think is only a product of our minds; we can also realize that what I think metaphorically exists outside the mind sensually.

The central goal of this book is not to identify, discuss, and debate every kind of religious idea. It is rather to formulate the framework within which such discussions can occur in a meaningful manner. The main goals of this book are to show that there is a hierarchy of theologies, from polytheism, to monism, to monotheism. However, even the single God has many facets, quite like our bodies have back and front, top and bottom. The soul is free to see one or more of the facets, and that perception of the different aspects of God creates a diversified understanding of God, even when God is only one.

There are hence two kinds of polytheism. First in which there are many different 'gods'. Second there are many aspects of the same person which can be individually experienced. Most people think that polytheism necessarily means the first type, but in this book, you will find the second type of polytheism in which God has many faces and each soul sees one or more of the faces. Seeing God in full involves the perception of contradictions—e.g., how could you simultaneously see the back and front of God? Seeing more than one facet therefore entails perceptual advancement beyond seeing one facet. An example of such perception is mentally perceiving the idea 'coin' different from the head and tail of the coin; as we look deeper into the personality of God, we see ideas that reconcile the opposites and make them visible at once.

Monotheism and polytheism are not contrary ideas when the second type of polytheism is adopted. Similarly, because the soul has expanded from God, the soul is said to be a part of God, which leads to the idea of monism, and even this idea is not entirely contrary to the monotheistic religions, although the part is never equal to the whole so being part of

God is not identical to being God. The monist position that identifies the soul with God is false, although there is a nuanced position within monism which is true. In this way, the so-called contradictions between diverse religious ideologies disappear.

The source of all this unity is ultimately the three aspects of the soul—which originally exist in God—and which create the subsequent diversity. Monism, polytheism, and monotheism are simply expansions of these three aspects. There are as many possible religions as there are branches on the trees expanded from a root. We can see their diversity and conflict if we choose to look at the leaves and neglect the higher branches and root. But we can see their unity if we are prepared to rise higher in our understanding and perception whereby the incompleteness of the leaf—without the root and branch—is evidenced, which then prompts the soul to ascend progressively.

I would consider this book a success if the reader can walk away with one idea: God created a tree of ideologies, and the soul chooses which branch of that ideological tree it wants to be on. That choice doesn't preclude the reality of the other branches, nor does it necessarily entail a contradiction. Hopefully, the study of this ideological tree will help us become better practitioners of our own currently chosen religion, and respect other religions as well.

2

Overview of Theogony

I tell you the solemn truth, that the doctrine of the Trinity is not so difficult to accept for a working proposition as any one of the axioms of physics

— *Henry Adams*

The Trinity of Gods

The Vedic system of demigods constitutes an administrative system for governing the universe, in which powers are delegated from top to bottom quite like in a bureaucracy. All the demigods are in turn manifest from a trinity of *Viṣṇu*, *Brahma*, and *Shiva*, who represent the three modes of nature—*sattva*, *rajas*, and *tamas*, which are material embodiments of the three facets of the soul called *chit*, *sat*, and *ānanda*, respectively. *Viṣṇu* embodies the judgment of truth manifest from *chit*, *Brahma* the judgment of right manifest from *sat*, and *Shiva* the judgment of good manifest from *ānanda*. The *chit* creates all that we can perceive in this world through senses. The *sat* represents relations between the things and to the things we perceive[1]. These relationships create our roles to other things, and hence the sense of being[2]. Finally, *ānanda* represents the goals and purposes and hence the pain or pleasure obtained through perception; if the goals are fulfilled the person is happy and the person is unhappy if they are not. Thus, *Viṣṇu* is the creator of all that exists materially. But everything that exists is not known or used by everyone. Hence, *Brahma* creates the roles which bring specific individuals in contact with other individuals. Finally, the fact that you come into contact with certain things doesn't mean you necessarily enjoy or suffer them. The pleasure depends on your goals and tastes, and *Shiva* is the creator of a variety of pleasures and intentions.

The three modes of nature, and the trinity that rules over them, are intimately tied to the nature of the soul. The system of gods is therefore not conceived arbitrarily. They are rather conceived as controllers of the three aspects of the soul. To change this trinity, one would have to change the soul.

The Vedic system of demigods has an advantage over other systems because it gets grounded into a theory of the soul, and the understanding of material nature derived from the nature of the soul, which are directly accessible to us without reference to the demigods. But it also means that in order to accept the system, we must know the theory of nature, and the nature of the soul on which it is based. When the understanding of nature and the soul disappears, only the system of gods remains, and there is nothing to verify its truth anymore. This has indeed been the fate of most systems that are presently called 'mythological'. The primary reason is that the worship of such gods was detached from the philosophical underpinnings of the nature of the self, why it exists in the material world, and how it evolves from one stage of life to another. When this knowledge is lost or disregarded, then the system of worship becomes tenuous and open to varied interpretations and changes. The Vedic system differs not so much in the system of demigods but in its surviving philosophical system based on which we can understand the system.

The understanding of the soul in the Vedic system is very intuitive—the soul has the capacities for knowledge and action called *chit*, it relates to other souls based on *sat,* also called 'awareness', and it enjoys these interactions through *ānanda*. Based on the understanding of the soul, Vedic texts describe a trinity that represents and manifests the properties that exist in the soul in primordial form. The assumption in this system is the nature of the soul. Since we are all souls, we have direct access to this nature through introspection. If the self is well-understood, then everything else is automatically understood. The worship of gods reinforces this understanding of the self, and knowledge of the nature of the self confirms the truth of the worship of gods.

There are some contentions about which of these three is superior to the others, and these contentions are based on different references to Vedic texts where each of the three is described as superior to the others.

I will quickly try to dispel these contentions. From a spiritual standpoint, God is originally *chit* or the six qualities called knowledge, beauty, heroism, wealth, power, and renunciation. He then develops the awareness of His qualities, and through that awareness becomes situated in the original role—the relation to the self. The process of becoming self-aware constitutes His *sat* which divides and expands His personality of six qualities into a tree. Finally, becoming aware of the nature of self creates happiness within God, leading to His *ānanda.*

As a result, from a spiritual standpoint, *chit* is highest, followed by *sat*, followed by *ānanda*. But these are things as understood from God's viewpoint. In the material world, morality or duty produced by *sat* is highest, the desires of *ānanda* are below the duty, and the truth created by *chit* is below these desires. As a result, *Viṣṇu* who represents *chit* or truth is highest from a spiritual viewpoint, but He takes a lower position in the material world[3]. Similarly, *sat* which has a lower position from a spiritual standpoint becomes the highest in the material world, and *Brahma* who represents *sat* becomes the highest. Although *chit* is the original reality, it only creates the material ingredients. The placement of the soul in matter, the relation between material objects, and the different types of species and ecosystems to live are created by *Brahma*. Normatively, our pleasure is subordinated to our duties, however, we would not enter the world if there wasn't some happiness. Thus, *Shiva* who represents *ānanda* is sometimes said to be subordinate to *Brahma* (when desires are subordinate to pleasure) and then called superior to *Brahma* and *Viṣṇu* (when desire is seen as the cause of the material sojourn). Factually, there is no contradiction in these descriptions if we understand the reasons underlying them.

From a spiritual standpoint, the *chit* and *ānanda* are embodied in God, but His awareness expands His person into the individual souls. This expansion of God's awareness into other forms of awareness is called His *Śakti*. Each *Śakti* is a particular way of knowing God, and we will see later how *Śakti* itself has 8 forms, which are 8 kinds of 'worlds' in which the soul can exist. These 8 forms constitute different varieties of choices which arise from prioritizing *sat*, *chit*, and *ānanda*. For example, we noted above how *chit* is higher than *ānanda* which is higher than *sat* from a spiritual standpoint, and *sat* is higher than *ānanda*, which is higher than *chit* from a material standpoint. These are different priorities within the soul, which constitute his free will. Based on this free will, the soul can choose a different type of world. When the soul prioritizes his *ānanda* over that of God, he falls into the material world, where his *ānanda* is subordinated to his duties and the laws of nature. However, when the soul prioritizes God's pleasure over his pleasure, he is liberated from the material world. *Śakti* as awareness expands God into the creation, which means awareness is subordinate to *chit* or truth and *ānanda* or desire for happiness: God becomes aware of things only when there is content and a desire for it.

In the material world, *Brahma* represents this *Śakti*. He is a soul, who has been empowered to manage and control the *dharma* or duties in the world. As the duties are the normative laws of the world, *Brahma* is the chief lawmaker. And yet, he is not God, only an empowered living entity managing the world. Thus, he is generally not worshipped on par with *Viṣṇu* and *Shiva* even though he is described as being superior to both because *sat* is higher than *ānanda* and *chit* in this world. Again, as we can see, there are profound philosophical reasons for these differences and if these reasons are not understood then one is led to believe that a higher deity must always be worshipped if the lower one is worshipped, or that the lower one need not be worshipped if a higher one is worshipped. Before we make any conclusions regarding such worship, we must understand the underlying philosophy and the reasons for them.

It is noteworthy that *Viṣṇu*, *Brahma*, and *Shiva* have the same qualities as the soul, although the quantities are significantly larger. Thus, *Viṣṇu*—who dominates in *chit* or *sattva*—creates all the concepts of knowing and acting, from which all material objects and their changes can be created. From these material concepts, *Brahma*—who dominates in *sat* or *rajas*—creates the roles of different species of life, structuring and organizing the society, and the rules of *dharma* which are different kinds of responsibilities for different kinds of roles. Once these roles and responsibilities are created, *Shiva*—who dominates in *ānanda* or *tamas*—creates the different kinds of desires, goals, and intentions, using which the soul enjoys different kinds of pleasures in the world. Ideally, a particular type of body is suited for a specific type of role, and a specific type of role is ideally needed to enjoy a unique type of pleasure. Therefore, the trinity is not mutually conflicting if the ideal scenario of matching the body with the role, and the role with the pleasure is employed. However, their separation creates the potential whereby a soul can enjoy different pleasures in the same body and the same role—some of them may not be righteous.

This separation is essential for free will because without it a certain body will mean a fixed role and a fixed pleasure, and the soul would have no choice once he obtained the body. We can say that *Viṣṇu* is the creator of knowledge and action, *Brahma* is the creator of all roles that cause societies, ecosystems, and civilizations, while *Shiva* is the cause of different kinds of desires within us. They are all creators and controllers, although of different kinds.

Expansion of the Trinity

This trinity is expressed in Abrahamic religions as the Father, the Son, and the Holy Ghost. *Viṣṇu* is the Father, *Brahma* is His Son, and *Shiva* is the Holy Ghost. The Holy Ghost gives 'life' to the body, because that 'life' is desire, purpose, and intention. The Son, on the other hand, defines the *dharma* of different roles and relations. The Son is the teacher who propagates the principles of righteous action in society and tells them what to do and how to live in different times, places, and under different circumstances. The Son of God creates many distinct 'religions', for different people at different places and times—Judaism, Christianity, and Islam accept this idea in modern times. The Father is the creator of the material world—the concepts—from which the Son has manifested different religious lives, which the Holy Ghost impels the soul to enjoy.

Shiva is described as the leader of the ghosts in numerous Vedic texts; He lives on a mountain, consumes intoxicants, dons a disheveled look with long matted hair, dresses in tiger skin, and smears his body with ashes. His appearance—by normal human standards—is 'ghastly', and He is appropriately the leader of ghosts. The ghosts have material desires, but not a material body by which they can fulfill these desires. The ghosts are also unable to form societies based on rules and duties. They are hence—in one sense—only the material embodiments of desires, and they follow *Shiva* because He is the creator of desires. The term 'Holy Ghost' likely references this fact from older times, and if this is indeed true, then *Shiva* and 'Holy Ghost' are identical persons.

It is said sometimes the ghosts enter the body of other living beings in order to enjoy through those bodies and their interrelations to other bodies. Many Hollywood films have been made depicting societies of ghosts where the ghosts talk, walk, and interact with each other. These movies are pure fictions, because the ghosts cannot have relations and cannot know and express. They embody only one of the three aspects of the soul—desire—as a result of which they cannot be perceived like ordinary things; we can say they don't have a body of *chit* or cognition and activity. They suffer simply because they have desires which can never be fulfilled except through another body.

The *Shaiva Tantra* system prescribes the worship of *Shiva* as a way to control and master one's desires. However, in degraded forms, this system has also been used for mind control over others. Ghosts are used for this purpose; when they enter the body, they force their desires on the person, and the person whose body they inhabit appears to lose control over their body. Again, Hollywood has made many movies on exorcism of ghosts; those stories have a basis in reality. But quite like mind control of others is a degraded form of self-control, similarly, these depictions while true are not spiritually elevating. Similarly, any type of mind control or ghost worship is degrading. It is good for ghosts to worship *Shiva* because they cannot fulfill their desires legitimately. But it is degrading for humans to worship ghosts for mind control. Hence, the Holy Ghost is one of the trinity but ghosts are not to be worshipped.

The Vedas describe how this trinity further expands into a system of 36 demigods. There are 12 *Āditya* expanded from *Viṣṇu*, 8 *Vasu* expanded from *Brahma*, and 16 *Rudra* expanded from *Shiva*. These divisions are not whimsical, and we will have a chance in the next chapter to discuss them in detail, illustrating the philosophical reasons for making these distinctions. Briefly, the 12-fold division from *Viṣṇu* represents 12 essential concepts; the 16-fold division from *Shiva* denotes 16 essential desires and pleasures; the 8-fold division from *Brahma* represents 8 distinct levels of conscious experience of the soul. These numbers are therefore not produced out of thin air. They are rather based on a type theory in which all ideas can be known in terms of 12 basic concepts, all desires can be reduced to 16 types of pleasures, and all consciousness can be understood in terms of 8 fundamental types of awareness.

In Vedic texts, the 36 gods are sometimes also described as 33 gods by removing the first among the list of 12 *Āditya*, 16 *Rudra*, and 8 *Vasu*. This is because the first person in this list is closely identified with *Viṣṇu*, *Shiva*, and *Brahma*. The first deity is like the parent of the entire family from whom the rest of the family is produced and is therefore considered the 'highest' in the family. The family of demigods therefore doesn't comprise of 'equals'. Some demigods are higher, and others are lower, quite like the head in your body is highest while the feet are the lowest. Together, they constitute a body—comprising ideas, desires, and relations—which has many distinct parts.

Understanding the unity in the system of demigods requires us to see this hierarchy, and how the demigods are parts of the same 'body' created originally from the trinity, which is in turn the logical representation of the soul. The universe as a whole is, in this description, a single body with parts, and the different demigods are higher level (i.e., more abstract) conceptual descriptions of the universe. For instance, your hands and legs are abstract descriptions of your body, because they can be further divided into parts. You don't necessarily speak about all the pores in your body; you can also speak about the hands and legs. Similarly, you can take the hand or leg itself as a 'body' and speak about its 'head' and 'legs', thus repeatedly subdividing it into smaller and smaller parts, using the same set of 36 concepts over and over. This hierarchical system of description creates a universe that can be experienced in the abstract or detailed manner, depending on the extent of its division.

The Four-Dimensional Space-Time

The material world is three dimensions of space, and one dimension of time. The time is produced by *ānanda* or the choice of pleasure. Space, in turn, in produced from *chit* and *sat* each of which is divided by the three modes of nature. The *chit* creates objects and the *sat* creates roles. In modern science, these are respectively called 'matter' and 'force'. Factually, there is no object which is also not situated in a role. Therefore, when we observe the real world, we only see the combination of *chit* and *sat*, although logically they are distinct. The three modes of nature dividing *chit* and *sat* create the three-dimensional space, but actually there is an overlay of two such spaces—of objects and roles—because both *sat* and *chit* are hierarchical. Hence, there are two kinds of overlaid spaces represented by *Brahma* (who defines the roles) and *Viṣṇu* (who defines the objects). Separately, *Shiva* defines the time. Due to this separation we tend to speak about the four-dimensional space-time, when the fact is that the space we see has to be described as two separate spaces.

In this section, I will describe the three dimensions of space which are created due to the combination of *sat* and *chit*. The three-dimensional space is comprised of a stack of two-dimensional planes. In each of the layers of the two-dimensional plane, the tree of *chit* (cognition and action) expands from a center, which constitutes the root of that plane. These constitute the material properties that we can perceive by our senses, mind, intellect, ego, and morality. Essentially, at each level of the plane, there is a different kind of sense, mind, intellect, ego, and morality. In addition to these material properties at each level in the plane, each of these properties is also situated in a *role*. However, the hierarchy of roles expands vertically such that a role is comprised of three parts—*ādidaivika*, *ādibhautika*, and *ādiatmika*. The *ādibhautika* and *ādiatmika* are two parts of the relation between two things—the *ādibhautika* representing the thing being observed, and the *ādiatmika* representing the sense, mind, intellect, ego, and moral sense that are perceiving these properties. In addition to these two-way relations, there is a third component in the relation which is sits *higher* than the two. This is the *ādidaivika* component, which represents the 'controllers' or demigods who mediate the relationship.

Thus, everything we perceive depends on a relation, the perceiver and the perceived are in the two-dimensional plane, but the relation between the two is controlled by a higher entity called the *ādidaivika* or the demigods. Thus, for example, the food we eat and the mouth that eats exist at the same plane. But who gets to eat which kind of food is decided by the higher level entity. Since all our experiences are produced through such relationships, the demigods can control what we experience. These relations are established due to *karma,* so the demigods are deliverers of this *karma.* The demigods are situated at a higher level than the level that they control. Therefore, the tree of diversification comprises of a root called the *ādidaivika* which divides into the *ādibhautika* and *ādiatmika.* This constitutes the *vertical* tree of expansion, in distinction to the horizontal plane in which the root is at the center.

Therefore, from the perspective of the material properties, the root is at the center of the plane, but from the perspective of roles the root is above the plane. This is the basis of saying that to advance in life, one must move *inward* and *upward* because the origin of material properties lies inward (toward the center of the plane) and the origin of roles lies upwards (in a higher plane).

When an object appears in a role, the relation between the object and the role is called *is-a* relation. For instance, when someone becomes the president of the country, the body and the mind that enter the role are designated by the title of a president—we say that so-and-so *is-a* president. Similarly, we can say that someone is a father, is a mother, is a child, is a citizen, etc. Conversely, the relation itself *has-a ādibhautika* and *ādiatmika* part. So, within the tree of roles, the relation between the whole and the part is *has-a*. But the relation between the material property and the role is the *is-a* relation. This leads to two kinds of designations for each material property—(a) we can say that is a part of the larger whole, and (b) we can say that it is performing a role. The relation from the whole to the part is always *has-a*. For example, the hand has fingers, the fingers have nails, the nails have tips, etc. Similarly, the roles also have their components which perform different functions under the supervision of a higher role. All this can get very confusing in terms of terminology, so, we must be very careful in how we are using these terms. The above description can be used to separate the *chit* (horizontal plane) and the *sat* (the vertical dimension) into the *has-a* and *is-a* trees. The relation from the whole to the part is always *has-a*, but the tree of roles becomes the *is-a* destination for the parts of the *chit* tree. Therefore, with the above caveats in mind, we can call the tree of roles the *is-a* tree and the tree of material properties the *has-a* tree.

The care to be exercised in this nomenclature is that both these trees involve a *has-a* relation between the whole and the part. So, we must not think that the *is-a* tree doesn't have a *has-a* relation between its whole and parts. We must just realize that the *is-a* tree is an additional designation of material properties because each such property exists in a relation and a role.

The descent from the higher to the lower plane involves a process of instantiation created by the *sat*, role, law, or "I am". We can also call this the *is-a* process. For instance, a mammal is an animal, a dog is a mammal, a poodle is a dog, etc. The animal kingdom includes dogs, and therefore dogs are parts of the animal kingdom. Going from top to bottom, therefore, there is a whole-part relation which is created through instantiation in which the property of an animal is instantiated into a mammal, a mammal into dog, a dog into a poodle, and so forth. All these instantiations create a functional *role* in the life tree.

For example, the big fish eat the smaller fish, the smaller fish even smaller fish, and so forth. The division of the whole into parts here creates ecosystems. You can describe the ecosystem at higher levels of taxonomic and ecosystem classification. At each level, you use the *is-a* method of dividing a whole into parts. Thus, every species is a life form, even though life itself is the highest taxonomy.

This life itself is *sat*, morality, role, and consciousness, which is called *mahattattva* in Vedic philosophy. When this consciousness divides, it expands into the different types of moralities followed by various species of life. *Śrīmad Bhāgavatam* notes how *mahattattva* expands into three parts—awareness, self-identity as a type of life form—e.g., that "I am human", "I am mammal", and so forth, and the connection between awareness and self-identity established by *prāna*, called the life-air or "life of activity". In other words, the first thing to emerge from consciousness is the self-identity or the sense of "I am".

> *Śrimad Bhāgavatam 3.6.7*[4]. *Translation: The total energy of the mahattattva, in the form of the gigantic virāṭ-rūpa, divided Himself by Himself into the consciousness of the living entities, the life of activity, and self-identification, which are subdivided into one, ten and three, respectively.*

The crucial point here is that when the soul enters the material world, he first acquires a self-identity, which constitutes his role in relation to other roles, and this identity is created in three parts—*manas*, *prāna*, and *vāk*. The *manas* is the awareness, *vāk* is the identity experienced, and *prāna* is the connection between the identity and the awareness. The identity is divided into three parts based on the three modes of nature (*sattva*, *rajas*, and *tamas*), but the connection to that identity is divided into ten parts (ten types of *prāna*). That connection is the process by which the identity is created and experienced.

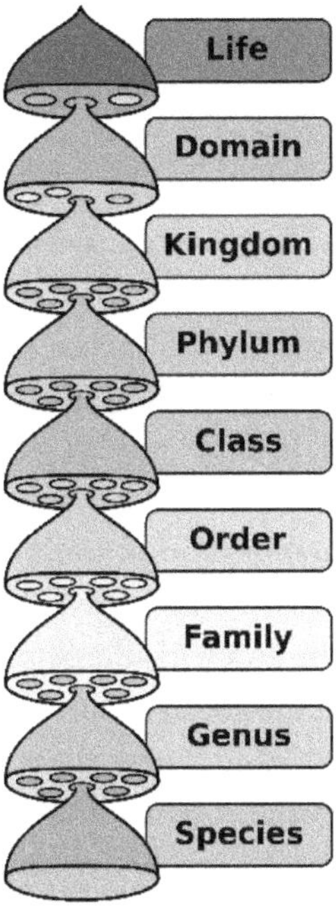

Figure-4 The Hierarchy of Taxonomic Classification

Thus, when a person says "I am human", there are three parts to it—(1) the "I" or awareness, (2) the "human" or identity defined by a role, and (3) the "am" which is the energy that expresses the "I" into a "human" and experiences that identity—as the *instantiation* of the self into a social character.

This identity is hierarchical. The first identity is also the ideal expression of "I" and constitutes the complete Self—also known as God. Subsequent expressions are incomplete *parts* of that completeness, which is succinctly described in the above verse by stating that God "divided Himself by Himself". The ideal expression of "I" as the first and primordial role is the leader of the society of all souls, sometimes called the *Supreme Personality of Godhead* who constitutes the taxonomy 'life itself'. This primordial role then further instantiates—quite like the kingdom, phylum, class, family, genus, species, etc.—creating more and more roles which constitute the individual souls. Śrīla Prabhupāda explained this idea by coining the phrase "life comes from life"—in the context of evolutionary theories that claim life to have emerged from matter. "Life comes from life" is a scientific theory in which there is an original life form (God) which instantiates into many individual life forms—souls.

Each soul is a combination of two things— (1) the original "I", and (2) the division of this "I" to create a role. This means that the soul's "I" cannot be defined without the original "I", and to know the self is to know the original "I" and the relation to that original "I". Thus, knowing God is an essential step to knowing the self. Just as an 'animal' exists inside 'mammal'—you could look at 'mammal' and call it an 'animal'—and yet doesn't fully contain it, similarly, God exists inside the soul, and yet the soul is neither equal to God, nor is God contained inside the soul. When Vedic texts exhort the spiritualist to meditate on the 'self', the true meaning is the self as defined in relation to the Super Self because it is not possible to know the self in any other way, as the self is a *role* defined in relation to other roles beginning with the Supreme Person.

In other words, the soul is a social creature by *definition*. Society is not an afterthought or formed as material elements aggregate. Rather, the soul has an identity by definition which makes our identity a social construct[5]—although in a spiritual sense, because the identity is defined in relation to God. In one sense, all the souls are created from the "I am" process of instantiation. In another sense, each soul is an individual because the suffix of the "I am" is different—each soul has a unique relationship to God. This relational suffix is sometimes called the soul's *Svarūpa* or 'form', which is not a body, but a self-identity (e.g., father, mother, child, friend, lover, servant, etc.) in relation to God[6]. The role can be performed in many different kinds of bodies; therefore, the soul can exhibit the *Svarūpa* even in the material world—with a material body. The role is the self-identity a person feels during any activity. For instance, a person in the act of cooking can feel to be a mother, father, friend, or lover, and the act of cooking is separate from this feeling, although it has an effect on it.

In the material world—created by *mahattattva*—the soul forgets the original role and adopts temporary roles (father, mother, citizen, employee, etc.). Impersonalist philosophers argue that if one gave up all such roles, one would find the true self, which is an incomplete understanding of the soul because it doesn't explain how the soul's limited "I" came into being. To overcome this problem, the impersonalist must also say that the limited "I" is necessarily an illusion, and therefore each "I" is itself the full identity—God. This is commonly known as *Advaita* in modern times, and in so far it posits the identity of the soul and God, it is false. A dog is a mammal, but a mammal is not a dog. In the same way, the soul's identity is instantiated from God's identity to create a particular life form, defined in relationship to God's life form. This instantiation and identity are eternal although it is possible to temporarily forget the identity.

If you were counting all the instantiations, you will count the best one first, followed by the next best, and so forth. To count we require two things— (1) the definition of the ideal, and (2) a method of measuring the distance between the ideal and the non-ideal. Thus, a single *manas* is instantiated in many ways; however, we instantiate the *manas* into the first or ideal, and then we instantiate this ideal into less-than-ideal, thereby creating the distance from the ideal. The plane produced due to *sat* begins with the first instantiation from the higher plane—the higher role is *manas*, its ideal instantiation process is *prāna*, and the ideal created by this process is *vāk*. This ideal is the *origin* of space and becomes the new *manas*. Then we apply a process of instantiating again and create the less than ideal from the ideal. Again, the process is *prāna* and the less than ideal instance of the ideal is the *vāk*. This process can repeat infinitely as we go further and further away from the ideal. If the ideal is the center of the space, then moving away from center is the non-ideal.

We normally think that species (at the bottom of the hierarchy) are the only real thing we can speak about. However, in Vedic philosophy, the higher levels of classification—namely, genus, family, order, class, phylum, etc.—are also real. In fact, there are higher living beings which embody these higher classes. The tree of diversification increases from top to bottom, so there are fewer classes at the higher level and more classes at the bottom. As a result, we can speak about higher living beings which embody the higher methods of classifying. These higher classes of life are present in higher planetary systems or planes. Since they are produced by the subdivision of *sat*, which represents consciousness and relationships, the higher planetary systems embody higher forms of consciousness, which is manifest in ecosystems organized on the basis of these higher types of consciousness. As an example, in the lower levels of life forms competition is the norm, and cooperation is the exception and hence ecosystems are created based on the idea of competition, which Herbert Spencer—after reading Charles Darwin's "On the Origin of Species"—called the "survival of the fittest"[7]. In higher levels of consciousness, found in higher levels of classification, we can find far more cooperation as opposed to competition. Those societies by way of cooperation are therefore better.

So far, we have spoken of how the *sat* creates classes, genus, phyla, species, etc. Now we will talk about the individual *members* of these species. Each member of the species also has a whole-part relationship, but that relation is of a different type. While the classification relation is called *is-a*, the member of the species creates the *has-a* relation from whole to part. Thus, the soul has a body, the body has hands, the hands have fingers, the fingers have nails, etc. This type of whole-part relationship is called *chit* or cognition where something is called 'nail' because it is part of the finger; something is called 'hand' because it is part of the body. The triad of *manas*, *prāna*, and *vāk* is again used, however, now *manas* is the whole body, *prāna* is the relation between whole and part, and *vāk* is the part. Just as previously we instantiated a meaning into a word or sentence (beginning with the ideal expression), now we can speak about the parts of the word or sentence—e.g., the alphabets and the grammatical structure of the sentence—that has the whole sentence as the tree root.

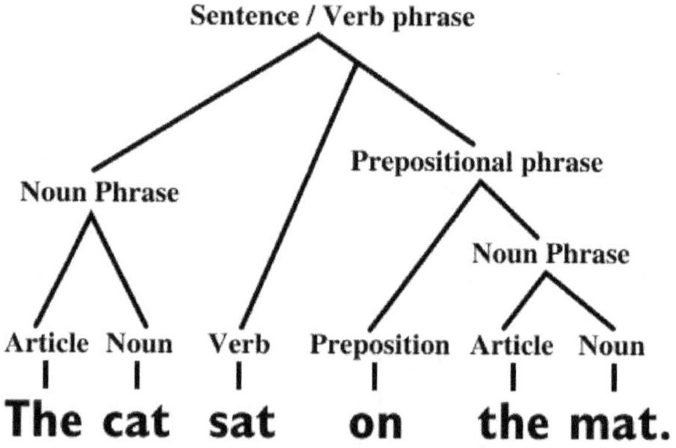

Figure-5 The Combination of Is-A and Has-A Elements

In Figure-5 we can see how the whole sentence has a noun phrase and a prepositional phrase as its parts. The noun phrase further has article and noun as its parts. The tree of grammatical structure therefore involves a *compositional* hierarchical relation in which the whole *contains* the parts. At the bottom of the tree, however, you can see the conversion of each part of speech (e.g., noun) into an example of the part of speech (e.g., a cat). The above sentence structure can remain unchanged in terms of grammatical form, but the actual sentence may change using different words which convert the noun, article, verb, preposition, etc. into different words. The parts of speech are the roles played by the words, while the words are the material entities. Similarly, the words may remain unchanged although they are now structured by a different grammatical form as depicted in Figure-6 where the sentence "I saw a man on a hill with a telescope" has several meanings; two are depicted here.

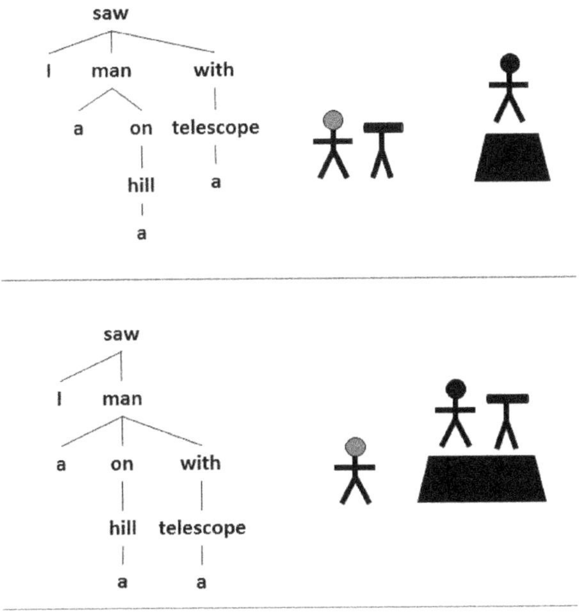

Figure-6 A Sentence Can Have Many Meanings

This hopefully gives us a sense of what we mean by the combination of *sat* and *chit*. The *sat* represents the grammatical structure of a sentence while the *chit* represents the words used in the sentence. Both have whole-part relations, but they are of two different kinds. When we form an actual sentence, we use both kinds of relationships, breaking down the whole sentence into parts in two different ways—(a) a grammatical structure, and (b) word selection. Each of these can be changed keeping the other unchanged; in that sense they are different. However, we cannot create an actual sentence without combining the two; in that sense they must always co-exist in a sentence.

Note that we used the words "noun phrase" and "prepositional phrase" to describe some parts of the whole sentence. There is a choice of words involved here too—i.e., we could have used different names for the same grammatical structure, or we could have changed the grammar itself and then named the sentence parts differently. Therefore, *chit* and *sat* are combined at all levels in the tree; in the above example, the grammatical elements called "noun phrase" and "prepositional phrase" are the *sat*, and the particular words used to instantiate these ideas into an observable reality—the words—are *chit*. Hence, we can say that the whole is being divided into parts in two different ways. This fact is commonly seen in ordinary languages when the same word denotes different parts of speech—e.g., noun vs. verb. Similarly, the role of noun or verb can be played by a different word. Therefore, apart from reading the word as part of a sentence, we have to also intuit the grammatical structure.

The words in higher planetary systems are therefore analogues of "noun phrase" and "prepositional phrase" while the words in the lower planetary systems are analogues of "cat", "mat", "hill" and "telescope". Obviously, one's consciousness must be advanced to understand more abstract concepts based on the context, even when sometimes the same words may be used. Similarly, if the higher part of speech were modified, the lower details in the sentence structure will be automatically changed. With this intuitive analogy we can understand how a higher being can control the lower being; how the higher being is a bigger whole as compared to the lower being—even though it is not physical bigger because a "verb phrase" is not bigger than "the cat sat on the mat". Finally, we can see how a higher being has a different kind of experience: dallying with "verb phrase" or "noun phrase" rather than "cat" or "mat".

Another way to understand the combination of *sat* and *chit* is to look at an ordinary organizational hierarchy. For example, a company has a functional structure comprised of roles such as CEO, CFO, CTO, etc. But in each of these roles there is a different person. We can say that a CEO *has-a* CFO, but that CFO is not a part of the CEO's body. The organizational structure is a conceptual description of the organization, while the actual members of the organization are the material description of the same organization. To transform the conceptual structure into the material structure, we use the *is-a* relation. Similarly, both the conceptual and the material structure have the *has-a* relation.

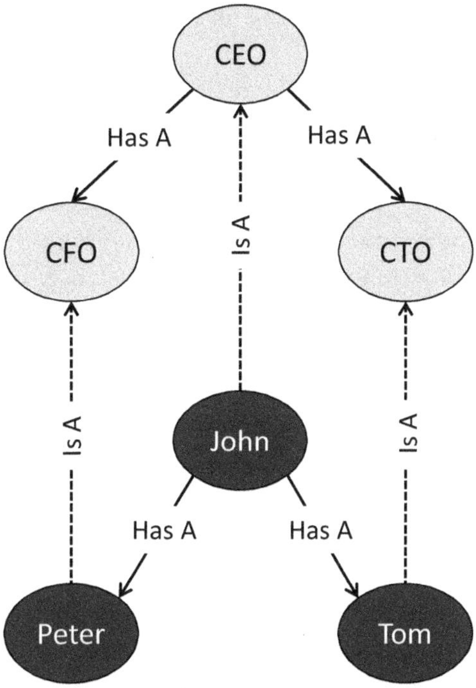

Figure-7 Horizontal and Vertical Dimensions

The instantiation and composition relation shown in Figure-7 illustrates two important facets of Vedic cosmology. First, it shows the relation between the higher and lower planes—the lower plane is an instantiation of the higher plane. Second, it shows a compositional relation within a given plane. Each plane is not truly flat; it is elevated in the center and depressed toward the edges. The plane actually looks like the roof of sacred buildings like temples, churches, synagogues, monasteries, etc. which have one thing in common—the center of the roof is elevated relative to the edges. In Vedic cosmology, similarly, the flat plane has an elevated center, surrounded by successively lower steps leading to the edge which is at the lowest level in the entire plane. Factually, this is a model of any kind of social organization with a leader in the center, the next level leadership close to the center at a slightly lower point, the people subordinate to the next level leadership even lower, and so forth. In one sense they can see each other, and they are therefore part of the same 'level'. In another sense, there is a whole-part system of division. Thus, there are two kinds of hierarchies—in between the levels, and within a given level.

We can also note the direction of arrows in Figure-7. The arrow for 'John is a CEO' goes from John to CEO—i.e., bottom-up. But, the arrow for 'CEO has a CFO' goes from CEO to CFO—i.e., top-down. The bottom-up order is responsible for materialism due to which we can say that a higher concept such as CEO is just a title given to a tangible person such as John and has no real existence. Indeed, owing to this fact, philosophers have summarily rejected the reality of concepts claiming that John is real, but CEO is unreal when the fact is that if these higher-level concepts did not exist then it would be impossible to define John's duties; he could do whatever he liked without a moral imperative. Thus, John's duties are derived from the imperatives for a CEO, and yet we count from the bottom of the hierarchy tracing the *is-a* relations upward.

Once we begin counting from the bottom, we also convert materialism into reductionism, due to which only the parts are real and the whole is unreal. The fact is that the *has-a* relation always flows downward, and as we saw above, even though the *is-a* relation is counted upward it flows downward. Looking at the tree in perspective we can see why both reductionism and materialism are false—reductionism because the whole divides into parts, and materialism because the whole is instantiated from an abstract idea.

Once we grasp how each part is connected to the whole in two different ways, we can then see how the instantiation and composition of the whole into parts is produced over time, due to a purpose, resulting in happiness. This time is not about linear change; it is rather about dividing the whole into parts or absorbing the parts into the whole. The former is called *creation* and the latter is called *destruction*. When the whole is manifest into parts and the parts are not being created or destroyed, the same time is called *maintenance*. The whole exists for a longer period of time and the parts for the shorter durations. As a result, time is also hierarchical and divides into parts—bigger and smaller. Therefore, the composition and instantiation relationships now have to be complemented by the duration relationship between whole and part. This means that to *sat* and *chit* we have to now add the *ānanda* aspect. Since each part exists for a finite duration, it is a combination of *sat*, *chit*, and *ānanda*. The three aspects called *manas*, *prāna*, and *vāk* act again. The *manas* is the larger duration of time, the *vāk* is the shorter duration, and *prāna* is the method of dividing the longer duration into the shorter duration. In this sense, we can see that there are three hierarchies or trees that divide the whole into part. And yet, these three trees are combined together to create the parts.

We can describe the world in terms of the three facets called *manas*, *prāna*, and *vāk*, which are the three modes of material nature as they create the hierarchy in each of the three trees. We must also divide reality as the combination of the three trees originating in the *sat*, *chit*, and *ānanda* of the soul. As a result, there are three orthogonal triads which combine to create 9 categories. As these divide successively, 9 becomes 27, 27 becomes 81, and so forth, and the tree successively diversifies, although it is rooted in the soul. *Sāñkhya* philosophy describes this tree of diversification from the soul; its 24 elements are diversifications of the *chit* or the compositional relationship. Similarly, there is an instantiation relation comprised of 8 elements. Finally, there is a duration relationship comprised of 16 elements. Together, the 8 + 16 + 24 elements create the 48 elementary categories symbolized by the alphabets of the Sanskrit language. The mapping of these categories to the alphabets is a more esoteric topic which I will not cover here[8], but the key point is that once we understand these alphabets then we can create the sentences. The world would then be described not as objects but as *symbols* of meaning.

The Eight Realms of Creation

We noted above that the flat plane originates in the center as the ideal part (due to *sat*). Similarly, the center also represents the best part (due to *chit*). In the human body, for example, the ideal and the best part is the head. From this head the rest of the body is expanded and controlled. The head is the center of the space, and the toes are the ends of the space. Similarly, the head is at the top and the toes are at the bottom. These facts are represented as two distinct descriptions of space as a flat plane and a sphere, respectively.

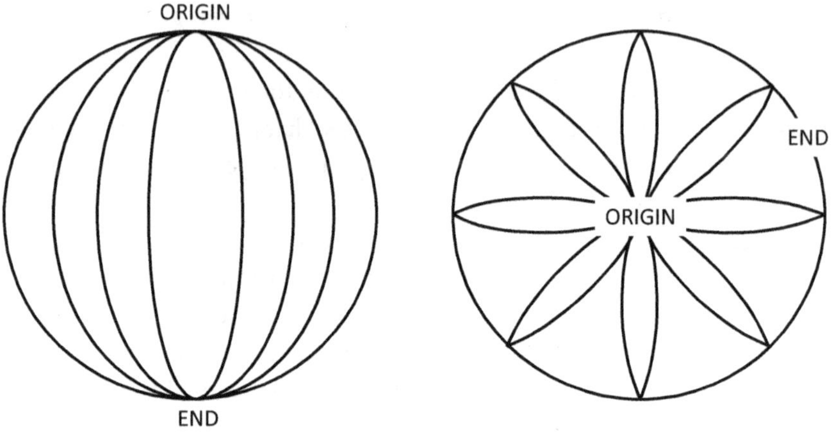

Figure-8 The Spherical and Lotus Models of Space

If we describe the space from top to bottom, we use the model of a sphere. But if we describe the space from center to edge, we use the flat plane. These are not two different descriptions. We can think of the sphere as an orange whose skin has been peeled and stretched out creating a flower or lotus-like structure. The origin at the top now becomes the whorl of the lotus. Each plane of the tree can be represented as a sphere if we demarcate the plane with a beginning and an end. Each plane can also be described as lotus if we keep the origin at the center and the non-ideal and non-best parts further from the center. The ideal and best in each plane is a representation of God, and the less than ideal and best are further removed from the center of the plane.

In spiritual cosmology, the planet of *Kṛṣṇa*—called *Goloka*—is described as a 'lotus', with *Kṛṣṇa* at the center of this lotus. The planet of *Kṛṣṇa* is also described as a sphere. These are not contradictory descriptions if we understand what they mean. In the highest plane of existence, *Kṛṣṇa* is the personification of *ānanda* and *Rāma* is the personification of *chit*. Both have the energy of consciousness or awareness which constitutes the *sat*. God also has consciousness, which is personified by *Narayana*; however, God's consciousness is different from the consciousness embodied by His energies. We will revert to this topic shortly and discuss the differences between the two.

Ramā is the personification of *chit* in relation to *Rāma* or the *chit*. The difference between the two is that *Rāma* is the known while *Ramā* is the knower. The *chit* comprises six qualities called knowledge, beauty, power, wealth, fame (or heroism), and renunciation, and *Ramā* is the cognition of these qualities. *Rāma* is the fullness of the qualities, and as *Ramā* focuses Her cognition on the six qualities, She analyzes the whole into parts. Her cognition is initially seeing *Rāma* from a distance—when the full thing is seen but the parts are not seen. We can liken it to seeing the forest but not the trees. Then She comes closer to *Rāma* and sees the different parts of the six qualities; this proximity converts the forest into the individual trees. As She looks even closer, the trees convert into leaves, the leaves into veins on each leaf, and so forth. The effect of *Ramā* is the subdivision of the whole into innumerable parts, and these parts are therefore said to 'expand' from the whole. *Rāma* is the male, and *Ramā* is the female. Her looking closer toward *Rāma* creates their 'children'.

Similarly, *Kṛṣṇa* is the completeness of pleasure, and *Hara* is the observer of that pleasure. When *Hara* looks at *Kṛṣṇa* from a distance, She can know Him fully. But as She looks closer, the fullness of a forest divides into individual trees, then leaves, then veins on each leaf, and so forth. Thus, *Kṛṣṇa* is the male and *Hara* is the female. As they come closer to each other, many children are crated. *Kṛṣṇa* being the embodiment of pleasure is the cause of all spiritual purpose, and hence time, but He is complete pleasure and hence the complete time. Subdivisions of this complete time into parts is due to *Hara*.

Hara and *Ramā* are the perceivers of pleasure and cognition, and they make God aware of His pleasure and knowledge. We can liken this perception to a mirror for a person. Without the mirror, the person has a body, but they cannot see that body. When the mirror is shown, the person who had the body becomes aware of their body. Therefore, *Hara* and *Ramā* are like the mirrors in which God sees Himself and thereby perceives His pleasure and knowledge. Quite aside from the perception of emotion and cognition is the awareness of God's ability to form relationships to others by being aware of them. God therefore has the ability for relation, and then there is a form of awareness that makes Him aware of this ability. The embodiment of awareness is called *Narayana*. His consort is *Lakshmi* and She embodies the awareness of God's awareness—and She makes God *self-conscious.* As the self-conscious form of God, *Narayana* is reserved, as opposed to the forms of God who are engaged in enjoyment and cognition. When *Lakshmi* sees *Narayana* from a distance, She finds the fullness of awareness. But as She gets closer to Him, this awareness is further divided into parts like the forest is divided into trees, leaves, and veins on closer look. The division of *Narayana* consciousness is called the soul. Again, *Narayana* is the father, *Lakshmi* is the mother, and the soul is the child.

In the self-conscious state, the soul serves *Narayana* as the supreme self-conscious person. In the state of being cognizant of the world, the soul serves *Rāma* as the supreme source of all cognition. And in the state of being perceptive of pleasure, the soul serves *Kṛṣṇa* as the supreme source of pleasure. The soul is factually *sat*, *chit*, and *ānanda*. However, depending on which of the three dominates, the soul comes under the influence of *Lakshmi*, *Ramā*, or *Hara*. It is therefore impossible to say whether the soul is an expansion of *Lakshmi*, *Ramā*, or *Hara*. The free will of the soul is that it can prioritize *sat*, *chit*, or *ānanda*, and thereby it can change its position among the three. The soul can therefore be the child of *Kṛṣṇa* and *Hara*, or *Rāma* and *Ramā*, or *Narayana* and *Lakshmi*, in a paradoxical case of the child selecting their parents!

Only one thing can be said with certainty, which is that God is the male, and His *Śakti* or consciousness is the female. Depending on whether this *Śakti* is used to make God aware of *ānanda*, *chit*, or *sat*, She is described differently. God originally exists as *chit*, which is described as the fullness of six qualities namely knowledge, beauty, power, wealth, fame, and renunciation. However, in such a state, He is not *aware* of His own qualities. His *Śakti* called *Ramā* makes Him aware that He is the completeness of knowledge, beauty, power, wealth, fame, and renunciation, and when God becomes aware of His qualities the cognition itself expands the whole into many compositional parts of the whole. Once these parts are expanded, God isn't aware that He could enjoy them. His *Śakti* called *Hara* makes Him aware that He has the ability to enjoy, and when God becomes aware of His capacity to enjoy, this perception itself expands into many types of pleasures. This enjoyment is like God playing with many kinds of toys, which are inanimate at this time. To truly enjoy, God must engage with animate persons, just like Himself. A person is self-aware of their existence, but the inanimate objects are not self-aware. However, God in the present state is not self-aware. His *Śakti* called *Lakshmi* makes Him realize that He is a self-conscious Being and so He can engage with other self-conscious beings. The dawn of self-awareness causes the expansion of the soul.

In the highest plane of existence, self-awareness and cognition of the six qualities are subordinated to the enjoyment of pleasure. We can say that *ānanda* is highest but *chit* and *sat* are dominated by *ānanda*. As a result, in the realm called *Goloka* self-awareness and God's six opulences are not given great importance. Only God's pleasure is given the highest importance.

As we descend from this highest plane, *ānanda* is subordinated to *chit*. Now, God's six opulences become very important. These opulences themselves are prioritized. Knowledge precedes the rest, fame follows knowledge and creates the perfect and most famous (heroic) person, from this fame four qualities, are successively created—wealth, power, beauty, and renunciation. Based on this prioritization of the six qualities, there are six different levels of reality, which produce 24 forms of God called (1) *Puruṣottama*, (2) *Acyuta*, (3) *Narasiṃha*, (4) *Trivikrama*, (5) *Hṛṣīkeśa*, (6) *Keśava*, (7) *Mādhava*, (8) *Aniruddha*, (9) *Pradyumna*, (10) *Saṅkarṣaṇa*, (11) *Śrīdhara*, (12) *Vāsudeva*, (13) *Dāmodara*, (14) *Janārdana*, (15) *Nārāyaṇa*, (16) *Hari*, (17) *Padmanābha*, (18) *Vāmana*, (19) *Madhusūdana*, (20) *Govinda*, (21) *Kṛṣṇa*, (22) *Viṣṇu-mūrti,* (23) *Adhokṣaja* and (24) *Upendra*. We will discuss the significance of the division by four at each tier shortly, but for now we can additionally note that at each tier the forms are also called *Vasudeva, Saṅkarṣaṇa, Pradyumna* and *Aniruddha*, if we only look at a single plane. However, if we look at 6 tiers, then they are named differently. These 24 realms are called *Vaikuṇṭha.*

As we descend from the realm of *Vaikuṇṭha* we come to the realm of *Narayana* who—as seen above—personifies self-consciousness due to *Lakshmi*. In this realm, *Narayana* is the supreme self-conscious person, and the individual souls are parts of this complete self-consciousness. Since the *sat* constitutes the *is-a* relation, the soul emanated from God as a part of His consciousness, can claim that the soul *is a* God, which is different from saying that the soul *is* God. Just as we can say that a dog is a mammal, but we don't say that the dog is mammal. Similarly, it is appropriate to say that the soul is one of the self-conscious beings, but we cannot say that the soul is the complete self-consciousness. Impersonal philosophers misinterpret the soul *is a* God into the soul *is* God. A deeper look at the soul's origin can correct this mistake.

Whether the awareness predominates in *ānanda*, *chit*, or *sat*, in all the above three realms there is recognition of some form of God, and the soul realizes that his emotion, cognition, and relation are meant to make God aware of His emotion, cognition, and relation, expand these further, and see oneself as a part of the whole. The material creation lies below the realm of *Narayana* and it is a place where the soul sees his emotion, cognition, and relation as being independent of God. Self-awareness leads to the notion of an individual, but this individual transforms from being the soul is a God to the soul is God. In other words, instead of viewing oneself as a part created due to division of relation, cognition, or emotion, the soul sees itself as an independent source of relations, cognition, and emotions. God is now replaced by the laws of nature, which frustrate this idea of independence by subordinating the soul's free will to the determinism of time and the moral consequences of the soul's choices.

The above four are the broad divisions of all creation, but these are further subdivided into two parts. The two-part division arises because among *sat*, *chit*, and *ānanda*, we have identified the facet that remains at the top, but there are still two possibilities of the second facet being dominant.

In the case of *Goloka*, there is a realm of *Kṛṣṇa* and another realm of *Sri Chaitanya*. Both dominate in *ānanda*, but the second order facet can be *sat* or *chit*. In the realm of *Kṛṣṇa*, *sat* is more dominant than *chit*, which means that God's self-aware individuality is known but subordinated to His enjoyment. The six opulences of *Kṛṣṇa* are almost totally ignored. In the realm of *Sri Chaitanya*, however, the *chit* is emphasized which means that God is known as the completeness of knowledge, beauty, fame, power, wealth, and renunciation, and God's self-awareness is almost totally ignored. We might note that self-awareness is synonymous with self-love. *Kṛṣṇa* is viewed as a self-loving narcissistic person[9] while *Sri Chaitanya* is seen as most munificent. We can say that *Kṛṣṇa* isn't tolerant, but *Sri Chaitanya* is most tolerant. Thus, the neophyte spiritualist is advised to worship *Sri Chaitanya* instead of *Kṛṣṇa* because the former is easy to please and difficult to offend relative to the latter.

Similarly, in the case of *Vaikuṇṭha*, the *chit* dominates overall but the second order facet can be *ānanda* or *sat*. Thus, some souls emphasize the happiness of God, while the others underscore His self-engrossment. In the former, God is all powerful and His happiness is in saving the soul; the soul is compared to the kitten carried in the mouth of the cat; the powerful jaws of the cat are felt as the savior and protector of the soul. In the latter, God is all powerful, but He is self-absorbed. Therefore, the soul has to make his own efforts. Now, the soul is compared to an infant monkey who latches onto the mother's underbelly as the mother jumps from one branch of the tree to another. The mother is not responsible for the baby because the mother is self-absorbed; it is the responsibility of the baby to hold tight to the mother to save itself.

In the realm of *Narayana*, *sat* dominates overall, but the second order facet can be *chit* or *ānanda*. Owing to the fact that *Narayana* is the source of self-consciousness, He is described as the original father in heaven. However, this father can be described as being great and therefore aloof because He has innumerable children and He cannot attend to each child individually. Alternatively, the child can believe that God is his father and therefore protection of the child is the child's natural birthright and protecting the child is the father's enjoyable liability. Accordingly, some souls glorify the greatness of *Narayana* as their father thinking Him to be somewhat distant because He has innumerable children. Others, instead, disregard His greatness and consider the relationship of being their father of greater importance, indulgently demanding His attention and protection. These two types of worship can be compared to the adult child and the infant child. The adult child keeps a respectful distance from the father, but the infant child is not afraid of climbing in His lap.

The key point of these descriptions is that the love of God is not monolithic. There are innumerable forms of this love, which are the choice of the soul. The soul is therefore free to choose how to love God. It also means that surrender to God doesn't necessarily mean loss of free will or choice. Rather, because loving is itself imbued with so many choices, the free will of the soul is subordinated to that of God, but the free will is not lost. Rather, God appears in many forms in order to accommodate the free will of the soul. Through such multifarious forms, the religion doesn't become polytheistic. Rather, there is infinite variety in the religion of love in choosing how to love God.

Below the realm of *Narayana* lies the material world which is divided into *Mahesh Dhāma* and *Devi Dhāma* corresponding to the two unique facets of the material realm called time and *karma.* The *Devi Dhāma* comprises all the universes where the soul enjoys or suffers due to their moral and immoral actions. In this realm, the soul's independence is subordinated to the moral laws; one is allowed to act independently (because the free will is never lost) but independence has a price—any violation of moral duty brings adverse consequences. The *Mahesh Dhāma* is the realm called time. Time simply means that when the soul is liberated from the clutches of *karma,* he attains eternity because *karma* causes repeated birth and death. Time also means being in the present—unafraid of the past, and not desirous of a future. This freedom from the effects of past and future is the body of *Shiva* who is also called *Mahesh.*

Shiva is the source of *Brahman*[10]; it is attained if the soul gives up the desire to enjoy and suffer under moral laws but hasn't given up his independence. The soul here remains self-absorbed thinking itself to be an independent individual unconcerned with and disengaged from any other soul or God. Vedic texts describe that the material world expands from the embodiment of time and all the souls which were thus far within the body of *Mahesh* are injected into the material energy. Similarly, when the creation is wound-up, the soul enters the body of *Mahesh,* waiting for the creation to begin again.

Sometimes, *Narayana* is described as *Kāraṇodakaśāyī Viṣṇu* and *Shiva* or *Mahesh* is described as *Saṅkarṣaṇa* as the embodiment of time. *Narayana* lies upon *Saṅkarṣaṇa*, which can be taken to mean that the *Narayana* is 'above' *Mahesh.* Similarly, because time is above *karma*, therefore, the soul can eternally maintain its independence and selfishness without falling into the trap of material enjoyment. The soul who attains *Brahman* or the eternity free from the cycle of birth and death is in a state where he can stay forever. However, the likelihood of maintaining an independent identity and not using it for enjoyment is very low. The soul thus eventually falls from eternity into temporariness unless he has transcended eternity to one of the higher realms. The domain of eternity is called *oneness* while the material domain below it is called *nothingness.* The soul falls from oneness into nothingness when he feels empty being himself because his existence cannot be given any meaning. Notably, meaning arises in relation to other things and for the soul to give meaning to his existence he must find a relation to something. When the soul feels his life is meaningless through staying independent of everything, he begins the material journey. This feeling of emptiness is also called *māyā,* which creates restlessness, fear, anxiety, despair, unhappiness, and meaninglessness.

It is often said that the material world came from nothingness or void. This is true in the sense that the soul is covered by the sense of existential void in his life. However, it is also false because the soul is still eternally real. The feeling of void is the effect of loneliness. By itself, the soul is unable to find emotion, cognition, and relation, and without these he feels empty. But that experience of emptiness is still the experience of the soul. It is not truly a void, because in that void there would never be any experience. Therefore, the material world is produced to solve the problem of emptiness in life. However, no matter how much the soul tries to fill his inner sense of vacuum through material occupations, the accumulation of power, wealth, knowledge, or through varieties of relationships, the vacuum is never overcome because all these things are temporary and because everything changes the soul never finds peace and rest. He keeps feeling lonely even in the crowded world.

The Geometry of the Flat Plane

We noted above that the center of a plane is created by instantiating the first and ideal instance of the idea from a higher plane. We briefly discussed how this ideal then expands into less than ideal. This is a paradoxical and important problem in the philosophy of religion called the problem of evil. Since evil exists in this world, and God created the world, therefore He must have created the evil too. As the source of this evil, God must be evil. This problem is false for two reasons. First, the good exists along with evil, so the soul has the *choice* for either of them; just because the evil exists doesn't mean the soul has to choose it. Second, if God did not create the evil, there would be no meaning to choice; God is the ideal and good; if only He existed and the evil did not, then the soul would be compelled to worship God due to lack of alternatives. By eliminating all the other choices, God would take away free will.

But there are further reasons why the flat plane is divided into four directions. As we noted earlier, the four directions represent *Vasudeva, Saṅkarṣaṇa, Pradyumna,* and *Aniruddha.* In the center of space resides a 5th form who is also sometimes called *Narayana* due which *Pāncharātra* texts describe five forms including *Narayana*. This fifth form is also sometimes called *Saṅkarṣaṇa* which expands into the other four forms and is different from the *Saṅkarṣaṇa* included in the four forms. Let's turn to understanding how the ideal has four facets and how these four facets represent a new profound idea.

> *Chaitanya Charitāmṛta 1.5.40[11]: Translation: In that spiritual sky, on the four sides of Narayana, are the second expansions of the quadruple expansions of Dwarka.*

> *Purport (excerpt): The Padma Purāna, as quoted by Śrīla Rūpa Gosvāmī in his Laghū-bhagavatāmrita, describes that in the spiritual sky there are four directions, corresponding to east, west, north and south, in which Vasudeva, Saṅkarṣaṇa, Aniruddha and Pradyumna are situated.*

The flat plane comprises two dimensions called *knowing* and *acting* which are subdivisions of *chit*[12]. To know something is to know what it *is* and what it can *do*. Accordingly, we employ two kinds of concepts and two kinds of senses—of knowing and acting—to describe cognition. The concepts of knowing include ordinary percepts such as sound, touch, sight, taste, and smell; by combining them we create many types of perceivable objects. The concepts of acting include ordinary concepts such as walking, talking, holding, running, swimming, eating, mating, etc. as performed by the senses of action.

When *Śakti* focuses on the full knowledge and action, She divides the whole into parts. However, since the part is created by dividing the whole, there is a latent sense in which the parts are excluded from the whole to bring something into focus. In ordinary cognition, this fact is present as the foreground and background of cognition. For instance, while reading this book your consciousness is probably defocused from the other things happening in the background. Each individual object is foreground from its perspective, while all the other objects are backgrounded. The result of this focus is that each object is something, but it is also *not* other things. We define the object in relation to the things it is not, and not independent of them. Thus, the foreground becomes meaningful only in contrast to the background.

The background becomes the *context* in which the object (considered the foreground) is placed. Thus, describing an object's negation is identical to describing its relation to other objects, or the context of its existence. Therefore, apart from dividing the object into its knowledge and action components, we have to also divide it into the foreground and background components. The key idea here is that the background is in some sense present in the foreground because only in that context we are able to give the foreground *meaning*. For example, if you have a table kept in the kitchen, the table is called a kitchen table, even though you are focusing on the table and not on the kitchen. The kitchen is the background, but it enters the foreground by modifying the table into a kitchen table. Effectively, our cognition involves the act of *contrasting* things; an imperfect round object would be called a 'circle' in contrast to another imperfect rectangular object being called a 'square'. In contrast to a perfect circle, the same thing may be called an octagon or a hexagon.

Therefore, we never cognize a thing by itself. We always cognize it in contrast to other things which lie in the background. Similarly, we never know the use of a thing by itself. We only know its use in relation to other things which lie in the background. The designation we apply to an object—e.g., circle vs. octagon—is driven by what we consider lies in the background. Now, remember that this background is also a choice. We can *choose* to include somethings in the background and leave other things out. The background is also therefore carved from the rest of the universe while focusing on an object. Therefore, not only do we require a background to know the foreground, but also that we make a choice in carving the background from everything else. Due to this carving, the background is something specific and not everything other than the foreground object. The foreground is already something specific.

Thus, each object has to be placed in a finite space which includes the foreground and some chosen background. And this foreground and background distinction has to be applied to both knowledge and action. This creates two dimensions and four directions. The two dimensions represent knowledge and action, while each dimension has both foreground and background.

The four deities of the *chatur-vyūha* are situated on the four directions of the plane. *Vasudeva* represents knowledge of what a thing *is*. *Pradyumna* represents what a thing cannot do. *Saṅkarṣaṇa* represents the knowledge of what a thing is not, or the contrast to other things. And *Aniruddha* denotes the activities that a thing can perform. Therefore, if *Aniruddha* is the foreground then *Pradyumna* is the background. Similarly, if *Vasudeva* is foreground, then *Saṅkarṣaṇa* is background. The East represents knowledge, and the North represents action. The West denotes the negation of a thing, and the South the negation of its actions. What we don't see by the senses is present in the mind, because the mind is able to perceive the relation between things while the senses only perceive the individual objects, and not their interrelations. Therefore, the mind is the essential instrument to cognize the world, which modifies the thing's meaning. Modern science relies on sense perception and believes that objects are independent and if we measure the object's properties, we don't need to account for the context in which they are being placed. Such measurements are ineffective in describing the meaning given to things.

We move clockwise in this space—East to South to West to North. As a result, we first observe what a thing is, but we cannot give it any meaning. However, just by seeing a thing we can know what it cannot do, even without placing it in a context. Then we give the thing meaning when we see the thing in its context. When the nature of the thing is known, then we understand all the things it can do in relation to the other things in the context. The negation comes handy in giving something meaning and value in a context.

The Four Directions of a Plane

One of the most fundamental properties discovered by atomic theory is that the atoms are not defined by themselves. They are rather defined in relation to other things, or what the thing is *not*. In classical physics, it was sufficient to say what a thing *is*, but in atomic theory we have to also say what a thing is *not*. This is a direct consequence of dividing a whole into parts, which not only asserts the prior reality of the whole but also changes the manner in which we describe each part. Owing to this fact, quantum theory uses terms such as 'inseparability', 'holism', 'complementarity' and others to describe how a thing is connected to every other thing within an *ensemble* context. The ensemble is the whole, or the description of reality at a given *level.* Things within that ensemble are described mutually through negation and assertion. Thus, the four-direction space is the space needed for *each individual object* because in defining that object we have to note its property and activity besides the summary of all the properties and activities that it doesn't constitute.

When an individual object is changed, its relation to every other object is altered. This fact is called *nonlocality* in quantum theory and it arises because we are cutting a picture into a jigsaw puzzle using the focus of consciousness. If one part of the jigsaw puzzle is altered, at least one other part must be altered, and potentially all the other parts within the ensemble may also be altered. As a result, we cannot simply change a single part independently, and this makes physicists squirm with discomfort as they are used to thinking of these parts as independent things which can be changed individually. Nonlocality tells us that by changing one part in the jigsaw puzzle, we have to change other parts, and this brings into question the meaning of change.

What is change to an individual object? An individual object is brought into focus by awareness like light shining on a part of the whole while the other parts remain dark. As consciousness changes its focus toward a different part, the thing in focus appears to change but factually the thing itself is not changing; we are instead seeing a different thing. The old thing we were seeing has disappeared from our vision and a new thing has appeared in the vision. The continuity in perception is established by the observer—the same observer is seeing a different thing—but there is no continuity in the things being perceived as the change is caused by the shift in the focus of awareness.

Therefore, factually, the material objects are not changing; the change is the *apparent* shift in experience by moving the torchlight elsewhere. The torchlight is also two separate things—the source of light and the focus of that torchlight. In focusing the torchlight from one object to another, the torchlight is itself not changed although the focus is altered. The torchlight here is the soul and light is the consciousness focusing on a part of the whole. While we have the experience of change, factually neither the soul nor matter are changing, and both are separately individual and real. Only the focus of the torchlight is altered due to which we *think* that something has changed. A spiritual science is one that treats both matter and soul as individual and real, while their connection evolves over time.

A material science is one that disregards the individuality of the observer and considers the material object changing. In the former case, the *continuity* of experience is established by the soul, and the change is caused by the moving focus of consciousness. In the latter case, the continuity of experience is caused by the movement of the object.

The fact is that the shift in focus from one thing to another is discrete, and if we carry the classical physical idea of change to small changes, the theory collapses—as has been the case in atomic theory—and we lose the objectivity that created the *continuity* across discrete states. If instead we attribute the change to the *focus* of consciousness, then both matter and soul are real, however, the change in focus is discrete. The focus is attributable to the individual observer (although it is separate from the observer), and we can speak about a science of *guna* and *karma,* which manipulate the focus. In Vedic philosophy, this focus is called *prāna* and it is controlled by *guna* and *karma* under the influence of time. At every moment of our life, our focus is diverted to different things, and at the time of death the focus is shifted to another body. The change of focus is always discrete, but the magnitude of this change varies. Therefore, the *change* is microscopic or macroscopic, and our ability to describe both big and small changes using the same theory requires a new science.

The change of the soul's focus is called the transmigration of the soul through successive bodies and it is the general paradigm of change. All these bodies exist simultaneously but the soul's torchlight is not pointing at them. When the torchlight is pointed, they become visible to us. During this lifetime the torchlight moves slowly—i.e., we see gradual change in the body from childhood to youth to old age. A sudden change in focus of the torchlight occurs at the time of death, due to which the soul changes the body at once. The basic paradigm of change in this life and at the time of death is identical; the difference is one of degree of change rather than type of change. Hence, we cannot describe change as 'motion' of particles because material objects are not moving. They are simply parts of a bigger picture which are illuminated or dark. Similarly, the torch is not changing; only the focus of the torchlight is altered, and this focus of the torchlight is called consciousness. Where the light is focused, the object comes distinctly into focus and becomes the foreground of experience. The area where the light is diffused is the background of experience. Finally, there is the dark part which we don't see due to focusing on a particular thing and hence we believe and claim that it doesn't exist.

If you move a torchlight above a picture, and slowly bring all the parts into focus one by one, eventually you will find that you have exhausted all the parts and now the torchlight must move to the original part again. To the materialist who thinks the motion of torchlight is an actual change to the object in focus, it appears that reality is a dice; you roll the dice again and again and after seeing all the six faces, the first face will appear again in your vision. Material change now appears to be *rotating* the object in space because the same thing is seen again and again, although when one face is seen, the others become invisible. This apparent 'rotation' is depicted by two facts— (1) the angle of rotation, and (2) the radius from which the rotated part is being seen.

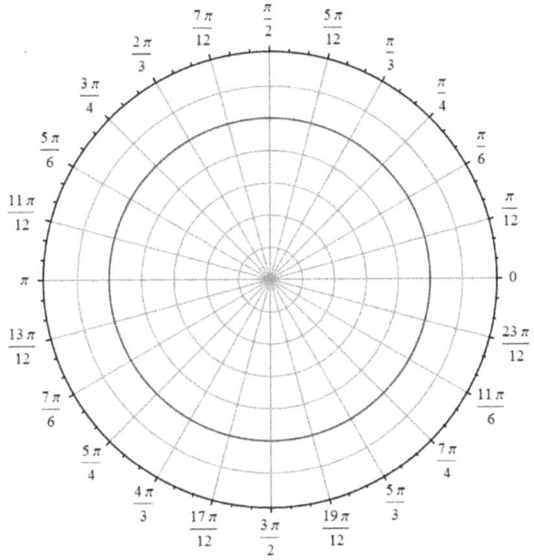

Figure-9 Flat Planes and Polar Coordinates

The angle of rotation represents a different part of the whole made visible through the focus of the torchlight because after scanning all the parts of the whole one must return to the same part again. The radius of the circle represents how closely the light is focused on the picture, which then defines the span of the foreground and the background. If the light is very close to the picture, then we dominantly see the foreground because the light is not significantly diffused and thus what a thing is comes sharply into focus but its relation to other things becomes invisible. This is the limit of vision of classical physics, where the proximity of the torchlight to the picture reveals a point particle. As the torchlight is withdrawn from the picture, there is a sharper central focus, but also diffusion of light around that focus, and this means that we can see both foreground and background and this is the vision of atomic theory. When the light is focused closely, then the diffusion is discarded and we only see what a thing is, and defocus on the relation to the other things.

When the diffusion is discarded from our vision, we fail to see how the light is shining on the different parts of the same picture. We just see a moving point particle and now classical physical laws of motion are defined.

In classical physics, the rotation of an object in space simply changes the position of the object. But the same rotation for a macroscopic object can be seen as revealing a different *facet* of the *same* object—like a dice. Therefore, when a planet rotates in its orbit, we see different facets of the same thing, and the planetary rotation insinuates different properties and effects, which constitutes the foundation of astrology in which planets have different effects in different positions. Two types of coordinate systems are employed in this description. The *radial* coordinate system—using the angles of rotation—denotes the different facets or parts of the whole. The *linear* coordinate system—using X and Y axes—denotes the knowing and acting dimensions of each facet. The combination of the radial and linear systems creates a tree.

As we move clockwise in this space from the East, we first observe the physical properties of an object, without giving them meaning. This only constitutes what a thing is, without taking into account the context. Hence, it represents the independent particle's position. As we move to the South, we add to this the cognition of what a thing can never do—not because the context will not allow it, but because simply knowing the properties of the object tells us what it is incapable of doing. Then we see the context and give the object a meaning in contrast to the other things. Finally, having eliminated what a thing cannot do due to its properties, and then seen how the thing is related to the other things in the context, we understand all the potential things it can do.

Both Euclidean and Polaris coordinates are *flat* rather than *hierarchical.*

As a result, neither numbering system completely depicts all the properties of the semantic plane which is like a tree. The conclusion is that the flat plane described as a 'lotus' with many directions denoted by its petals is not the physical plane—Euclidean or Polar number—but it has properties of both. Once the nature of the flat plane is understood, then we can realize the importance of the third dimension which creates a hierarchy of multiple planes. Similarly, when the flat plane is understood, then we can understand how change is cyclic because the system is closed—the torchlight must move back to the original state—due to which time must produce repeating patterns.

This closed and cyclic nature of space and time is described by using three words—*deśh*, *kāla*, and *pātra*—which refer to place, time, and circumstance (euphemistically described as a 'pot' or 'container'). The *pātra* or situation represents the context or what a thing is not. The term *deśh* represents the object's location in the knowledge and activity plane. Finally, *kāla* denotes the cyclic change in the situation within the knowledge and activity plane. The plane is the space for the motion of an individual particle, although the particle is described through a distinction with its surrounding context. If we look at the world in a third-person way, we only see many objects. But if we look at the world from a first-person perspective, we are defined by our situation; the situation selects some properties in us and hides other properties.

The Description of Material Space

The material world in Vedic philosophy is described as the combination of three *modes* called *sattva*, *rajas*, and *tamas*, which form the three dimensions of space. Why does nature have three modes of nature? Could they not be four or nine? We have empirical experience of the 3-dimensional space, so it is confirmed by ordinary experience. But is there something fundamental about these dimensions, or are they merely accidents of nature that seem to be true, but could have been different? Modern science, for example, has generalized the idea of dimensions, and it is not uncommon to hear the use of terms such as four-dimensional space-time, or 10-dimensional string theory, in which the number of dimensions being three just seems an accident of nature.

The material world, in Vedic philosophy, originates in *sound* or words; this is sometimes called *śabda brahmān* or the eternal existence of a vibration, which is sometimes characterized by the sound *OM*, which then separates into three individual sounds called *A*, *U*, and *M*, when in contact with the three modes of nature. To understand the three dimensions of space, we have to understand how sound or words are divided into three basic categories.

These three categories constitute the three ways in which words are used; we can call them the *interpretation* of words, in the act of giving them *meaning*. In essence, the sound, prior to the manifestation of the universe, doesn't have meaning; it just exists, but it is not *understood*. Understanding this sound implies experiencing it, and that experience involves interpreting the sound, or giving it meaning. There are three dominant modes of interpreting the sound, which we call *names*, *concepts*, and *activities*. The concept is the meaning. The name is a word or specific object. And the verb denotes an activity; quite specifically, it is the activity of converting a meaning into a word, found in the act of speaking by which an idea is expressed into a sentence. The spoken word is the name or the individual object, the general concept is the idea in the mind which is converted into the word by the activity.

The three modes of nature are therefore sometimes identified with the terms *manas* which represents the concept, *prāna* which denotes the activity, and *vāk* which is the specific object created by the activity. Factually, the same sound can be interpreted as a *name*, a *concept*, and an *activity*. Such interpretation thus often creates confusion as to the exact meaning denoted by the sound. For instance, the term *present* can denote a noun (as in 'He was given a present') or a verb (as in 'I will present to you a gift'). If you combine these two kinds of usage, you can see glaring examples of such interpretation (e.g., 'I will present to you a present'). This fact has now come to light in interesting ways in mathematics, where logical paradoxes are produced if we don't distinguish between the three different uses of a sound.

In mathematics, these sounds are simply numbers. However, a number can—under the three types of interpretations—denote a concept, a name, or an activity. The confusion between names and concepts appears in the well-known mathematical result called *Gödel's Incompleteness Theorem*[13], which indicates that unless mathematics distinguishes between names and concepts it will be prone to paradoxes such as "P: P is false". In such a statement, the first P is a *meaning*—it embodies the meaning that "P is false". The second *P* is used as a name, and it refers to a sentence called *P*. The paradox is that if *P* is true, then its meaning is that it is false. If, however, *P* is false, then its claim that "*P* is false" entails that *P* is true. There is no way to solve this problem except by precluding the *creation* of such contradictory sentences that refer to themselves. A sentence is a material object; it cannot refer to itself, because self-reference is a property of the soul, and even in self-reference, Vedic philosophy delineates a difference between the knower and the power by which he knows, as *puruṣa* and its *śakti*. Self-references can lead to paradoxes, for example, in the famous sentence "I am a liar". If I was indeed telling the truth, then by the truth of that statement, I must be lying. But if I was indeed lying, then by the falsity of that statement I must be telling the truth. The only way to solve the paradox is to separate the person from the act of lying, which involves the distinction between the person and the power that creates the action. There is, hence, simply no scenario in which an object can refer to itself. In the case of the soul, self-awareness is caused by the knower and the power of knowing. The *chit* is the knower, and to know, it uses the power of knowing.

Similarly, the confusion between name and activity in the context of numbers leads to *Turing's Halting Problem*[14] where the name of a program doesn't exactly tell us what the program *does*. You could call a program that adds two numbers a "word processor", but that name is not indicative of what it actually does. Indeed, if we interpreted the name as the activity, we can create a paradox in which a program that claims to be useful is actually malicious. Such programs abound today as viruses, Trojans, and a variety of malware. They claim to be useful based on their innocuous names, but they are actually malicious. Thus, their names are contrary to their activities or program semantics. The inability to distinguish between the names and activities in mathematics leads to the inability to identify which program is malicious. Indeed, we cannot even know if the program's name correctly indicates the class of the program—e.g., a word processor. In essence, the bits in a program are just sound or symbols, but their meaning or interpretation is not in the program. Program semantics requires the ability to decode when a symbol indicates names, concepts, and activities—i.e., distinguishing between the three modes of nature.

The material world in modern science is *objects.* In Vedic philosophy, the same material world is *symbols.* The difference between the two is that in a physical space, the dimensions of space can be easily substituted through coordinate transforms. Thus, there is no absolute meaning to dimensions such as X, Y, and Z. However, when the dimensions are denoted by name, concept, and activity, substituting these dimensions amounts to interpreting a name as a concept, or a concept as an activity, which leads to semantic confusions. The dimensions X, Y, and Z—when these dimensions are used to denote a figure of speech, have an absolute interpretation, which should not be substituted. If I view a sound as a verb and you think it is a noun, then our communication will break down, or will be mired in differences of understanding between us. To communicate, our personal space or coordinate reference frame must refer to an absolute frame, to consistently interpret the sound's meaning.

Therefore, the difference between object and symbol manifests in a problem: the space of objects can be made to undergo coordinate transforms, while the space of symbols cannot. One such transform involves flipping the directions of space by which X is converted into –X. If the name of a symbol is P, and we flip the concept axis, we will map the name P to the concept *not* P, but the meaning is not flipped because the inverted tree always grows in a single direction—top to bottom. By flipping the coordinate axes, the parts become the root and the whole becomes the leaf or the part. Now we have a paradox in which the whole contains the parts, but when the picture has been inverted, the part contains the whole but the other parts of the whole logically contradict it.

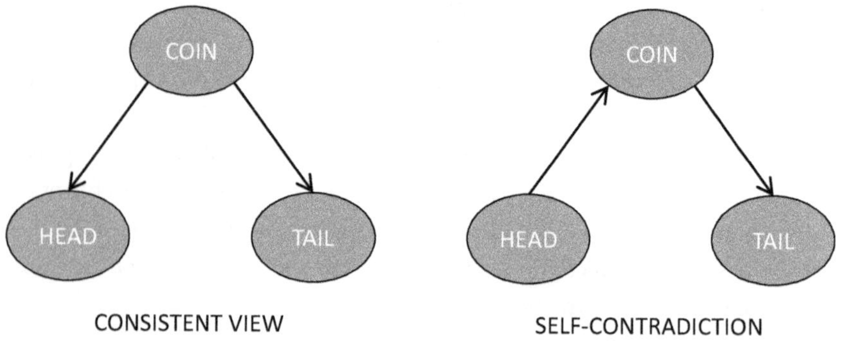

Figure-10 Coordinate Transform Creates Self-Contradiction

For example, consider a coin which has two sides—head and tail. The coin contains head and tail as its parts, and when we view the tree from top to bottom, we find no contradiction. However, if we invert the coordinate axes and look at the same tree from bottom to top, then the head seems to contain the coin, but the coin also contains the tail. As a result, the tail is inside the head, but since head and tail are logically contradictory, by including the head within the tail a self-contradiction is created. These contradictions are the outcomes of performing coordinate transformations within an absolute space.

The essence of these mathematical paradoxes is three-fold. First, we must describe space as a tree because otherwise we can never give the symbols any meaning. Second, the root of the tree must be described as the whole which is then subdivided into parts because otherwise the tree is unbounded and anything unbounded cannot be given meaning. Third, the tree has an absolute direction which has to be preserved in order to avoid logical paradoxes.

The space of objects is relative—i.e., each observer can view an object from their perspective, and all such spaces are *equivalent*. The space of symbols is absolute—i.e., an observer can view the object from their perspective, but all such spaces are not equivalent because they will misinterpret the true meaning of a symbol. In fact, only one interpretation can be true, and all others must be false. This fact permits a *choice* in the observer by which he can view the world differently, but those choices simply result in falsities. Thus, our ability to interpret the world doesn't indicate the truth; rather, we have to understand that space is absolute, and hence we have to get to the absolute viewpoint in order to discover that truth, rather than interpret it freely.

We are free to see either the head or the tail if we so choose. However, we cannot consider ourselves as the origin of space because such a view only leads to a self-contradiction because the opposite is contained within. Therefore, while seeing the head or tail, we must know that there is an absolute origin in the coin, from which head and tail (our experiences) have emanated.

The sound prior to interpreting is zero-dimensional—i.e., it exists as an object, but that object is not in the material space. This sound is hence often called *transcendental* because it is outside material space. The same sound, if covered by matter is placed in the material space, which means that it is given a meaning. Thus, a zero-dimensional entity becomes three-dimensional because the transcendent entity is 'covered' by meaning or interpretation.

Quite separate from the act of giving meanings to sounds, is this meaning being used by the soul as its pleasure, knowledge, or relationship? The original sound is called *OM* which represents *I*. Through association with the three properties of the soul—*sat*, *chit*, and *ānanda*—it divides into three parts called "I am", "I have", and "I want". For instance, you can say that "I am a father", "I have a father", and "I want to be a father". In the first case, 'father' is a relationship, in the second case 'father' is an object, and in the third case it has become a goal. You can prefix "I am", "I have", and "I want" to any word (which can be interpreted as name, concept, or activity) and it will create a different meaning for the individual soul. The prefixing of "I am", "I have", and "I want" is the distinction produced by the soul when it comes into contact with the sound *I* quite like verbs, names, and concepts are produced when *I* comes in contact with matter. Thus, there are two orthogonal ways to divide *I* into parts.

Through the division of "I am" you could say "I am Mr. Smith", "I am a lawyer", and "I am running", which involve, respectively, the use of a name, a concept, and a verb. Similarly, you could say "I have a house on South Avenue", "I have a tall body", and "I have read this book", which involve, respectively, the use of a name, a concept, and a verb. Likewise, you can say "I want a Ferrari", "I want expensive clothes", and "I want to be swimming", which involve, respectively, the use of a name, a concept, and a verb. Therefore, the singular reality—*I*, also called *Śabda Brahman*—initially becomes three parts (I am, I have, and I want) when the soul associates with it, and it then becomes nine parts (names, concepts, and activities) when it contacts matter.

At present, in modern science there is no self or *I*, and the distinction between "I have", "I am" and "I want" doesn't exist. The non-existence of "I am" means that we never talk about the person and his awareness in science; a person is simply an object, which is divisible and hence subject to mutations. The non-existence of "I have" implies that the whole is reduced to the parts, because the whole—in this case *I*—is simply a composition of all the parts (the things that he has—e.g., hands, legs, head, stomach, etc.). Finally, the non-existence of "I want" entails that we never talk about choice in matter; we assume that everything works according to deterministic mathematical laws.

Similarly, since modern science employs mathematics, but mathematics cannot distinguish between names, concepts, and verbs, the rest of science also doesn't. Effectively, the starting point of the world in the soul and material energy and their divisions into parts is missing in modern science. Since Vedic philosophy has a different starting point, it incorporates the ideas of the self, its varying identities through roles, the ownership of the body by the soul, and the existence of desires and goals that lead to pleasure and suffering. Similarly, the world is not just objects, but symbols with meaning, which means that we can distinguish between particles—some are parts of a whole, others are relations to other parts and wholes, and yet others are goals in the future.

The Influence of Duality

However, this three-fold division of sound into meaning is still incomplete, because meanings are always defined by opposites. In Vedic texts, material nature or *prakriti* is sometimes described as three modes, and at other times described as *duality*. Duality means that 'hot' is not defined without 'cold', 'black' is not defined without 'white', etc. Thus, if there is something 'hot' in this world, then there must also be something 'cold' elsewhere. Heat by itself cannot exist; it has to exist only in opposition to cold. If there were no black men on this planet, nobody will use the term 'white man' because it would be sufficient to just use the term 'man' to describe everyone. Without black men, 'white' would just be part of the definition of humanity. The world as a whole therefore contains logical contradictions—hot and cold—but each object is individually consistent because it is either hot or cold. This presents grave problems for logic, because a logical system—comprised of many propositions—cannot have contradictions. In Vedic philosophy, the universe collectively is contradictory, but individually each object is consistent. To solve the problems of consistency, therefore, we have to induct space and time in logic itself! Through such induction, we solve the logical contradictions without taking away the duality itself. This duality now combines with the three modes of nature, and creates opposites in the names, concepts, and activities.

In this theory, there is often confusion between the *duality* or opposites which exist as the positive and negative directions on a given dimension, and the *three* modes of nature, which manifest as the three dimensions. The confusion arises because *prakriti* is described as the combination of three modes, as well as duality. The fact is that there is no contradiction between these two descriptions if we see the three modes of nature as the three *dimensions* of space, and the duality of nature producing the two *directions* on each dimension. Thus, the x-axis can have East and West, the y-axis can have North and South, while the z-axis can have Up and Down. The duality is East vs. West, North vs. South, and Up vs. Down. This duality is in the three modes.

An example of colors will help clarity this point further, where the duality is black and white, and the three modes of nature are cyan, magenta, and yellow. White here represents the positive direction on the three-color axes, and it is generally ignored as a color assuming that the *paper* on which the color is printed is white. The black on the other hand represents the negative direction, and is mixed with cyan, magenta, and yellow, to create further shades of color. Thus, we call the color scheme CMYK, where K is the 'key' called black. Since you can mix black or white with each of the three colors (cyan, magenta, and yellow) there are three axes, and then there are two directions. There is hence a three-dimensional space from which six *directions* are produced. The three dimensions are yellow, cyan, and magenta, and the two directions are white and black. In Figure-11 white and black are respectively the top and the bottom. This only means that the colors are *unsaturated* at the top and *saturated* at the bottom. The limit of the three-color saturation is the color black.

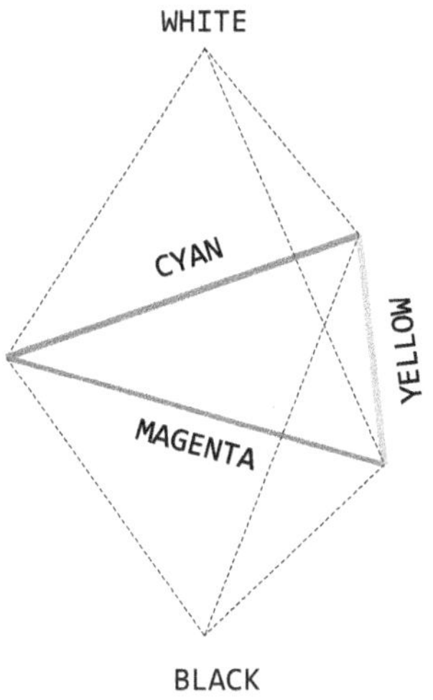

Figure-11 The Space of Five Colors

This color sphere can be given a meaning in which the top or white is the complete whole, and it is gradually divided into parts until the parts are so small that they cannot be further divided. The act of division is the act of adding the three colors—cyan, magenta, and yellow—to white. As we go on adding the colors, the whole is successively divided into smaller and smaller parts, and the saturation of all colors (black) represents the smallest parts. The successive additions of colors therefore represent many *tiers* of reality—the higher tiers are closer to white or everything and the lower tiers are closer to black or nothing. The individual things—*something*—exists between the extremes of everything and nothing. White is the balance of all three colors, and the cyan, magenta, and yellow are created by *removing* something from white. Therefore, another way to look at the same scheme is that when we are adding more and more colors from top to bottom, we are actually hiding some parts of the whole. As a result of this hiding, less and less is visible as we get to the bottom, and more and more is revealed as we move toward the top. In effect, the top is fully enlightened, and the bottom is completely dark. These notions about top and bottom are common even in today's world where 'going up' means becoming more enlightened and 'going down' means greater ignorance.

The three dimensions of name, concept, and activity, combined with the distinctions brought by duality, produce a three *dimensional* but six *directional* space. These directions are very important because they indicate opposites, and therefore we can think of space as these six directions. This space is the place for contradictions or duality, and yet each thing in this space is by itself consistent. There are hence contradictions, but no self-contradiction. As a result, you can expect clashes and fights in this world, but no logical paradox. Indeed, the existence of opposites creates *completeness* and the avoidance of logical paradoxes creates *consistency*. The world is thus both consistent and complete, although it is also necessarily a place for clash and conflict.

Motion in Material Space

If you move to a higher location on the z-axis, you move to a higher role. If you move inward, to the center, on the x-axis and y-axis you move onto a higher activity and a higher concept. Thus, in the semantic space, moving inward and upward, is better than moving outward and downward. The inward and upward movement represents a 'rise' while the outward and downward movement denotes a 'fall'. The center of this space—called the *axis* of the universe—represents the perfection in two ways— (1) each point on that axis represents the highest concept and the highest activity within a given plane, and (2) as we move upward on that axis, we also go to higher roles. Thus, perfection of knowledge is to be gained by moving inward in this space, and the higher levels of the universe are meant for those who are entitled to control the lower levels. However, even a living entity at a given level in the space can still advance in their actions and knowledge by moving to the center.

This structure of the space is mimicked in the structure of nerves in the body—emanating from the spinal cord. The spinal cord represents the inward and the upward path, which means that information flows from the rest of the body to the center—the spinal cord—and then it moves upward to the brain. Similarly, the signals are sent down from the brain as commands or instructions through the spinal cord, and they are then distributed to the rest of the body. The structure of the spinal cord is emblematic of the structure of the universal space of three dimensions, and accordingly, Vedic philosophy describes the universe as a body, and the body as a universe. The advanced *yogi* who has perfected the inward and the upward journey understands this structure because he realizes that the only path to move upward is to first move inward. If we cannot move inward, we also cannot move upward in this space.

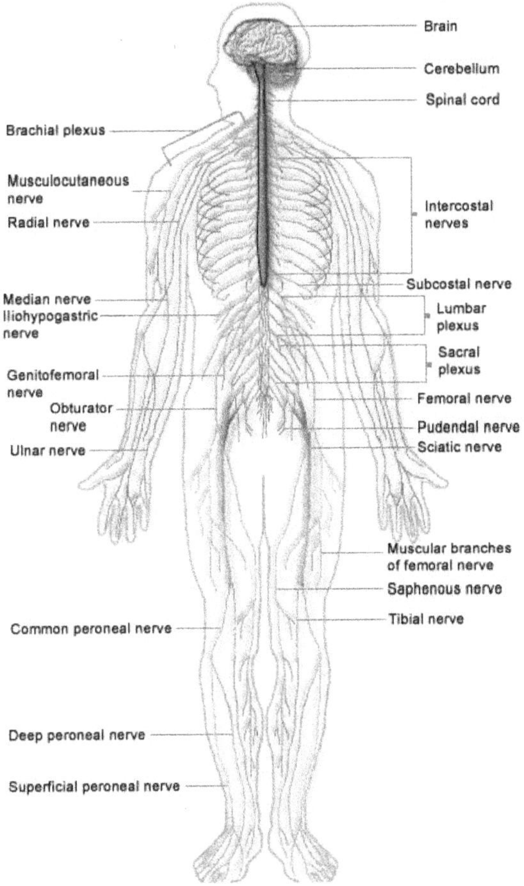

Figure-12 Space as Veins in the Human Body

Thus, those people who continually look outward cannot see anything higher than their current existence. They imagine that since they cannot see the higher reality, it must not exist, and hence they are not even inclined to pursue it. The problem is their flawed understanding of space itself. To see a higher reality, one must necessarily move inward, because only that type of change opens the path to the vision of the existence of higher reality.

> *SB 3.26.34*[15]. *Translation: The activities and characteristics of the ethereal element can be observed as the accommodation of room for the external and internal existences of all living entities, namely the field of activities of the vital air, the senses and the mind.*
>
> *Purport by Śrīla Prabhupāda (excerpt): The mind, the senses and the vital force, or living entity, have forms, although they are not visible to the naked eye. Form rests in subtle existence in the sky, and internally it is perceived as the veins within the body and the circulation of the vital air. Externally there are invisible forms of sense objects. (Emphasis mine).*

From this verse we can understand that the structure of space (or what is called 'ether') can be internally perceived as the veins within the body. The *yogi* draws his concentration inward, which means he loses the bodily sensations, and then moves the consciousness upward. Thus, simply by understanding the nature of his body, and how consciousness can be drawn inward and upward, he realizes the structure of space, and hence, of the universe.

The highest point in the body is called the *brahmarandhra*—the 'hole' from which the soul leaves for *Brahman* at the point of death. It is also called the *sahasrāra chakra* or the crown chakra which lies at the top and in the center of the head. For some people, if this point is touched, very pleasurable tingling sensations are created in the body. The process of *yoga* is meant to raise the consciousness to this highest point and then escape through it. In Vedic cosmology, the highest center-most point is occupied by *Vasudeva*, a form of *Viṣṇu*, and the *yogi* can go that place simply by the process of *yoga*.

The location in this space—i.e., where the consciousness is situated—constitutes a type of experience comprised of name, concept, and activity. Every location therefore has these three properties which represent the true name by which the thing should be called, its properties by which it should be understood, and the different types of changes that it can cause. Simply knowing the location of an experience in space constitutes true knowledge. We don't have to know dozens of properties like mass, charge, energy, temperature, pressure, surface tension, friction, voltage, current, resistance, etc. We have to know just one property—the *position* of the object in the universal space.

All these positions are forever fixed, which means the experiences corresponding to these positions are always *possible*. The soul, however, moves in this space, jumping from one position to another, thereby experiencing diverse things. Therefore, *dynamics* or what we call 'motion' does not pertain to the change in the state of *objects* because these objects are *states* in the space—fixed forever. The dynamics instead pertains to the soul, who is moving from one state to another. Therefore, science—as the theory of motion—should never be about the change of position of an object; it should be about the position of the soul. Furthermore, the change in position is not factually the soul's motion. It is only a change in the attachment between the soul and the material reality by which the soul becomes aware of the reality—this attachment is called *prāna*. The jumping from one state to another is called *reincarnation*. That jump is discrete at the time of death, when the body is changed drastically, and the soul is born into a new body—i.e., a position far away. But even within this lifetime, every new experience constitutes a change in position.

Therefore, science—as the theory of motion—is identical to the theory of reincarnation or how the soul jumps from one state to another. Any science that talks about the motion of objects is utterly false because matter is inert, and never moves; it doesn't move because it is simply a location in space. Space doesn't move; rather the soul becomes aware of different things in that space, and by that change in awareness it *appears* to move. The actual motion pertains to *prāna* which is refocused due to *guna*, *karma*, and time, and if a person can control their *guna* or 'nature' they can change their focus in life.

When the soul moves into a new location, that location is automatically 'illuminated' by the soul's presence and we can perceive the existence of a body. If our perception is advanced, we can also perceive the mental state, the intellectual biases, the egoistic goals, and the moral values. But if the perception is not advanced, then we only see the body—and the most superficial outer covering of that body. If we cannot see the deeper levels of reality, we think that these bodies are just objects, which is how science begins modeling them in terms of a physical world. Modern science claims to be empirical, but factually it is built by people who had underdeveloped perception. Under this impoverished perception they modeled the world as objects, because they simply could not perceive the existence of deeper realities. Furthermore, because they are motivated by an outward and downward motion, they seek to look at other things rather than bring their consciousness inward. Similarly, they want to look deeper into the details rather than into the higher concepts. Due to this outward and downward movement, they cannot see the nature of reality, even though they have an inner life of mind, intellect, ego, and morality. They simply ignore that reality and focus on the existence of molecules.

I call this space *semantic space* because the locations in this space are symbols, and the motion of the soul in the semantic space creates a *semantic time* because it constitutes a change in experience. To do real science, we have to produce a theory of the soul's motion which *appears* to be object motion, but factually involves the change in the soul's experiences. The motions of planets and stars are therefore not motions of objects. They are rather the motion of souls; whose bodily change appears to us as celestial motion. There is hence no object without a soul, and nothing moves if a soul is not present. Everything is moving because the soul is changing its location in space[16]. The personalization of nature therefore is not simply about imagining the existence of demigods within material objects. It is rather a more profound understanding of space, time, causality, and motion itself. If these essential ideas are not understood, then the personalization would remain a caricature ridiculed in many modern religions (let alone in the scientific description of nature).

A true science is not different from religion; it involves the understanding of space and time, not because we are interested in the nature of the world, but because we want to understand how the soul is forced to move in matter. Unless this understanding is obtained, the soul will remain bound to matter, and the real purpose of religion—as liberation from material existence—cannot be achieved. To see the celestial bodies as demigods therefore involves spiritual advancement; it is not perfection, but it is a far superior alternative.

Therefore, Vedic texts expend a considerable amount of time and space explaining the nature of matter and the structure of the cosmos. One really wonders what these things have to do with transcendence: If the purpose of life is to transcend the material world, then why study the material world at all? The short answer is that before we can transcend the world, we have to understand how we are stuck in this world, and the process of going inward and upward by which we can transcend it. If we don't understand the structure of the cosmos, then we cannot understand the importance of going inward and upward, and we will never transcend the world. Therefore, the study of matter and cosmos lays the *theoretical* background on which a *practice* can be built. Without such a theory, we cannot understand the value in practice.

The Creation of Life Forms

We saw above how the *sat* hierarchy creates the different species of life. We saw how they are not different bodies but different roles, which prescribe the behaviors of a species within an ecosystem. *Brahma* creates the species, which are *instantiation* relationships, not the compositional relationship. The compositional relation is the body of different parts, and the parts are elements of *Sāñkhya* created by *Viṣṇu*. Therefore, *Viṣṇu* creates the material elements, and *Brahma* fashions these elements into a functional design which indicates the interaction between the parts within a body, and the interactions of the body as a whole within an ecosystem. In a system with N parts, each part can interact with the other N-1 parts. Thus, a single material composition of N parts can behave in N * (N-1) ways and knowing the material composition is inadequate to know how the parts combine to create the functional interaction. Similarly, the interaction between the parts can have different sequences, giving rise to permutations of the same parts. Finally, the order in interaction can change with time, leading to even greater variety. Thus, the knowledge of the parts is grossly inadequate to describe the behavior of the whole.

Even in modern biology, a species is defined by the is-a relation, namely, that a mammal is an animal, a dog is a mammal, a poodle is a dog, etc. Therefore, ideally, species must be defined by the functional model of the body rather than its material composition. Modern biologists, however, are obsessed with body parts. They focus on long or short necks, spotted or clear skin, and hoofed or non-hoofed legs. Of course, these are things that we can clearly observe. What we cannot always observe clearly is the internal interaction between the parts—what we call the biology which involves not just the chemical that we can see, but the interactions or chemical reactions in the body.

Similarly, we don't always see the interaction between the various animals within an ecosystem, or even between the members of the species. How would a species be defined differently if we focused on the interaction model rather than the bodily structure? For example, a person who hunts deer in the forest in order to eat them is like a tiger because of his behavior in the forest ecosystem. It doesn't matter if has a body that looks like a human because the tiger is a species defined by the behavior rather than the body parts.

The functional behavior of the body—in relation to the other species and life forms—is called its *dharma.* It is a prescription of duty and role-play. Ideally, the functional behavior of the body must be aligned with the bodily structure, but these are not necessarily identical. As we noted earlier, the material world is comprised of three overlapping trees, which should ideally be identical, but they are not owing to the free will of the soul. A tree is loop-free but if the trees are overlapped or combined in disjoint ways then loops are created. These loops are the cause of material consequences or *karma.* If the tree is loop-free then the duty is aligned with the bodily structure which is aligned with the happiness of the soul: the soul enjoys the life in the body. However, if the three trees are disjointed, then the parts in the body don't work correctly because they are interacting with the wrong parts, and pleasure derived from such functioning parts becomes the pain experienced in the body.

In the same way, if a person performs their duty according to the body type, and enjoys the pleasures aligned with the duty, then the three trees are identically overlapped, and no *karma* is created. Even while living within the body, the person is considered liberated from the laws of nature, which means that through his actions he is not producing new good or bad *karma* which will compel him to enter a body and role contrary to his desire for pleasure. The three trees become discordant when the desire contradicts the body type, and under that desire the person violates the *dharma* expected of them.

There is hence—based on the definition of a species—a clear and succinct criterion for understanding the definition of *dharma,* and how it is violated based on one's desires (also called *guna*) thereby producing consequences of actions called *karma.* If the laws of moral action apply when the three trees are discordant, but they disappear when the three trees are mutually aligned, and the soul attains salvation from the material existence, then even while living in the body he performs the duties allocated to the body living peacefully and harmoniously with the surroundings. This is the basic definition of religion—identify the duty based on the body type, and align the desires to those duties, because by desiring something incompatible with the body type and the role allotted to the body type, inner loops will be created which will then produce moral consequences, which will result in birth, death, and suffering.

The suffering can be caused due to the inner functioning of the body going haywire. It can be caused through adverse interactions with the other members of the ecosystem. Finally, it can be caused by the entire ecosystem being disrupted through natural calamities such as famines, wars, epidemics, or even social, political, and economic upheavals which are beyond the control of any person. Many people suffer from their own body and mind, even when they are not being troubled by society or other people. Other people have a healthy body and mind, but they suffer due to other living entities; these may be their friends, family, colleagues, neighbors, etc. Then there are others who have a healthy body and mind, and are not troubled by other living entities, but the situation in their surrounding is itself disturbed in uncontrollable ways. There are numerous other combinations of the above three types of suffering.

Thus, the definition of a 'species' can be provided in three different ways—as a body type, as a type of role or duty, and as a type of pleasure. A true human being is one who inhabits the human body, performs the human role, and enjoys the human pleasures. Thus, just because someone inhabits a human body, doesn't necessarily mean he is a human if he doesn't perform the duties expected of the human life, or enjoys pleasure contrary to human life. The human body enables the abilities of thinking and understanding, but the meaning of 'human' is also a certain type of *dharma* or duty, not merely the body.

One such duty is making offerings to demigods by recognizing their control of nature, which is called *yajña* or sacrifice. Similarly, social customs like marriage, division of society into four classes for division of labor, and the division of life into four stages to fulfill all purposes of life[17] are unique to humans. We don't expect animals to follow a division of labor (although in species such as bees and ants such a division of labor exists). Similarly, we don't expect animals to follow a life of training, enjoyment, retirement, and renunciation (although in many animal species such orders are found). We don't expect animals to perform *yajña* or practice marriage vows. Thus, the human *dharma* is not always performed in other species because the human body is different from the human duty, and humanity is to be defined by its duties rather than just the body. Animal bodies cannot enact human duties, but many human bodies may also not perform the human duties. Hence, a 'human' is only one who performs the human duties in the human body; a rare class today.

Modern science misses the fact that life is created for the purpose of fulfilling the soul's desires while remaining in the confines of morality. Science discards the desires and intentions of the soul, and the dictates of moral imperatives arising from social roles. It hypothesizes that only material particles are real, and hence there is neither role nor goal. Even these particles are treated as things rather than symbols, so, there cannot be a mind that understands the world via symbols. How these particles organize into a body, why this body is capable of cognition, how the bodies organize into societies and ecosystems are all problems that the physical theory doesn't solve.

Evolutionary biology is expected to explain the organization of particles into living bodies and economic competitiveness is supposed to explain the origin of social systems. At each level—beginning with the particles themselves—there is randomness: the particles are governed by atomic theory which is probabilistic, the living bodies are created by random mutation which cannot be predicted, and societies are supposedly governed by free choices, but the choice has no moral imperative and is made without a moral consequence. At each level of material organization, there is randomness, and as randomness aggregates, the uncertainty at the higher levels or organization grows exponentially. Exponential growth means that the existence of molecules, living bodies, and societies is highly unlikely, as the number of alternatives in which such things exist are miniscule relative to those where they don't.

Many people believe that even a small amount of possibility will become reality given sufficient time; they have a flawed understanding of this possibility because it is like a tree which creates new branches at every moment, which means that uncertainty *grows* instead of declining over time. This idea is presented in the *Many Worlds Interpretation* of atomic theory[18] in which every time a man is picking his nose in this universe, there is another universe in which he is not. The total number of universes grows exponentially over time as the universe in which the man picked his nose divides into two universes where he again picks his nose and another one where he does not. Accordingly, passing time doesn't increase the chance of something occurring eventually. Instead, the uncertainty grows exponentially with time, which means that if life was unlikely at the start of the universe, then it is even more unlikely now. As a result, if you cannot postulate that life existed prior to the creation of the universe, then every passing moment has made its existence harder.

The personalization of nature—where particles are organized into living bodies, the bodies are organized into societies, and the soul enjoys morally through such organization—represents an answer to the question: Why does the world exist the way it does? The answer is that nature is not random. Rather, through a hierarchy, the abstract predetermines the details, and hence the 'complex' is a level of organization beyond the 'simple'. Similarly, this material organization—which we perceive sensually—is not the only reality: roles and goals are also real, but we cannot perceive them by the senses. The goals help us enjoy life, but that enjoyment is restricted through the moral imperatives of roles. The hierarchy of organization, together with a purpose and moral law of behavior eliminates the randomness in nature, without removing choices. In fact, the law of nature is how an intent translates into roles, and how the imperatives of the role are rewarded or punished contextually.

This new understanding hinges on perception by the mind because the mind can perceive *could*, *should*, and *would*, but the senses can only see objects. The senses give us knowledge of what the world *is* but not what it *could be*, *should be*, or *would be*. By the mind we can see possibility, we can understand a person's role and responsibilities, and perceive desire as the source of happiness, which acts to exploit the opportunities of a role. Without the mind we can obtain sensations, and at best suppose that these sensations existed even before I perceived them (objectivity of the world). Such a view about nature misses the point that the world is created from the combination of could, should, and would—each of which cannot be perceived by the senses.

The Significance of the Trinity

Thus, we can see how the whole divides into parts creating space, time, and matter. *Viṣṇu* creates all matter manifest from *chit*, *Brahma* creates the functional forms in a hierarchy that we call space (and science sometimes calls it 'force'). *Shiva* creates the material desires and time. The smallest part of the whole is called 'atom', but this atom is created by dividing the whole successively through numerous stages, such that the higher part, function, and purpose becomes the controller of the lower part, function, and purpose.

Once we grasp this basic understanding of the soul, and its three different aspects, we can see why a trinity exists—namely, to create concepts, roles, and pleasures. The trinity is not three disparate components; it is rather expressing the three aspects of the soul and creating the freedom to combine them in new ways to create any experience. The three individual parts of the soul are therefore the possibilities of a role, knowledge, and pleasure. In combination, they constitute a pleasurable experience of some external reality.

This brief overview of the Vedic system of gods entails a personalist description of the world, different from the impersonalist system employed in modern science. However, as we saw above, all the fundamental concepts of modern science exist in a different form in the Vedic system. We can use these differences to revise science—i.e., the idea of space, time, and matter. We can also use the same ideas to understand the Cosmic Theogony, or the system of God and demigods. Finally, we can use the same method to understand the nature of the soul, and its various psychological manifestations. How powerful is that system that encompasses the theory of space, time, and matter, the study of the soul and psychology, as well as the system of God and demigods into a single, coherent, and might I add—rather simple—description of reality? The personalist system therefore doesn't have to be grounded in stories and myths. It can be grounded into the science and philosophy of nature and life.

The trinity is also described in Vedic texts as three schools of Vedic philosophy called *Shaivism*, *Shaktism*, and *Vaishnavism*. Of these three, *Shaivism* and *Vaishnavism* are common with the trinity, but *Shaktism* appears to be different. *Śakti* is the female counterpart of *Shiva* and *Viṣṇu*.

Śakti is involved in expanding emotion and cognition, and this *Śakti* is called *Pārvati* in relation to *Shiva* and *Lakshmi* in relation to *Viṣṇu*. In that sense, the notion of *Śakti* is subsumed under both schools, although by the inclusion of *Śakti* the sexual aspect of the male-female relation is emphasized in these schools of philosophy.

Śakti is a general concept of being the perceiver and servant and is required to divide and expand God into smaller parts. It can denote the awareness of God's pleasure, in which case She is called *Pārvati* and *Hara*. It can denote the awareness of God's cognition, in which case She is called *Lakshmi* and *Ramā*. Finally, it can be the awareness of God's awareness, which is the recognition that God is a living being and not an inanimate principle, in which case She is called *Narāyanī* in relation to a form of God called *Narāyana*.

The soul can be a 'child' of any of these three forms of *Śakti*. When the soul is situated in relation to God, either being aware of God as a conscious being (*Narayana*), or being aware of God as the fullness of six qualities (*Viṣṇu* forms and *Rāma*) or being aware of God as the fullness of happiness (*Kṛṣṇa*), it behaves like the *Śakti* of God. The description of the theology in terms of *Shaivism*, *Shaktism*, and *Vaishnavism* is slightly different in emphasis than the description of theology in terms of *Viṣṇu*, *Shiva*, and *Brahma*. The former emphasizes the male-female division of the reality into knower and known, while the latter emphasizes the three aspects of the reality as *sat*, *chit*, and *ānanda*. They are not contradictory, but they are different emphasis in theology.

In the *Svetaśvatāra Upanishad*[19] it is said that the *Śakti* of God has three parts—*jnana* (tied to the *chit*), *bala* (the will power tied to *ānanda*), and *kriya* or activity (tied to *sat*). This is an explanation for how the *Śakti* is one, but it becomes many by initially dividing into three parts. Therefore, even when *Śakti* is described in a separate school, the three aspects of the soul as *sat, chit,* and *ānanda* are described as the expansions from this *Śakti*. Ultimately, the whole truth is the combination of the masculine and the feminine, each of which have three aspects. Thus, rather than seeing these two as different systems of philosophy, we can see them as different emphasis in the same system.

3

The Religion of the Sun

If I had to choose a religion, the sun as the universal giver of life would be my god.

—*Napoléon Bonaparte*

Sun, Moon, and Star Worship

As we noted in the previous chapter, there are three dominant systems of religion to which all other religions can be related, sometimes directly, and sometimes seemingly through a cross-fertilization of the ideas between the systems. These three systems are founded on the trinity of *Viṣṇu*, *Shiva*, and *Brahma* as noted earlier. These three respectively represent the three facets of the soul called *chit* (*Viṣṇu*), *ānanda* (*Shiva*), and *sat* (*Brahma*), who are the respective controllers of the material world, the desire for the material world, and the relationships in the material world. The material world is what we perceive through the senses, mind, intellect, ego, and morality. However, we don't perceive all the material world at once; therefore, to see something we have to be in a particular relationship to this world. Similarly, we don't always enjoy what we perceive; to enjoy we must have the desire for the particular relation. Thus, the trinity of *Viṣṇu*, *Shiva*, and *Brahma* represent aspects of *experience*.

Religion has a role in life as the process of improving our experience. This can mean having a better body and mind in order to perceive the world differently. It can mean being situated in a different relation to the world in order to experience different things. And it can mean changing our desires to enjoy what we can perceive by the current body, which is available through the current relationships. Religion therefore has three facets, once we understand the nature of experience, and the trinity represents the controllers of matter, desire, and relations. Vedic texts call these three by many different names. For instance, in the Rig Veda matter is called *Agni*, desire is called *Soma*, and relation is called *Vayu*[1]. These are also represented by the sun, the moon, and the stars, respectively. The worship of *Viṣṇu* became the worship of the sun as the source of material energy. The worship of *Shiva* manifested as the worship of desire and pleasure through moon worship. Finally, the worship of *Brahma* has manifested in different societies as the worship of different stars.

The sun, the moon, and the stars are given *meanings* in religion; they are not merely celestial bodies; they have an influence over our experience. To understand religion, we must understand the philosophy and science of that experience, grasp the original controllers of that experience, and then comprehend the various ways in which our need to define and control that experience manifests through the worship of the sun, the moon, and the stars.

In this chapter, I will focus on the religion of the sun, and the next chapter will discuss the religion of the moon and stars. In order to enunciate these religions, we have to delve deeper into cosmological topics, but this cosmology is not simply astronomy. Astronomy constitutes empirical observations, while cosmology forms the explanation of those observations. Astronomy involves sense perception, and cosmology entails theories used to explain these perceptions. To an extent, we may focus on the sense experience, but any sense experience can be explained using many different theories. In particular, as we have seen earlier, there are two dominant explanations of the world—*personal* and *impersonal*. Modern cosmology involves an impersonal explanation of sense experience, while Vedic cosmology—and other religious systems which emanated from or emulated this system—follow a personalist explanation. It is notable that we cannot use empirical measurements to distinguish the two, because they try to explain the same empirical data in a different way.

By cosmology therefore I mean a discussion of the concepts and theories that underlie the astronomical observations. Since this cosmology is the expression of the soul—namely, relation, cognition, and emotion—to study this cosmology we have to delve into the philosophy of the soul, the various subdivisions of the three aspects, and how they create our experience.

Facts like the rising and setting of the sun, the changing of the seasons, the cyclic nature of day and night, extending over long ages, are all empirical facts common to both systems. The difference is that when the Vedic system personalizes the world, it provides a *qualitative* account of experience that includes the body, but also the experiences of the mind, intellect, ego, and morality. Modern astronomy instead restricts itself to sense perception of the motion of the planets and stars themselves, with the premise that these motions have no effect on our lives, and hence the problem of explaining those effects doesn't arise. As a result, when we study modern cosmology, we restrict ourselves to explaining the motion of the sun, the moon, and the stars. But when we study Vedic cosmology, we talk about their effects on our life.

The type-based description of the cosmos emanates from this difference. To explain the effect of planets and stars on our life, we have to change the theoretical model in cosmology and describe it using *types* rather than *quantities*. The quantities don't disappear, and we still measure distances, times, rates of revolutions, the tilt of angles, etc. However, these numbers are now indicative of qualities rather than quantities. For instance, the different positions of the sun, the moon, and the stars are not just places; they are also *meanings*, and their presence in a position indicates a type of influence. Owing to these influences, as the position changes, the influences also change.

The key task in understanding the worship of the sun, the moon, and the stars is to comprehend the meanings of different positions, angles, and times, because these are identified as different properties embodied by demigods. Thus, as the sun passes through signs of the zodiac, it acquires different properties, represented by the *Aditya*. Similarly, as the moon changes its phases going over the zodiac, it has different facets represented by the *Rudra*. The zodiac also rotates once per day represented by the *Vasu*. In short, the meanings are associated with the position, and the planets acquire that meaning when situated on that position at that time. In one sense, the entire study relies on the nature of space and time as differences in meaning. In another sense, those meanings are visible to us through planetary motion[2], and the change in meanings is thus attributed to their motion. But the motion—as we have seen previously—is caused by their desire to perform their duties, and hence the results of such actions are attributed to the demigods doing their work.

With this background, we can now delve into the cosmological types. Most of us are familiar with these types through the different calendars, the names of zodiac signs, and properties generally associated with planets, all of which are embodied in the practice of astrology. In this chapter and the next, we will take a closer look at the relation between these widely-known ideas and demigod worship. For example, why does the zodiac have 12 signs? Why is the system of stars divided into 28 parts? Why does the moon have a 30-day cycle? By finding the answers to these questions, we can see the relation to the aforementioned deities, across diverse cultures, ages, and civilizations.

The Division of the Zodiac

We are familiar with the fact that the zodiac is divided into 12 parts, and star signs such as Cancer, Taurus, Aquarius, and Capricorn are associated with these divisions. As the sun passes through each of the 12 zodiac signs once per year, a tradition of building calendars with 12 months in a year has existed across the world. The question is: Why do calendars almost universally employ 12 months, when they very seldom agree on the start dates for the calendars, the beginning and the end of the years, and often even the number of days within a year? This agreement is not an accident. There is a history to the universality of 12 months, based on the division of the zodiac into 12 parts. The following description of the sun found in the *Śrīmad Bhāgavatam* presents a number of details about personalities relevant to our discussion here.

> *SB 12.11.29 — Sūta Gosvāmī said: The sun travels among all the planets and thus regulates their movements. It has been created by Lord Viṣṇu, the Supreme Soul of all embodied beings, through His beginningless material energy.*

> *SB 12.11.32 — The Supreme Personality of Godhead, manifesting His potency of time as the sun-god, travels about in each of the twelve months, beginning with Madhu, to regulate planetary motion within the universe. Traveling with the sun-god in each of the twelve months is a different set of six associates.*

SB 12.11.33[3] *— My dear sage, Dhātā as the sun-god, Kṛtasthalī as the Apsarā, Heti as the Rākṣasa, Vāsuki as the Nāga, Rathakṛt as the Yakṣa, Pulastya as the sage and Tumburu as the Gandharva rule the month of Madhu.*

SB 12.11.34 — Aryamā as the sun-god, Pulaha as the sage, Athaujā as the Yakṣa, Praheti as the Rākṣasa, Puñjikasthalī as the Apsarā, Nārada as the Gandharva and Kacchanīra as the Nāga rule the month of Mādhava.

SB 12.11.35 — Mitra as the sun-god, Atri as the sage, Pauruṣeya as the Rākṣasa, Takṣaka as the Nāga, Menakā as the Apsarā, Hāhā as the Gandharva and Rathasvana as the Yakṣa rule the month of Śukra.

SB 12.11.36 — Vasiṣṭha as the sage, Varuṇa as the sun-god, Rambhā as the Apsarā, Sahajanya as the Rākṣasa, Hūhū as the Gandharva, Śukra as the Nāga and Citrasvana as the Yakṣa rule the month of Śuci.

SB 12.11.37 — Indra as the sun-god, Viśvāvasu as the Gandharva, Śrotā as the Yakṣa, Elāpatra as the Nāga, Aṅgirā as the sage, Pramlocā as the Apsarā and Varya as the Rākṣasa rule the month of Nabhas.

SB 12.11.38 — Vivasvān as the sun-god, Ugrasena as the Gandharva, Vyāghra as the Rākṣasa, Āsāraṇa as the Yakṣa, Bhṛgu as the sage, Anumlocā as the Apsarā and Śaṅkhapāla as the Nāga rule the month of Nabhasya.

SB 12.11.39 — Pūṣā as the sun-god, Dhanañjaya as the Nāga, Vāta as the Rākṣasa, Suṣeṇa as the Gandharva, Suruci as the Yakṣa, Ghṛtācī as the Apsarā and Gautama as the sage rule the month of Tapas.

SB 12.11.40 — Ṛtu as the Yakṣa, Varcā as the Rākṣasa, Bharadvāja as the sage, Parjanya as the sun-god, Senajit as the Apsarā, Viśva as the Gandharva and Airāvata as the Nāga rule the month known as Tapasya.

SB 12.11.41 — Aṁśu as the sun-god, Kaśyapa as the sage, Tārkṣya as the Yakṣa, Ṛtasena as the Gandharva, Urvaśī as the Apsarā, Vidyucchatru as the Rākṣasa and Mahāśaṅkha as the Nāga rule the month of Sahas.

SB 12.11.42 — Bhaga as the sun-god, Sphūrja as the Rākṣasa, Ariṣṭanemi as the Gandharva, Ūrṇa as the Yakṣa, Āyur as the sage, Karkoṭaka as the Nāga and Pūrvacitti as the Apsarā rule the month of Puṣya.

SB 12.11.43 — Tvaṣṭā as the sun-god; Jamadagni, the son of Ṛcīka, as the sage; Kambalāśva as the Nāga; Tilottamā as the Apsarā; Brahmāpeta as the Rākṣasa; Śatajit as the Yakṣa; and Dhṛtarāṣṭra as the Gandharva maintain the month of Iṣa.

SB 12.11.44 — Viṣṇu as the sun-god, Aśvatara as the Nāga, Rambhā as the Apsarā, Sūryavarcā as the Gandharva, Satyajit as the Yakṣa, Viśvāmitra as the sage and Makhāpeta as the Rākṣasa rule the month of Ūrja.

Month	Form	Apsarā	Rākṣasa	Nāga	Yakṣa	Sage	Gandharva
Madhu	Dhātā	Kṛtasthalī	Heti	Vāsuki	Rathakṛt	Pulastya	Tumburu
Mādhava	Aryamā	Puñjikasthalī	Praheti	Kacchanīra	Athaujā	Pulaha	Nārada
Śukra	Mitra	Menakā	Pauruṣeya	Takṣaka	Rathasvana	Atri	Hāhā
Śuci	Varuṇa	Rambhā	Sahajanya	Śukra	Citrasvana	Vasiṣṭha	Hūhū
Nabhas	Indra	Pramlocā	Varya	Elāpatra	Śrotā	Aṅgirā	Viśvāvasu
Nabhasya	Vivasvān	Anumlocā	Vyāghra	Śaṅkhapāla	Āsāraṇa	Bhṛgu	Ugrasena
Tapas	Pūṣā	Ghṛtācī	Vāta	Dhanañjaya	Suruci	Gautama	Suṣeṇa
Tapasya	Parjanya	Senajit	Varcā	Airāvata	Ṛtu	Bharadvāja	Viśva
Sahas	Aṁśu	Urvaśī	Vidyucchatru	Mahāśaṅkha	Tārkṣya	Kaśyapa	Ṛtasena
Puṣya	Bhaga	Pūrvacitti	Sphūrja	Karkoṭaka	Ūrṇa	Āyur	Ariṣṭanemi
Iṣa	Tvaṣṭā	Tilottamā	Brahmāpeta	Kambalāśva	Śatajit	Jamadagni	Dhṛtarāṣṭra
Ūrja	Viṣṇu	Rambhā	Makhāpeta	Aśvatara	Satyajit	Viśvāmitra	Sūryavarcā

Table-1: The Eighty-Four Expansions of the Sun

I don't expect us to remember all the names in the foregoing description including the names associated with the different forms of the sun. But there are two important facts provided in the above description. First, the sun has many forms—and names—as it passes through the twelve months. Second, there is a recurring pattern of 6 associates in each of the 12 phases of the sun. The above description is summarized in Table-1 for easy reference. Put together, these constitute the 84 expansions or divisions of the sun of which 12 are the signs of the zodiac, and 72 are 6 associates in each of the signs.

SB 12.11.45[4] *— All these personalities are the opulent expansions of the Supreme Personality of Godhead, Viṣṇu, in the form of the sun-god. These deities take away all the sinful reactions of those who remember them each day at dawn and sunset.*

SB 12.11.46 — Thus, throughout the twelve months, the lord of the sun travels in all directions with his six types of associates, disseminating among the inhabitants of this universe purity of consciousness for both this life and the next.

SB 12.11.47-48 — While the sages glorify the sun-god with the hymns of the Sāma, Ṛg and Yajur Vedas, which reveal his identity, the Gandharvas also sing his praises and the Apsarās dance before his chariot. The Nāgas arrange the chariot ropes and the Yakṣas harness the horses to the chariot, while the powerful Rākṣasas push from behind.

SB 12.11.49 — Facing the chariot, the sixty thousand brāhmaṇa sages known as Vālakhilyas travel in front and offer prayers to the almighty sun-god with Vedic mantras.

SB 12.11.50 — For the protection of all the worlds, the Supreme Personality of Godhead Hari, who is unborn and without beginning or end, thus expands Himself during each day of Brahmā into these specific categories of His personal representations.

There are several important things that we need to understand here. First, why is the orbit of the sun divided into 12 parts when it could have been divided into more or less parts? Second, why is each of the positions of the sun described along with associates? Third, why do we speak precisely about 6 associates—called *Gandharvā*, *Rākshsa*, *Apsarā*, *Yakshā*, *Sage*, and *Nāga*—leading to a total of 84 forms when there could be more or less forms? I will return to these questions shortly after discussing some additional facts, namely, that even within the orbit of the sun, all the positions are not at the same *level*. The orbit of the sun is described to be tilted, which is in modern astronomy attributed to the tilt in the earth's orbit of rotation. The tilt leads to the difference between the *equator* and the *ecliptic*. The equator is the circle that we will project in the sky assuming the earth were not tilted. The ecliptic is the circle that we project in the sky by looking at the orbit the sun itself follows.

Tilting in the Sun's Orbit

The 12 forms of the sun are not at the same 'level', which means some positions of the sun—which are placed higher—are better than others. In fact, the orbit is tilted twice, and that tilt creates a hierarchy—increase and decrease. As the sun goes in its orbit, therefore, it also rises and falls.

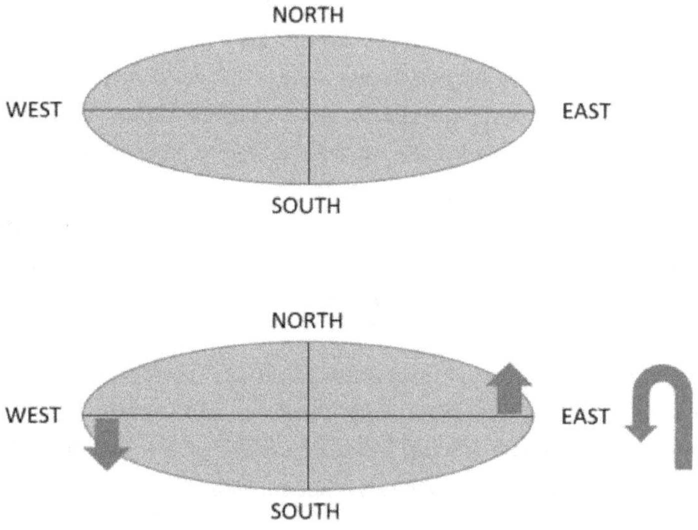

Figure-13 Twisting a Circle by Two Turns

The 12 divisions constitute a linear hierarchy (because they are counted from one to twelve) and yet these are represented in a circle (which appears to be a closed loop). The linearity in the hierarchy and the loop in the circle appear contradictory, but this contradiction is non-existent because the circle is tilted twice—the North is higher than South, and the East is higher than the West. The method of this tilting and its implications are shown below.

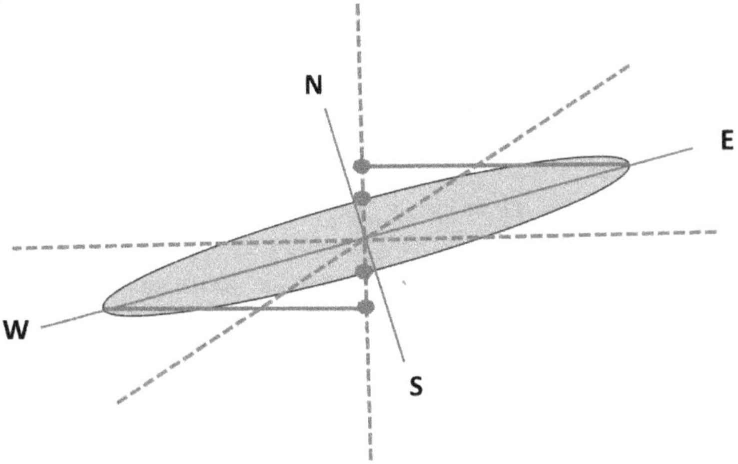

Figure-14 Twisted Circle Creates Hierarchy

We can see that every point on the circle going from East to West through the North has a lower counterpoint in going from West to East through the South. The circle is loopy, but there is a hierarchy. Therefore, we can count the divisions from 1 to 12, and yet, when we reach 12, the next number is again 1, rather than 13. The reason for this loopy nature is that the circle describes the transformation of increase and decrease, and hence time is cyclic.

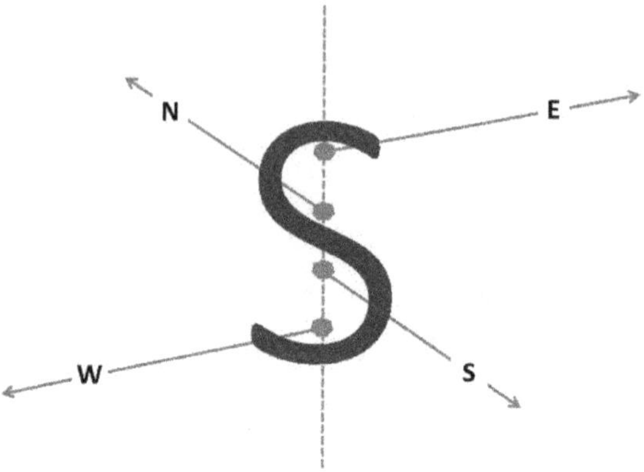

Figure-15 Twisted Circle Has Two Paths

The twelve divisions are both places and times; the places are 30^0 sectors in the rotation of the sun, commonly denoted as the 12 signs of the zodiac, and the times are produced by the rotation of the sun commonly known as the 12 months of the year. But since the sun acquires 12 distinct names, forms, and activities in the divisions in the zodiac, therefore, it is not the 'same' sun that moves through the months; those are considered different *types*.

Bhagavad-Gita 8.24[5]. *Those who know the Supreme Brahman pass away from the world during the influence of the fiery god, in the light, at an auspicious moment, during the fortnight of the moon and the six months when the sun travels in the north.*

Bhagavad-Gita 8.25. The mystic who passes away from this world during the smoke, the night, the moonlight fortnight, or in the six months when the sun passes to the south, or who reaches the moon planet, again comes back.

Śrimad Bhāgavatam 7.14.20-23 Purport[6]. *The six months when the sun moves toward the north are called Uttarāyaṇa, or the northern path, and the six months when it moves south are called Dakshināyana, or the southern path. These are mentioned in Bhagavad-gītā (8.24-25). The first day when the sun begins to move north and enter the zodiacal sign of Capricorn is called Makara-saṅkrānti, and the first day when the sun begins to move south and enter the sign of Cancer is called Karkaṭa-saṅkrānti.*

The sun thus has two paths—upward and downward—called *Uttarāyaṇa* and *Dakshināyana* which are, respectively, the paths of good and evil. For six months in a year, the sun moves downward which is called *Dakshināyana* or moving southward. For the following six months, the sun moves upward which is called *Uttarāyaṇa* or moving northward. It is said that those who die during the *Uttarāyaṇa* phase go upward to the heavenly planets where the demigods reside. Similarly, those who die during the *Dakshināyana* phase are said to go to nether planets where the demons reside. In the semantic space, up represents higher levels of consciousness which reside in more abstract life forms involving more cooperation and unity. Similarly, down represents lower levels of consciousness, which reside in more detailed life forms involving more competition and disunity. The times when the sun passes through *Uttarāyaṇa* are the daytime of the demigods, and the following 6 months are their nights. Conversely, the 6 months of *Dakshināyana* are the days of the demons and the following 6 months are their night. Thus, demigods and demons are awake and asleep during different times, which means that they become more powerful during their waking phases, and weaker during their sleeping times. Accordingly, a single year of the sun's rotation constitutes a single day of demigods, with 6 months each spent in waking and sleeping periods. The human duration of life is 100 years, and the demigod duration of life is 36,500 years.

Meanings of the Solar Motion

We have previously discussed two types of meanings associated with the flat plane, based on its structure. First, when the plane is truly flat, we can describe four directions—two of these represent knowledge and action, while the other two denote meanings arising from a relation to the context. Second, we discussed how the flat plane is sometimes elevated in the center and tapers toward the edges because the center represents the compositional whole and the edges the smallest compositional parts. While the whole represents the ideal, the origin, and the first member of the plane, the parts are non-ideal and ordered relative to the origin in the center. The trajectory of the sun differs from both these cases for two reasons. First, there is no center—elevated or otherwise—in the sun's trajectory so we are not speaking about how the compositional whole divides into parts. Second, the trajectory of the sun is not flat; it rises and falls due to the twisting of the plane in two directions.

Hence, in understanding the meaning of the solar motion, we must focus upon the significance of the double twisting, instead of the elevated central origin, or the division of the plane into knowledge and action. The vertical dimension in Vedic cosmology denotes a hierarchy of planes; the upper planes are the residences of the demigods and the lower planes those of demons. Therefore, as the sun rises and falls, it creates phases of relative domination of the demons and the demigods. As seen above, the *Uttarāyaṇa* path represents the relative domination (and daytime) of demigods, while the *Dakshināyana* path denotes the relative preponderance (and daytime) of demons. Within each path, there are different stages of greater or lesser domination. Thus, the sun's position can be described as a combination of positive and negative traits that combine to describe the qualities of the signs of the zodiac.

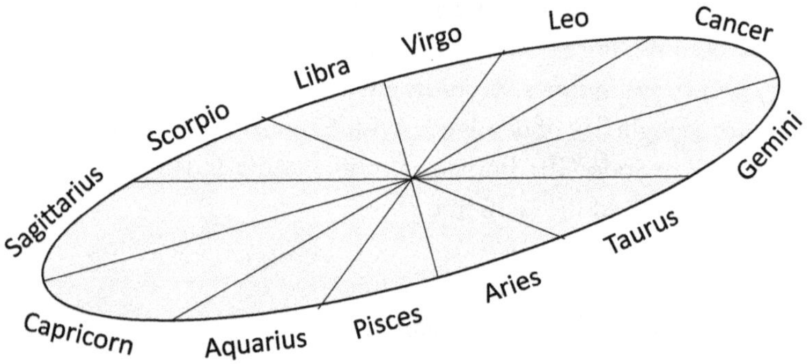

Figure-16 The Twelve Signs of the Zodiac

We might additionally note that the *apparent* motion of the sun is clockwise, but the *actual* motion of the sun is counterclockwise. In Vedic cosmology, the sun is dragged clockwise due to the movement of the zodiac—which is much faster—relative to the counterclockwise motion of the sun. Due to the combination of the two motions, the apparent motion is clockwise although the sun is moving in the counterclockwise direction[7]. If we combine this with that of the orbital tilt, and the positions of the zodiac signs known from the Earth's motion, then the upward motion of the sun begins at the lowest constellation called Capricorn, reaches the zenith at Gemini. Then, the downward motion begins at Cancer until it reaches the nadir at Sagittarius. If we order these positions along a vertical dimension, the picture would look like alternating positions on the upward and downward paths as in Figure-17.

To describe the sun's position on this vertical dimension, we need to know two things—(a) the path of motion (upward or downward), and (b) distance along the path (greater or lesser). There is a quality associated with the fact that the sign is higher or lower. Similarly, there is a quality associated with the fact that the path is upward or downward. Based on these four qualities—higher, lower, upward, and downward—we can divide the ecliptic plane of the sun's motion into 4 directions which are different from the 4 directions of the flat plane (which represent knowledge and action) and the 4 directions of the tapering plane (which represent the decomposition of the whole into parts). This flat plane is to be seen differently than the planes seen earlier.

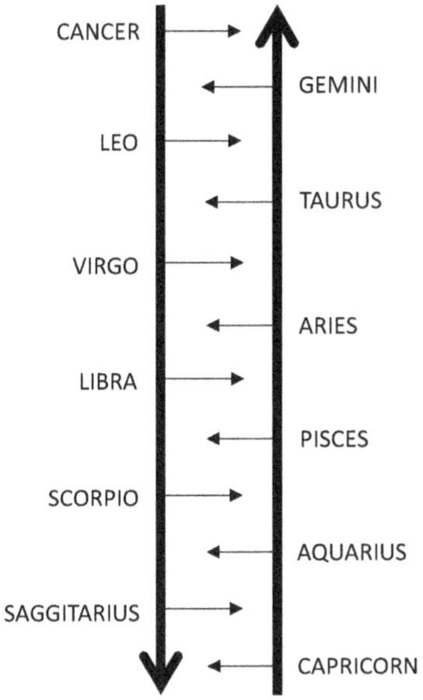

Figure-17 Alternating Positions of the Zodiac Signs

The sun is a representation[8] of *Viṣṇu*. However, due to its upward and downward movement, the sun is associated with both demons and demigods. This seems rather paradoxical because it suggests that the representation of God has evil properties; however, this paradox is not unique to God. We can see a similar type of paradox even in the case of fire—which is associated with the sun—where fire is associated with purification, just as it is associated with destruction. To understand this paradox, we need to recognize that God is not Himself demigods or demons; rather, he rewards the pious and punishes the impious. Piety involves sacrifice and self-restraint, and its reward is abundance and lavishness. Impiety involves self-indulgence and sensual stimulation, and its punishment is deprivation and constraint. We can see a contradiction in both cases; the difference is that in the case of piety the restriction is self-enforced and in case of impiety restriction is externally enforced.

The contradiction is not in God, but in the moral law. Those who use their choices morally get greater freedom. Those who use their choices immorally obtain greater restriction. Therefore, goodness is morality combined with freedom and evil is immorality combined with restriction. God is free from the moral law; therefore, His choices are not judged as moral or immoral. In that sense, God is neutral to both demons and demigods and simply awards them the consequences of their choices. The fact that *we* value freedom more than restriction means that *we* must have a preference toward morality. If instead we prefer immorality, then we must prefer restriction over freedom. This is a well-known fact about the conflict between choice and responsibility; if one is more responsible then he or she obtains greater freedom; conversely, if one is more irresponsible then he or she gradually loses their freedom.

In Abrahamic religions, Satan is the contrast to God. The devil lives in the dark, and although he is powerful, he is also vain, proud, and envious of the goodness above. In the Zoroastrian religion, the supreme deity, *Ormazd*, created two entities: the unruly and damaging spirit *Ahriman* and his benevolent and altruistic twin brother, *Spenta Mainyu*. In Judaism, Satan is viewed as limiting the authority and omnipotence of God, and while God is depicted as the more powerful personality, Satan is also powerful and deviates people away from

God. Judaic mystical teachings in the *Kabbalah* note two sides—one light, one dark—but the dark is never equal to the light one. Christianity similarly describes Satan as a 'fallen angel', which means he has the power of the angels, but he has an evil and dark side contrasted to the goodness. In many cases, the Devil is portrayed as having the same property as the sun—e.g., he lives in a hot place and 'burns' people, but that place is also dark and dingy. Common representations of the Devil thus invoke images of fire in a dark place, of a serpentine creature[9] with burning eyes, and a strong but dark body.

The divine and the demonic represent the moral and immoral use of freedom, resulting in greater or lesser freedom. Therefore, God has two sides—He rewards the moral use of freedom and punishes its immoral use. The realm of the demigods is occupied by those who have performed sacrifices and have the proclivity toward self-restraint. Due to their self-restraint, they are afforded a greater amount of freedom. The realm of the demons is occupied by those who have the proclivity toward unrestricted indulgence and therefore restraint is externally enforced upon them. This fact is nicely clarified in the six qualities of *Viṣṇu* which the sun represents—knowledge, beauty, fame, wealth, power, and renunciation. Of these six qualities, the last—i.e., renunciation—represents self-restraint. The upward path therefore represents growth in knowledge, beauty, fame, wealth, and power *because* of growing renunciation. Conversely, the downward path declines knowledge, beauty, wealth, power, and fame *because* of declining renunciation. As a result, the upward path is increase of all six qualities, and the downward path is decline in all six qualities.

The Meanings of the Zodiac Signs

By viewing the sun as embodying the six qualities of *Viṣṇu*, we can provide an understanding of the qualities of the zodiac signs. The understanding is simply that the six signs on the upward path represent the increase in six qualities, while the six signs on the downward path denote the decrease in these qualities. Personally, I also consider such an attempt a stepping stone to seeing God's qualities in human beings and using astrological signs as a way to understand how the fullness of all the six qualities in God is expressed partially in humans. When the qualities are fully manifest, then the person is also perfect. When one quality is manifest to the exclusion of the others, then the same quality sometimes appears to be a positive trait and at other times a negative trait. For example, when knowledge is presented in an ugly manner, then there is imperfection in the presentation. If knowledge is not used for the benefit of others, again there is imperfection in the use of knowledge even though the knowledge may be correct. Therefore, only the combination of six qualities is perfect, and when one quality is present without the other, the representation is imperfect. Thus, humans under the zodiac signs have positive and negative traits even though they are embodying God's qualities because only some of the qualities are dominantly present, while the others are missing.

The challenge is that using the relative dominant and subordinate relationship within the six qualities, we can create 6 * 5 * 4 * 3 * 2 * 1 = 720 different signs, although we only have 12 signs. This is then the source of the interpretive problem in giving meanings to zodiac signs—there are many more possibilities being accommodated within a fewer signs. But this, in general, has never been an issue in astrology because of the use of *hierarchy*. We assign a meaning to the sign as a whole, then divide the sign into different number of parts, which are tied to different meanings. Thus, you can obtain an approximate picture through the 12 signs. A more accurate picture can be obtained by further dividing the signs into 4, 6, 10, or 12 parts. These sub-divisional locations are used in astrology to answer specific types of questions accurately; only the general tendencies are sufficiently clear from the 12 signs.

These sub-divisional or hierarchical locations are called *varga* in astrology. Given the fact that there is a total of 720 possible divisions, each zodiac sign can be divided into 720 / 12 = 60 parts at most. This is the basis of the divisional chart system which divides each sign into up to 60 parts, creating ever more precise—although hierarchical positions; this means that even when we divide each sign by a factor of 60 (to determine past birth), we must keep the smaller divisors such as by a factor of 10 (to determine current profession and actions) in mind. Not every type of division has to be taken into account, and the factorization hierarchy helps us decide the meaning.

Varga	Divisor	Chart	Influence Determination
Rāśi	1	D-1	All General Features of Life
Hora	2	D-2	Wealth and Family
Drekana	3	D-3	Siblings and Personal Nature
Chaturthāmsa	4	D-4	Fortune and Property
Saptāmsa	7	D-7	Children
Navāmsa	9	D-9	Wife and Relationships
Dasāmsa	10	D-10	Actions in Society and Profession
Dvadasāmsa	12	D-12	Parents
Shodasāmsa	16	D-16	Vehicles, Travel and Comforts
Vimsāmsa	20	D-20	Spiritual Pursuits
Chaturvimsāmsa	24	D-24	Education and Learning
Saptavimsāmsa	27	D-27	Strengths and Weakness
Trimsāmsa	30	D-30	Evils, Failure, and Bad Luck
Khavedāmsa	40	D-40	Maternal Legacy
Akshavedāmsa	45	D-45	Paternal Legacy
Shastāmsa	60	D-60	Past birth or Karma

Table-2: The System of Varga Charts for Meaning

There is natural hierarchy in the six qualities themselves. The Absolute Truth is the *knowledge* to which every other quality is applied. This knowledge stands on its own merit and must therefore be objective, detached, and independent of everything else, which is represented by renunciation. From this independent, detached, and sovereign Absolute Truth manifests the famous hero, the leader, the icon, or the star, who controls the creation. God as the supreme controller is therefore the first and ideal manifestation of knowledge. This perfection represents *greatness, owing to which we say that God is great, after we say that He is the Absolute Truth.* Once greatness manifest, it is further qualified by other qualities. The first such quality is power—using the power the hero expresses his greatness and performs prodigious deeds. Great deeds bring prosperity, so wealth follows power. With prosperity a person is able to acquire name, fame, reputation, etc. and thereby enjoys the wealth.

If this natural hierarchy is preserved, then all the six qualities grow, which means that the highest point in the zodiac—the border between Cancer and Gemini—represents this perfection. If this natural hierarchy is changed, such as by putting power and reputation ahead of knowledge then all the six qualities decline. Thus, the person or the society that pursues power and wealth but undermines knowledge, detachment, and heroism will decline in all the six qualities; this pattern has been evidenced in the transformation of civilizations and societies over centuries; great societies emerge out of true ideas and valorous leaders. But over time, the true ideas and the valorous people are replaced by those hungry for power, wealth, and reputation, and the result is the destruction of all the six qualities. The society that prioritizes knowledge and detachment (the *Brahmana*) followed by valor and power (the *Kshatriya*) followed by wealth and beauty (the *Vaisya*), becomes successful. Conversely, the society that changes this order gradually reduces in all the qualities.

In this way, we can see how the rise and fall of the six qualities is related to the *order* in which they are prioritized. It is a mistake of modern civilization to think that wealth and beauty are the highest qualities, power and valor are only the means to attain the wealth and beauty, while knowledge is to be used to accumulate power, and detachment is completely obsolete. The result of this ideology will be the gradual destruction of all the six qualities of *Viṣṇu*.

The highest point in the zodiac—namely the border between Gemini and Cancer—represents the natural priority among the six qualities. The lowest point in the zodiac—the border between Capricorn and Sagittarius—represents the inversion of the six qualities. With *inversion* comes *reduction*; therefore, in one sense, all the 12 signs of the zodiac seem similar because they may have all the six qualities. In another sense, the difference is caused not by their possession of knowledge, wealth, beauty, power, heroism, etc. but what they prioritize—i.e., what is viewed as the most valuable—and what is used in the pursuit of the greatest value. For instance, a person who values knowledge will not mind renouncing power, wealth, fame, and beauty to obtain knowledge. Conversely, the person who prioritizes wealth and beauty would not mind selling his knowledge in order to attain material wealth or power. The differentiation is therefore not so much in the possession of the six qualities but in the prioritization of these qualities—which lead to rise or decline. Furthermore, even if a person is born with a certain type of priority, he or she can change that order in this life, thereby changing their destiny. The possession of the six qualities is predetermined by *karma* but the *ordering* is our free will.

The precise composition of qualities of *Viṣṇu* in the 12 zodiac signs is not found in the Vedic texts, nor can we find the relative values of the six qualities in the different signs. But using the above discussed ideas—(1) the signs are created by 6 qualities, (2) the qualities can be ordered differently, (3) there is a natural hierarchy which increases all six qualities and its inversion declines all six of them, and (4) there is hierarchy within the signs, which represents the rise and fall of the six qualities—we can explain not just the 12 signs but the successive subdivisions of each sign by larger divisions until 60.

I will not attempt this description here because although we can speak about the general trend of rise and decline as the order is upright or inverted, the exact magnitude by which it rises and falls needs a semantic science which has to be understood prior. To an extent, the gap between the highest and the lowest points of the zodiac is presented in Vedic texts, and this gap is also noted as the tilt of the earth's axis of rotation by 23.5^0 in astronomy. If space were treated semantically, then this distance between the highest and the lowest points would represent the absolute values of the highest and lowest points, which will then indicate the rise and fall of qualities due to the change in order. However, there are nuances to this computation because the six qualities are components of *chit* which has to be treated compositionally—i.e., the whole is *divided* into six parts which combine to create the whole—due to which the distance between the highest and the lowest points must be divided into 6 parts, such that each quality contributes a certain fraction to the whole.

This subdivision of the whole into parts can be viewed as a pie chart and a bar chart; the bar chart determines the sum total of the six qualities, and the pie chart represents the fraction of each part within the whole. The bar chart gets shorter as we move from the highest to the lowest points in the zodiac and therefore, we can speak about the net decline in the six qualities; we can also measure this decline based on astronomical observations. However, by knowing the sum of the six values we cannot know the relative proportions of the six qualities within the sum. The relative contribution of each quality to the total requires a *theory* in addition to the *observation* of the heights. The theory would predict and explain how changes in the order of the six qualities alters their individual and total magnitudes and thus the relative proportions.

Once these relative and absolute values are understood, then we can also speak about the *effects* resulting from the variation of the six qualities. For example, if detachment dominates knowledge, then knowledge would manifest as philosophy and science. But if wealth and fame dominate knowledge then knowledge would appear as economics, sociology, and political science. Similarly, if knowledge dominates beauty then forms will be precise and detailed; but if beauty dominates knowledge then beautiful forms will be emphasized over meaningful content. Thus, the change in the order of qualities not only alters their absolute values and their relative proportions, but also the observed effects. Such effects of the order, relative, and absolute magnitudes of qualities constitute the empirical predictions of the theory—the kind that astrology attempts. The essence of this prediction is that if one quality dominates over others, it also changes the nature of the subordinate qualities.

We cannot describe the six qualities as 'independent particles' because such particles can be counted in any order and change in the order of counting independent particles brings no difference in their effects, nor does it change the particles themselves. In the case of the six qualities, a change in order alters the absolute and relative magnitudes, and their effects. Therefore, we require a radically different kind of predictive model in which the total meaning is comprised of parts, although by reordering the parts we change the absolute and relative values of the parts, and hence their effects. One could visualize this type of prediction in terms of a bag of marbles. If the marbles are treated as independent particles, their motion doesn't change the marbles. However, if these marbles are treated as symbols of meaning, then as the marbles are moved inside the bag, they change their sizes due to which the relative contributions of the marbles to the size of the bag also changes. Then, the effects of such an altered bag on the other bags (the effects) are also altered.

At present, we have the astronomical observations, which correspond to the change in the bag sizes, but we lack the understanding of the six qualities, how they can be ordered in 720 ways, how each of these 720 orders changes the absolute magnitude of each quality and their relative proportions, and as a consequence the effects caused by these changes. In effect, astrology has been dissociated from the understanding of *Viṣṇu*, and the scientific understanding of God has been replaced with a collection of heuristic tools. The tools are not false, but which tool must be used in which situation is not well-known. One such tool is the meaning of zodiac signs—e.g., if the sun is situated at birth in a particular sun sign, then the person would exhibit certain qualities. Why a sign brings certain qualities remains unknown and unexplained today. Since the foundation is weak and there is no way to know the true causality underlying these claims, astrology is open to numerous interpretations. Such interpretive difficulties then result in predictive challenges because the calculations underlying the prediction are linearly additive and do not take into account the alterations to each part resulting from the reordering of the parts.

In this regard we can also note that a similar change in the order of qualities can be employed to understand the different forms of God, which is originally the fullness of all the six qualities and is called the *Absolute Truth* which means that knowledge is the primordial quality, while heroism, power, wealth, and beauty are subordinate. God's expansion into many forms can be understood as the change in order of these qualities—attributed to His *free will.* As the order is changed, the relative proportions of the qualities are also reduced, as a result of which the successive manifestations are called parts, part of the part, etc. Furthermore, as the order of the six qualities is changed, the meaning associated with the quality undergoes a transformation, due to which the Personality of God manifests different behaviors, forms, and pastimes.

God is therefore amenable to the same kind of scientific study simply by understanding (a) the six qualities, (b) the order of these qualities determined by free will, (c) the change in the absolute magnitude of the qualities caused by the change in the order, and (d) the change in the effect of the qualities as a result of the change in the order and magnitude of the six qualities. The understanding of astrology is therefore a stepping stone to the understanding of God, *if* we treat this knowledge not merely as astronomical observations of height, distance, and angle, but semantically as the change in six qualities.

The Six Associates of the Sun

Having looked at effects wrought by the changes in the order of the six qualities, we can now speak about the manifestation of the six qualities through the three modes of nature employing two different methods.

As seen earlier, the three modes of nature are *manas* (concepts), *prāna* (activity), and *vāk* (things). Each of the six qualities manifests into a theoretical understanding of the quality represented by *manas*. In the case of wealth for example, there are numerous economic theories that describe the nature of wealth—e.g., that the monetary value of something is in the perception of the buyers and sellers vs. that the monetary value must have absolute upper and lower bounds based on the minimum cost required to produce and the highest price that can be commanded to prevent economic exploitation[10]. Based on such theories, economic activity or *prāna* is carried out; this includes activities like manufacturing products, agriculture, extraction of natural resources, and even trading of virtual entities such as currency, stocks, and bonds. Finally, as a result of such economic activity one obtains numerous products and services; these include commodities such as food, clothing, housing, cars, etc. but can also include virtual entities likes currency, stocks, and bonds.

As the sun's motion causes a rise and fall in the six qualities, the changes will manifest in corresponding changes in ideas, activities, and products as well. For instance, decline in knowledge will produce theories that fragment our knowledge into disparate and disjointed theories which seem to work in limited domains but are useless, or counterproductive outside those domains. The upward path unifies our understanding and the downward path fragments it[11]. When fragmented knowledge rises, then activities look at cause-effect relationships in a very narrow sense. For instance, industrial activity can be used to produce chemicals without regard to the environment; medical research can focus on making human life better while making the life of the animals which are experimented upon much worse. Finally, you can also see fragmented products. They may be tasty but injure health; they may entertain for the moment but damage the person psychologically in the long run.

Therefore, the rise and fall of the six qualities changes the nature of the theories, activities, and products. The six associates of the sun represent the two types of theories, activities, and products. On the upward path, the sages represent the unification of knowledge, the *apsara* represent the cooperation in the work, and the *gandharva* represent the consistency of things. On the downward path, the *nāga* represent the fragmentation of knowledge, the *yakshā* the competition in activities, and the *rākshasa* represent the contradictions in the world. There are hence three expressions of coherence, harmony, and unification. Similarly, there are three symbols of fragmentation, disorder, and chaos. The former creates enlightenment, cooperation, and peace; the latter produces confusion, competition, and conflicts. The six associates therefore are manifestations of the deeper cause in the change of six qualities.

It is commonly said that good and evil are present in each person, and the difference lies in their relative proportions. This change in proportions creates the patterns of subordination and domination. Therefore, in the upward path, there is progress toward greater unity, harmonization, and cooperation, but only God is completely unified. Even though one progresses toward the perfect, unless one reaches proximity to God (or the sun in this case) there is still some level of fragmentation, disunity, and disorder. As a result, even though demigods signify the upward trajectory, there is still competition between the demigods. Similarly, just because the downward path represents disorder, chaos, and conflict, there is still a level of unity that produces a society. These things become evident when we look at the universe as a tree; the upper part of the tree has greater unity and fewer branches; but the fewer branches are not the root. Similarly, the lower part of the tree has many leaves, which sway individually, although they are still bound to the tree as a whole.

Associate	**Mode**	**Parity**
Gandharvā	Tamas	Positive
Rākshasa	Tamas	Negative
Apsarā	Rajas	Positive
Yakshā	Rajas	Negative
Sage	Sattva	Positive
Nāga	Sattva	Negative

Table-3: The Six Guardians of the Sun-God

The six associates of the sun are principles embodied as personalities. The sages denote the principle of unifying ideas, the *apsara* the principle of harmonized activities, and the *gandharva* the principle of consistent things. Conversely, the *nāga* denote the principle of fragmenting ideas, the *yakshā* of competitive activities, and the *rākshasa* of conflicting things. If we keep these principles in mind, then we can easily grasp their role in the universe. In a very simple sense, the former denotes the principle of order and the latter, of chaos. The sun is the cause of both order and chaos. Clearly, order is more desirable than chaos. And yet God creates both order and chaos to fulfill different kinds of desires in the living beings, who aim to enjoy in different ways.

This is a common problem in theology and religion—the problem of God-created evil. God-created evil exists in this world both to fulfill the desires of the living entities who enjoy a life of evil, as well as to punish such evil adopted in the past. God enables the option to choose the evil, and then delivers the punishment for such choices. The choice and the responsibility of both good and evil rest with the individual; God only creates the possibility of both in order to fulfill the soul's desires. Nature is designed to reward and punish. The punishment is not itself the evil; it is a *response* to the evil, in order to correct it. The cooperative person will not cooperate with the competitive; he will create hurdles in their path. The kind person will not enlighten those who love war and destruction; he will rather rely on confusing and bewildering them. The organized person will not help overcome the chaos for those who aim to create more chaos; he will rely on chaos to hinder their progress.

The path of greater unity, cooperation, and harmony is self-reinforcing. As a result, as some organization and unity are achieved, it becomes easier to organize and unify even more. Conversely, the path of disunity, competition, and disorganization is self-limiting. Hence, as you fragment, your power and ability to fragment declines. Therefore, retribution is a natural principle in which a destructive person only needs to be co-located with other destructive persons and they will be appropriate company for each other. Similarly, reward is also a natural principle in which a cooperative person is co-located with other cooperative people, and they will help each other progress.

God's reward and punishment is thus not delivered directly. His hand only nudges the person in the appropriate company, which then takes care of the rest. This nudging is based on the person's *guna* and *karma*—or desiring and deserving. If you desire destruction and you have performed the good deeds to enjoy according to your desires, then you will be nudged into a company where the others are helpless against the force of your destructive ability. When the good deeds are over, you will be nudged into a situation where you have no power over others, but they have the power over your will. God's reward and punishment are disbursed by arranging the suitable interactions. When a person is confused, baffled, and troubled by evil but like-minded association, he realizes the nature of the evil and changes. Bafflement is also a route to enlightenment, competition is also a route to cooperation, and chaos is also a route to order. The route is longer—but it leads to the destination. Thus, Vedic texts describe that the universe is 'round'. You can go downward but there will be growing motivation to move back upward. Similarly, you can move upward but there will be growing temptation to move downward.

The Role of the Six Associates

The sages recite verses from the *Sāma, Ṛg and Yajur Vedas*, so they represent the differences in the style of knowledge presentation. The verses in the *Ṛg Veda* encode terse conclusions; the verses in the *Sāma Veda* are songs that extoll the same knowledge as poetry; the verses in *Yajur Veda* are procedures that explain how to attain the same truth. Thus, in one form, the knowledge is expressed as terse but precise conclusions, in another form it is expressed lucidly as poetry, and in yet another form the same knowledge is presented as processes and procedures to acquire to above-said understanding. These are disparities of style and presentation, not those in knowledge itself.

The *apsara* are dancers par excellence, and their dancing is the epitome of coordination and cooperation: there is coordination within the different parts of the body, and then cooperation with the other dancers. The *gandharva* are skilled musicians, they create the sounds consistent with the time, place, and situation of expression; these sounds are emblems of harmony.

The *gandharva, apsara,* and the *sages* represent the music, dance, and style within a performance. This performance expresses the 6 divine qualities of the sun. Therefore, we can say that the style, dance, and music are used to express knowledge, beauty, power, fame, wealth, and renunciation. The six qualities of the sun are not meant for himself; rather he distributes these qualities throughout the universe. The light of the sun is thus not a physical property; rather, light is the expansion of the six kinds of meanings. In other words, when plants, animals, and humans absorb the sun's light, they are gaining knowledge (because they see due to the presence of light). But by being under the sun's light, they also gain beauty, power, fame, wealth, and detachment. Being out in the sun, or worshiping the sun, is thus useful if you want to be healthy, resplendent, beautiful, well-informed, and wealthy. People know that being out in the sun makes their life richer, progressive, and healthier. But they don't understand that it is because the sun imparts these qualities.

The songs sung by the sages are especially taken from the *Vedic* texts, which means they are describing *Viṣṇu* as the Supreme Being. The songs of the sages represent the literary style to glorify *Viṣṇu*, the dance is the *activity* performed to glorify Him, and the music is the composition that converts the knowledge into a symbolic expression. The combination of style, dance, and music expands the sun's body or persona. Just as a knowledgeable person emanates knowledge, a rich person spends his wealth, a powerful person demonstrates his power, a beautiful person creates expressions of the beauty, and a renounced person teaches and inspires others to become more detached, similarly, the sun exudes his qualities for everyone to assimilate. This expression of the sun's qualities constitutes the empirical evidence of their existence in the sun. If something exists in me, but I don't express it externally, then what evidence can exist for its existence? The sun as the representative of *Viṣṇu* exudes His qualities by creating their empirical evidence around him.

The *nāga*, *yaksha*, and *rākshasa*, on the other hand embody the negative sides of the same six qualities. Their purpose is to increase the bafflement in knowledge, create greater hurdles in the completion of activities, and keep destroying the value of the things that one may have already acquired.

The *nāga* are teachers who enlighten the student by baffling them. In Zen Buddhism, for example, knowledge is presented through paradoxical riddles called *koans* rather than through direct revelation. The humble mind can be educated through direct revelation, but the vain mind needs to be perplexed. For example, you can go to a classroom to learn from a teacher, and if you are humble then you will be knowledgeable having understood the ideas being imparted in the class. Conversely, if you are arrogant, you will keep challenging the teacher, doubting the process of knowledge acquisition, and try to refute the teacher. The teacher will therefore not impart you knowledge directly. He will rather ask you to think about problems and propose the solution. If and when you propose that solution, the teacher will critique the answers, turning the tables on the student. The teacher thus makes the student aware of the extent of his ignorance and uses the hurt pride to move him forward.

The modern Western method of knowledge is an example of such teaching methods because the students are individualistic, arrogant, and distrusting by innate nature. The teacher asks the student to think on their own, in what is called 'creativity', and the created ideas are then tested in exams by subjecting them to problems, questions, etc. In the traditional Vedic system of education, the teacher never asks the student any questions and doesn't subject them to problems. After all, if the student is ignorant, what can be expected from such questioning? There is no concept of testing the student, and the students are not subjected to exams. Life is the exam in which the student will be tested. To prepare for that life, the student asks the teacher questions in a humble manner and accepts the answers, asking further questions to clear his doubts rather than to challenge, doubt, or ridicule the teacher itself.

You can seek knowledge because you are inquisitive, or because you are confused and perplexed. Both are useful techniques for teaching; if the person is humble, then they can be taught what they don't know. But if they are vain or arrogant, first they have to be humbled. The teacher can either give the student answers, or problems which baffle and shame him of his inability. The positive process of education involves the student asking questions with humility, which the teacher answers appropriately. The negative process of education is that the teacher humbles them by enlightening their students about the extent of their ignorance. The *nāga* are the negative teachers. Their method involves humiliating and shaming their students with questions and problems that the students are unable to solve or showing the contradictions in their thinking. When students are humbled, they can learn new ideas.

The *nāga* have been worshipped as snakes and dragons in Southeast Asian countries such as Malaysia, Cambodia, Indonesia, and China, due to which the dragon or the snake has become a prominent symbol for Asia. Unlike the *sages* who have been revered in Vedic culture, the *nāga* have been revered in Buddhism; indeed, *Sariputta* and *Moggallāna*—two chief disciples of Buddha—are referred to as *Mahānāga* or "Great *Nāga*", and many important historical Buddhist figures—e.g., *Dignāga, Nāgāsēna, Nāgārjuna*—are *nāga*. The Vedic process of knowledge involves humility, surrender, and acceptance of the information imparted by the *guru*. But in this age, people suffer from doubt and confusion; they consider themselves the best judges of the truth, and instead of surrendering to an enlightened master, they speculate on the truth. When one speculates on the truth, the teacher presents them with counterexamples to disprove their speculation. The teacher will not impart the truth directly because he knows that the suspicious mind cannot accept it. The teacher will rather challenge the student with problems, because the impertinent minds have to be baffled through contradictions, paradoxes, and by pointing out mistakes in the insubordinate person's thinking before they can even be educated about truth. This baffling is teaching, meant for the arrogant.

The Buddhist system relies on the use of *buddhi*—intelligence. The intellect is symbolized by the sun (as opposed to the mind which is symbolized by the moon). But the Buddhist system is a self-driven investigation in which the person finds the truth by his effort rather than being told about the truth. There is little by way of describing what the truth is; there is so much more description of how to get to that truth. In the process you will be baffled and confused, and when the confusion grows unlimitedly, one discards the process of thinking and empties the mind. When the mind is emptied, it becomes quiet, but that isn't *knowledge*; it is only freedom from confusion. In essence, one has moved from the negative side of confusion to the midpoint between knowledge and confusion. Progressive realization means the seeker must now surrender to the enlightened teacher in order to learn more. Thus, the *nāga* have a role to play—they bewilder and confuse to force surrender. Once the person surrenders, he has to move to the positive side of the sages.

The *yakshā* are the rich, playful, sexually aggressive, capricious protectors of natural wealth. Like the *nāga* confuse the speculator toward surrender, similarly, the *yakshā* create greater hurdles in one's work by holding the access to natural resources. They will provide the natural resources, but they are not going to give them away in charity. Instead, you have to struggle and endure hardships to obtain anything. This is the path of diminishing returns because the access to natural resources needed to succeed becomes harder and harder. In that sense, they are 'protectors' of the wealth; they keep it safe under their control and ration it to people if they have endeavored for it. They are going to give it to others eventually, but they want the person to struggle and strive for it. They are described as the caretakers of natural wealth such as forests, mountains, lakes, and rivers. They are attractive, and in the work of Indian poet *Kalidāsa* the *yakshā* is described as a romantic and amorous figure. But this love is unlike the love of the *apsara* who voluntarily entertain the demigods. The love of the *yakshā* is like teasing—or playing hard to get. For example, the *yakshī*—the female of the *yakshā*—makes the *yakshā* lovelorn.

The *yakshā* represent the *activity* of this material world. But it is also a negative type of activity where you work to break down barriers to your opportunities. That work is not a work of art—like that in case of the *apsara*—who dance to create forms out of their own body. The *yakshā* represent the struggle for existence and survival. They are taskmasters who will give the results only if you have toiled, but if you toil, you will get results. In the Vedic descriptions, *Kubera*—the god of wealth—is a *yakshā*. That means he controls the wealth to be obtained through hard work. In Buddhist descriptions, the *yakshā* are fearsome warriors, shown protecting the access to Buddhist temples, which means you have to obtain the *yakshā*'s permission to enter the temple. That permission represents building the qualification before you enter a sanctum, and the job of the *yakshā* is to raise the bar for anyone's entry. Like the *nāga* baffle the attempts at knowledge, and only one who is truly serious surmounts the ocean of unceasing confusion, similarly, the *yakshā* protect the access to the place of worship where sacred activities are performed.

The *rākshasa* are thugs and thieves who steal your property. *Rāvana* is described as a famous king of *rākshasa*, who stole everyone's wealth—including their wives. The *rākshasa* destroy property and desecrate it by urinating and defecating on it. They also rape women. Vedic texts describe that when *Shiva* is upset with *Daksha* because he insulted His wife *Sati*, He sends *rākshasa* who urinate and defecate on his *yajña*, break the pots, and chase the *Brahmana* out of the place. They hence embody a destructive force which terminates whatever you have built through your knowledge and hard work. Like the *nāga* baffle our knowledge, and *yakshā* hinder our work, the *rākshasa* destroy the things we obtain even after we get the knowledge and surmount the hindrances on the path of performing our activities toward our goal. Our greatest prized possession is our body, and the *rākshasa* are sometimes described as man-eaters; they want to steal and consume your property, and since the body is indeed everyone's valuable possession, they want to consume it too.

The *rākshasa* are the harbingers of death, destruction, disorder, and chaos. They act on the *vāk* or the individual *names* and things manifest from our activities operating on the concepts. If the positive side of *vāk* represents well-designed and beautifully crafted words and things, then the negative side represents ugliness and disorder. The *rākshasa* thus have ugly bodies, they lead unclean lives, and they have highly disorganized societies. Their ruler is one who encourages and empowers them to bring more death, destruction, and chaos. Even in modern society some people advocate war to plunder the wealth of other countries, bring destruction through weapons, or enjoy the suffering of others. Some nations consider the possession of advanced weapons of destruction a matter of their fame and power. Others mutilate their bodies with piercings, or listen to heavy metal and grunge music, and consider that a sign of beauty. Leading lives of crime, prostitution, and killing, they consider themselves successful. Such sadistic people are akin to *rākshasa*.

God is absolute and His representation through the sun is also absolute. However, this absolute person is manifest in two opposing ways. For the arrogant, proud, and vain people, the six qualities are imparted by distracting, confusing, creating hurdles, and destruction, harnessing their ego and vanity for their progress. For the humble and sincere, the same qualities are attained by modest, unassuming, and meek inquiry, service to the teacher, and offering the results of their work back to God as gifts. The same God is perceived in two different ways by the humble and the arrogant. The duality therefore lies in the soul because he sees God in two ways, but God is not good nor evil.

Verse, Music, Dance, and Literature

We noted previously that the sun represents the cognition of six types of qualities. But beyond these qualities are various methods of expressing them. All these methods can be understood in the context of meanings encoded in language. Language expression, for instance, employs prosody or verse formation. Sentence length plays an important role in expressing the meaning. For example, shorter sentences are necessary to get to the punchline quickly, and longer sentences are employed to create the tension about where the sentence is truly headed before you deliver the punchline. Both are useful techniques to delivering the meaning, but they have to be applied in different ways, based on the type of meaning you aim to deliver. Punctuation within a sentence, and pauses between the sentences, are similarly employed for greater effect. Speech also includes the use of correct intonation and pitch. Facial expressions, hand gestures, and bodily posture accompany speech. And the content can be delivered in various literary forms—fiction or non-fiction, theoretical or historical, transcendental or mundane, treatises or drama.

Beyond the content of what you are speaking, there is an equal—if not greater—role for linguistic *style* such as the intonation of the words, variations in pitch, the speaker's body language, facial and hand gestures, pauses within and in between sentences, sentence length, speed of speaking and the pace of the narration, the use of simple and short words vs. complex and flowery expressions, the use of sarcasm, irony, rhetorical questioning, active or passive voice, the use of examples, vivid and colorful imagery, the expression of content through various literary forms such as fiction vs. non-fiction, and many others. It would be a grave mistake to talk about meaning and not consider the role of style in expressing it. Fortunately, we don't have to do that here because the associates of the sun naturally represent the elements of style.

The singing of the *gandharvā* represents the use of pitch and intonation. The dancing of the *apsarā* represents the use of body language, facial and hand gestures. The horses tied to the sun's chariot represent sentence length, the number of syllables in metric prosody, and breaking the expression into different parts through the usage of punctuation and pauses. Rhythm and speed are spoken of as the wheel of the sun's chariots as it changes the durations of days and nights. Terse language is dominantly represented in the *Rig Veda,* flowing flowery language dominantly in the *Sāma Veda*, and simple plain language dominantly in the *Yajur Veda*, so the sages speaking these verses embody the positive literary styles. The *nāga* embody the use of the negative literary styles—irony, sarcasm, hypothesis, paradoxes, rhetoric, pedantic nitpicking, ambiguity, sophistry, criticism, ridicule, poking fun at things, etc.

As the *apsarā* express the style through dance—which embodies harmony, symmetry, balance, and poise, the *yakshā* are their very opposites;

they fight, compete, battle, and attack personally. Similarly, as the *gandharvā* employ beautiful tunes, the *rākshasa* use harsh tones; their composition is rough and crude and presents itself as clatter and blast instead of melody.

The world around us doesn't just come to us as facts. It also appears as problems, challenges, hurdles, delays, confusion, possibility, as well as restrictions. Similarly, sometimes the picture of the self we see in the world is endearing, while at other times it appears to mock, deride, and devalue us. We find the meaning in these and many other ways. The *content* of the meaning—i.e., the conclusion we arrive at—may be presented straightforwardly or paradoxically. Hence, there is an equal role for style in reaching the conclusion. For some people, simple and straightforward descriptions suffice. For others, the conclusion must be presented poetically, musically, or with amplifying gestures and bodily language to appear convincing. There are yet others who would be unmoved by straightforward description or even poetic and flowery language. They instead require hard-hitting criticism, rude awakening, and paradoxes to rule out the alternative before they are convinced. For novel ideas, none of the above methods work by themselves; we have to employ repetition, examples, and illustrations as an essential element of style.

The conclusion or meaning doesn't change, but the vehicle or method of its presentation may vary. Verse, music, gestures and body language, simple vs. complex, are the normal or upward looking elements of style. Conversely, paradoxes, problems, criticisms, counterfactuals, and personal attacks are the downward elements of style. As we have noted, God is absolute—neither good nor bad. This means that the meaning being presented in both cases is the same. However, the style of presenting the meaning can be varied, depending on what the person wants to hear, is prepared to hear, or deserves to hear. The study of style—and how it influences the presentation of meaning—is a very complex topic, and I don't think I can do it any justice here. Nevertheless, having breached the topic of style, I will spend a few paragraphs describing a few of the elements of style—namely, verse, music, gestures, and literary styles. Through this we can see how style is itself a science comprising numerous elements which are combined to produce a meaningful expression. If the combination of meaning and its effects seemed daunting, the combination of the elements of style is not any easier. Nevertheless, to the extent that meaning is natural, style is also natural; we just don't know enough about the natural embodiments of style because we don't approach nature semantically.

The Vedic music system of *rāga* is a collection of 72 *sampūrna* or complete *rāga*, with a scale comprising 12 semitones and each *rāga* having 7 notes. The 12 semitones are S, R1, R2=G1, R3=G2, G3, M1, M2, P, D1, D2=N1, D3=N2, N3. Since two notes—S and P—are fixed, we can divide the possible *rāga* into two parts based on the note variations before and after P. There are six possible variations between D and N (D1-N1, D1-N2, D1-N3, D2-N2, D2-N3, D3-N3). Similarly, there are two possible variations between R and G (R1-G1, R1-G2, R1-G3, R2-G2, R2-G3, and R3-G3). Finally, there are two variations of M (M1 and M2). As a result, the total possible combinations of the *rāga* turn out to be 6 (R and G variants) * 6 (D and N variants) * 2 (M variants) = 72.

Figure-18 The Katapayādi System of Counting Rāga[12]

These 72 *rāga* are the *janak* or the parents. Then there are other *janya* or child *rāga*, for which no particular count is described. All the child *rāga* are parts of the parent *rāga* which means they use the scales of one of the 72 *rāga* but employ less than 7 notes. As we have seen earlier, the parent-child relationship in the case of *chit* is that the child is a part of the whole. Therefore, if the complete *rāga* are known, their parts are included within them.

The above method of describing the 72 *rāga* is sometimes referred to as the *Katapayādi* system[13]. The two M in this system refer to the two halves of the circle. Each half is then further divided into 6 parts based on R and G variations, producing a total of 12 divisions, which are then compared to the 12 signs of the zodiac. Finally, each of the 12 divisions is further divided into 6 parts based on the D and N variants, producing a total of 72 divisions. Therefore, when it is said that the *gandharvā* compose the music for the sun, we can understand that a system of 72 *rāga* is being referred to in the process. Although only 12 *gandharvā* are referred to (associated with each sign of the zodiac), from the *Katapayādi* system of describing *rāga* we can see these 12 are further divided into 6 parts each— we can guess—based on the six qualities of the sun which we have extensively noted in previous sections.

The use of facial expressions and hand gestures is well-known, but I think most people may be unaware that there is a classification of gestures which sets the mood in which something is said. For instance, pointing the index finger at someone implies accusation, holding the fingers in a tight fist indicates the forceful controlling of rage, raising both hands simultaneously is a well-known synonym for surrender and helplessness, holding the hand up at the chest level is meant to convey reassurance and calmness. These types of gestures are different from those employed to directly convey meaning. For instance, a thumbs-up and the A-OK gesture indicate that everything is great. Some of these gestures—such as the V sign for victory—are specific to a culture. Raising the middle finger upward has a derogatory significance[14], but raising the index finger upward can mean a warning in social settings.

Gestures therefore are a language in themselves, and it should not be surprising that the deaf and mute people employ a language of gestures to convey meaning. In such cases, gestures are simply symbols of content, not an element of style. Nevertheless, since the gesture could be used to convey some content, or a similar idea as the mood, only the context indicates the meaning and the purpose of the gesture; in general, they can be used in either way.

Indian classical dance identifies many such gestures; similarly, gestures are prominently used in *yoga*. Since there are many Indian classical dance forms[15], which have some overlap but also many differences, and there isn't an easy mathematical or numerical way to establish a precise number of forms, it is hard to say the exact number of gestures. In the *Bharatanatyam* school of dance, 55 root gestures are used like the alphabet of expression[16]. Similarly, some authors have identified 72 unique gestures employed in *yoga*[17].

Finally, there are many kinds of literary styles. The *Nātya-śāstra* notes 10 types of drama. There are also texts that present philosophical and scientific information. There are stories, histories, and genealogies. There are manuals on how to perform rituals and practices. There are songs and poems. There are condensed *mantra* or formulas to be recited regularly. There are prescriptive styles employed in books on moral conduct, social organization, economic practices, and how to govern different kinds of people. Commentaries are often employed to explain and elaborate the above. And then, as we have seen above, the direct information can also be presented indirectly by forcing and challenging the student with hypothesis-conclusion-paradox, semantic analysis, the use of irony, sarcasm, rhetoric, and criticism. If a detailed genealogy of the literary styles was ever presented in the Vedic system, we cannot find it today. But in similar ways that music, rhythm, verse, and gestures have been systematized, I expect that literary styles have a system too. We might not know about this system but discovering this classification and hierarchical genealogy should be the primary goal for any theory of literature.

The Cognition of Emotion

All these elements of style are the *cognitive* counterparts of *emotion*. There is an emotional undercurrent in the use of different musical forms, dance, verse formation, and literary styles, because the same information could be expressed through alternative forms. In the dramatic art forms, music, poetry, dance, and rhythm are combined with linguistic style, which makes drama a complete art form relative to the other incomplete forms.

Emotion is the byproduct of *ānanda,* and it is separate from the *chit*, which manifests into the body and the various cognitive instruments. A consequence of the separation between *chit* and *ānanda* is that one can be happy in adverse situations or unhappy in favorable situations. Emotion or feeling is an internal experience; others may not *experience* your feelings although they can *know* what you feel. This knowing is the *chit* expression of *ānanda*. Due to this expression, emotions affect the body; they show up in the tone of the voice, the gestures on the face and hands, and in psychosomatic illnesses. Even though others may not feel what we feel, it is important to *communicate* this feeling to others cognitively. Thus, we have words such as 'fear', 'joy', 'happiness', 'anger', and 'envy' as the cognitive counterparts of the feelings. By hearing those words, one may understand what the other person is feeling but may not necessarily feel those same emotions. Cognitive expression of emotions generally only produces a cognitive understanding, not necessarily an emotion.

If these forms did not exist, then there would be no way for one person to convey their feelings to another. Even as we express those feelings through words, sounds, gestures, etc. the expressions are not the feelings, but if we are empathetic to those things, we can ourselves reconvert the cognition into emotion and feel the emotions that are only being cognitively expressed.

Thus, some people cry on watching a movie, while others understand what is going on but don't feel the emotions. Some people are exhilarated or feel sad on listening to some music, while others simply analyze the musical tones being used in the composition. Some people relish the movement of poetry and verse, while others seem to find no interest in such things, even though they can understand the meanings in the poetry. Owing to these differences, there is a clear distinction between *understanding* and *feeling*. The conversion of cognition into feeling is called *empathy*. The psychopath sees the suffering of other people and understands it. But he doesn't suffer as a result of that understanding. There are others who are unable to express their feelings through words, gestures, tone changes, and others; this doesn't mean they don't feel the same emotions as others. It just means that they are unable to convert emotion into cognition. Thus, we can identify a faculty in each one of us that converts emotion into cognition and cognition into emotion.

This faculty is the capacity called *sat* due to which we can feel the pain of near and dear ones but don't feel the same kind of expression in others who are distant. The *sat* is also called awareness, but the question is: What are we becoming aware of when we know the world? Does our consciousness actually contact the world by going beyond the body? Or is the consciousness perceiving something *in* the body—e.g., the perception of sounds and colors in the brain? The short answer is that the world is *represented* in the body. This representation is called *ādibhautika* or the "other" as opposed to the *ādiatmika* or the "self". We have discussed these two parts of the *chit* previously. The world is within our body; it exists as one of the *leaves* of the bodily branch. The leaves are different from the actual branches they represent, which means that my representation of the world can be illusory or false. And yet, I'm the cause of that illusion, because the illusion is attached as a leaf to my branch.

The representation of the world in the body—i.e., the creation of additional leaves of the trunk—is caused by *karma.* Thereafter *awareness* of this representation is created by *sat,* which exists in the body as *prāna.* Through this awareness, the emotion or pleasure of experience is created. Therefore, the pleasure is *manas,* the objective representation of the self and the world are the *vāk,* and the connection between the two is *prāna.* If we change this *prāna,* then three things will happen. First, the focus of consciousness will change; instead of focusing on the things that make you unhappy, you will focus on the things that make you happy automatically. Second, the conversion of the bodily representation into emotion will be altered; for instance, even if you have to focus on something unpleasant, you will remain happy. Third, emotions will be converted into the bodily representation differently; some emotions may be expressed while others are not; consciousness becomes the mechanism by which one is able to choose what to hide or reveal.

Thus, *yoga* texts focus on the purification of consciousness by altering the *prāna.* This process is called *aśtānga-yoga.* Then *jnana-yoga* focuses on changing the mental representation of the world itself—you understand the world differently. *Karma-yoga* is the other leg of *chit*—comprised of knowledge and action; as you change your knowledge, your actions are modified naturally. Finally, *bhakti-yoga* focuses directly on changing the emotions—i.e., becoming happy—by which consciousness and the bodily representation are modified. These processes are part of the same triad of *sat, chit*, and *ānanda*, with *chit* comprising the two dimensions of knowledge and action. Furthermore, our consciousness is not 'going out' in the world to know it[18]. Rather, the world is 'coming in' as a representation. However, the entry of the external world into our body and mind is controlled by *karma* and even if it enters our body and mind, through consciousness, we can ignore it, or focus upon it. Finally, if and when we focus on the chosen parts of *chit*, different pleasures can be created. Thus, our consciousness is the *link* between matter and happiness. The link is bidirectional but owing to the dominant-subordinate structure of the three facets of the soul, sometimes the worldly representation dominates our consciousness, sometimes consciousness chooses to focus and ignore certain parts of the worldly representation, and then, finally, our pleasure ability experiences the chosen parts of the internal representation as pleasure or pain.

For expression to work, there must be a consciousness. As a result, only a living entity can change his style—e.g., through changes in tone, verse, gestures—because he or she feels the cognitive world variously based on choice and awareness. A machine can perform all the cognitive functions—provided we understand the process of mental representation—but it cannot choose to focus on some parts and ignore others because that necessitates consciousness. Similarly, a machine cannot become a person because doing so requires acquiring a unique style based on the experience of emotion. Hence, we cannot expect a robot to create music, poetry, dance, and drama, although the robot can quite intelligently engage in conversation and understanding without being able to determine a particular focus, and without enjoying it.

A person with advanced consciousness is able to convert the cognitive representation of other's emotive expression into their own emotions. Thus, they can feel the pain and happiness of others as their own. Conversely, the person whose consciousness is not elevated may understand the cognitive component but feel nothing; such persons become cold, calculating, and manipulative psychopaths. Since *sat* is relationality, to convert the cognitive representation into an emotional feeling, the person must consider themselves involved in a close relationship with the others whose pain or happiness he feels. The elevated consciousness easily establishes close relationships to others, and because of his ability to feel a person's pain and happiness, the others become closely attached to such a person, because they can see that he or she feels what they feel, and a bond of proximity is naturally established.

We previously saw that the different divisions of the zodiac are different relative priorities among the six qualities. We have now also seen that this prioritization is the ability of consciousness to focus on certain things and ignore others. Therefore, the prioritization of the six qualities represents the *focus* of consciousness. This focus is in turn driven by a personality called *guna* (plural) which are responsible for creating our sense of happiness and unhappiness. Obviously, everyone seeks happiness, and they can focus their attention onto the relevant parts and ignore the rest. However, because we don't understand the mechanism of happiness, we are dragged by the changes of the body and mind—which are produced automatically—accepting them as the facts that we need to attend to. This compulsion to attend to the mind and body is sometimes called *sangha*— 'association' or 'attachment'—of the body. *Bhagavad-Gita* 2.62-63 states that emotions are created from the attachment.

> *Bhagavad-Gita 2.62-63*[19]*: While contemplating the objects of the senses, a person develops attachment for them, and from such attachment lust develops, and from lust anger arises. From anger, delusion arises, and from delusion bewilderment of memory. When memory is bewildered, intelligence is lost, and when intelligence is lost, one falls down again into the material pool.*

Conversely, once these emotions are created, then they are also expressed in the body cognitively, depending on the nature of consciousness. Hence, there is always a back and forth between emotion and cognition, caused by the presence of consciousness. When the soul leaves the body, you can still see the chemistry working, because that is the *chit* expression. In fact, in some cases, if you touch a dead body, you might be surprised to see the limbs moving. Even that movement is within the cognitive interaction, although there is no soul. The presence of the soul simply means that there will be an emotional feeling. When a person goes into a coma, their body—the cognitive part—keeps working, but there is no emotional expression. The soul may or may not be present and it is very hard to tell when a coma patient has actually died, because the bodies of these patients can be kept alive through chemistry, although consciousness is not interacting with the body to create happiness or suffering. The coma patient is therefore not suffering or enjoying, because the connection between the *guna* personality and the *karma* body—created by the consciousness—has been severed. The symptom of such severance is that the effects of *prāna*—e.g., breathing and circulation—stop. If breathing and circulation continue without life support, then the soul is present in the body. If the body cannot breathe and circulate blood on its own, then the soul has left the body. The existence of the soul is indicated by *prāna* and its effects.

As we move through the zodiac signs, a different *gandharvā* means the tonality—caused by a feeling—has changed; a different *apsarā* means the gestures—caused by a feeling—have changed; a different sage means that the prioritization of the six qualities—caused by a feeling—has changed. All these associates of the sun are therefore expressing his feelings outwardly.

Aesthetics - Rasa and Bhāva

Indian treatises on drama provide a very detailed description of the process of experiencing emotion. This process is divided into 4 parts:

Vibhāva – this is the *ādibhautika* component of experience, which causes the experience. For example, if you are feeling the emotion of love then the *vibhāva* can be seeing a beautiful person; if you are feeling fear, then the *vibhāva* may be someone attacking you.

Anubhāva – this is the *ādiatmika c*omponent of experience, which may cause, or may be caused by emotion. For example, if you are feeling the emotion of love, sidelong glances or smiling expressions may be seen. If you are feeling fear, then hands may cross in defense, the eyes may flutter, and you may retreat from the danger.

Bhāva – this is the consciousness that attaches to the *ādibhautika* and *ādiatmika* in order to experience them. There are 8 primary *bhāva* called *sthāyi* or stable and then 33 *sanchāri* or temporary *bhāva.* The *sthāyi* are described below; the *sanchāri* are not discussed here.

Rati (Love)

Hāsya (Mirth)

Śoka (Sorrow)

Krodha (Anger)

Utsāha (Energy)

Bhaya (Terror)

Jugupsā (Disgust)

Vismaya (Astonishment)

Rasa – this is the outcome of consciousness coming into contact with *vibhāva* and *anubhāva* through *bhāva.* Literally, the term *rasa* means the "liquid essence". But the term is employed to indicate pleasure. There are several descriptions of *rasa*—some note 8 primary *rasa*, others add a 9th *rasa* called *Śānta* or calmness, while others add 4 more to this list to indicate a unique pleasure enjoyed by a servant, a friend, a parent, and a lover. Then there are others who add two more pleasures to this to indicate the pleasure of being a master and a child, producing a total of 7 relational *rasas.* Finally, all these *rasas* are experienced differently based on gender—male or female—so gender experience is the 16th *rasa.* As a result, we can count up to 15 such divisions of *rasa,* and a 16th *rasa* of being a particular gender.

Eight experiential *rasas*:

Śṛungār: Beauty, attractiveness.

Hāsya: Laughter, comedy.

Raudra: Fury, destructive anger.

Kāruṇya: Compassion, mercy.

Bībhatsa: Disgust, aversion.

Bhayānaka: Horror, terror.

Veera: Heroism, leadership.

Adbhuta: Wonder, amazement.

Seven relational *rasas*:

Śānta: Peace and tranquility.

Dāsya: Servitor, dependent, faithful.

Sakhya: Friendly, cordial, supportive.

Vātsalya: Parental, elderly, caretaker.

Mādhurya: Romantic, amorous, sexual.

Prabhu: Master, lord, controller.

Bālya: Child, minor, irresponsible.

Gender rasa:

Masculine

Feminine

Based on the gender differences, the 8 experiential *rasas* and the 7 relational *rasas*—constituting a total of 15 *rasa*—can be further divided into two parts, creating a total of 30 divisions of *rasa*. Half of these are enjoyments of the males and the other half those of the females. We will see later that these 15, 16, or 30 *rasas*—depending on how you count them—are represented in the phases of the moon, owing to which the moon has two phases of rising and falling each lasting 15 days, and the lunar month is 30 days long.

The *rasa* are produced by the *bhāva*, which is the type of consciousness focusing on the bodily representation comprising the self and the other. This means that the soul's consciousness itself has different facets due to which it is predisposed to interpret the bodily representation in different ways. For example, under the *bhāva* of love, a bad situation can lead to the *rasa* of compassion (to protect the loved one), disgust (against the perpetrator), wonderment (of how such a bad situation can arise), heroism (the feeling to protect the loved one from the perpetrator), horror (at how the loved person has been subjected to a difficulty), comedy (at how the loved one has been fooled), or even attractiveness (because a situation that makes a person vulnerable also makes him attractive). Under the mood of anger, the same situation will lead to the above *rasa* but now there would be a sense of astonishment about how a person can subject himself or herself to such a condition, disgust that previous warnings of impending problems were ignored, comedy that foolishness naturally leads to punishment, heroism that despite a weak and foolish person subjecting themselves to a difficulty he or she must be rescued, terror that if the situation were not corrected it would become much worse, enthusiasm that the problem can still be fixed if an effort were made, and sorrow on the realization that even if it were fixed it would recur again in the future.

Each of these feelings can be experienced through the above 7 types of relationships and then by the male and female genders. Thus, there are some objective facts about the world denoted by *vibhāva* and *anubhāva*. Then there is a process of interpreting these facts called *bhāva*. Finally, there is an emotional experience resulting from this interpretation which is called *rasa*. In this process, the distinction between *rasa* and *bhāva* is often a cause of confusion because the *bhāva* leads to *rasa* and this can be described as follows:

Rati bhāva (love) leads to the *Śṛungār rasa* (erotic).

Hāsya bhāva (mirth) leads to the *Hāsya rasa* (laughter).

Śoka bhāva (sorrow) leads to the *Kāruṇya rasa* (compassion).

Krodha bhāva (anger) leads to the *Raudra rasa* (fury).

Utsāha bhāva (heroism) leads to the *Veer rasa* (heroic).

Bhaya bhāva of (fear) leads to the *Bhayānaka rasa* (fearful).

Jugupsā bhāva (disgust) leads to the *Bībhatsa rasa* (revulsion).

Vismaya bhāva (astonishment) leads to the *Adbhuta rasa* (wonder).

However, these are only the dominant tendencies. As we saw above, love may dominantly lead to erotic feeling, but depending on the situation (*vibhāva* and *anubhāva*) it can also lead to all the other emotions. The co-existence of the numerous emotions leads to the dominant-subordinate structure in which one emotion dominates while the others are subordinated. This structure can be stable or changeable; as a result, a person can be conflicted alternatively between a feeling of anger or compassion along with love. In the pastimes of *Kṛṣṇa*, for example, His mother *Yaśoda* feels several emotions at once—compassion because *Kṛṣṇa* is her child, fury because he is naughty, fear that he might be hurt by naughtiness, and heroic as she wants to protect him from dangers. And all these emotions are caused simply by the *bhāva* of love for *Kṛṣṇa*. She is the embodiment of the parental emotion as manifest in the feminine form. It is not uncommon for us to experience many emotions simultaneously, and the multitude of emotions can sometimes get confusing.

The distinction between *bhāva* and *rasa* is therefore subtle but important. *Bhāva* is the instrument for feeling emotion, *Vibhāva* and *Anubhāva* are the reality measured by the instrument, and *rasa* is the outcome of measurement—the value obtained as a result of that measurement. The 8 types of *bhāva* represent 8 distinct types of instruments used for measuring emotion. Quite like you can measure a table using a meter or a kilogram, which are the instruments of cognition, similarly, we can measure the same reality using the instruments of emotion. The same reality—as measured by different instruments—produces different types of values, and the same world can therefore lead to both cognition and emotion. The resulting values of measurement are different because the instruments are different, and the instrument is different from the value (emotion vs. cognition) it produces. The value is not meaningful unless defined in relation to the measuring instrument, and the instrument, the value, and the reality must all be known for a full understanding.

For example, if you are feeling emotionally vulnerable, then a joke about you will make you angry. On the other hand, if you are feeling emotionally confident, then the joke may make you happy and cause you to laugh out loud. Here, the joke is the reality, vulnerability vs. confidence is the instrument of measuring, and anger vs. laughter is the value obtained by the measurement.

Through *bhāva* we appraise the cognitive situation to feel the *rasa*. Similarly, through *bhāva* we convert the *rasa* into the cognitive situation. For instance, if you feel the love for a person, but the *bhāva* is anger, then love would manifest as compassionate criticism to correct the shortcomings. On the other hand, the *rasa* of love will be manifest as jokes under the *bhāva* of humor. Thus, we can distinguish between *mood* and *feeling*. The *bhāva* is the mood under which the world is interpreted and expressed while *rasa* is the feeling we experience, which can be different from the mood. An anxious mother's feeling of love is expressed by being too protective about her children. And a sad mother's love may be expressed by making the children independent.

Emotion and Morality

There are certain ideal expectations on how to measure the situation for emotional response. For example, we should not love a thief, we should not mock the disabled, and we should not be angry at the faultless. Thus, even though we have the freedom to use any instrument, we must *choose* these instruments appropriately. There are hence *appropriate* and *inappropriate* or right and wrong instruments to be employed for different situations. Once a particular type of instrument has been chosen, the emotional experience, and the decision caused by that feeling become automatic. Therefore, the choice of the instrument is the primary agency by which we change our behavior. The purification of emotion means that we are able to choose the instrument for emotion measurement appropriately. Thus, mockery and sarcasm are appropriate instruments for certain situations, but not for all situations. If one is permanently imbued with a cynical attitude, then sarcasm would be employed in all situations; it can lead to laughter in all situations, but it is often at the expense of those people which are not deserving of this disparagement.

If you look at a situation cynically, then ask disparaging and rhetorical questions, you are unlikely to receive love in return, because the other person also has a sense of right and wrong and would respond in kind. And this is true even if you did not actually feel disregard for the person or mean to insult him. In that sense we disconnect our actual feelings and focus only on the instrument that perceives and creates the cognitively accessible response.

The cognitive expression of emotion is therefore not the expression of *rasa* but that of *bhāva.* We cannot express the feeling of being a mother, father, child, lover, or master, but we can express the love, anger, fear, astonishment, humor, disgust, heroism, and sorrow in the different situations. Based on that expression others may try to judge what you feel. For instance, if someone is protective toward a child, the natural conclusion is that he or she might be a parent or elder brother or sister. But these conclusions are simply interpretations and it is hard to know what the person feels internally. Thus, 8 experiential *rasas* have corresponding *bhāva*, but the 7 relational *rasa* and the gender *rasa* are internal. We express the *bhāva,* but we cannot express the *rasa*. Similarly, there is a difference between the social relation and the emotional feeling. Two people may be married to each other and may also perform the requisite duties but may not express love for each other. A child doesn't necessarily feel loved and cared by the parent, even though the parent provides food and shelter to the child (children of many rich and illustrious parents thus feel lonely and abandoned). The emotional *bhāva* of being loved as a child, parent, husband, wife, friend etc. is different from the duties of these roles.

Nevertheless, since there is an appropriate emotional response for each situation, the *bhāva* can also be associated with our moral duties. This means that it is our duty to express the correct emotional response to situations. Getting angry at the wrongdoers, expressing affection toward children, or speaking heroically to inspire others, are therefore duties for certain people in certain situations. One should not be attached to the world, and anger, greed, envy, or pride arising from these attachments should be rejected. But the rejection of emotion arising from attachment is different from the emotion essential to the performance of duties. For example, *Kṛṣṇa* exhorts *Arjuna* to fight in the battle of *Kurukśhetra* and yet teaches him to remain detached. How can anyone fight a battle without expressing anger—even as a matter of duty? This constitutes the key difference between *bhāva* and *rasa. Arjuna* can express the *bhāva* of anger, but his *rasa* will still be friendly devotion to *Kṛṣṇa*. Likewise, when *Viṣṇu* appears as *Narasiṃha* (a fearsome man-lion) to kill *Hiraṇyakaśipu*, He exhibits the *bhāva* of anger but the *rasa* of paternal affection toward *Prahlāda* for whose protection He takes the superficially terrifying form. Only *Prahlāda* understands the *rasa* while everyone else sees the *bhāva*.

In the material world, the recommended way of living is to practice detachment—i.e., perform the necessary duties without getting entangled by attachment in order to enjoy the pleasure and distress of the world. This is often taken to incorrectly mean that one must not display anger, love, laughter, etc. because these are emotions, which follow from attachment. But how can a person live in the world without expressing any emotion? Would he or she not appear to be a machine that only has cognition without emotion? The short answer is that the *bhāva* is different from the *rasa*. It is the duty of a parent to get angry with a naughty child and display that anger to correct their behavior. But that anger is only a symptom of the paternal love felt internally. Conversely, not displaying the anger on the pretext of loving the child would constitute a violation of duties. Thus, even though emotion is felt by the *ānanda* aspect of the soul, and separate from the *sat* which represents duties, in the material world ideally the emotion is subordinated to the duties. Expressing certain forms of *bhāva* is therefore a duty, and the 8 types of *bhāva* used appropriately (i.e., the correct context) also constitute our duty. Thus, loving and hating are not per se immoral as long as they are bound by duty. Similarly, detachment from desires contrary to moral principles is recommended.

> *Bhagavad-Gita 7.11 Translation*[20]*: I am the strength of the strong, devoid of passion and desire. I am sex life which is not contrary to religious principles, O Lord of the Bharatas [Arjuna].*

In terms of the artistic expressions of emotion, only the *bhāva* (and not the *rasa*) is emphasized, because that is what you express to others. An actor on a stage playing the part of a mother or father cannot experience the *rasa* toward another actor because deep within they know they are not the true parent. Nevertheless, to act the part properly on the stage, they have to express the *bhāva* because otherwise the drama would not be realistic. Again, we can see that the actor in the drama must express the *bhāva* even though he or she doesn't feel the *rasa*. The material journey is also like that drama in which we have to act the part correctly without feeling the *rasa* because there is nothing real about the stage actor acting a particular type of role. In the *Nātya-śāstra* or the treatises on drama, only the 8 experiential *rasas* corresponding to the 8 *bhāva* are noted. Hence, when we speak about the expression of emotion through poetry, music, dance, and drama, we only refer to the *bhāva* and not to *rasa*. The *bhāva* are expressions of moods as the feeling of a father, mother, son, daughter, husband, wife, etc. cannot be expressed although they can be inferred from the cognitive expression but being in a body doesn't mean you feel the emotions[21]. As a result, the emotional feeling of being male or female is not reflected in the body, although the *bhāva* does manifest in different behaviors; for instance, a male may act in a female role, or vice versa.

The descriptions of *bhakti* in which the soul truly feels himself or herself to be in a particular type of relation to God, however, include the 8 relational and gender *rasa* because the person is no longer in a temporary stage drama acting out a part. The person is truly and eternally in a particular relation and their actions are not merely playing a part; they are indeed the reality. Thus, dressing like a *gopi* doesn't mean you feel the *rasa* of being a *gopi*, although you can express all the moods—i.e., the *bhāva*—of being a *gopi*. Factually, there is no need to indulge in such expression because *rasa* is not *bhāva*. Conversely, there are indeed bodily expressions of *bhāva* called *sattvika-vikāra* which manifest in the body as trembling, crying, hairs standing on end, etc. The true *rasa* of a devotee cannot be known through such bodily expression, although it is possible to know the *bhāva* when the *sattvika-vikāra* are manifest.

The *genre* in artistic expression are expressions of *bhāva*—love, fear, comedy, heroism, sadness, etc. These emotions are expressed in three ways through literary style, music, and gestures—in the case of speech—which is always used as a cardinal example of expression in Vedic philosophy. Each of these three ways also has a positive and negative side, which makes for the six associates of the sun. In one sense, the six associates of the sun are expressing the emotion as style, as opposed to content. In another sense, they are responding correctly to the different situations according to moral duty. Finally, style is also available to us cognitively. Should we speak of style cognitively, morally, or emotionally? The short answer is that the six elements of style are cognitive. The eight types of *bhāva* are morally correct behaviors. Like in a drama, where a person can express certain feelings without actually feeling them, similarly, *bhāva* is not truly emotion; it is just the expression of emotion. This helps us nuance the understanding of *sat* or awareness: by correct behavior we don't just mean the mechanical action of performing the duties but doing it in the right *style*—e.g., with the expression of the right emotion.

Symbolic Expressions of Rasa

While the *rasa* themselves are not expressed externally, the representation of desire—which manifests in time—is said to be represented by rhythms and meters as per the below reference from *Aitareya Brahmana*. Since the horses of the sun's chariots pull the chariot, and these horses are said to be the 7 meters, time is driving the motion of the sun through the horses. This time has two distinct manifestations. First, through the rhythms it indicates the speed of their motion. Second, through the use of the meters it represents the longer or shorter steps they take. We can also say that the content is divided into smaller or larger parts, then expressed slowly or quickly.

> *Now (he) glorifies the arts,*
> *The arts are refinement of the self (atma-samskrti).*
> *With these the worshipper recreates his self,*
> *That is made of rhythms, meters.*
> *—Aitareya Brahmana 6.27*[22]

It is now also possible to interpret the 7 meters as corresponding to the 7 rhythms which are called *tāla* in Indian classical music. 7 prominent rhythms are identified in the *Carnatic School* of music[23]. Each of these rhythms has further 5 types of divisions. All these are described in Table-4 below. The system of *tāla* is well-known to be hierarchical. For example, the larger cyclic *tāla* pattern has embedded smaller cyclic patterns, which is quite unlike the system of rhythm used often in Western music. Thus, a single beat in a *tāla* can be representative of the entire cycle of beats in another *tāla* and through such successive hierarchical patterns different instruments can play at different rates—following slower or faster embedded patterns—in a single composition. This hierarchical and cyclic view of time is typical to Vedic philosophy.

Tāla	Notation	Tisra	Chatusra	Khanda	Misra	Sankeerna
Dhruva	1011	11	14	17	23	29
Matya	101	8	10	12	16	20
Rūpaka	01	5	6	7	9	11
Jhampā	1U0	6	7	8	10	12
Tripūta	100	7	8	9	11	13
Ata	1100	10	12	14	18	22
Ekā	1	3	4	5	7	9

Table-4: The System of Rhythms in Indian Music

Śrīmad Bhāgavatam 5.21.15 provides the description of how the qualities of the sun are composed into 'verses' of meaning. These verses are also described as the 'horses' that pull the sun's chariot. Similarly, apart from the horses pulling the chariot from the front, rākshasa push it from behind. The yakshā guard the chariot from the sides, while the nāga bind the horses to the chariot. Then there are apsarā dancing, gandharvā singing, and the sages reciting. This is obviously a complex arrangement, and every part in it is significant. They represent the various styles in which the meanings are delivered. There are 7 types of verses in the Vedic texts. These are described as follows.

Translation: My dear King, the carriage of the sun-god's chariot is estimated to be 3,600,000 yojanas [28,800,000 miles] long and one-fourth as wide [900,000 yojanas, or 7,200,000 miles]. The chariot's horses, which are named after Gāyatrī and other Vedic meters, are harnessed by Aruṇadeva to a yoke that is also 900,000 yojanas wide. This chariot continuously carries the sun-god.

Purport: In the Viṣṇu Purāṇa it is stated:

gāyatrī ca bṛhaty uṣṇig jagatī triṣṭup eva ca anuṣṭup paṅktir ity uktāś chandāṁsi harayo raveḥ

The seven horses yoked to the sun-god's chariot are named Gāyatrī, Bṛhati, Uṣṇik, Jagatī, Triṣṭup, Anuṣṭup and Paṅkti. These names of various Vedic meters designate the seven horses that carry the sun-god's chariot.

	Gāyatrī	Uṣṇik	Anuṣṭup	Bṛhati	Paṅkti	Triṣṭup	Jagatī
Deva	1	2	3	4	5	6	7
Asura	15	14	13	12	11	10	9
Pra-jāpati	8	12	16	20	24	28	32
Rṣi	24	28	32	36	40	44	48
Yajur	6	7	8	9	10	11	12
Sāma	12	14	16	18	20	22	24
Ṛg	18	21	24	27	30	33	36
Brah-mana	36	42	48	54	60	66	72

Table-5: The Seven Meters of the Sanskrit Verse

The above mentioned 7 meters have several manifestations as illustrated in Table-5[24]. Of these, a common expression of the 7 meters is that used for the *Rṣi* and the *Gāyatrī* in this system has 24 syllables, which are the result of adding the syllables of *Asura*, *Prajāpati*, and *Deva*. The *Yajur*, *Sāma*, and *Rig Veda* conversely employ a different system, and the number of syllables in the verses of the *Brahmana* are the result of adding the syllables of *Yajur*, *Sāma*, and *Rig*. Therefore, when it is said that the sages recite the verses from *Yajur*, *Sāma*, and *Rig Veda* we can understand that a verse system extending up to 72 syllables is being referred, although parts of this system may be used.

We can see from the above that the *Yajur* verses are the smallest. The *Sāma* verses are twice in length, the *Rig* verses are three times in length, and the *Brahmana* verses are six times in length. It is therefore possible to view the *Yajur* verses as representing the 12 zodiac signs divided further into 6 parts using the six qualities of the sun that we have extensively discussed.

Once prosody and rhythms are combined in this way—as representations of time and thereby the expressions of *rasa*—the shorter meters and slower rhythms represent the attainment of the *Śānta rasa* or the emotion of calmness and respect, and as the relation becomes more complex and exciting, one needs to employ longer meters and faster rhythms. Although we cannot experience the emotion, there is an indirect expression of that feeling as the speech involves shorter or longer sentences, uttered slowly or quickly. The inner emotion therefore manifests as the structure of time externally. Similarly, gestures, music, and literary style manifest as structure of space externally. Even though the sun only represents the cognitive expression, the fact is that this expression also contains the imprints of a deeper reality that we call pleasure.

4

Moon and Star Religions

Praised be You, My Lord, through Sister Moon and the stars.
—Saint Francis of Assisi

Meaning vs. Judgment

Before we get into the discussion of the nature of the moon and the stars, we need to discuss an important distinction between meaning which exists in the mind, and the judgments which exist in the intellect, ego, and the moral sense. The mind is said to perform three functions called thinking, feeling, and willing. The intellect performs the judgment of truth corresponding to the thinking, the ego performs the judgment of good corresponding to the feeling, and the moral sense performs the judgment of right corresponding to the willing. And yet, the mind, intellect, ego, and the moral sense are all manifestations of the *chit* or cognition; these are therefore not truly the feelings enjoyed by the *ānanda* aspect of the soul (experienced as *rasa*), or the morality as embodied by the *sat* aspect of the soul (experienced as *bhāva*). These are rather simply the cognitive expressions of the feeling and willing. This distinction between feeling and willing, and then the cognitive expression needs some elaboration, which I will try to undertake in the following paragraphs.

> *Śrimad Bhāgavatam 10.1.42 Translation*[1]*. At the time of death, according to the thinking, feeling and willing of the mind, which is involved in fruitive activities, one receives a particular body. In other words, the body develops according to the activities of the mind. Changes of body are due to the flickering of the mind, for otherwise the*

soul could remain in its original, spiritual body.

Śrimad Bhāgavatam 1.9.32 Translation[2]*. Bhīṣmadeva said: Let me now invest my thinking, feeling and willing, which were so long engaged in different subjects and occupational duties, in the all-powerful Lord Śrī Kṛṣṇa. He is always self-satisfied, but sometimes, being the leader of the devotees, He enjoys transcendental pleasure by descending on the material world, although from Him only the material world is created.*

We all have experience of the fact that having a feeling is different from *knowing* what that feeling is. For instance, if you are feeling upset, you may not necessarily know if that feeling is anger, depression, frustration, fear, or something else. You just feel restless because of these feelings, and if you went to a psychiatrist to talk about these feelings, he or she would first prompt you to categorize these feelings using the appropriate words—e.g., fear, anger, sadness, frustration, etc. This categorization of the feeling is the *concept* corresponding to the feeling and arises when the mind *cognizes* the feeling. Since the feeling in you can exist without the cognition, the cognition is separate from the feeling. Similarly, because you can cognize the feeling in others without feeling the same emotion yourself, the cognition is distinct from the feeling. Emotional problems in people are thus often treated by a method known as *Cognitive Behavioral Therapy*[3], which means that you have to first classify and cognize what you are feeling, before you can attempt to change it.

In the same way, we carry an intuitive understanding of right and wrong which automatically makes us comfortable and uncomfortable, although we might not be able to precisely define what gives us that sense of comfort or discomfort. For example, if a stranger talks to you openly and frankly, many people—especially from the cultures that are reserved with strangers—will feel uncomfortable. Similarly, if a person stares at you or gives you undue attention, you might be uncomfortable. The reason for the discomfort in these cases is that, in certain cultures, privacy is considered a moral value, and someone being too open too quickly, or staring at you, is viewed as the invasion of your privacy. In other cultures, where privacy is not a moral value—e.g., those cultures which don't value individualism—openness and staring are considered invitations to be friendly, and expressions of one's openness. Since you can unconsciously appreciate the fact that openness can be morally good, but you hold privacy as a moral value, you become confused by your discomfort. To truly understand the reason for this discomfort, you have to convert your moral values into a cognition—giving it names such as 'privacy' and 'openness'—before you can explain why you feel the sense of discomfort.

Similarly, when you listen to a person, you often tend to believe or disbelieve them innately, and judge what they are saying as true or false, although you cannot exactly pinpoint the reasons. The situation becomes even more paradoxical when the person you distrust presents the information based on facts and figures, because you cannot explain why you innately distrust them. The reason for this trust and distrust is the harmony or disharmony in our belief systems. The facts and figures you present can be explained using many alternative theories. Each such theory postulates a certain number of *axioms* which constitute our *beliefs*. Most scientists, for example, believe in reductionism, materialism, atheism, and evolutionism, and if a religious person were to talk to them about the nature of reality scientifically, they will innately distrust them because of the differences in the belief systems. Facts and figures don't matter anymore, nor does reason and argument, because there is a basic clash in the axioms based on which we judge something to be true or false. It takes considerable amount of philosophy to even articulate what those assumptions are. For instance, the assumption underlying Vedic philosophy is that the world is comprised of three fundamental properties—cognition, emotion, and relation—which originally exist as the three properties of the soul. Articulating these axioms also therefore necessitates a cognition of our beliefs.

As a result, beliefs, morals, and feelings are essential parts of the process of judgment of truth, right, and good, and yet much of this might remain unconscious. The mind helps us convert the beliefs, morals, and feelings into concepts by which they are expressed and communicated to others.

The sun represents the judgment of truth, and the sun has been associated with the intellect. Those religions which evolved from the worship of the sun place greater emphasis on theology and philosophy, relative to rituals, worship, prayer, or even the need for emotional satisfaction from religion; they are after the discovery of truth as the supreme purpose of the religion.

The moon represents the judgment of good, and the moon has therefore been associated with pleasure and feelings of happiness and sadness. Those religions which evolved from the worship of the moon therefore place greater emphasis on the love of God, singing, dancing, poetry, and music, relative to philosophy and theology, and even avoid complex rituals and elaborate systems of worship. Religion, in this view, is the pursuit of ultimate happiness and satisfaction; it cannot be obtained simply by philosophy or rituals; it has to be instead developed through the development of devotion, humility, and compassion, and the spiritually advanced person is emotionally strong.

The stars represent the judgment of right, and the religions which evolved from the worship of stars emphasize morality, duty, rituals, and worship according to strict rules of individual and social disciplined behavior. Philosophy and theology for such people are merely theoretical conclusions; what does one *do* after one arrives at such conclusions? Similarly, those who haven't arrived at the final understanding of God and the soul need a *process* by which they can attain such a conclusion. Without a disciplined method of practice, how can the ignorant be enlightened? Finally, society needs to be organized on the principles of morality—which is viewed as the laws ordained by God. What good would philosophy be if we were not leading a moral and disciplined life? What could singing, dancing, and poetry yield without a set of rules by which people live cordially, harmoniously, and with clarity regarding their duty?

Factually, no religious system is complete without these three judgments. Indeed, no living being can lead a fulfilling life without judging the truth, right, and good, so the problem is not limited to religion but extends to any form of life. These judgments are weak in the case of animals and they are pronounced in the case of humans and other higher forms of life. Accordingly, the mind—which converts beliefs, morals, and feelings into concepts—is also significantly advanced in humans as compared to animals. Therefore, when we speak about the religious importance of the sun, the moon, and the stars, we are not just referring to the historical facts about myriad religious ideologies centered on these cosmological entities. We are actually referring to the three aspects of the soul and how these manifest into the three kinds of judgments.

The Meaning of the Moon

Quite specifically, when we speak about the moon, we refer to the judgment of good, or what constitutes our pleasure and happiness. The moon represents our emotions and feelings. It is described as the place for *soma* or enjoyment. In terms of *Sāṅkhya* philosophy, the moon affects a person's ego. In common parlance, the ego has negative connotations such as pride and vanity. However, the ego is not limited to these. In broader terms, the ego constitutes the sense of the self—our *personality*—or what we like and dislike. From this personality emerge the goals and purposes which drive us forward in life toward the quest for happiness. The pursuit of goals creates the forward movement and hence the sense of time. The ego therefore has many meanings in a broader sense which include emotions, goals, personality, and even time. All these meanings naturally emerge from the idea that the ego is the manifestation of *ānanda*, and constitutes the basis of desire, which leads to happiness and distress on the one hand, and goals, purposes, and time on the other.

Shiva represents all these ideas; He is identified as the primordial enjoyer of the material creation; He is identified as time; and He is identified as the personification of *ahamkāra* which is another name for the ego.

Many people wonder why the Vedic system uses the lunar calendar instead of the solar one, when the primary cause of the day and night, the changes in the seasons, and the concept of a year depend on the sun. The reason is that the moon as the representation of *Shiva* is identified as time. Even the horses of the sun—which drive the sun's chariots—are identified as the 7 meters, and these meters are then the representations of emotion. All these ideas point toward a single direction—namely, that time is desire, and change is caused due to our desire, not due to mechanical forces of motion. We measure this time through changes in the sun's position, but those changes are not the real cause; the cause is the changes in the desires themselves. Thus, the solar calendar denotes the *measurement* of time as *change*, while the lunar calendar denotes the *cause* of time as it originates in shifting desires.

Specifically, the motion of the moon is unlike the motion of the sun; the former denotes the changes in desires, and the latter in effects produced due to contact with the world. The sun represents the judgment of truth, and the moon the judgment of good. Therefore, the motion of the sun indicates the changes in the truths and the motion of the moon represents the changing notions of what constitutes good. The truth in Vedic philosophy is not a fixed material reality. This truth exists as a *possibility* from which the *guna* can make a selection. In a sense, there are many possible facts that can potentially exist; these may not be eternally true, but they can appear temporarily. If the truth were not a possibility, then there would be simply no room for choice.

This truth is foremost our material body and mind—constituted of our *abilities* and *opportunities*. The sun represents the *chit* and hence this body, and the body is the possibility of performing many actions and knowing many things through the opportunities afforded to it through interactions. The moon represents what we enjoy knowing and doing and helps us make a selection from the abilities afforded by the body. Finally, despite the fact that we have abilities, opportunities, and desires, there is also morality of action, which determines which alternatives from the possibility are right or wrong.

The change we see in this world is a combination of three things changing represented by three types of motion—sun, moon, and stars. The motion of the sun represents the changes in the truth as abilities and opportunities. The motion of the moon denotes the changes in our goals, purposes, and desires which exploit the abilities and opportunities. Finally, even as the opportunities are changing, so are our roles and duties, which normatively determine the contextual sense of right and wrong. Therefore, even morality is not universal; the sense of right and wrong depends on the person's role, which evolves with time. The prediction of the future depends on the combination of the changes in abilities, opportunities, desires, and moral values. The natural law of this prediction is whether we act morally given the abilities and opportunities. In other words, can we be happy to subordinate our desires to morality? By understanding the nature of the soul, we can see why these must combine to produce the actual facts and events of this world. However, this three-fold change only concerns the changes in the *individual* desires, abilities, morals, and opportunities. Beyond this individual change lies the *cosmic* change.

The universe is like a drama whose events have been fixed, but the actors in the drama are yet to be decided. The motion of the sun determines if an individual actor is qualified to play a certain role. The motion of the stars determines if the actor deserves—based on their past deeds—to get the role. And the motion of the moon decides if the actor wants to play the role. Sometimes due to past deeds, a person may not get the opportunity to play the part even though they have the ability and desire to perform the role. At other times, a person may have the ability and opportunity but no desire. Finally, one may have the desire and the opportunity but doesn't have the ability. These combinations therefore determine myriad types of events at the individual level. However, at the cosmic level, the events of the drama are predetermined. Regardless of which actor can or will play the role, the show will go on.

The moon—as the representation of *Shiva* Who embodies this time—therefore has a dual role: individual and cosmic. The individual role of the moon is to impel a person's ego to desire to participate in the events. But the cosmic role of the moon is to create the events of the time itself. Thus, the changes in desires act at the individual level, and the changes in the events are effected at the cosmic level. Owing to this, the moon forms the basis of the calendar in the Vedic system, because it represents the cosmic time. And yet, it also represents the individual desire, passion, and goal because it causes the changes in our desires, and thereby impels us toward many goals.

The individual and cosmic functions of the moon can be reconciled if we recognize the fact that time is *Shiva*'s desires; cosmic change is simply caused by His desire. But as this desire changes, there is natural change effected even in our desires due to the presence of the ego. The ego is—in this sense—a repository of innumerable desires, but these are not manifest at once. Rather as time moves forward due to *Shiva*'s desire, time itself selects some of these desires present in the ego, and they naturally manifest as *our* goals. Factually, these desires are not *our* desires because they are impelled due to the passing time; as a result of this one could argue that we have no free will because the desires are being naturally and automatically created within us. However, two factors reinstate the role of free will. First, after these desires have been created, we can *reject* them[4]. Second, not everyone gets the same types of desires; even the desires lying dormant in the ego are based on which desires we have entertained in the past and converted them into habits by repetition.

Through His effect on the ego, God proposes the desires and man disposes them by accepting or rejecting them. However, through the effect of *karma,* which creates opportunities, and through the effect of changing abilities, God acts as the person who disposes the desires proposed by man. Thus, both man and God are proposing and disposing desires, but in different ways.

The effect of the moon on the individual person is to perform a selection on the dormant repository of desires. This dormant repository is sometimes called the *chitta* and desires are compared to the waves in an ocean. The *chitta* that is devoid of desires is like the calm ocean; the *chitta* that is inundated by desires is like the stormy ocean. The moon therefore creates the waves in the ocean of the *chitta*. This fact is also sometimes compared to the moon causing high and low tides in the earthly oceans; as the moon grows through the rising phase, the tides get bigger, and when the moon declines through the falling phase, the tides get smaller. The ego is therefore like the ocean, and desires are like the waves in the ocean. The moon tugs at the ego and creates waves of desires. If the ego was dried up, there would be no desire, and the moon cannot act on us. Conversely, the bigger the ocean, the bigger the waves can be. Accordingly, the shrinking of the material ego—resulting in the decline of material desires—is the primary purpose of spiritual advancement by which a person becomes free from the influence of *Shiva* who tempts the soul with material enjoyment whereby the soul then becomes a victim of this temptation.

As we have seen previously, the *rasa* of pleasure is internal and enjoyed by the *ānanda* of the soul. The moon doesn't affect the soul's *ānanda*; however, it creates the *desire* for this pleasure, even when none exists. For example, with the effect of the moon, a woman will naturally develop the desire to be a wife and a mother, in what we call the natural progression of time. Similarly, a man will develop natural desires to be a boss, a husband, and a father. As time passes, the sun gives us the abilities, the stars give us the roles or duties, and the moon creates the desires to use the abilities and opportunities[5].

This is important because if the pleasure is internal then how can it have an objective manifestation as the moon? The answer to this quandary is that the moon is not actually the pleasure; it is rather the desire or temptation for this pleasure; the temptation arises automatically due to time when the moon acts upon a person's ego, creating a wave in an ocean that was previously populated through innumerable lifetimes of enjoying material pleasures. Accordingly, the 16 divisions of *rasa* that we spoke about previously can now be understood in the context of the moon as 16 types of *desires* for pleasure.

Sixteen Forms of the Moon God

The *Śrīmad Bhāgavatam* gives a description of the nature of the moon, which has been translated and explained in many ways by different teachers, and all those explanations are useful and relevant here. Let us begin by discussing the relevant points of these translations and explanations below.

SB 5.22.8[6] *— Above the rays of the sunshine by a distance of 100,000 yojanas [800,000 miles] is the moon, which travels at a speed faster than that of the sun. In two lunar fortnights the moon travels through the equivalent of a saṁvatsara of the sun, in two and a quarter days it passes through a month of the sun, and in one day it passes through a fortnight of the sun.*

SB 5.22.9 — When the moon is waxing, the illuminating portions of it increase daily, thus creating day for the demigods and night for the pitās. When the moon is waning, however, it causes night for the demigods and day for the pitās. In this way the moon passes through each constellation of stars in thirty muhūrtas [an entire day]. The moon is the source of nectarean coolness that influences the growth of food grains, and therefore the moon-god is considered the life of all living entities. He is consequently called Jīva, the chief living being within the universe.

SB 5.22.10
ya eṣa ṣoḍaśa-kalaḥ puruṣo bhagavān manomayo
'nnamayo 'mṛtamayo deva-pitṛ-manuṣya-bhūta-
paśu-pakṣi-sarīsṛpa-vīrudhāṁ prāṇāpy
āyana-śīlatvāt sarvamaya iti varṇayanti.

Translation by Śrīla Prabhupāda: Because the moon is full of all potentialities, it represents the influence of the Supreme Personality of Godhead. The moon is the predominating deity of everyone's mind, and therefore the moon-god is called Manomaya. He is also called Annamaya because he gives potency to all herbs and plants, and he is called Amṛtamaya because he is the source of life for all living entities.

The moon pleases the demigods, pitās, human beings, animals, birds, reptiles, trees, plants and all other living entities. Everyone is satisfied by the presence of the moon. Therefore, the moon is also called Sarvamaya [all-pervading].

In the above verse, the term *ṣoḍaśa-kalaḥ* or sixteen parts has been used but the translation by Śrīla Prabhupāda doesn't emphasize it. This has been emphasized by other translators and commentators as follows[7].

Commentary by Bhagavatprasadacharya: The moon has sixteen faculties. He is the god of the mind. He is the ruler of all plants and thus is called annamaya. He is responsible for sustaining the lives of all creations and thus he is called amrtamaya. In short, he is the lord of everything.

Commentary by Sri Giridhara Lala: The elders say that the moon is endowed with 16 faculties—the five sensory organs, five motor organs, five great elements, and the mind. He is the mind of Lord Narayana, and is hence endowed with such extraordinary powers.

Based on the above we can identify some notable points. First, the moon covers the full rotation in a month (that the sun covers in a year), which means a month is not an arbitrary division of the orbit of the sun by 12. Rather, there is another entity—the moon—which completes the full revolution in 30 days, and the concept of a 'month' is based on the moon's revolution. The 'month' therefore has two separate interpretations—(a) as the 12th division of the year defined by the sun, and (b) as the completion of the orbit by the moon. However, the month defined by the sun is not the same as the month created by the moon; the lunar month always has 30 days, due to which the full year has 360 days. The solar year has 365.25 days which means the months have different days. We therefore treat the year and the month differently.

Second, the moon's rotation in 30 days constitutes a day and night of the demigods and the ancestors. The first 15 days during the ascent of the moon constitute the day of the demigods, and the next 15 days during the descent constitutes their night. Similarly, the descent of the moon constitutes the day of the ancestors and the ascent brings their night.

The demigods enjoy one half of the circle and hence they are 'awake' at that time, while the ancestors are 'asleep' at that time. Conversely, the ancestors enjoy the other half of the circle and they are 'awake' at that time, while the demigods are 'asleep'. For 15 days the demigods control the world, and for the other 15 days the ancestors control the world. The ancestors or *pitr* have been worshipped in many traditions, and they were the primary deities for the aborigines. We might also say that these two rule our waking and sleeping pleasures. Thus, one who has a positive influence of demigods will have a pleasurable day life—e.g., work, money, social interactions. But one who has a negative influence of the ancestors will have a painful night life—e.g., lack of sexuality, sleep, restfulness, etc.

Element	**Knowing Sense**	**Action Sense**
Ether	Ear	Tongue
Air	Skin	Legs
Fire	Eye	Hands
Water	Tongue	Genitals
Earth	Nose	Anus

Table-6: The Five Elements, Knowing and Action Senses

Third, the moon has 16 aspects, called *ṣoḍaśa-kalaḥ*, which are identified with the mind, the senses, and the objects of the senses. In *Sāñkhya* philosophy, there are 5 objects of the senses, 5 senses of knowledge, and 5 senses of action. Together with the mind, these constitute the 16 aspects described above. The moon is also the repository of desire and pleasure, so the sixteen aspects above represent not the elements themselves but the 16 ways of desiring and enjoying via the senses and the mind. There is desire and pleasure in the senses by which we enjoy the material world. But this desire is not just 'created' by the senses. Rather, the objects of the senses also have desire objectively, due to which the senses are naturally 'attracted' to the objects, and the objects are naturally 'attracted' to the senses. We have intuitive experience of this fact—sometimes the senses are inexorably drawn toward their objects, and it appears that the objects are 'pulling' the senses, which leads to the problem of 'sense control' where we have to withdraw the senses away from the objects. The senses and the mind are the 'subjective' part of pleasure, and the objects of the senses are 'objective' pleasure[8]. Of these 16, only 15 are visible to the senses, because the 16th aspect is the mind, invisible to the senses.

Thus, the three types—*name*, *concept*, and *activity*—are divided by the five elements to create the 15 parts. These parts have their opposites which constitute the rising and setting of the moon, and they combine to create the 30 day month. The ideas of rising and setting are not themselves seen as *objects* although they can be seen mentally by correlating the succession of the states. In that sense, 'rising' and 'setting' are pure ideas, but the individual states such as full moon, half moon, and no moon, can be perceived sensually. Thus, day and night are mutual opposites, but nothing is *simultaneously* day and night. The existence of the day presupposes the existence of the night (rather than *logically* ruling it out) although when it is day, it could not be night. Thus, logical contradictions are resolved by inducting the concept of space and time within logic: the opposites are opposite locations seen at opposite times. As a result of this semantic structure, the world undergoes cyclic change.

The 16-fold division of the moon's state is a way of describing how the world is enjoyed, as opposed to the 12-fold division of the sun's state which denotes how the world is to be seen via the intellect. The perception through the intellect corresponds to the *chit* of the soul, and the perception through the ego corresponds to the *ānanda* of the soul and denotes how the world is amenable to enjoyment. These two descriptions are combined when a month is divided into 30 days, and a year is divided into 12 months. In this combination, we denote both the material objective existence, and its enjoyment by the soul. Therefore, these are not mutually exclusive constructs. Rather, time is divided into 360 days—each denoting a different phase of the sun and moon. It is notable here that in the Vedic system, the year doesn't have 365 days, even though the sun completes a revolution in 365 and 1/4th day. The calendar is constructed with each month having 30 days (unlike Gregorian calendars which have 28, 30, or 31 days), and the year having 12 months. Properly speaking, this is a lunar calendar because the months are 30 days. But it is also a solar calendar because we take into account 12 months. The notable feature is that the 12 months are multiples of the 30-day lunar month, which means that we first provide a definition of the month before defining the year, instead of first defining the year and then defining the month's duration (as is the case in the Gregorian calendars which are based on the sun's revolutions).

The combination of the sun and the moon creates interesting outcomes. As an example, in the context of wealth, if the pleasure given by the moon is weak, then even if one has a lot of wealth, one won't be able to enjoy that money or the things that one buys with it. A strong sun will make one wealthy, but a weak moon means that the money will be spent wastefully and although one has money, there is no happiness from owning it. Similarly, in a marriage, one may have a spouse, but a weak moon will mean there is no happiness through the spouse. A strong sun will prevent the occurrence of a divorce or separation, but a weak moon will prevent the enjoyment of marital pleasure. Perversion of the moon may mean that there are extra-marital affairs, or someone else's money is enjoyed by stealing or deception. Thus, the role of the sun and the moon remain distinct, but both play an important role in life.

The Five Divisions of the Moon

The material world is described as 24 elements in *Sāñkhya* philosophy, organized at 7 tiers. The first 4 tiers are morality, ego, intellect, and the mind, and the next 3 tiers are senses, sensations, and sense objects. Each of these tiers is divided by the three modes of nature—concepts, activity, and names—and each of the divisions is further divided by a five-fold distinction. The concepts in relation to the eye are color, form, and size. The process of measuring the world is the activity. Finally, the names in question are the objects, which become the *standards* of measurement. Everyone considers their senses the standard for how things have to be perceived; in other words, if I can't see it, it doesn't exist. Thus, every part of the 15-fold division has a further 3-fold division. In the context of the senses, these three divisions are the property being measured, the process by which is measured, and the standard of measurement. Philosophers of science have emphasized one of these three aspects of perception; thus the Realists claim that scientific concepts are real; the Operationalists insist that scientific concepts are nothing other than the process by which they are measured; and the Instrumentalists argue that scientific concepts are useful instruments of describing nature and scientific progress cannot be couched in terms of concepts and theories mirroring reality.

As the Greek philosopher Protagoras said with "Man is the measure of all things", there is an inherent ego in our senses by which they become the standard. In *Sāñkhya* philosophy, the senses are said to manifest from the ego, or the idea that I can measure the world because I am indeed the measure.

The same three-fold distinction exists at the level of sensations or *tanmātra*. For instance, in the measurement of length, the property 'length' is the concept; the process of measuring length is the activity; and the unit of length—e.g., a meter—is the name. Thus, measurement involves a concept (e.g., length), an activity (of measuring length), and the unit of measurement (e.g., meter). Similarly, the objects are divided into concepts or how they are known, activities or how they are used, and as things prior to being known and used. The process of knowing and using things modifies them because knowledge and activity involve transfer of energy or information. Therefore, the need to define the object as something prior to being known and used arises. The thing being known and used is the *name*. The knowing of the thing is the *concept* and the use is the *activity*. Alternately, we can say that in the process of creativity we conceive an idea—*concept*—then we employ a process—*activity*—in order to create a thing—*name*. Each of these is further divided into 5 parts.

In *Sāñkhya* this five-fold division is called Earth, Water, Fire, Air, and Ether. It a denotes hierarchical model because the Ether produces sound which can only be heard, Air produces touch which can both be heard and touched, Fire produces sight which can be seen, touched, and heard, Water produces taste which can be tasted, seen, touched, and heard, and finally, Earth produces smell which can be smelt, tasted, seen, touched, and heard. The question is: why do we have 5 knowledge senses? In principle, we could have 10 or 3 senses. What creates the 5 senses? The moon's five qualities are based on the fact that our pleasure is divided into five parts, which we saw previously manifests into five senses of knowledge, five senses of action, and five objects of these senses. When combined with duality, the five-fold division results in the 10 directions which are denoted by the 10 *Dikpāla* or the "guardians of the directions" as shown in Table-7. Half of these directions are opposites.

Name	Direction	Planet
Kubera	North	Mercury
Yama	South	Mars
Indra	East	Sun
Varuṇa	West	Saturn
Īśāna	Northeast	Jupiter
Agni	Southeast	Venus
Vāyu	Northwest	Moon
Nirṛti	Southwest	Rāhu
Brahmā	Zenith	Ketu
Viṣṇu	Nadir	Lagna

Table-7: The Ten Directions

The senses exist for pleasure. The five-fold division of the senses is an outcome of a five-fold division in desire; we could potentially live with fewer or greater number of senses, but we would have greater or lesser variety in pleasure. To understand the five-fold division, therefore, we have to describe the types of pleasure, and why there are only five such unique types.

The *yoga* philosophy describes the body at five levels. These are called *anna-maya*, *prāna-maya*, *mano-maya*, *vijñāna-maya*, and *ānanda-maya*. The *anna-maya* represents the existence of eating food, or the pleasure of the body built out of food; this pleasure is obtained by our external interactions with the world, such as eating, talking, sex, etc. The *prāna-maya* represents the pleasure of a healthy body. As we know, a healthy body creates happiness, and a sick body makes us unhappy; health is thus considered a basic wealth. This means that having the ability to enjoy is itself pleasurable, whether or not we actually use the body for enjoyment. The practice of *yoga*—at the most basic level—demands the control of eating, sleeping, sex, talking, etc. and accumulate the power of *prāna* that makes the body *capable*. The goal, of course, it to use the capacity for a higher purpose, and a side-effect of curtailing sense pleasure is that one obtains a higher form of pleasure—the healthy body. A healthy body leads to a healthy mind, and the third level is thus called *mano-maya* or the existence at the level of mind. We ordinarily call this happiness 'positive thinking' by which we become optimistic and enthusiastic. When the mind is surcharged with optimism, it can engage in constructive thoughts. But the mind is prone to fall into depression and unhappiness due to confusion. The *vijñāna-maya* level is that of realized knowledge that destroys all confusion. The mind becomes fixed when one knows the truth. However, the truth involves both an understating of the world, as well as the understanding of the self. If we only know the external world, but don't know who we are, we cannot be happy. The *ānanda-maya* level involves the understanding that happiness lies within; that the soul is the only creator of its own happiness and unhappiness. With that realization, the person becomes fully self-sufficient for her happiness.

Thus, we begin by seeking happiness from the outside through bodily interactions. Then we advance into the realization that I don't need the external world if only I have a healthy body. But a healthy body would not suffice unless we have a positive, optimistic, and constructive outlook toward our life. The change in thought patterns, and adopting a bright outlook is the next stage of obtaining happiness. Of course, why should one be optimistic rather than pessimistic? Isn't life an existence of struggle and pain, which makes us pessimistic? For the mind to be happy, one needs to know that the world is a fair place. Our positive thoughts are predicated on the understanding that our experience is not fundamentally an illusion, there is no evil genius controlling our minds, that there is integrity and honesty in nature, that one gets results in proportion to their efforts, and that the pursuit of happiness is a legitimate activity. Note that if you have seen the evils of this world, you may have many doubts. You might think that the world is not a fair place; that things happen randomly and not for a purpose, that you cannot explain why someone is rich and powerful while others are destitute and sick, and that you don't get the best results in spite of best efforts, which means effort doesn't determine outcomes.

If you have such doubts you cannot be happy. Your optimism about life would disappear, and a healthy body or worldly interactions won't make sense. Doubt is the nemesis of happiness, and one must have some 'faith' in the goodness of life in order to be happy. Doubt destroys this faith, and knowledge restores it. In that sense, realized knowledge that destroys the doubts and uncertainty about the true nature of the world—and restores the faith in its inherent goodness—is the next form of happiness. If you have faith in the natural justice, you will be satisfied and content in the knowledge that you have done the right thing, that even if you haven't obtained the best results at the moment, there is natural justice due to which your efforts are not in vain. The *vijñāna-maya* pleasure constitutes the happiness of having faith in the goodness of life, based on which the mind has optimism, the body has health, and the worldly interactions can then be employed for enjoyment.

Now, even if you have faith in the goodness of life, you might still commit mistakes inadvertently. Similarly, due to *karma* one has to bear the consequences of past actions. Even though you may have faith in the goodness of life, life may not seem all that good at the moment. How do you deal with the fact that you desire something for your happiness, but you are unable to obtain it? Ultimately happiness depends on what we desire. Realizing that we are the creators of this desire, and our happiness is fully in our control if we can control the desires, is the pinnacle of realizing the nature of the self. Thus, we may not be in control of the situations; we may not have a healthy body; the mind may be sick, and remembrance of knowledge may wax and wane; but the advanced *yogi* is able to remain happy by controlling his desires.

The soul is by itself full of happiness, and it wants to expand this happiness through the successive levels, thus creating the five levels of existence. The soul becomes unhappy in this world if he forgets that happiness and distress are the creations of the soul; he starts thinking that happiness depends on others—the material situations, the body, the mind, faith in the goodness of life, etc. When these things fail, one's faith is shattered, the mind is depressed, the body is unhealthy, and our external interactions are not successful, then one is compelled to take shelter in the fact that we still have complete control over our desires. Thus, the realization that one is happy by himself is far higher than obtaining happiness through worldly relations, by having a healthy body, positive thoughts in the mind, and even the happiness of realizing the truth. In a simple sense, all mystic traditions teach us that happiness is within, not without. Accordingly, the quest for happiness must be accompanied by gradual withdrawal from external engagements to the body, from the body to thoughts, from thoughts to truth, and from truth to the eternal nature of the self.

We can also think of these as the five ways in which we seek happiness—from the external world, from our body, from our thoughts and feelings, from our understanding of reality, and from the innate nature of the self. These five levels are hierarchical in the sense that the deeper levels of pleasure precede the grosser levels, and we can discard the gross level, but the deeper level will still be present. Indeed, we realize the existence of the deeper levels when we defocus from the grosser levels. This five-fold division, as we saw above, divides the three modes of nature—name, concept, and activity—which means that each of these three produces five kinds of concepts, activities, and names. That five-fold division is then known as the five senses of knowledge, five senses of action, and five kinds of objects. The hierarchy ends with five levels because the fifth level involves the interaction with other things, and the soul—which began with the self—has now reached out into the other.

This five-fold division of pleasure is described in the *Bhagavad-Gita* and it contrasts to the seven-fold division of experience noted above. In the five-fold division, the five parts are: objects, senses, mind, intellect, and the soul, which leaves out two elements in *Sāñkhya*, namely, the ego and morality. That this division denotes the division of pleasure is evident from the context where *Kṛṣṇa* describes the nature of lust prior to illustrating its five-fold division. Below is the succession of verses that demonstrate the context.

> *BG 3.38*[9]*: As fire is covered by smoke, as a mirror is covered by dust, or as the embryo is covered by the womb, similarly, the living entity is covered by different degrees of this lust.*

> *BG 3.39: Thus, a man's pure consciousness is covered by his eternal enemy in the form of lust, which is never satisfied and which burns like fire.*

> *BG 3.40: The senses, the mind and the intelligence are the sitting places of this lust, which veils the real knowledge of the living entity and bewilders him.*

> *BG 3.41: Therefore, O Arjuna, best of the Bharatas, in the very beginning curb this great symbol of sin [lust] by regulating the senses, and slay this destroyer of knowledge and self-realization.*

> *BG 3.42: The working senses are superior to dull matter; mind is higher than the senses; intelligence is still higher than the mind; and he [the soul] is even higher than the intelligence.*

> *BG 3.43: Thus knowing oneself to be transcendental to material senses, mind and intelligence, one should control the lower self by the higher self and thus—by spiritual strength—conquer this insatiable enemy known as lust.*

The verse of interest to us here is BG 3.42 which notes the five-fold distinction—presented hierarchically—between objects, senses, mind, intellect, and the soul. However, that this description pertains to pleasure or "lust" is evidenced from the preceding and following verses. This description corresponds to the five-fold division called *anna-maya*, *prāna-maya*, *mano-maya*, *vijñāna-maya*, and *ānanda-maya* which are successive levels of pleasure. While the senses are not directly equated to *prāna* in all cases, in this context, the term 'working senses' is employed to indicate that the pleasure is derived from the functioning of the senses rather than sense contact with the objects. There is hence a pleasure obtained when the senses contact 'dull matter' and then there is pleasure just because the body is healthy and functional.

This five-fold division represents a typology of pleasure; we might say that there are five unique types of pleasure, which are experienced as body, senses, mind, intellect, and the soul. However, since the *ānanda* of the soul is organized like a tree, the same types manifest at different levels again and again, and they are then used to divide the tree of pleasure over and over, creating the holographic nature of pleasure in which there are gross forms of pleasure that follow the subtle pleasures, and the same type division can be reemployed to further divide the pleasure of objects, the senses of knowledge, and the senses of action into five parts. The 15 parts of the moon are therefore not literally representative of the 5 elements, 5 senses of knowledge, and 5 senses of actions. They are rather indicative of a typology in which five types of pleasure are divided by three modes of nature—concepts, activities, and objects—and these 15 parts then have their opposites to create the 30 phases of the moon in which the moon waxes for 15 days and wanes for 15 days.

	Pleasure	Guna	Parity	
1	Objects	Concept	Waxing	
2	Objects	Activity	Waxing	
3	Objects	Object	Waxing	
4	Senses	Concept	Waxing	
5	Senses	Activity	Waxing	
6	Senses	Object	Waxing	
7	Mind	Concept	Waxing	
8	Mind	Activity	Waxing	
9	Mind	Object	Waxing	
10	Intellect	Concept	Waxing	
11	Intellect	Activity	Waxing	
12	Intellect	Object	Waxing	
13	Soul	Concept	Waxing	
14	Soul	Activity	Waxing	
15	Soul	Object	Waxing	Full Moon
16	Soul	Concept	Waning	
17	Soul	Activity	Waning	
18	Soul	Object	Waning	
19	Intellect	Concept	Waning	
20	Intellect	Activity	Waning	
21	Intellect	Object	Waning	
22	Mind	Concept	Waning	
23	Mind	Activity	Waning	
24	Mind	Object	Waning	
25	Senses	Concept	Waning	
26	Senses	Activity	Waning	
27	Senses	Object	Waning	
28	Objects	Concept	Waning	
29	Objects	Activity	Waning	
30	Objects	Object	Waning	No Moon

Table-8: The Thirty Days of a Lunar Month

Each day of the moon, therefore, is not the same as any other day. Instead, each day represents a unique type of meaning, and the meanings repeat after 30 days. This repetition can be seen if we loop from day 30 to day 1. The nature of the cycle is such that the *waxing* path represents the journey from objects to the senses to the mind to the intellect to the soul, and the *waning* path involves going from the soul, to the intellect, to the mind, to the senses, to the objects. In other words, we can call the waxing path *ascending* (because it goes from gross to subtle) and the waning path *descending* (because it goes from subtle to gross). The lunar cycle is a complete round of ascent and descent.

The Significance of Moon Worship

The moon represents desire, and in the material world, this desire is created by *Shiva* and His *Śakti*. We have seen how the moon has 16 parts, but only 15 are visible. In other *Tantra* scriptures, the same 16 parts are described but now each phase of the moon is also associated with 16 different forms of *Śakti*. Out of these, *Mahā Tripura Sundarī* is called *Para Śakti*, and hence the phase ruled by her is not visible to normal mortals. It is said that on the full moon day all the 15 *Śakti* are in the moon; on each successive day after the full moon day, one *Śakti* leaves the moon and goes to the sun and the moon is reduced slightly in size, until the no moon day (the 15th day). The full moon day is called *Pūrnima* and the no moon day is called *Amāvasya*. Then after *Amāvasya* the *Śakti* return to the moon one by one until the full moon or *Pūrnima*.

	Moon Phase Name	Śakti Devi Name
1	Amrita	Mahā Tripura Sundari
2	Manada	Kameswari
3	Poosha	Bhagamalini
4	Tusthi	Nityaklinna
5	Pusthi	Bherunda
6	Rati	Vanhivasini
7	Dhruti	Maha Vajreswari
8	Sasichini	Shivadooti (Roudri)
9	Chandrika	Twarita
10	Kanta	Kulasundari

11	Jyostna	Nitya
12	Shree	Neelapataka
13	Preeti	Vijaya
14	Angada	Sarvamangala
15	Poorna	Jwalamalini
16	Poornamruta	Chidroopa (Chitra)

Table-9: The Sixteen Divisions of Material Desire

Material desire has three aspects. First, desire entails *aggression*, the need to dominate, win, conquer, and control. Second, with aggression comes the *fear* of being unsuccessful; anxiety and insecurity result from that. Third, there is often *frustration* associated with most material desires because they may have been unfulfilled and when a person is frustrated, he or she is likely to become passive or depressed. Since most desires are unfulfilled, a person goes through a cycle of aggression, fear, and frustration. These feed on each other. For example, fear leads to aggression and frustration, and when a person is fearful, they are prone to oscillate between being aggressive and passive. But, of course, if you become passive then others will be even more aggressive with you, and that incites more fear and aggression. In this way, to understand material desire, we have to disentangle it into aggression, fear, and frustration. The rise and fall of the moon represent this cycle of desire in which one first starts aggressively, then realizes that aggression is not working and fears the outcomes, and finally if the desire is unfulfilled the result is depression.

We might note that people seek happiness even in frustration, when they wallow in self-pity. Playing the victim of circumstances, shifting the blame onto something other than our desire, and rationalizing the frustration is a very important feature of material desire due to which the soul remains stuck to the material world. If one stops playing the victim, and ends the rationalization of frustration, he or she will quickly realize the futility of material desires because these always begin in aggression, but the aggression of others causes fear in us, and when we succumb to our fears we descend into victimhood.

There is hence a *Śakti* of *Shiva* that creates aggression and desire within us; She is called *Sati*, and by Her influence we feel powerful, and capable of conquering the world; She constitutes what we generally call self-confidence in our ability to fulfill our desires; She gives us hope, courage, and optimism in life. Another *Śakti* creates fear in us; She is called *Durga* and by Her influence we become afraid and strike fear in others. Fear has an important function too—it acts as a counterbalance to unbridled optimism; as the saying goes: "fools rush in where angels fear to tread", fear forces us to reexamine our assumptions and plans rather than simply rely on our self-confidence. Finally, another *Śakti* creates the power of rationalizing the frustration and telling ourselves that we are correct in our approach and the problem lies with someone else; She is called *Kāli*. If this rationalizing energy goes missing, then one falls into depression and starts blaming oneself for every kind of problem. Guilt overtakes the person, and because of the guilt they are paralyzed. However, if this energy is very strong, then one rationalizes every kind of problem into someone else's fault and refuses to take any type of responsibility. Such a person becomes inert and blames 'fate' and 'destiny' for their suffering.

These three energies—optimism, fear, and inertia—are also sometimes compared to the three modes of nature: *sattva*, *rajas*, and *tamas*. The decline in the phases of the moon represents the path from optimism where one acts constructively, to fear where one is paralyzed by overanalyzing, to resignation where one can only blame someone else for their fate. Similarly, the ascent in the moon's phases represents the path from resignation to fear to optimism. If one is suffering from depression, they are even unable to rationalize and blame others; they simply blame themselves, and such people cannot be lifted by giving them more analysis and fear of what might happen if they don't act. They have to be lifted first by helping them rationalize their problem to their bad circumstances—which we generally call 'empathizing' and 'listening'. By helping them rationalize their suffering, at least they get the ability to stand up and find a new situation which might be better than the previous ones. Once they are thus active, some level of fear will further propel them to planning. And if this planning—under the influence of fear—has been done properly, then the person automatically gains confidence in their ability because they think that they have devised a fool-proof plan that caters to all eventualities.

The divisions of the moon therefore are not arbitrarily chosen. Rather the cycle of the moon represents the cycle of emotions experienced by a person in their life. Understanding this cycle only means realizing that every person who is optimistic today will be fearful tomorrow and blaming their fate later on. Similarly, everyone who is blaming their fate today will eventually get the energy to put together a plan and execute it fervently, and successes in that plan will then make them self-confident—sometimes even feel invincible. Thus every proud person is made to lick the dust, and everyone down in the dust receives the energy to work hard and then become confident again. If their confidence becomes overconfidence, they will be licking dust again.

The ideal state of a person is to remain confident—without fear and needless rationalization of one's problems to their fate—but also without overconfidence in their own ability as the sole cause of their happiness. In that sense, one 'surrenders' to *Sati* to ask Her for confidence but realizes that this confidence is a power given to a person by the grace of *Sati*. It is not their own power, and if one's power is lost, then many desires—e.g., for eating, sleeping, sex, etc.—naturally disappear. A depressed person thus loses weight because he stops eating, their drive for sexual enjoyment disappears, and they are unable to sleep, fundamentally because the confidence in the self is gone. By the grace of *Sati* one can get the requisite confidence and lead a happy life, provided he doesn't fall prey to unnecessary pride. Similarly, by praying to *Durga* one obtains the power to deal with their fear, which means that fear is used constructively to propel systematic planning and organization. If one is able to put their fear to constructive use through hard work, planning, and execution of their plans, then their ability to handle fear itself strikes dread in the hearts of those who are unable to use their fear for such constructive purposes. This power is generally employed in battlefields to make the enemy fearful because superior preparation and planning naturally makes the opposition fearful. Finally, surrender to *Kāli* gives one the brute-force stamina to tolerate and suffer one adverse situation after another, without becoming dejected.

Fear plays a very important role in our lives because it forces us to conjure 'what if' scenarios by which we can plan and execute our work carefully and avoid future potential problems. But if one is overwhelmed by fear then the need to be careful in order to avoid potential problems paralyzes the person into not taking any risk and most of the time is spent in fearing fear itself. Similarly, resistance and stamina to face existing problems is also important because through the ability to suffer pain and anguish one crosses over the troublesome situations. However, if one becomes too thick-skinned in dealing with such problems then he is resigned into thinking that he will just tolerate whatever happens and not try to improve the situation to avoid such problems. Finally, optimism is essential to have a constructive approach to life and believe that things will work out okay in the end. But if one is overly optimistic, he doesn't plan for the eventualities and when they happen isn't prepared to face the adverse situations. Thus, fear, resistance, and optimism are not adequate on their own; they have a value, but they are incomplete by themselves. As a result, there are multiple deities ruling over different emotions.

Note that we are only talking about our emotional state at the moment. Having the optimism doesn't actually mean the results will conform to our positive thinking. Those positive results are governed by *Viṣṇu*—the owner of the material energy—and *Lakshmi* Who provides the boons for such success. However, optimism is an essential state to even enjoy such boons because even if one has adequate wealth, power, fame, knowledge, beauty, etc. one may still be afflicted by a negative thought process. Indeed, depression doesn't uniquely affect the poor and weak; it equally well affects the rich and powerful. In that sense, the deities governing our emotional state are different from those that govern the material body, health, wealth, beauty, power, fame, etc.

The sun represents the cycle of material and cognitive well-being and the moon denotes the cycle of emotions and happiness. They are complementary because one might be rich and depressed or poor and happy. Those suffering from emotional health issues, lack of optimism and confidence, lack the ability to tolerate some anxiety to endeavor hard, or feel helpless and weak against the onslaught of difficult situations can thus worship *Shiva*, and He then provides the emotional strength to conquer such adversities. Those, on the other hand, who are emotionally confident, healthy, and forbearing, but desire the material wealth, power, fame, knowledge, beauty, and detachment to enjoy the world compatible with their emotional health worship *Viṣṇu*. When the separation between cognition and emotion is understood, then the difference between the sun and the moon is also grasped, and then their successive subdivisions which identify different emotional and cognitive states are realized. Their reality doesn't depend on seeing them face to face. We can also understand their reality simply by analyzing our conscious experiences.

The Role of Sidereal Motion

One difference between Vedic and modern astronomy is that modern astronomy considers the stars in the sky to be stationary while the sun, the moon, and the earth are considered moving. In Vedic astronomy, the earth is stationary, the sun and the moon are moving, but the system of stars moves the fastest. This system of stars 'drags' the sun, which in turn 'drags' the moon. Thus, there are three moving things in Vedic astronomy—the system of stars or *Nakṣatra*, the sun, and the moon, while the earth is stationary. A single rotation of the zodiac constitutes a *Nakṣatra Ahorātra* or a *sidereal day*. It is the time in which the stars regain the original position in relation to the earth, which means that the stars cover a full revolution within a single day. Thus, one full revolution of the sun is one solar *year*, one full revolution of the moon is a lunar *month*, and one full revolution of the stars is a sidereal *day*. 30 sidereal days make a sidereal month, and 12 sidereal months make a sidereal year. The sidereal year is therefore different from solar and lunar years.

The zodiac moves in the clockwise direction, while the sun moves in the counterclockwise direction. The zodiac 'drags' the sun in the clockwise direction, and therefore we observe the relative motion of the sun in relation to the zodiac. The sun appears to move clockwise (due to the motion of the zodiac), although the sun is moving counterclockwise in an absolute sense.

The *Surya Siddhānta* states that the system of stars goes around *Meru* 1,582,237,828 times in the period of a *chaturyugi*, i.e., 4,320,000 *solar* years. Hence, the zodiac does 1,582,237,828 / 4,320,000 = 366.2587565 revolutions in a year. Meanwhile, the sun moves in the opposite direction, although much more slowly, covering the 12 signs of the zodiac. A solar year is that time which the sun takes to cover all the 12 parts of the zodiac moving counterclockwise. The star signs perform 366.258 rotations in a year, and the sun performs 365.258 rotations; the resulting gap of one rotation corresponds to the sun's revolution through the zodiac denoting the duration of a year. Thus, the zodiac goes clockwise creating 366.258 sidereal days in a solar year, and the sun goes counterclockwise, passing through the 12 signs of the zodiac in 365.258 solar days. In a *chaturyugi* the zodiac will do 1,582,237,828 rotations while the sun will do 1,577,917,828 rotations, creating a difference of 4,320,000 rotations. This *difference* between the rotations is used for various kinds of solar times.

The *Surya Siddhānta* also describes the motion of the moon, which goes counterclockwise 57,753,336 times in 4,320,000 solar years. However, the *Surya Siddhānta* describes an interesting fact, that to find the number of lunar months, we must *subtract* the number of the sun's rotations from the number of the moon's rotations. This is interesting because it implies that just as the sun is dragged clockwise by the rotation of the zodiac, the moon is dragged by the counterclockwise motion of the sun. The relative rotation of the moon is only that which is in addition to the motion caused by the sun's rotation. If the sun is an ant on the potter's wheel of the zodiac, then the moon is another ant sitting on a secondary potter's wheel created by the sun's motion.

Thus, if the moon rotates 57,753,336 times in 4,320,000 years while the sun rotates 4,320,000 times in the same duration, then the real rotation attributable to the moon must be 57,753,336 - 4,320,000 = 53,433,336 rotations. This number is called *adhimāsa* or "additive month", which implies: (a) the real lunar motion is in *addition* to the solar motion, and (b) their difference is viewed as a *lunar month* (rather than a year, as was the case for the sun's additional motion in relation to the zodiac). To get the total number of days for the above lunar month, we just multiply the months by 30 days.

1,582,237,828 – 4,320,000 = 1,577,917,828 solar days
53,433,336 x 30 = 1,603,000,080 lunar days

Thus, a solar year has 365.258 days, and the lunar year has 12 * 30 = 360 days. These are based on the *relative motion* of the sun and the moon, obtained by subtracting the zodiac rotations from the sun's rotations, and subtracting the sun's rotations from the moon's rotations. Thus, the sidereal year is more fundamental than the solar year, and the solar year is more fundamental than the lunar year. Nevertheless, if you just take into account the lunar year, you have also incorporated the motion of the sun and the zodiac because the lunar rotations are obtained by subtracting the solar and the zodiac rotations. Thus, in one sense there are three types of years—solar, lunar, and sidereal—and in another sense the lunar year is more fundamental because it includes solar and zodiac motions. Hence, the lunar year is widely used in Vedic culture.

The sidereal year has traditionally been the basis of seasonal calendars. The rotation of the zodiac is a *sidereal day* and if a day is 24 hours, then the sidereal day is 24 * 60 / 366.25 = 3.93 solar minutes shorter than the solar day. In modern astronomy, this day is attributed to the earth's rotation about its axis, while in Vedic cosmology the same day is attributed to the motion of the zodiac. From an observational standpoint the two are identical, but the cosmological models underlying the two systems are radically different. In modern astronomy, a sidereal day is defined as the earth's rate of rotation relative to the fixed stars—assuming that the stars are fixed, and the earth is rotating. The sidereal day gains 3.93 solar minutes in every 24-hour solar duration, until the gain adds up to a full additional sidereal day in any given solar year.

As we have seen earlier, the zodiac is not a flat plane, but is twisted twice leading to the hierarchy from East -> North -> South -> West. This twisting of the star system corresponds to the tilted axis of the earth's rotation in modern astronomy. Similarly, the sun's orbit is not flat, and the sun rises and falls in its orbit. Now comes the interesting question on the *cause* of this tilt. Since the sun is described as an ant moving on the potter's wheel, it is impractical to suppose that the sun causes the potter's wheel to tilt. Furthermore, if we attributed the cause of the tilt to be the sun, then the potter's wheel would tilt in the direction that the sun was currently situated, and that would contradict the precession of the equinoxes. Therefore, the tilt is attributed to the zodiac itself.

We can say that the potter's wheel is a bit wobbly. It rotates very fast (once per day), but once per solar year it also does a slower up and down motion, which causes the sun to go up and down along with the zodiac. The cause of the wobble lies is the stars themselves, but it appears that the sun is coming closer or going farther. This wobble in the zodiac creates the seasonal changes on earth, which modern astronomy attributes to the rotation and revolution of the earth, with the earth's axis wobbling—i.e., the precession of the axes. Thus, the earth's northern hemisphere comes closer to the sun during 'summer' in the northern hemisphere, although it is the 'winter' in the southern hemisphere. This change is called *Dakshināyana*, when the sun lowers its orbit. Conversely, the rise in orbit is called *Uttarāyaṇa*. Unlike modern astronomy where the seasonal change is due to the earth's motion, the same change is attributed in Vedic cosmology to zodiac wobbling, as the earth is stationary.

As a result, the true cause of the seasonal changes is the zodiac, and hence the sidereal calendar is associated with seasonal change, which dramatically affects human life: different kinds of fruits and vegetables are eaten in different seasons, the clothing changes with seasons, and different kinds of activities are performed in different seasons—e.g., sowing vs. harvesting, traveling vs. resting, building vs. preserving. We might not realize this effect in modern times as much, due to industrialized life, but all things that depend on nature—e.g., growing crops, flowers, and fruits, or even when to wage a war and when to rest in peace—still depend heavily on the seasons. Vedic cosmology identifies 6 seasons in a year, each lasting a period of two months.

Four Types of Relationships

We noted previously that the material world is described in *Sāñkhya* at 7 levels—morality, ego, intellect, mind, senses, sensations, and objects. *Prakriti* divides them by 3, *māyā* divides them by 2, the qualities of knowledge, beauty, power, wealth, fame, and detachment divide them by 6, and our desires divide them by 5. Each of the 7 levels constitutes a sense and an object, which are then bound into a relation—according to *Sāñkhya*, by a higher deity. The object is called *ādibhautika*, the sense is called *ādiatmika*, and the higher deity is called *ādidaivika*. In essence, an 'agent' brings two things together into an interaction, and that interaction is therefore called their 'relationship' denoted by *sat*. The *sat* of the soul is sometimes called 'consciousness' or 'awareness' because it is the power by which the soul connects to the self and to others. To study the *sat*, we have to know two things— (1) the different levels at which we can relate to other things, and (2) the different ways in which we can relate to them. Of these, the former (i.e., the levels) is said to be 7 as they are tiers of material organization from deep and abstract to gross and detailed. I will devote this section to the discussion of the latter—the different ways to relate.

Relationships are conceived very formally in mathematics—especially in set theory. But the mathematical conception does not give these relations a meaning. I will therefore use a different approach of describing the same relationship types through an intuitive medium of man-woman relations. Once we grasp the differences between these types, I will return to describing how these ideas about relationships have been formalized in set theory.

The best relationship is one of *mutuality* in which two partners care about each other's well-being. They are genuinely attracted to each other, and that attraction is based on their complementary personalities which make them mutually compatible. Through this complementarity, the two partners complete each other—i.e., they cover each other's flaws, and they don't compete on their respective strengths. Due to this complementarity they find strength in each other because the other person overcomes the flaws of the self. Their primary commitment is to each other, and everything else takes a back seat. That means that they prioritize each other's happiness over the other relationships. As a result, their bonds to others are weakened, as they spend most of their time and attention on each other, and the weakening of bonds to others further strengthens their mutual bond. Thus, in a relation of mutuality, the bond between the partners strengthens continually over time, while other relationships tend to weaken. Ultimately, they have each other for support, but if one partner dies or leaves, the other is left exceptionally lonely because of the enormous amount of commitment that was built between the two of them.

The next best relationship is one of *asymmetry*. Two individuals are attracted to each other due to some complementary qualities in them, but there are also areas of difference. The differences can arise because one person is not as committed to the relationship as the other, because he or she has other commitments and responsibilities and is compelled to share his time in many relationships. For example, a person may stay away from the partner due to long hours at work, have an extended family that demands their time, or may be involved in social and political commitments that take time away from their partner. As one partner craves for another's time and attention, an asymmetry in the relation is created due to the imbalance in the respective desires for each other. One symptom of the asymmetry is that the partner who feels isolated begins to lose interest in their shared life and starts neglecting their duties. The busy partner is then overburdened with responsibilities and finds even lesser time and opportunity to fix the imbalance that led to the conflicts. A possible path to reconciliation in such cases is for the isolated partner to accept that their commitment to the partner doesn't have to be reciprocated. In most cases, the asymmetry results in the breakdown of the relationship.

The third best relationship is *social.* When one partner gets busy in other relationships, the isolated partner also seeks other relationships. A stay-at-home mom may, for example, go out for work, or socialize more with friends. That external engagement relieves the unhappiness of being isolated, and the balance in the relationship is restored because each partner has reduced their mutual commitment in exchange for multiple relationships. In fact, if the two people have active social lives, their friends help them keep the relationship together. They might have children who keep them bonded because separation would mean pain for themselves and the children. Their parents might be mutually friendly, and they could pressure the couple into staying together. In short, they stay together not because of intense commitment to each other but because other people or things keep them together. They reconcile to the fact that their happiness lies in diversifying their relationship options. They give priority to things other than their mutual relationship—children, parents, friends, social life, etc.—and while the relationship itself is not particularly exciting, the prospect of separation seems overwhelmingly painful.

The fourth relationship is *opportunistic.* The parties involved enjoy certain things about each other but don't have the commitment to deal with the problems of the other person. Thus, as one person goes through a difficult patch in life, the other wants to focus on their own happiness, rather than helping their partner overcome the problems. The partner interested in their happiness avoids discussing the problems in their partner's life, shuts down their complaints, and tells them to become more positive and lift themselves. This isolates the other person who was wanted when they had something to give, but unwanted when they have something to take. The opportunistic partner avoids difficult situations and seeks solace in others. And the isolated partner is driven out of that relationship into the arms of another person. Such relationships are short-lived because they are not about commitment; they are rather business arrangements that work so long as they are profitable.

The relationship types are ideal and natural for different kinds of material roles. The relationship between loving couples is ideally one of mutuality. Their intimacy requires that they avoid conflicts, because marital conflicts hurt the deepest. The asymmetric relationship is well-suited for a child who is in demand from parents, grandparents, relatives, and sometimes even friends of their parents. The parents don't resent when their child gets attention from grandparents, their relatives, or their friends. And the child loves to receive gifts, affection, and friends from many individuals. Thus, the child receiving attention from many individuals divides his or her attention among them, and there is no resentment from either party. We might also note that the child is in control of the relationship because the child makes the demands and the parents fulfill them. Even though the parents seem to be the elders and hence more powerful than the child, in the relationship they serve the child.

The relationship between friends is a social relationship; they have other friends and each person relates to many other individuals without an exclusive commitment to any single person. Thus, a friend is not offended if some friend is spending more time with one person as opposed to them; they find other friends to spend time with. Finally, the master-servant relationship is ideally opportunistic; the master employs a servant to complete a job, and the servant is employed by the master who offers the best compensation. We call this 'equal opportunity employment' which means that the employer and the employee are free to leave each other's association without a grudge. Furthermore, the employment is offered by the employer and cannot be demanded by the employee. In that sense, the employer is in greater control.

The above description hopefully helps us see the different types of relationships, and how they manifest through different social roles. With this background, we can now look at the same ideas in the context of set theory.

- The mutuality relation is one-to-one
- The asymmetric relation is many-to-one
- The social relation is many-to-many
- The opportunistic relation is one-to-many

Man-Woman Relation	Family Relation	Set Theory Relation
Mutual	Husband-Wife	One-to-One
Asymmetric	Child-Parent	Many-to-One
Social	Friend-Friend	Many-to-Many
Opportunistic	Master-Servant	One-to-Many

Table-10: Four Types of Relationships

In the context of a man-woman relationship, the mutuality relation of one-to-one is the best, and all other types of relations become problematic. However, the parent-child relationship is best if there are many elders to take care of the child; the parents love the fact that the children are spending time with grandparents or their relatives, and sometimes they employ nurses and babysitters to take care of their children. The fact that a child has many 'parents' doesn't make the parents unhappy; in fact, parents are delighted by the fact that their child is loved by others. The children, however, desire an exclusive attention and resent the siblings dividing the attention of their parents. Therefore, the parent-child relation is ideally many-to-one. The many-to-many relationship weakens the marital tie, and makes the child jealous, but it is the ideal form of friendship in which each friend divides their time with many friends without resentment. A boss would not like their employee working for many bosses, although the boss is likely to employ many employees. The employees don't consider themselves bound to a particular boss, just as the boss reserves the right to replace one employee with another. Thus, both parties are satisfied if they focus on their needs over the needs of others.

We might emphasize that the above examples help us identify *types* through mutual contrast, but once we know these types, we can recall that relations are hierarchical, and the same types can be reused over and over. For instance, a man and a woman may have a dominantly mutual relation but also a subordinate social relation. That would mean that they spend time with family and friends, but even in such crowded places they remain attached to each other far more than they associate with the family and friends. If this dominant subordinate order is inverted, then the primary relation would be social and the secondary relation would be mutual, which means they will consider each other primarily friends and secondarily husband and wife; they might discuss their problems like friends, but they will not own the burden of solving them for the other person. Thus, one person's problems aren't owned by their partner, because the dominant relation is social rather than mutuality.

Through the above analysis we can also see that no type is ideal for all cases. But we can also see that each type is ideally suited for some relation. This background is important to understand two important facts. First, Vedic philosophy describes relations between the soul and God in the above four forms—conjugal, parental, friendly, and service—but they are described as the *ideal* forms of relationship. The soul becomes happy in relation to God because he is situated in the ideal relation. Second, the relations in the material world are not ideal, which makes us unhappy, but there is still a need to model the relationship in objective terms if only to understand why the relation doesn't work. For instance, one partner in a marriage may act like a child, a friend, or a boss, when the relation is supposedly one of mutuality. Similarly, a boss might act like a lover, friend, or child, instead of being the boss. If we understand the relationship types and the ideal form of the relation, then we can not only form a logical theory of relations but also diagnose their problems.

Material relationships are not ideal because we seek to fulfill the shortcomings of one relation through another. For example, if a person is unable to fulfill his or her need to be a boss at the workplace, they try to be boss at home or in their relationship to friends. Similarly, a person who became accustomed to being a child, or had an unfulfilling childhood, tries to play a child—seeking the unmitigated attention and adoration of the others—even in relation to friends. A person with unrequited love in married life seeks mutuality at work or with friends. And one dissatisfied with their friendships wants to become a friend—quite like many other friends—with their spouse in married life. Thus, some married couples seek a relationship of equality and friendship—asking each other to give them 'space' and 'time'—even in a marital life, while others expect their spouse to become their guardian and caretaker even as adults. Once we understand the different types of relationships, and their ideal use—i.e., where they are best suited—we can analyze the flaws in relationships arising from trying to overcome the dissatisfaction of one unfulfilled relationship through another unfit for it, and thereby failing even in that attempt.

The soul needs to be satisfied in each type of relationship. Thus, he needs to be a lover, a child, a parent, a friend, a master, and a servant. No relationship is complete, but one may have preference of one over another, depending on their natural proclivities or based on what remains unfulfilled. Thus, as a child grows up, and has led a fulfilling childhood, he loses the desire to be a child again. He now wants to be a parent, a lover, and a servant. Over time, as his children grow up—and he has been a good parent—he loses the desire to be a parent. Similarly, if one has been a good servant, he loses the desire for servitude, and wants to be a master. Over time, if one has been a good master, he loses that desire too. Likewise, if one has been a good faithful lover, or a faithful and genuine friend, and has received adequate reciprocation in those relationships, the need for that relationship reduces or goes away. A satisfying life of relationships thus prepares one for detachment from the material world. Conversely, dissatisfying relations compel one to desire their fulfillment.

Of course, dissatisfying relations can also help one transcend the material relationship desires, especially if one realizes that the material relationships can never be completely satisfying, and there is no end to trying to fulfill one dissatisfying relation through another dissatisfying relationship. Thus, the Vedic texts also describe how the relationships become perfectly satisfying in relation to God. The study of these relationships, and their ideal place, and how a person seeks multiple kinds of relations in their life, and how one relationship is destroyed by the attempt to fulfill another relationship is the vista to a general theory of how relationships are created, destroyed, or mended.

The Twenty-Eight Star Signs

Brahma is the definer of *dharma* in the material world and he has four heads. To perform *dharma,* one must know the duty, and the duty is defined by the relationship. The four heads of *Brahma* correspond to four kinds of relationships, and each relationship then defines a unique type of duty and *dharma.* Each of these relationships can be enacted at 7 levels of matter, which means that each person has 28 duties corresponding to the four kinds of relations and 7 levels of matter. For instance, a husband and a wife are connected to each other not just at the level of the body, but also at the level of sensations, senses, mind, intellect, ego, and morality, and therefore have a duty to each other at each of these levels. A couple may have a sexual relationship of mutuality at the level of the body, a friendly relation at the level of the mind, a parent-child relation at the level of the ego, and a master-servant relation at the level of morality. This would mean that one partner subordinates their moral values to those of the other, one person has desires like that of a child while the other nurtures like a parent, they exchange ideas at the level of mind like friends, and they enjoy conjugal relationship at the level of the body.

In such a case, to check the compatibility between a man and woman, we cannot assume a relation of mutuality at all the material levels. Compatibility would be determined by considering all the levels of each person, and conflicts can arise at each level. Deeper levels of incompatibility will naturally produce greater adverse consequences even if the superficial levels are compatible. For example, a man and a woman may be sexually compatible but morally incompatible. Their sexual happiness will not easily overcome grave moral differences. Conversely, if there is deep moral compatibility, then even incompatibility in their mutual sexual union would not create grave problems. There is hence an objective method of evaluating compatibility issues.

We are now in a position to discuss the 7 main stars, and their four-fold division by the above types of relations to create 28-star signs, which are called *Nakṣatra* in Vedic cosmology. The 7 stars correspond to the *dharma* at the 7 levels of matter, and the four-fold division corresponds to four types of relations. There is hence an ideal duty at the level of body, sensation, senses, mind, intellect, ego, and morality in each of the four relations—friendly, parent-child, master-servant, and husband-wife—leading to 28 ideal forms of duty. Of course, these ideal duties may not always be ideally placed in the world. For instance, a husband might behave like a child in relation to his wife, or a child might act like a friend to her parents. Therefore, it is not enough to just understand the 28 types of duties, but also their ideal application in the world.

The duties to be performed at 7 levels of matter are represented by the 7 prominent stars, which are also called the *manas-putra* or "mental sons" of *Brahma*, who enunciates the *dharma* for this world. This means that *Brahma* first defines the duty of the four ideal relationships, and then delegates the definition of duty at each of the 7 levels of matter to his "mental sons". Each person is in many relationships with regard to different people. For instance, each person typically has a parent and some children, they have friends, they are masters of some and servants of others, they may be conjugally related to a spouse, etc. Thus, each person has 28 types of duties. At different times, some duty might take precedence over the others, which means prioritizing the duties is also a duty. Indeed, prioritization of duties is the primary duty after which the duty performance comes into play. This prioritization is the choice of the soul, who is transcendent to the 7 levels of matter; we can call this the primary duty, not to others, but to oneself in the relationship to the self. As a result, there is also the pole star—sometimes called *Dhruva*—which is sometimes counted as one of the sons of *Brahma* who are together called the 8 *Vasu*. At other times, the pole star is kept aside from this description and only 7 stars are counted. Once we understand their meanings, we can see why both are true.

Manu	Saptarishis						
Swayambhu	Mariche	Atri	Angiras	Pulaha	Kratu	Pulastya	Vasishtha
Swarochisha	Urja	Stambha	Prana	Nanda	Rishabha	Nischara	Arvarivat
Auttami	Kaukundihi	Kurundi	Dalaya	Sankha	Pravahita	Mita	Sammita
Tamasa	Jyotirdhama	Prithu	Kavya	Chaitra	Agni	Vanaka	Pivara
Raivata	Hiranyaroma	Vedasri	Urddhabatu	Vedabahu	Sudhaman	Parjanya	Mahamuni
Chakshusha	Sumedhas	Virajas	Havishmat	Uttama	Madhu	Abhinaman	Sahishnu
Vaivasvata	Kashyapa	Atri	Vasistha	Vishvamitra	Gautama	Jamdagni	Bharadvaja
Savarni	Diptimat	Gslava	Parasurama	Kripa	Ashwatthama	Vyasa	Rishyasringa
Daksha-savarni	Savana	Dyutimat	Bhavya	Vasu	Medhatithi	Jyotishman	Satya
Brahma-savarni	Havishman	Sukriti	Satya	Apammurtti	Nabhaga	Apratimaujas	Satyaketu
Dharma-savarni	Nischara	Agnitejas	Vapushman	Vishnu	Aruni	Havishman	Anagha
Rudra-Savarni	Tapaswi	Sutapas	Taopmurti	Taporati	Tapodhriti	Tapodyuti	Tapodhana
Rauchya	Nirmoha	Tatwadersin	Nishprakampa	Nirutsuka	Dhritimat	Avyaya	Sutapas
Bhautya	Agnibhisu	Suchi	Aukra	Magadha	Gridhra	Yukta	Ajita

Table-11: The Seven Sages in Fourteen Manavantara

Since duty is a hierarchy, the 28 stars are only the 'elements' from which individual relationships can be constructed. Some relations are *dharma* and others are *adharma*. The duality of *dharma* and *adharma* is the result of applying the duality of *māyā* to the relationship and its duty. Similarly, the duties can be divided by the three modes of nature—concepts, activity, and names. Thus, *dharma* is also divided into *manas* (mind), *prāna* (work), and *vāk* (words). In Vedic cosmology, in the upper planetary systems *dharma* is prominent which means the persons are engaged in proper duties according to their different relationships, while in the lower planetary systems *adharma* dominates which means nobody is interested in performing their duties and chaos rules. Of course, if the parents don't perform their duties, then their children will also not do their duties; if the husband is not dutiful, then the wife will also not be dutiful. So, the world of *adharma* is painful to everyone because every person is unreliable, and one person's dereliction of duty reinforces the same callousness in others. Thus, even though they have relationships with each other, they are only in namesake. No friend will stand by his friend's side, no couple will be chaste to each other, no parent will care for their children adequately, and no master will give their servants their due after their service.

To escape from this nether world, one must become dutiful to whatever extent then can; as they become more dutiful, they are constantly cheated in their life (because the others are not performing their duty) but after death the soul is promoted to the next level where people are more dutiful, the cheating reduces, and the person who performs *dharma* feels more satisfied.

Any deviation from *dharma* produces *karma*, which then places the person in a new role and responsibility with a different set of expectations. Thus, the soul is forced from one role to another by the laws of *dharma* created by *Brahma*. The laws of mankind, for example, are delineated by *Manu*. These personalities live for extraordinary durations of time, and they outline the duties for the living entities under their rule. The change in duties with the change in *Manu* only represents the changes to the tree of relationships. That is, in some age, the king may be expected to act more as a friend and parent to the citizens, while in another age he would be expected to act as their master.

With every change in *Manu* there is an associated change of the 7 sages. The different *Manu* are therefore the sons of *Brahma* and the 7 sages are in turn subordinate to these *Manu*. As the *Manu* changes the presiding principles for a given age, the 7 sages then delineate the subordinate *dharma* principles based on the higher principles. The Vedic texts thus describe the 14 *Manu* in one day of *Brahma*, and the 7 sages with each of the *Manu*. Table-11 lists the names of the 14 *Manu* and the respective 7 sages associated with them.

The Changing of Dharma

This list is pertinent to see that the laws of *dharma* are not constant over time. Rather, as time passes, the meaning of *dharma* or 'duty' changes. Since the sun and the moon are also moving in this time, the soul is subjected to changing desires under the influence of the moon, and a changing body under the influence of the sun. This means that sometimes you may not be able to perform your duty to the fullest because the body is incapable due to the influence of the sun. At other times, you may be capable but may not feel like doing the duty due to the influence of the moon. The differences between the cycles of the sun, the moon, and the zodiac entail that duty performance is not easy because sometimes we are motivated and sometimes, we are not.

> *SB 12.2.27-28[10]: Of the seven stars forming the constellation of the seven sages, Pulaha and Kratu are the first to rise in the night sky. If a line running north and south were drawn through their midpoint, whichever of the lunar mansions this line passes through is said to be the ruling asterism of the constellation for that time. The Seven Sages will remain connected with that particular lunar mansion for one hundred human years. Currently, during your lifetime, they are situated in the Nakṣatra called Maghā.*

An even more profound problem emerges through the motion of the 7 stars relative to the zodiac. The above verse describes that the 7 sages remain in one of the 28 *Nakṣatra* for a period of 100 human years. As the sages move into a different *Nakṣatra*, a particular type of experience in a particular type of relationship will become important, and when that experience gains prominence there will be more attention to define its duties. The last few hundred years, for instance, have been marked by an immense increase in labor laws, union laws, institutionalizing the labor contracts, etc. which did not exist previously. We can say that labor or master-servant relationship is the dominant *dharma* of this age, because the virtues of hard work are extolled, and for people prestige is associated with the company or organization they serve. Industrialization is designed to undermine every other relationship—children, parents, spouse, and friends—to emphasize labor. When a particular relation is emphasized over the others, the others naturally weaken. As a result, the children's bonds with their parents or grandparents, the commitment of friends to each other, and even spousal relationships have weakened. All that matters at present is for a person to have a job and financial independence.

The *Nakṣatra* are often associated with the moon, rather than the sun, because *dharma* is the space in which our desires must operate. Thus, each *Nakṣatra* represents a certain amount of freedom within which the moon moves, and in the time it moves in that space, we are expected to exercise our freedom (the moon representing the desire) but within the bounds of the duties. For instance, if we are supposed to do 3 things as our duty, we might do them in different orders (unless a specific order is prescribed); or, we might flavor them with our personality, such as eating one kind of food vs. another, or giving charity to one person vs. another, etc. The prescription of *dharma* doesn't take away our desires or free will. *Dharma* however bounds these desires in the sense that we are not expected to go outside their ambit.

The number 28 appears twice in Vedic texts—once in describing the number of constellations or *dharma* and the other in describing the number of hells or *Naraka* denoting 28 different kinds of *adharma* or dereliction of duties. Just as *Manu* is the supervisor for *dharma*, similarly, *Yama* is the supervisor for the punishment due to *adharma*. The 28 hells exist at the bottom of the universe, a theme common to practically all religions where the hells are below. The 'above' and 'below' are conceived in the semantic sense, not physically. Thus, the duality inherent in *māyā* is manifest in the existence of heaven and hell, and it constitutes the vertical dimension for *dharma* and *adharma*.

The Reflection of the Sun's Light

The sun is the source of all light in the universe, and every other visible planet and star is described to reflect the sun's light. In modern cosmology, the planets are indeed reflecting the sun's light, but the stars are considered to be just like suns—i.e., independent sources of light. Indeed, by that comparison, the sun is simply described as yet another star. Vedic cosmology differs significantly in this respect[11]. It identifies the sun as the source of light, and every other luminary in the sky reflects the light of the sun. Of all these luminaries, the moon is said to be the most prominent. The *Bhagavad-Gita* affirms that the moon is the prominent star, and hence stars reflect the sun's light.

> *Bhagavad-Gita 10.21 Translation: Of the Ādityas I am Visnu, of lights I am the radiant sun, I am Marici of the Maruts, and among the stars I am the moon.*

As we have noted previously, the *chit* or the truth of this world exists as the *ability* in the body. This fact is now affirmed by modern atomic theory where atoms are described as possibilities which need to be converted into a reality through *choice*. The choice in question here is the consciousness that interacts with the body to create the pleasure; the choice is also the desire for pleasure that is used to exploit the abilities of the body. However, many of you would have noticed that a sick body loses the desire for pleasure. If you are running a fever, for example, you don't feel like eating. If you are having a headache, then you lose the passion for sex. If your body is weak, you don't feel like working, although you may enjoy your work otherwise. Similarly, a person who is incapable of performing great deeds doesn't develop the desire for such deeds no matter how much you exhort them toward greatness. Before you can motivate them toward greatness, you must motivate them to acquire the skills and abilities by which they can *believe* that greatness is achievable. Only when they can believe in their own abilities, can they even desire greatness. The greatest motivators therefore don't simply create a desire and temptation. They rather focus on creating the belief in one's ability to achieve it.

The key point is that ability precedes desire. A person desiring knowledge may not have the intellect to learn, but he desires knowledge based on underestimating the intellect needed to learn. When he realizes that he is incapable of learning, he loses the desire itself. On the other hand, when a person is highly capable, he or she naturally develops the motivation to use the ability. Thus, rare are those cases when one has a desire but not the ability; such cases are based on overestimating one's ability and underestimating the true ability needed to fulfill the desire. The common case is where ability leads to desire; as we develop our abilities, we also develop greater aspirations from them.

Once we have the desires for enjoyment, we need the opportunities for enjoyment. These opportunities are available to us in the form of roles through which we interact with other living beings. They are also available to us through the *karma* realized through these roles. Each such role brings a duty or *dharma* which we are expected to fulfill if we accept the role. Once we accept the role, we will see success and failure based on the previous *karma.*

Karma is objective but it is delivered relative to our desires. For instance, if you are a hard-working person, then the situation that keeps you idle will be felt as suffering. Conversely, for a lazy person, idling would be happiness and hard work would be suffering. Therefore, the desire (based on *guna*) must be known before the effect of *karma* can be determined. If you are lazy and have good *karma* you will be able to lead a life of luxury without doing anything. But if you are lazy and you have bad *karma* then you will be forced to work hard. Conversely, if you are hard-working and have good *karma* then you will get opportunities to work hard. And if you are hard-working and have bad *karma* then you will not get the opportunities to work. Thus, *karma* entails happiness or suffering, but it is relative to what makes you happy or unhappy.

Karma is also delivered in accordance with what the body is capable of bearing. Thus, a person in a demigod role is accorded a different body, because the *karma* can be utilized in a more capable body. Similarly, the living entity in hell is given a body that doesn't die even when it is tortured or burnt. The human body cannot withstand such punishment; a person will die if such a punishment was meted to them. The hellish body however is very strong and capable of withstanding an enormous amount of torture and suffering. Therefore, before the person can be tortured, he is given a resilient body.

Finally, the actual events are caused by the combination of *guna* and *karma*—i.e., suffering or pleasure coupled with what constitutes suffering or pleasure for *you*. This process is shown by a hierarchy in Figure-19.

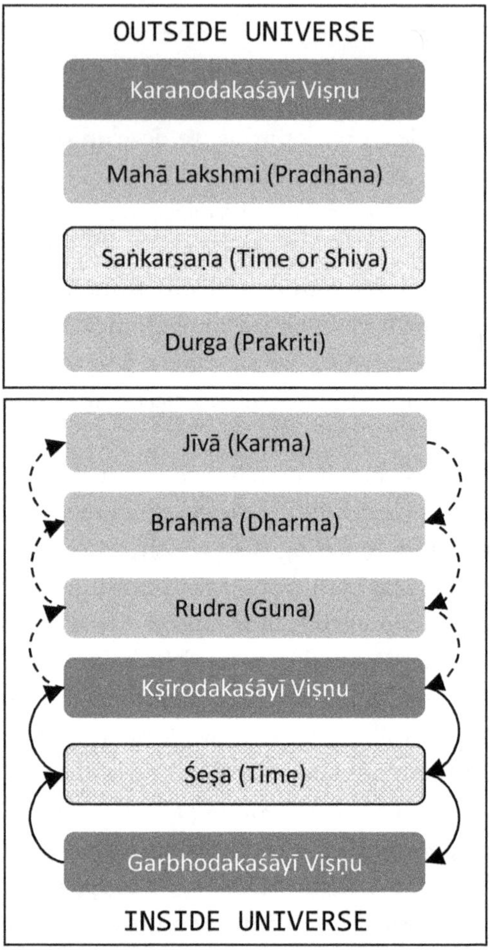

Figure-19 The Hierarchy in the Material Creation

Starting at the bottom of the hierarchy, *Kṣīrodakaśāyī Viṣṇu* represents the material possibilities available at a given time. He constitutes all the atoms, or the ideas built by combining the six qualities of *Viṣṇu*. Even though the combination is divisible, the atoms are indivisible—you cannot reduce the six qualities into anything more fundamental. At the top of the hierarchy is *Garbhodakaśāyi Viṣṇu* who represents all the material possibilities at all times. *Śeṣa* is the person who represents time and selects some possibilities out of all possibilities for any given time. The result of selection is still a possibility because even though something has been made available, it may not be desired, known, and used. The sun—as the representation of *Kṣīrodakaśāyī Viṣṇu*—manifests the possibilities so that they can be desired, known, and used. Through the intellect we can see the axioms in each of the manifest combinations.

The upward solid arrows in Figure-19 represent the selection of a possibility out of all the possibilities to create the material world which can be desired, known, and used by the soul. The downward solid arrows represent the disappearance of this desirable, knowable, and usable world back into an unmanifest state of matter where it cannot be desired, known, or used. The dashed arrows on the other hand represent the cycle of causality for a living entity dependent on the cosmic cycle. This cycle has two parts—upward and downward—and we will begin with the upward path, then discuss the downward path, and then discuss the implications of this cyclic causal model.

As the combination of atoms is perceived through the intellect, a desire for enjoyment is created automatically. For instance, we naturally feel the urges for hunger, thirst, sex, sleep, etc. owing to which many people argue that our free will is controlled by the bodily needs. *Rudra* creates the desires in the ego which rests above the intellect, and the desires become goals.

Due to this desire we seek out a particular role through which we can fulfill the desire. These roles are governed by rules, commandments, injunctions, do's and don'ts, prescribed by *Brahma* which constitute the normative concept of religion. And within that role one obtains success or failure (in fulfilling their desires) based on *karma* (which was previously produced due to performance or nonperformance of duties). A form of *Viṣṇu* called *Śeṣa* delivers this *karma* based on the desire, which means that as you change your desires and enter a new role, you will still be reaping the *karma* although it will be delivered differently. For instance, if a lazy person—who was suffering because he is made to indulge in hard work—begins to enjoy the work, then adverse *karma* will now push him out of work, and he will suffer again due to inaction.

The meaning of the fact that the moon reflects the sun's light is that the desires denoted by the moon are produced from the abilities given by the sun. As you feel more capable, powerful, virile, accomplished, and potent, you want to enjoy through your mind and body, and you seek out roles and responsibilities that are governed by the rules of *dharma* denoted by the stars. Finally, the results of *karma* are enjoyed or suffered in that role governed by *Śeṣa*.

But this is only the bottom-up path in which the body creates desire, desire selects a role, and *karma* manifests within the role. There is also a top-down path in which *karma* picks a role, the role limits our choices forcing us to act in accordance with the situation, using the abilities of our body. In the former case, we think we are the doers because desire follows ability, the situation is chosen by the desire, and success or failure follow the situation; a person in the doer mindset attributes this success or failure to the actions of other doers. In the latter case, we think we are pushed by the worldly situation because our role is determined by some unforeseen causes; that we are compelled to act according to the present circumstances, and the best possible action we can perform is limited by the abilities of the present body. This is the mindset of the fatalist, or one who has lost control over his life.

These two paths are represented within the body by the *idā* and *pingalā* as two directions of the flow of *prāna*. The *pingalā* is the bottom-up path—i.e., reflecting the light of the sun onto to the rest of the universe; it is the path in which we acquire the ability, then develop the desire, then select the role we want, and then create the deeds within the chosen role to enjoy life. *Pingalā* represents the optimist person's worldview. Conversely, *idā* is the pessimist's worldview in which destiny puts us in a predetermined situation, which determines our obligations, which we are compelled to fulfill by force of circumstances, by making the best of all the available abilities within us. *Prāna* is said to flow through *idā* and *pingalā*. Sometimes it is flowing upward—when the body creates desire, the desire seeks out a situation, and the situation consumes *karma* to deliver a result. At other times, *prāna* is flowing downward—when we are pushed into a situation due to *karma*, the situation forces the choice on us, and the choice then uses the bodily abilities to deliver a result. We cannot universally describe the process because there are two different processes—one moving upward and the other moving downward.

Both these paths—top-down and bottom-up—are described in Vedic texts. For example, time causes the zodiac to move, the moon is higher than the sun, which means that the zodiac must move the moon, which must then move the sun. This is the top-down path. In the bottom-up path, the moon reflects the light of the sun, the stars reflect the light of the moon, and the motion of the stars represents the passing of time. Now, it appears that since the moon reflects the sun's light, the sun must be the cause of the moon's motion. Similarly, since the stars reflect the moon's light, the moon must be the cause of the zodiac's motion. All calculations are consistent with either path, but these paths are different explanations of that calculation. The use of contrary explanations presents a paradox because two paths—top-down and bottom-up—are involved due to which the causality becomes cyclic instead of linear.

In this cyclic causality, *karma* is created by desires (based on *guna* which select a desired situation) and *karma* then pushes the soul into new situations where the situation becomes the cause of desires which become the new *guna*. For example, based on desires, a person may want to be a politician; he takes the role of a politician where his desire for power and wealth makes him indulge in corruption, creating adverse *karma*. Due to this *karma* the person is subsequently stripped of his political position, and now he might become honest in order to get back to this previous position of power. Thus, good *karma* makes the person corrupt, and bad *karma* makes him honest. In the first case, *karma* is caused by the *guna* and in the latter case *guna* is caused by *karma*. Both *karma* and *guna* can therefore be causes and effects. Which one is the cause and which one is the effect is hard to determine *a priori*. As a result, we must suppose that both *guna* and *karma* are acting in conjunction—sometimes *karma* dominates and *guna* is manifest in relation to that *karma*, at other times *guna* dominates and *karma* is delivered in relation to that *guna*.

This cycle of *guna* and *karma* operates within the cosmic cycle of creation, maintenance, and destruction, which means that *guna* and *karma* are simply repositories of our past habits and consequences of those habits, but the cosmic cycle will select a particular habit and consequence from the repository. If our repositories of *guna* and *karma* are cleaned out, then there is nothing to select, and the soul will be liberated. Conversely, if the repository is large, then there are numerous possible alternatives where the soul can go based upon all that is possible in the universe at a given time, *guna* and *karma*.

The Problem of Retrograde Motion

Any time we have a causal loop, the behavior is inevitably oscillatory. When the loop's feedback is constructive, the system moves forward; when the loop's feedback is destructive, the system moves backward. This oscillation appears in planetary motion too as prograde and retrograde phases. Now, in modern astronomy, retrograde motions are only apparent; since the earth is moving, sometimes its motion causes the planets to *seem* moving backwards. When the earth is stationary—as in the case of Vedic cosmology—the prograde and retrograde motions have to be explained differently. All the planets except the sun and moon undergo prograde and retrograde phases. In the case of the sun, the change appears as longer and shorter durations of days and nights. Therefore, before we consider the retrograde and prograde motions of the different planets, I will describe this issue in the context of the sun.

> *Viṣṇu Purāṇa, Book II, Chapter 8, Translation*[12]. *As the circumference of a potter's wheel revolves most rapidly, so the sun travels rapidly on his southern journey: he flies along his path with the velocity of wind, and traverses a great distance in a short time. In twelve Muhūrta he passes through thirteen lunar asterisms and a half during the day; and during the night he passes through the same distance, only in eighteen Muhūrta. As the center of the potter's wheel revolves more slowly than the circumference, so the sun in his northern path again revolves with less rapidity, and moves over a less space of the earth in a longer time, until, at the end of his northern route, the day is again eighteen Muhūrta, and the night twelve; the sun passing through half the lunar mansions by day and by night in those periods respectively. As the lump of clay on the center of the potter's wheel moves most slowly, so the polar-star, which is in the center of the zodiacal wheel, revolves very tardily, and ever remains in the center, as the clay continues in the center of the wheel of the potter. The relative length of the day or night depends upon the greater or less velocity with which the sun revolves through the degrees between the two points of the horizon. In the solstitial period, in which his diurnal path is quickest, his nocturnal is slowest; and in that in which he moves quick by night, he travels slowly by day. The extent of his journey is in either case the same; for*

in the course of the day and night he passes through all the signs of the Zodiac, or six by night, and the same number by day: the length and shortness of the day are measured by the extent of the signs; and the duration of day and night by the period which the sun takes to pass through them. In his northern declination the sun moves quickest by night, and slowest by day; in his southern declination the reverse is the case.

There are some important points in the above description.

- The sun travels 6 zodiac signs during the day and 6 signs during the night. Similarly, in the *Dakshināyana* path, the sun covers 13.5 *Nakṣatra* in 12 *Muhūrta* during the day, and the other 13.5 *Nakṣatra* in 18 *Muhūrta* during the night. There are 27 *Nakṣatra*[13] and 30 *Muhūrta* in a day; the 13.5 *Nakṣatra* correspond to the 6 zodiac signs.
- Therefore, the "extent" of the travel in terms of zodiac signs and *Nakṣatra* is equal during the day and night. As the lengths of the days and nights changes, this speed of the sun changes to cover the same distance in longer or shorter times. This is clearly an area of discrepancy with modern astrology where the signs at sunrise and sunset are changed based on the season that is presently ongoing.
- The movement at the center is slower and at the periphery is faster. If the sun were moving at a constant linear speed, then it would move faster at the center. If it were instead moving at a constant angular speed, then it would not change the duration of the days. Both of these are incorrect notions based on the descriptions given above.
- The correct way to think of this motion is to think of space semantically such that the center is higher concepts and the periphery is lower concepts. To change the higher concepts, all lower concepts must be modified, and the energy spent in making the higher-level change is also consumed in lower level changes, which slows the motion. If instead the sun is at the periphery, then only the lower level is modified, and the higher level remains unchanged. Thus, lesser energy is consumed so that

the sun moves faster. We will revisit this topic shortly and discuss the phenomena again in greater detail.

SB 5.22.7 Translation: The sun-god has three speeds — slow, fast and moderate. The time he takes to travel entirely around the spheres of heaven, earth and space at these three speeds is referred to, by learned scholars, by the five names Saṁvatsara, Parivatsara, Iḍāvatsara, Anuvatsara and Vatsara.

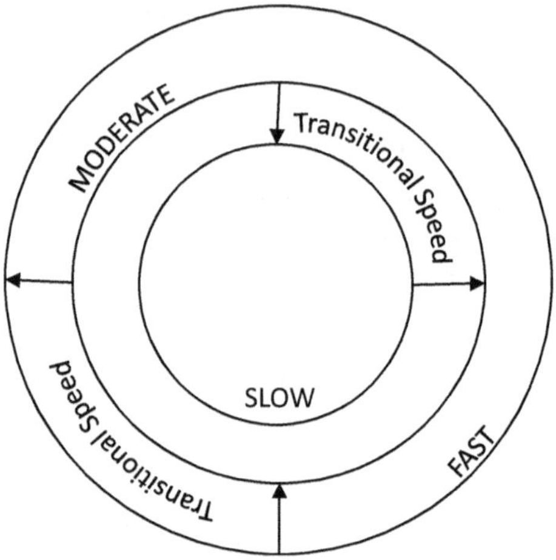

Figure-20 The Five Speeds of the Sun

Since the sun is moving inward and outward causing changes to the durations of days and nights, and then at the equinoxes, the days and nights are equal in length, we can see that there are three stable zones in which the duration is fast, slow, and moderate. As the sun shifts from one state to another, it will get another transitional state which will be between slow and moderate, or between moderate and fast. As a result, given three stable angular speeds, through which the sun transitions inward and outward, there must be five angular speeds, which include two additional transitional speeds. The transitional speeds serve as smooth transitions from one stable speed to another. Factually, however, as the sun falls inward, it will see an angular *deceleration* rather than a constant speed. Similarly, as the sun falls outward, it will see an angular *acceleration* rather than a constant speed. Therefore, two of the 'speeds' are not constant; they must likely represent acceleration and deceleration;

the former used to increase the speed from slow to moderate to fast, and the latter used to decrease the speed from fast to moderate to slow.

Once we grasp the manner in which the sun changes its angular speed, we can extend the understanding to the prograde and retrograde movements of the planets. The basic mechanism will be that in the retrograde movement, the planet moves inward and the planet's angular speed decreases. But since it is dragged in the opposite direction, it would seem to move *backward.* As the planet moves back outward, it will again resume its prograde movement. Due to inward and outward shifts, the planetary orbit must be *elliptical.*

Thus, the duration of day and night for the sun, and the retrograde and prograde motions of the planets, can have the same explanation with the exception that the sun never moves inward enough to go retrograde; the inward movement only elongates the day or night for the sun, while the other planets move sufficiently inward to go retrograde. In effect, the orbit of the sun and moon have inner and outer bounds which keep them moving forward rather than backward, while the inner and outer bounds of other planets span through a range that includes both prograde and retrograde motions. Thus, the decoupling of the motion into two parts—a wheel and a planet—is the generic solution to all kinds of planetary speed changes. Accordingly, the retrograde motion of the planets other than the moon and the sun can be likened to the days of the summer or the nights of the winter: things will naturally slow down during the period, and their effects may also in some cases be reversed.

We might note that in modern astronomy, the longer and shorter durations of the day are attributed to the tilt in the earth's axis. In Vedic cosmology, the same fact is attributed to the faster and slower angular speed of the sun by moving outward or inward on its orbit. When the sun moves inward during the day, the day goes slower, and the sun appears bigger because it has moved into a conceptually more abstract position which is bigger (i.e., comprised of more parts). Conversely, when the sun moves outward during the day, the day goes faster, and the sun appears smaller because it has moved into a conceptually detailed position which is smaller (i.e., comprised of fewer parts). These observations are consistent with summer and winter respectively where the sun appears bigger and smaller, and we attribute it to the earth being nearer or farther from the sun (due the earth's tilt in modern astronomy).

Space as a Rotating Wheel

In Vedic cosmology, there are several levels of planetary systems, each constituting a wheel on which the planets move. Each of these wheels constitutes a different spatial plane, which means that space is attributed a material reality and is called *ether.* Moving on different parts of the ether changes the speeds of motion, for the same type of energy being spent. If we viewed the energy spent per unit of time as the *power* of the planet, then this power remains unchanged, although the distance—angular or linear—traveled using that power changes based on the place where the planet is moving.

The notion of an 'ether' as the medium for the propagation of material objects existed in science prior to the dawn of relativity. If such an ether existed, then all speeds would be measured relative to this ether. Consider the experiment shown in Figure-21 where a beam of light leaves a bulb and is being observed by two observers—one inside the train and the other outside it. According to the observer outside the train, the observer inside the train is moving toward the light (because both light and the observer are moving relative to the ether) and hence he must receive the light sooner than if he was not moving. When actual measurements were performed, it was found that the motion of the train has no effect on the time taken to receive the light. This came to be known as the 'equivalence of frames' because whether you are moving or not, the time taken for light to reach you remains unchanged.

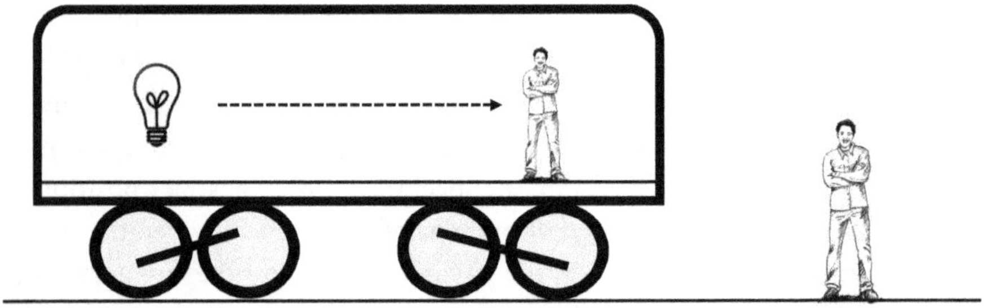

Figure-21 The Relativity of Simultaneity

This experiment could have been interpreted in a quantum theoretic way, but as history would have it, quantum theory had not yet been invented. In the quantum interpretation, the light bulb and the observer in the train become 'entangled' prior to the transmission of a photon. How they become entangled is not known and outside present quantum theory, but once they are entangled, then the light bulb undergoes a state transition *correlated* with the observer undergoing another transition, although nothing is 'going between' the two systems. In fact, as experiments have shown, the transition in the observer can occur faster than light can reach the observer from the light source—which is a problem now called *nonlocality* because we are compelled to violate the premise of a photon 'traveling' from a light source to the observer. There are also experiments that prove that the light can be slowed down. In short, light can take shorter, longer, or equal to the 'speed of light' to reach its destination, which means that the experiment proves nothing about the ether.

The right way to think about this problem is that any change requires some *effort*, and that effort requires time. In present relativity, this effort is disregarded, and the time taken to cause a change is attributed to the travel from the source to destination. However, the time consumed in making the change can also be interpreted in terms of the effort, and the 'distance' between the source and destination should be measured in terms of the effort, while the time to cover the distance depends on the rate of effort application. This is a definition of distance different from the physical distance; it depends on how the source and destination are different from each other, not how far apart they are. If the source and destination are similar, then the time taken to cause a change is small, for the same effort. If the source and destination are dissimilar then the time taken to cause the change is larger, regardless of the physical distance between them. Therefore, space and time can be redefined as the magnitude of effort required to bring any change. Hence, even if the physical distance appears to be great, if the dissimilarity is small, then the change can be quick—provided we had the systems entangled as in quantum theory—regardless of how far the object appears to be *physically*. From a physical perspective, given the distance between source and destination, change must take a long time. But from an effort perspective, the distance doesn't matter; what truly matter is the quantum of change that is being made. Therefore, even if the observer in the train is moving toward the light source, the quantum of change is not altered, and hence the time taken is not modified.

With this revised definition of distance, we can speak of the 'ether' in a new way—it represents the quantum of change needed for one object to *become* another object. If you had two trees—apple and orange—whose fruits appeared to be close in space, they are very far apart from an effort perspective because the 'distance' between the fruits is the amount of effort needed to convert an apple into an orange or vice versa. In short, we have to think of distance in terms of concepts—e.g., apple and orange—rather than physically.

The quantum represents energy, and when divided by time, it represents *power* which is used to overcome the resistance to change. We can symbolically write this as C / T = R where C is the change, T is the time taken to cause the change, and R is the resistance offered to the change. If the resistance is increased, then the change takes more time, based on the power. If the resistance is less, then the change can be carried out faster. The physical distance between source and destination doesn't enter this equation. Such a 'space' can be called the 'field of activities' because 'distance' in this space represents the quantum of change. Modern atomic theory calls energy the 'quantum of action', but 'action' is not itself described as space or distance to be covered in time. If we redefine distance as the quantum of change, then the 'speed' or 'rate' of change would become a function of the 'resistance' offered by space.

In other words, to think of ether in a new way, we have to think of the quantum objects not merely as independent things, but also *defining* their difference from other things. This is the novelty of atomic theory because in classical physics, you could place any particle at any location, and therefore particles and space were two separate things. Now, in atomic theory, *being* at a particular place adequately describes the particle, which means that all its properties simply reduce to its location in space. There is no such thing as mass, charge, energy, spin, etc. These are simply properties of the space, and how it connects the different parts of reality or what we call 'entanglement'. The rejection of 'ether' in classical physics is therefore flawed. What we really mean by the 'ether' is that parts of this world are interconnected, and you cannot separate space from the object; to the extent that space is real, the connection between things is real, and that connection is *objectively* called *ether*.

Now we can get back to the concept of the *wheel*; this 'wheel' is the 'field of activities' in which 'distance' is the measure of changes, and time taken to make the change is a symptom of the resistance offered by the field in making a change. If the resistance is high, then greater effort is needed to make the change. If the resistance is low, then the change occurs quickly. This idea of resistance can also be phrased differently as the opposite movement of space which resists change and sometimes (in the case of retrograde motion) even reverses the change. In classical physics, resistance is *passive*—i.e., unless you push forward, you will not face is backward push. But in Vedic theory, resistance is *active*—even if you are not pushing forward, you will be pushed backward. Thus, a struggle is needed even to stay in the same place.

The backward motion of the wheel is called 'destruction' by which one is pushed back in life. The forward motion of the planet is called 'creation' by which a desired change is brought about. And the object itself—which is being created or destroyed—represents 'maintenance'. *Viṣṇu* as the creator of material objects represents 'maintenance'. *Shiva* is the destroyer of the world as He causes the wheel of time to move backward. *Brahma* is the creator as he gives the power of *karma* by which a person can bring changes. The trinity is therefore present in each change as creation, destruction, and maintenance.

The resistance in the space—caused by the backward motion—is not uniform; as we move outward, the resistance decreases because only minor changes have to be made and the planet therefore moves quickly. As we move inward, the resistance increases because major changes have to be made and the change occurs slowly. The 'effort' needed to cause a change is therefore either spent in a few major changes or numerous minor changes. Many small changes take a lesser effort, and a few major changes take greater effort, due to the tree structure of space because in causing a few major changes, many minor changes are already included. You cannot make a major change without affecting many small changes, but you can make many small changes without causing a major change. Thus, people can be busy their entire life, but at the end of their life you can see that they did not achieve anything significant because they focused on making lots of small changes, neglecting the bigger alterations. Conversely, the person who focuses on the big changes, appears to move very slowly in life but at the end of their life they achieve something significant. When these simple ideas about change—as we can know from everyday life—are incorporated into a theory of motion, we can begin to see how planetary motion can be described in a novel manner, and these descriptions are not unscientific. Rather, the current scientific theories are limited caricatures of change incompatible with everyday concepts of change.

The Cyclic Flow of Energy

This way of looking at space seems to undermine the law of conservation of energy, because for the same effort sometimes you get a lot of change and at other times you obtain little change. If change is the goal of effort, then effort seems to be lost when the resistance is high. In classical physics, this resistance comes in different forms. In one form, the resistance can be called 'friction' which hinders the motion of objects. In another form, the resistance is called 'conductance' through an electrical conductor. In yet another form, the resistance is called 'refractive index' of a medium when light travels through the medium. When electricity is passed through a resistor, the resistor heats up and some of the energy is lost. When light is passed through a material with a high refractive index, the medium heats up and some energy is lost. When an object is moved on a surface with friction, the surface heats up and some energy is lost. While energy is conserved in all cases, the *useful* output you get from that energy is lesser than the energy consumed in the process.

This idea is now recognized in science as the Second Law of Thermodynamics[14]. The total energy is always conserved, however, some of the energy is spent in overcoming the resistance before the change can be attained. The output obtained from the use of energy is always lesser than the input, because some energy is always lost. The problem is that there are numerous definitions of this 'resistance'—e.g., friction, conductance, refractive index, etc.—which are all hypothetical properties useful in modeling, but not good explanations. For example, why should the speed of light be changed in water vs. glass when light should either pass through or be absorbed by the medium of travel?

In the Vedic model, all change originates from within a person. Even if you are pushing a cart, the movement of the cart is secondary; the primary movement or the cause of change is within you. Therefore, what we call 'force' in science is not mechanical; it lies under the control of free will and you can choose to push or not to push the cart. Then matter is the resistance to that change, which means that all the energy we apply to cause a change is not converted into change. Rather, some energy is lost in the process.

We can compare this situation to buying a product where the value of the product you get is lesser than the value of the money you have paid because—(1) the seller makes a profit, and (2) the government collects part of your payment as taxes. In the process of buying, your wealth is divided into three parts— (1) what you get, (2) what the seller gets, and (3) what the government gets. These three parts are called *ādiatmika*, *ādibhautika*, and *ādidaivika* as we have seen. In the cosmic scenario, the *ādidaivika* is the demigods, and every time we bring some change, the demigods take part of that effort. Similarly, other people—the *ādibhautika*—profit from your payment, giving you something whose price is higher than the cost. The existence of profits and taxes in the monetary world is an example of how the wealth you spend in buying the products is less than the value of the products themselves. So, some of your wealth is lost due to profits of the seller and taxes by the government.

We need a generic mechanism to understand the process by which energy is lost. This mechanism is the nature of space as a tree. In the tree topology, all the parts are interconnected. As a result, when we change a part, we must change the parts of that part. You will also change the roles of the other parts within the whole. The whole still performs the same function; the roles of the parts are swapped within the whole, which means their parts will also be altered. In a simple sense, when we change a part, we change all the parts at the same or lower level in the tree. As a result, change to a part isn't restricted to that part alone; rather, it ripples downward in the tree. This is the reason for energy dissipation—a part cannot change independently. To bring a change in a part, other parts and the parts of those parts must be changed, and the energy needed for a change includes the energy needed for many changes.

The resistance to change is nothing but the tree structure of space, which represents the connectedness of things. It creates an inertia to change. Depending on the place on the tree, and based on the change being made, the inertia can vary. Inertia is therefore an objective property of space, but it is not a universal property like 'mass' as in gravitational theory. The same object would exhibit a different inertia to a different type of change at different locations, because the inertia is caused not by the object but the space.

Remember that we are speaking about the inertia that an object faces in changing itself, not the resistance faced in changing *other* things. Factually, there is no such thing as changing other things; all change involves changing the self in different ways. Hence, in order to cause an external change, prior internal change is required. By the Second Law of Thermodynamics, even if you use a machine to do most of the work for you, you still have to push a button. And the benefit you get from the machine must be compensated by an effort in building, maintaining, and running the machine. Thus, while it seems like you are just pushing a button while the machine is doing the work, the reality is that you have previously spent a lot more energy in creating the machine. There is simply no scenario in which you can get more than what you put in; that would violate the conservation of energy. However, there is also no scenario in which you can get a result equal to the effort you put in. By the Second Law of Thermodynamics, you will always be the loser[15].

This fact is seen when you lose some money as profits and taxes to others, and the value of things you buy is always lesser than what you pay. But this is not a bad thing per se because when others make some profit from you, then they have the money to spend on goods or services that you might be selling. Similarly, when the government takes away wealth from you, you receive several amenities such as roads, police, education, or healthcare that you could not built all by yourself. In a limited sense of a single transaction you don't get as much as you put in, but in a larger sense, you get other things that you haven't paid for. When things are taken in the broader sense, the Second Law of Thermodynamics becomes false; because energy is conserved.

The changes we cause are based on the prior earned *karma*. And the results we receive in return are also based on the prior *karma*. As a result, when someone takes from you—as profit or taxes—it is based on their *karma*; in the process of taking, they are spending their *karma*, which was created prior through their work. The process is similar to that of an employee who works unpaid for a month and gets paid at the end of the month. There is hence a *delay* in the remuneration but eventually everyone gets back what they have put in. Thus, even if a government collects taxes from its citizens, it has to return the money back to the citizens in the form of shared amenities.

Karma is like wealth; it must circulate in society. To create this circulation, there must be a delay in effort and reward, because the changes you make take *time* to benefit other people. There is a minimum delay in nature which physicists call the 'speed of light', which occurs *after* an effort drawing on previously created *karma.* If *karma* is missing, then we cannot apply the effort to make a change. Thus, to obtain a result, we must have the requisite *karma*, we must use that *karma* based on choice, and the changes caused by that effort must reach their destination. When the results don't reach their destination, the effort is wasted. For example, if you do your job diligently to produce some products, but the person responsible for shipping them to the retailer is absent, then the products will be shipped late, the retailer will sell them later, the manufacturer will be paid late, and then your salary would be delayed. If you did your job diligently but the product was never shipped, then your efforts have been wasted. This means that you have spent your *karma* in effort, but you are not going to get a return on that effort. As society goes through wasteful activities, most of the good *karma* wealth is destroyed due to wastage.

We saw that the money spent by us goes out both as profits and taxes. In the cosmic case, this 'tax' is collected by demigods, who profit from our work because they have earned good *karma* prior, and they can keep taking from others so long as their *karma* lasts. To make their *karma* last longer, they must also give back what they are receiving, because otherwise their *karma* will run out faster and they will be forced to relinquish their position. The living beings in the higher position therefore reward the lower living beings by—(1) reducing the tax rates which would appear as lesser resistance to change, (2) giving more ability to the person by which he or she can obtain things by their own effort, and (3) supplying the benefits of taxation as shared amenities such as rain, wind, sunshine, etc. The demigods remunerate in all these ways. They move the living entity outward where the gratification is quicker, although the person is lost in making small changes, losing the bigger opportunities. The demigods also empower the living entity to overcome the resistance better and thereby obtain greater results. Finally, the demigods supply natural resources like sunshine, water, air, minerals, and nutrition in food, which the humans cannot create through their own effort. In all these ways, the demigods are not just taking from us; they are also returning it to us. The taxation by demigods is the method by which a living entity obtains the environment in which he lives, although he doesn't pay for it directly to the demigods.

The Planets of the Demons

However, the demigods don't collect taxes on all activities; they only take the *karma* when the activity constitutes our duty or *dharma*. For the activities that are not our *dharma*, the *karma* is taken by the other living entities who reside in the lower planetary systems and thrive on *adharma* activities. They too return the taxes that they have collected but by helping the person perform even more *adharma*. The problem is that they cannot provide human society with the things that demigods provide—namely, fresh air, clean water, fertile soil, adequate rain and sunshine, etc. They can instead enable things like oil and gas, chemical technology, drugs and pharmaceuticals, artificial foods, artificial fabrics, and many other things that we are familiar with in the industrial world. As *dharma* declines, the demigods stop receiving the taxes from our work, and stop compensating us back in the ways noted above. Instead, the demons begin to receive the taxes and they compensate us with the fruits of *adharma*. Human society cannot survive on technology alone. Therefore, as *adharma* increases, and *dharma* declines, life becomes impossible.

We marvel at the technological advancement of modern society and think that the previous societies were not advanced. The fact is that even the modern advancement is not our creation; yes, we have put in the effort, and part of that effort has been grabbed by the demons, who then further the development of even more *adharma* because they are allowed to only tax such activities. If *adharma* declines, then the demons cannot tax our work, and they will decline too. Thus, both demons and demigods can profit from our activities and there are periodic phases constituting the rise and decline of the demons and the demigods—driven by the type of work that dominates the world.

There is a subtle but important difference between the non-performance of duties, and performance of non-duties. The non-performance of duties weakens the person—the ability for doing duties declines, the hardships in doing duties increases, and the resources needed to perform the duties become scarce. When the person is so weakened, he becomes inclined toward the performance of non-duties, where he is empowered by the demons.

A common misconception in religions is that *adharma* naturally leads to hell, which is false. The demons can also be truthful, diligent, hard-working, and honest. They are just opposed to the worship of God; theirs is the sense of morality devoid of a conception of God. The demons can therefore live happily with demons; there is no hell in this type of life. The trouble starts when the demons start troubling the demigods or the people engaged in *dharma*. Ideally, the societies of demigods and demons are completely separate, and *bhū-mandala*—which includes the earth—is considered a part of the divine society. So, the demons are not expected to enter this society, because they have a hierarchy of 7 planetary systems just like 7 planetary systems are allocated for the divine persons. However, if the demons become powerful, they interfere in the divine societies and start torturing the divine persons. This is when the possibility of hellish punishment is created. The Bhagavad-Gita notes:

> *Bhagavad-Gita 4.7-8. Translation. Whenever and wherever there is a decline in religious practice, O descendant of Bharata, and a predominant rise of irreligion—at that time I descend Myself. In order to deliver the pious and to annihilate the miscreants, as well as to reestablish the principles of religion, I advent Myself millennium after millennium.*

The divine and the demonic are two non-overlapping societies in Vedic cosmology, each with their own lifestyles. The sun and the moon don't shine in the demonic planets, nor is there rain, grains, fruits, and vegetables enabled by the demigods. We can think of the planet of demons like an air-conditioned palace where the living entities consume animals, create food using energy produced from nuclear reactions, drink water from chemical synthesis etc. They are advanced scientifically; they just don't rely on the demigods. The demonic civilization needs a different kind of mind and body well-suited to lead a life based on moral principles of their choosing but without a conception of God. They just consider rulers of their planets as the ultimate gods.

Their hierarchy is also inverted—the bottommost planet is the highest for them. And their 'religion' is the manipulation of matter for sense enjoyment. Many of these demons worship *Shiva* or *Śeṣa* who creates time. As we have seen, time is produced from desire, and *Shiva* is the master of desires. So, their religion is sense enjoyment and they want it to continue eternally.

The main difference with the demigods is that the divine enjoy serving God and the demonic enjoy rejecting God's existence. They may still recognize *Shiva* or *Śeṣa* as God but only because this worship enhances their desires for enjoyment such that the person never gets bored of material life. The fact is that most people get bored of enjoying the same things over and over again. As you get older, the desire for working hard, romantic and sexual pleasures, or eating voraciously, tend to decline—and one largely withdraws from such types of pursuits to lead a life of relative simplicity and detachment. The demonic don't want to get bored of eating, sex, and hard work. They want to continue enjoying these things till the very end of their lives. This is possible if one's desires for pleasure are significantly magnified. So, their worship of *Shiva* is to give them intense desire to keep desiring eating, sex, work, etc.

In traditional Vedic society, a man enjoys life between the ages of 25 to 50, leads a retired life of simplicity from 50 to 75, and then renounces home, family, and all comforts at 75. These are respectively called the *Grihastha*, *Vānaprastha*, and *Sannyāsa* stages of life. But it is not uncommon to find old people today who take drugs for sexual arousal, want to continue working as long as the body permits, enjoy playing games and sports, etc. Instead of pursuing a life of seclusion, simplicity, and renunciation, they yearn to reenergize themselves for enjoyment as they were during their youth. The worship of *Shiva* by the demons is an atheistic type of religion in the sense that pleasure is regarded as the greatest happiness, and if this happiness seems to decline because the pleasure potency in the person has decreased, then worshiping *Shiva* to increase that potency in order to enjoy more constitutes 'religion'.

Shiva therefore manifests in two kinds of religions. The divine living beings worship *Shiva* to become free of material desires, and the demonic living beings worship Him to enjoy even more. In the *yoga* system, as the *kundalini* rises, it reaches the *sahasrāra chakra* which is described as a thousand petal lotus with *Shiva* and *Śakti* united in an embrace. Similarly, *Śeṣa* lives at the bottom of the universe (which is the topmost place for the demons as their view of the universe is inverted) and is said to have a thousand heads. *Shiva* and *Śeṣa* are therefore the same person viewed in two different ways.

Therefore, in Vedic cosmology, the planets of the demons are clearly distinguished from the places demarcated as hell. The 'Devil' in Abrahamic religions are the demons, but they are not ugly, foolish, or lazy. They have, in many cases, better amenities than the demigods. But they are always fearful of the demigods because *Viṣṇu* supports them and gives them power. Therefore, even though they are more powerful than the demigods in most cases, they are unable to counteract the benedictions of *Viṣṇu*, and their primary envy is directed toward Him. In Vedic texts, the demons often worship *Brahma* and *Shiva* and obtain benedictions from them, but they never worship *Viṣṇu*. This means that they are prepared to lead a moral life, with the aim of sense enjoyment, devoid of the worship of *Viṣṇu*. In that sense, the main difference between the divine and the demonic person is not morality because both can be moral.

The difference is also not in the recognition of the soul and free will because both worship *Shiva*. The main difference is worship of *Viṣṇu* by the demigods and the envy of *Viṣṇu* by the demons. This fact alone attests to the superiority of *Viṣṇu* because His worship constitutes the difference between the divine and the demonic. What we call 'atheism' today—i.e., the rejection of morality, the soul, and free will—is ugly, foolish, and lazy. This type of atheism is easily debunked by anyone who has some understanding, intelligence, and mental tenacity. Even a person with a mild understanding of modern science knows about the numerous problems of incompleteness and indeterminism, which create room for choice. More advanced scientists understand the inability to represent meaning and thought in matter without revising the definition of matter. The modern atheists are therefore largely ignorant. The real atheists—the demons—are far more advanced because they accept morality, the soul and free will for the enjoyment of life, but they don't accept the service of the personality called *Viṣṇu*. They live happily so long as they don't interfere in the lives of the devotees of *Viṣṇu*—i.e., keep their atheism to themselves and to others who like to follow a similar ideology. When, however, they try to propagate their ideology to the divine personalities they meet their end.

Brahma creates the *dharma* for both demigods and demons. In the *dharma* of demigods, the purpose of duty and responsibility is to satisfy God; this *dharma* is also called *karma-yoga* by which a person discharges their duty but the duties are defined in a way to satisfy God. Even the laws of society are organized to satisfy God, the ruler is believed to be a representation of God, and the work of governing is considered to be the work of God. Conversely, in the *dharma* of demons, the purpose of duty and responsibility is to satisfy oneself. Everyone is free to choose what they like—including the selection of a ruler who views his work not as God's work but meant for his satisfaction. The Vedic texts, for instance, describe how both demigods and demons are children of *Kaśyapa* (one of the sons of *Brahma*) through two wives—*Aditi* (demigods) and *Diti* (demons)—and hence they have a 'religion' too which is devoid of a genuine conception of God, but includes secular ideas about morality.

The modern world is under the grip of demons through the demonic ideologies. We don't have to see them as rulers of this world to conclude that the world is controlled by demons. We just have to understand the ideological differences between demigods and demons to see how secular morality replaces a theistic morality in the case of the demons; it advances the study of nature, the practice of choice and responsibility, and the elongation of material life for sensual enjoyment. This is a 'religion' of *Brahma* too, but it is not given importance in the Vedic texts, except to describe how the demons torture and trouble the demigods, how both are children of *Brahma*, how they live in different parts of the universe, and how *Viṣṇu* defeats and destroys them every time when they start interfering in the life and work of the demigods.

Solar vs. Lunar Zodiacs

The zodiac is divided in two ways, and the divisions are associated with the sun and the moon. As seen previously, the zodiac is divided into 12 parts in relation to the sun, and into 27 parts in relation to the moon. The zodiac represents the *dharma*, or the duties a person has to perform. The sun represents the *karma* or the results of the performance or non-performance of duties. But this *karma* is effected in relation to the *guna* or what we desire or hate. Thus, good *karma* for a lazy person allows him or her to enjoy laziness whereas bad *karma* forces them to work hard. The *guna*, *karma*, and *dharma*, are therefore three essential parts of a triad which works in conjunction with time.

There is some confusion in the Vedic texts regarding the number of *Nakṣatra*. First, Vedic texts such as the *Surya Siddhānta* describe 28 *Nakṣatra* instead of 27. Second, these texts attribute longer and shorter degrees to these *Nakṣatra*, different from the equal degrees attributed to them when the system of 27 *Nakṣatra* is employed. This difficulty can be resolved if the 28th *Nakṣatra* (called *Abhijit*) is treated as the whole zodiac with 27 parts[16]. This interpretation is supported by several Vedic texts. For example, in SB 11.16.27 *Kṛṣṇa* states that He is the *Abhijit Nakṣatra*[17]. Also, in the *Mahabharata* it is stated that *Kṛṣṇa* is born in the *Abhijit Nakṣatra*, asserting its importance.

Nakshatra	Ruler	Longitude		Zodiac Sign
		From	To	
Ashwini	Ketu	00 Aries 00	13 Aries 20	Aries
Bharani	Venus	13 Aries 20	26 Aries 40	
Krittika	Sun	26 Aries 40	10 Taurus 00	Taurus
Rohini	Moon	10 Taurus 00	23 Taurus 20	
Mrigashira	Mars	23 Taurus 20	06 Gemini 40	Gemini
Ardra	Rahu	06 Gemini 40	20 Gemini 00	
Punarvasu	Jupiter	20 Gemini 00	03 Cancer 20	Cancer
Pushya	Saturn	03 Cancer 20	16 Cancer 40	
Ashalesh	Mercury	16 Cancer 40	30 Cancer 00	
Magha	Ketu	30 Cancer 00	13 Leo 20	Leo
Poorva Phalguni	Venus	13 Leo 20	26 Leo 40	
Uttara Phalguni	Sun	26 Leo 40	10 Virgo 00	Virgo
Hasta	Moon	10 Virgo 00	23 Virgo 20	
Chitra	Mars	23 Virgo 20	06 Libra 40	Libra
Swati	Rahu	06 Libra 40	20 LIbra 00	
Vishakha	Jupiter	20 Libra 00	03 Scorpio 20	Scorpio
Anuradha	Saturn	03 Scorpio 20	16 Scorpio 40	
Jyeshta	Mercury	16 Scorpio 40	30 Scorpio 00	
Moola	Ketu	30 Scorpio 00	13 Sagittarius 20	Sagittarius
Purava Ashadha	Venus	13 Sagittarius 20	26 Sagittarius 40	
Uttara Ashadha	Sun	26 Sagittarius 40	10 Capricorn 00	Capricorn
Sharavana	Moon	10 Capricorn 00	23 Capricorn 20	
Dhanistha	Mars	23 Capricorn 20	06 Aquarius 40	Aquarius
Shatabhisha	Rahu	06 Aquarius 40	20 Aquarius 00	
Poorva Bhadrapada	Jupiter	20 Aquarius 00	03 Pisces 20	Pisces
Uttara Bhadrapada	Saturn	03 Pisces 20	16 Pisces 40	
Revathi	Mercury	16 Pisces 40	30 Pisces 00	

Table-12: The Combination of Sun and Moon Signs

A further evidence comes from the fact that the presiding deities of the *Nakṣatra* are described as the 27 daughters of *Daksha* who were married to *Chandra*—the presiding deity of the moon[18]—but *Chandra* was partial to one wife (*Rohini*, also a *Nakṣatra*). As a result, he was cursed by *Daksha*. This 'partiality' again represents that the moon doesn't spend equal time in each of the *Nakṣatra* and hence they are described as longer or shorter. In other words, there are many references to the special status of the 28th *Nakṣatra* and then several descriptions of the 27 divisions, of which the 26 are equal. Owing to these factors, I will consider the 28th *Nakṣatra* indeed a special one—representing the complete zodiac—and the other 27 as its parts. This helps us reconcile the contradiction between the different descriptions of *Nakṣatra*.

When the division by 12 and 27 are combined, the zodiac as a whole is divided into 108 parts which is accorded a special mystical status in Vedic texts[19].

Table-12 illustrates the division of the zodiac in two ways.

The division by 108 is further reinforced in Vedic astrology where each *Nakṣatra* is divided into 4 *pāda* or parts and all the planetary positions are therefore described in three ways— (1) as part of the solar zodiac signs, (2) as part of the lunar *Nakṣatra*, and (3) as parts of the *pāda* of the *Nakṣatra*. The astrological texts accord great significance to the *pāda*, and the properties of the planets change greatly depending on their location in the *pāda*.

Buddhists consider that the process of enlightenment comprises of 108 steps, and often these steps are represented in the construction of a temple or a *stupa*—ranging from the stairs that you have to climb to reach the floor of the temple, along with the steps along the body of the temple, and then the steps on the spire atop the temple itself. Mystically speaking, we can think of 108 as representing unique types of roles or duties, and the placement of planets in these roles depicts the influence of that planet on that role. This idea has important applications in organizational theory where a complete organization needs to perform 108 distinct duties or roles, which could be hierarchically organized either as 9 parts of 12 parts, or 12 parts of 9 parts. This topic is more involved, and I will therefore not delve into it further here.

5

Principles of Religious Universalism

Just as a candle cannot burn without fire, men cannot live without a spiritual life.

—*Buddha*

A Framework for Universalism

I will use this chapter to illustrate a framework for understanding religious universalism in which three types of religions—monotheism, polytheism, and monism—are viewed as different sects of a single religion. There are numerous members of these classes, and the classification identifies three kinds of existence—matter, soul, and God. If you emphasize the existence of God, then you are a monotheist. If you emphasize the personalized control of this material world then you are a polytheist. And if you have transcended the material world but not entered the association of God, then you are aware of your individuality, but you don't know how to distinguish yourself from other souls. Without such distinction, one cannot know if anything other than the self exists, and without such knowledge, one is left with an impersonal monism where one (erroneously) concludes that everything is a single existent.

Let's begin with monism. If we recall the tree with God as its root, you will notice that it doesn't support straight line paths from leaf to leaf. To go from one leaf to another, one must go to the higher branch where both leaves are joined. Therefore, to go to the other leaf, one must reach the branch prior. In this case, the soul is a leaf, but God is the root. To go from one branch to another, one must go to the root prior. This 'going' is not physical motion; it is the change of awareness which results in a *path* to reach the destination. Our awareness of other souls depends on our awareness of God, because God lies in the *path* connecting us to the other souls. There is no direct connection between two souls, like two leaves are connected only by a branch. Therefore, there cannot be love between two souls unless there is love of God[1].

The monist realizes that he is different from matter and becomes aware of his own existence. But because the monist doesn't know the nature of God, he cannot know anything other than himself. As the diversity of the material world disappears, the monist supposes that they have all merged into a single existence—i.e., that you and me are the same person, when the fact is that I don't know anything about you if I don't know God. That ignorance of God manifests in the inability to see anything other than the self. And that ignorance is called monism. It is better than considering the material body to be the person, but not as good as seeing one's spiritual identity in relation to God. Thus, the soul is independent in the sense that he can know his own existence. But the soul is dependent on God to know anything and anybody else. This dependence exists even for the demons, but they don't acknowledge it. They rather attribute the connection between individuals to *karma*—i.e., individual choice and responsibility—which is then constituted of the laws of society.

God, on the other hand, as the root of the tree, is fully independent because He can know anything—and He is thus *omniscient*. If the soul knows God, then he also becomes omniscient—i.e., he can know anything he wishes. Therefore, self-knowledge is incomplete without God knowledge. If the self is known but God is not known, then other souls are also not known, and as the variety of the world disappears, one is only left with self-awareness, which one erroneously interprets as the only reality. This understanding is called *Brahman*; it is a place of light where one can see the self; but it is a place of darkness because one cannot know the existence of anything other than the self. It is like you sitting in a dark room, aware of yourself, but unaware of all else.

The position of monism illustrates a major flaw in the humanist theories of morality or religion; we cannot love anyone else truly unless we love God. This position also demonstrates the flaws in charity without a conception of God. The soul cannot know anything else except via awareness of God.

The light by which we see other things, become aware of their existence, and obtain knowledge about them, is actually *karma* forcing an interaction. This *karma* travels up and down the tree—passing through the higher nodes such as branches, trunks, and trees—until it reaches the lowest point on the tree where two leaves are connected. This lowest point constitutes the *shortest path* on a tree between two points, but it is not a *straight line*. Thus, our knowledge of the world is caused by *karma*; when *karma* ceases, we cease to know the world—unless, of course, we develop knowledge of God in order to see other things beyond our own existence. Thus, cessation of *karma* is a good thing; but it is incomplete without the perfection of knowledge via God.

In Vedic philosophy, *karma* is tied to *dharma*. *Dharma* indicates our duties, which arise because we are placed in a certain role, and we have obligations to fulfill that which we call our responsibilities. If these obligations are fulfilled, there is no *karma*. However, we often exceed the demands of the obligations or fall short of these demands. For example, we might over endeavor in our jobs because we desire promotion, success, and fame. Or we might neglect our work because we don't enjoy doing it. Either behavior produces *karma*—the former is positive *karma* while the latter is negative *karma*. If one desires to enjoy their life, they tend to over endeavor to obtain this pleasure. The results are positive, but the cycle of hard work and enjoyment is never ending; it binds the soul to the material world through work and its fruits. On the other hand, neglecting our work is also undesirable because it causes suffering to others, and the soul is again bound in the material world to suffer.

Thus, both extremes of over endeavor and neglecting the responsibility fail to result in liberation. But if you are in this world, and desire to stay here, then you will desire positive *karma* through over endeavor. Once good *karma* has been acquired, it can be spent in different ways—depending on our desire. This *karma* is like currency which you can use to buy different things. But in order to get these different things, you have to go to different shops. Thus, there is a bookstore that sells knowledge, a garment store that sells clothes, an automotive dealer who sells cars, and a movie theater that sells entertainment. The demigods are the pathways that connect us to different stores. Just having the money to spend is therefore not enough; one must also get connected to the right seller who can give us things we desire for pleasure. And the seller must not have a better option to give those things to others. The demigods arrange exchanges of goods based on *karma*. They bring living beings into contact whereby they can enjoy or suffer the results of the *karma*. Thus, the enjoyment or suffering we will obtain is fixed; it is either money to be spent or the loan to be repaid. However, the money can be spent in different ways, and the loan can be repaid in several ways. The demigods represent the *choice* of how we want to spend our earnings, or how we wish to pay our debts.

You might have the money but still not be able to enjoy it, because the things you want are not made available to you at the right time. Therefore, the worship of demigods only arranges the right type of interaction based on our desire although what is obtained in that interaction is based on our *karma.* In that sense, the demigods don't help us create new *karma*—good or bad. However, they can help us spend or repay the *karma* in the most appropriate way we like. The worship of demigods is meant to fulfill our desires by finding the most desired method of spending and repaying the *karma.* For example, one might wish to enjoy one's *karma* through career success instead of family happiness; the demigod responsible for career can arrange that encounter—based on our *karma.* Similarly, we might wish to repay our debts by serving our parents—who don't pay us in return—while protecting our already earned wealth from thieves. The demigods perceive the soul's desire and fulfill it in the most appropriate manner possible—based on their *karma* and their desire.

The demigods are thus both important and unimportant. They are important because they arrange the contacts through which you obtain the desired results of your previous good or bad *karma*. They are unimportant because if you did not desire a particular type of outcome, or are unaware of impending *karma*, the demigods will deliver the outcomes nevertheless in the best way they deem fit. By worshiping the demigods, we can influence them to alter our interactions and shift the effect of *karma* to a different interaction. There is hence considerable free will in the soul in how he wants to spend his *karma* and that free will can be used to request the demigods for a change. The process of making that request involves additional effort—e.g., that you have to perform a particular ritual—which in turn consumes some *karma.* Therefore, in the process of shifting our *karma* to a chosen avenue, we lose some *karma*. You can think of this request as the money spent in transporting oneself to a different place, in order to enjoy or suffer in a different manner.

At the time of birth each soul is preordained to enjoy or suffer in a particular manner—e.g., that you might obtain good education but remain poor. We can change this preordained enjoyment or suffering—e.g., that we might remain uneducated but can become rich—in a zero-sum game. That is, every time you gain something additional, you will lose something else. Such a change can come about if the soul changes his desires in the course of their life. For example, you might stop valuing education and start valuing money. Your *karma* will still manifest as success or failure, but in the new venture. In that sense, our destiny of enjoyment or suffering is fixed, but that pleasure or pain can be obtained through several different avenues by the assistance of demigods. That shifting of avenues in life constitutes our free will. Thus, you can change your job or profession if you so desire; the success or failure that you will obtain in that new job or profession will be decided by *karma*. You would have received as much success or failure even in the old profession, but you have the choice to enjoy or suffer in new ways, chosen by free will.

The essential thing here is to understand the existence of *karma* itself, because its creation depends on *dharma*—i.e., the definition of the responsibilities of a role, the understanding of one's true role, and determining which of the potentially conflicting roles and responsibilities must take precedence. We must also understand that the laws of nature are for the performance of duties. These laws are not the impersonal laws of particles and forces; they are based on the choice of over endeavoring, working adequately, or neglecting one's duties. The material world is the marketplace of earning and selling, in which both earner and seller are persons. Similarly, the contact between a buyer and a seller is also arranged by a higher person. The seller takes your money in order to spend it on something else. And you earn your money in order to buy goods. Nature is therefore personalized even in things that we think are happening automatically. This personalization only informs about the laws of morality, how the consequences of moral actions are given by persons like us.

The polytheistic religions of demigods are true in so far as the control of material transactions of give and take is concerned. But monotheism is superior as it gives more importance to transcendence. However, that importance is not at the cost of misunderstanding or not understanding the moral law and its working. Just because I don't like the marketplace of buying and selling doesn't mean I can break its laws. Monotheistic religions—when they neglect this simple idea about how the material world works—become prey to immoral activities. Many monotheistic religions, for example, just command their followers to accept that religion, and salvation is ensured. The followers of such religions forget that they are still in the material marketplace and have to follow its rules. They consider themselves already liberated by their acceptance of religion and proceed to over endeavor for pleasure, or neglect their moral duties, prescribed according to their role by the natural laws. The result of such religious acceptance is not transcendence; it continues to bind the soul to repeated pleasures from over endeavor or suffering from neglect.

Monotheism therefore becomes flawed when it neglects the fact that the soul is still bound to the world ruled by demigods, under the laws of moral conduct. Hence, rejection of demigods doesn't actually uplift the soul. It rather risks pushing the soul into sinful activities for enjoyment and suffering. The worship of demigods is not essential, but it is essential to know that the demigods exist and control the nature through the laws of moral conduct. We must conduct the duties of our material role honestly and honorably; we must certainly refrain from the endless pursuit of material enjoyment, as well as the indulgence in crimes, killing, hurting, deceiving, dishonesty, etc.

Polytheism similarly becomes flawed when, realizing the role of demigods in this world, the soul over endeavors to earn good *karma* in order to enjoy according to his desires. One forgets that revectoring *karma* from one type of happiness to another is not the purpose of human life. It binds the soul to endless birth and death. How different can suffering be whether it is obtained through one avenue or another? Similarly, how different can pleasure be whether it is obtained in one way or another? The soul caught in an intense desire forgets that he is only consuming his *karma* for his pleasure, which would be obtained regardless of worshiping the demigods although in a different way—which may not be the most desirable—but is still necessary.

When monotheism rejects this understanding of material exchanges caused by *karma*, the process of the repeated cycle of birth and death is also rejected. Typical to most monotheistic religions is the idea of a single life followed by eternal heaven or hell. Those who accept the religion supposedly go to heaven, while everyone else goes to hell. Innate in this conception of religion is a hardened fanaticism which leads to interreligious conflicts because each religion believes that everyone else is a heretic and therefore due for punishment. Meting out that punishment becomes the sacred duty of the believer, which is a totally flawed notion of religion because God doesn't need the believer to reward or punish other believers or non-believers; there is already a fully functional system of reward and punishment in place—with designated roles and responsibilities—run by the demigods. The demigods don't need a religious believer to kill a heretic; if they want, they can kill through natural causes such as earthquakes, famines, or even arranging contact with a deadly disease. The believer, in trying to punish the heretic also spends their good *karma* of pleasure in the act of punishing others. This kind of endeavor degrades the believer as his pleasure now takes the form of sadism.

The monotheist—when he rejects *karma*, reincarnation, and demigods—becomes bound by his own misunderstanding of human responsibilities assuming himself to be already liberated just by accepting a religion. The polytheist is much better placed in this regard—he understands the difference between good and bad actions, and at least avoids suffering through that process, although, ultimately, he also remains bound to the cycle of birth and death.

The position of monism rejects both monotheism and polytheism. The monist sees that the cycle of enjoyment and suffering is not satisfying him. He wants to renounce the world and be liberated. But he also doesn't wish to accept a superior person beyond his self. He wishes to remain alone, neither bound by the laws of material nature, nor in the association of other persons—including God. In Vedic philosophy, there are two kinds of monism.

In the first kind the soul ends material experience but keeps the desire to enjoy the world. In fact, given that so many desires have caused him suffering in the past, he seeks that thing which will not give him suffering. He explores the universe of desires, imagining what it would be like to enjoy something else. This state of existence—where one is enjoying the imagination of enjoyment—is called the realm of *Shiva* or *Mahesh Dhāma*. This realm is infinite in the sense that there is no end to material desires; you can therefore spend eternity just going through all the possible desires and never come to an end. *Shiva* is also therefore called *time* or *kāla*. This time is *personal time* in the sense that it creates the sense of passing time because of the changing desires.

As we know, a time of happiness passes quickly, but the time of pain goes slowly. The passing of time is associated with pleasure or suffering. But when one is not enjoying or suffering—because the actual material contacts are absent—then time doesn't appear to pass in the above sense, as there is neither pleasure nor suffering; without these you feel timeless. This realm of timelessness is called the realm of *Shiva*—beyond the material world.

However, being in the realm of desire without indulgence is a precarious position, and the soul can fall into matter again. Therefore, in the second kind of monism, the soul realizes the problem of entertaining the desire but not indulging in it and decides to focus the desires on himself in the act of self-knowledge and self-experience. Now the soul experiences a different kind of timelessness because the self is eternal. By knowing the self, one doesn't run the greater risk of falling down. But self-knowledge is boring. The soul is finite and gets bored by just knowing himself. He wants to know the infinite world outside the self, which is then the cause of a different type of falldown if one has not become aware of God—and doesn't seek knowledge through Him.

In both cases there is an object of experience—the possibilities of enjoyment which can be desired, or the self which is eternal and separate from these possibilities. The monistic philosophy has a truth in it—it asserts the individuality and independence of the soul, and the limitlessness of material desires and the possibilities of pleasure. It indicates that we have free will by which we can yearn for pleasure unlimitedly or choose to give up all such yearning (which are external to us) and just focus on the existence of the self.

These three religious doctrines are manifestations of *Viṣṇu*, *Brahma*, and *Shiva*. The religion of *Viṣṇu* is monotheism; He is the transcendent and supreme person Whom we call God. The religion of *Brahma* is polytheism; he is the organizer and supervisor of the process of *karma* in this world—work and its reward through the demigods. The religion of *Shiva* is the mastery over the desires arising in the self; He is called *time* because He creates all material desires which propel the living entity to roam endlessly in search of pleasure, never finding the end of this enjoyment; but if one realizes that this realm of desire is endless he comes to the conclusion that he can never be satisfied in this realm because there is ever more to enjoy; at that point the soul recognizes that desiring something else other than the self is ultimately pointless; the soul now focuses his desire on the self—and experiences his eternity.

The soul—as we have seen—has three aspects of relation, cognition, and emotion. In principle, therefore, no doctrine by itself can be complete. Therefore, the Vedic texts prescribe these doctrines in a hierarchy. The religion of *Brahma*—which embodies the performance of material duties and the enjoyment of *karma*—is the lowest form of religion; it is called paganism or polytheism. Higher than this doctrine is the religion of *Shiva*—which emphasizes the conquest of material desires and focusing the attention inward rather than outward to realize the eternity of the self and the difference between the self and the material world; it is called impersonalism or monism. Higher than monism is the religion of *Viṣṇu*; it is called monotheism, but it involves progressive realization from the acceptance of material control by demigods, and the eternality of the soul and its difference from the material nature; the progression is that the soul recognizes that he is an individual but not the supreme individual; therefore, he must accept God's superiority for his experience.

Thus, monotheism is the greatest religion, provided one has understood that matter is controlled by persons—i.e., the *personalization* of nature—and that the self is independent of this nature. The subsequent association with the supreme person is not an association with the material personalities.

This overview of the three forms of religion, and how they are progressively more advanced than the previous religion, constitutes the framework in which (a) we can resolve the conflicts between religions, (b) without conceding that all the religions are equivalent. The first step in this progressive realization is the recognition that nature is personalized and governed by demigods. The next higher step is to recognize that we are different from the material nature. The final step is to understand that though we are independent individuals, we are not the supreme individual; asserting the equivalence or identity of all individual souls is tantamount to competing with the supreme. That competition doesn't make the soul the supreme soul; monism is purely imaginary although the soul is indeed an independent individual.

The three types of religions appear to be mutually contradictory when they emphasize three different realities, but the fact is that the complete answer to the problem lies in (a) accepting the existence of each of the three, and (b) and recognizing that monotheism is higher than monism, and monism is higher than polytheism. Unless all three are accepted, the religious doctrine remains incomplete. And unless the hierarchy is seen, the religious doctrines remain inconsistent. We want a consistent and complete religious doctrine, but it cannot be obtained unless each of the three types are recognized and given a place in our understanding of the complete reality, while not equating them to each other because they are individually acknowledged as true. This speaks to the need for *dialogue*—not just in order to understand the other and live peacefully, but also in order to advance one's own understanding.

The reality at present is that the three doctrines are mutually opposed. The monotheists reject the monists and the polytheists. The monists reject both monotheists and polytheists. Finally, the polytheists reject both monotheists and monists. I am, to an extent, generalizing. I'm not denying the existence of a monotheist who might incorporate some elements of monism, or a polytheist who might also recognize some elements of monotheism. My goal is to identify those logically orthogonal categories—which can be understood in the most logically simple sense—before we mix the doctrines and induct elements of one into another to formulate an individual doctrine. This method has the advantage that you can *place* a particular doctrine along the three dimensions of monotheism, polytheism, and monism. My effort throughout the rest of the book will be to show these three doctrines are indeed exhaustive[2].

The Problem of the Soul's Falldown

The dominant wisdom today regarding the various religions is that these are different 'faiths', which describe different notions of God, a plethora of different human practices, and have little to no agreement on what God or transcendence truly is. In that sense, we speak about multiple 'religions'. I will use this chapter to argue that these diverse religions are actually different 'sects' of a single system that exists as the trinity of *Brahma*, *Shiva*, and *Viṣṇu*, representing the three features of the soul. However, these sects are not equivalent. Instead, the sect of *Brahma* is lower than the sect of *Shiva*, which is lower than the sect of *Viṣṇu*. These sects have in turn manifested into the philosophies of polytheism, monism, and monotheism. The rejection of polytheism doesn't automatically take one to monotheism—as most monotheists imagine. Rather, in between the rejection of many gods and the acceptance of a single God there lies the realm of the soul's desires and that of knowing the self.

That single religion—which divides into three through *Brahma*, *Shiva*, and *Viṣṇu*—through the manifestation of subordinate deities, became the worship of the sun, the moon, and the stars, as we have seen previously. These celestial entities exist as manifestations of the effect of *Brahma*, *Shiva*, and *Viṣṇu* on the material world, although the sun, the moon, and the stars are visible while the previous three deities are not. By understanding and studying their influence—e.g., through a scientific theory of material nature—we infer the existence of what cannot be perceived by the senses. The practice of astrology and its influence on our life thus constituted in the past an empirical evidence for the theory that the *sat*, *chit*, and *ānanda* of the soul are controlled by higher personalities, and thereby of the existence of *Brahma*, *Viṣṇu*, and *Shiva*. However, as time passed, and the scientific understanding of nature declined, the meanings attributed to celestial bodies got confused and convoluted to the point where some religions even invented new deities, because the *philosophical* underpinnings of these deities, and their subordinate divisions, was forgotten. As we have seen in the previous chapter, the number of divisions of the sun, the moon, and the stars, is not arbitrary. Every division has a philosophical basis, but if we miss that basis then it might seem arbitrary to us.

As diverse as they might seem to us from what is overtly visible, it is possible to view diverse religions as embodying different 'sects' of a universal religion that prevailed in a time that appears too distant right now, because the philosophy underlying that religion has been lost, misunderstood, and discounted. That philosophy is Vedic philosophy. But it is not a sectarian ideology, because it describes the nature of the soul, how this soul is entangled in the material body, how the soul enters newer bodies from life to life, including the change of body within this life. While many authorities from other religions might find it offensive to have traced their history into a past that they seem opposed to, and a matter of personal pride for the remaining followers of the Vedic traditions—in whatever meager form they survive today—the intent of such a description is neither to offend other religions, nor to claim some kind of racial, cultural, or religious superiority. The goal of our life is not to feel good about who we are—racially, culturally, or religiously. The goal is to transcend the material existence of the cycle of repeated birth and death. But before we can transcend this cycle, we must know how we are bound, how we got here, and how the transcendental world looks different from this one.

As time passed, and the philosophical understanding was lost, deity worship became meaningless, and was eventually rejected in numerous religions propounded in the last 3000 years. This included the rejection of not only deities of the demigods manifest from *Brahma*, but also the deities of *Shiva* and *Viṣṇu*. The Abrahamic religions thus rejected paganism, but in the proverbial throwing of the baby out along with the bathwater, also undermined monotheism because the form of *Viṣṇu*—presented as a deity—is considered heresy. The result of that rejection is that the religious person loses a profound understanding of the nature of God and the soul—e.g., that God has six primordial qualities, and both the soul and God have three aspects of *sat*, *chit*, and *ānanda*. Thereon, the monotheist speaks about the worship of God and the soul's liberation from the world, but only has a vague grasp of either of the two.

This rejection of all deities has a lot to do with certain philosophical problems concerning the interaction between matter and the soul, which have existed for a really long time in the Western world and continue unresolved to this day. The main problem is that in all religions there is a need to explain how the soul fell into matter, if indeed the soul is spiritual and was with God originally. This falldown was typically attributed in all religions to a disobedience of God's order. While this thesis is correct, it also leads to the question of how God can appear in this world, if the primary reason for falldown is disobedience of God's word. Just as the material body of the soul entails the soul's 'fall' into matter, similarly, giving God a form would mean that God too fell. Such a proposition would now entail that God is Himself fallible, and if God is fallible then how could He be considered the supreme infallible personality?

The problem of the soul's falldown leads to the conclusion that if God is worshipped as a deity, then His appearance in this world must entail His falldown. Thus, the ideology about the soul's falldown in matter, when applied to God's manifesting as a deity, entails that God must never appear in this world, and hence any deity formed to worship God must constitute a religious heresy. Once these deities are rejected from religion, the result is indistinguishable from impersonalism where a supreme person is recognized but His form is not described in order to avoid the problem arising from God's falldown. This is the position in the Abrahamic religions today, which don't permit the formation of God's deities because such images would entail God's falldown.

Now, it is worth remembering that we are talking about throwing the baby along with the bathwater, not claiming that the bathwater is itself clean. The realm of *Shiva* and *Viṣṇu* exist beyond the material world, so their worship is superior to the demigods who are not permanently situated in their roles. Therefore, demigod worship has been rejected, although their *existence* and control over material nature is not denied. Indeed, they are often described as worshippers of *Viṣṇu* or *Shiva*, never on par with them. The rejection of demigod worship—without rejecting their existence—followed by the worship of *Viṣṇu* or *Shiva* constitutes true monotheism. And this ideology has been described and practiced even within the Vedic tradition. The fact that it also advents in the Abrahamic religions is not novel. The novelty in Abrahamic religions is extending the rejection of pagan gods to all deities of God[3].

A detailed discussion of this problem first appears in Greek philosophy—the idea of *form* and *substance* in Aristotle's thinking. Aristotle was trying to solve the problem of how a soul gets the body, and how the two interact. He formulated the idea—based on Plato and Socrates—that there are two distinct things: form and substance. The soul is the form, and the body is the substance. Thus, a statue—think of a deity of some Greek god—is not a material object; rather, there is an *idea* which exists in another world which *incarnates* into the material substance. Through that substance the mind perceives the idea and once this idea has been obtained the mind can continue meditating on the form without needing the deity itself. In other words, the deity is like a message by which we obtain a meaning but the stone in which the deity is built is not itself a god. You can see where Aristotle was going with this and why he would want to do something like this: he was trying to give a rational basis to the worship of Greek gods—a kind of theological philosophy. Aristotle's work set the precedent for a long time where philosophy was used to explain theology.

But there is a problem in this philosophy—the problem of falldown. If the gods are descending into material substance, and the soul's descent into the body is called its falldown, then the descent of gods into matter must also be their falldown. How can the gods be worshipped if they are so fallible? There is a further problem of the soul's mutability. If the gods can descend into many deities and exist simultaneously in all the temples where these gods are worshipped, then the soul would appear to have been divided into many parts. How can the same god—a soul—exist in many deities at the same time? By that analogy we could say that there is only one soul—a universal soul—who descends into many bodies, which will then beg the question of how one thing becomes many things, and the form of the body would now be attributed to the body rather than the soul, forcing a collapse in this entire ideology.

Owing to these problems—(a) explaining the soul's immutability, (b) the infallibility of gods, and (c) without a universal soul who descends into many bodies—and their pending resolution in philosophy—it became essential to reject deities as forms of god. And this logic had to be applied not just to the worship of pagan gods (the equivalent of the Vedic demigods) but even to the single God. It now came to pass that if God cannot appear in matter, then He also cannot appear before our eyes—because the incarnation of God would imply God's falldown into matter, and God must be infallible. Therefore, we cannot know about God except through His messengers. These messengers must 'fall down' into matter and therefore be 'punished' like every other falling soul, but the falling messenger is a benevolent soul who accepts to fall into matter in order to deliver the message of God. The theme of a devotee of God falling into matter and taking the punishment became central to some of the later monotheistic doctrines—prominent being that of Christianity.

The issue arises because of the soul-body interaction problem, or what Aristotle called the form-substance duality. To claim that a deity of God or gods actually is that person, we must first solve the above problems.

Soul-Body Interaction in Vedic Philosophy

In Vedic philosophy, the soul interacts with the body through *prāna*—which is the energy or *Śakti* of God. The soul is considered 'male' and the energy or *Śakti* is 'female'[4]. The material body is then considered inert. This inert material body is described as a space of possibilities in which all the alternatives exist simultaneously, but they are not visible at once—after all, they are mere possibilities. The body becomes visible when the soul attaches to the possibility through the energy called *prāna*. Thus, every living body is marked by the presence of *prāna*, and if the body dies, *prāna* leaves the body and attaches the soul to another body. Ordinary mortals can only exist in one body. An advanced *yogi* can simultaneously expand his presence into 8 bodies. And God—as the originator of this energy—can expand Himself unlimitedly.

Through this expansion, the soul is not mutated into many bodies. Rather, God appears in many bodies through His energy or *Śakti*. If you break the stone or deity, God is not destroyed, because He is not "in" the stone, and yet He is attached to that stone through His *prāna*. This is quite like how plucking the fruit on a tree doesn't destroy the tree; and yet, when the fruit is on the tree, it receives the energy of the root and thereby remains alive. Breaking the deity is like plucking the fruit; that particular fruit will die, but many more fruits can spring forth. God's appearance in matter is therefore not His falldown, because this appearance is effected through His *Śakti*. Thus, in the Vedic tradition, both God and His *Śakti*—male and female—are worshipped and venerated.

At the root of the Greek philosophical problems lies the use of the word *incarnation* which is comprised of two roots—inside and carnal—indicating that the soul is 'inside' the body. Factually, the soul is never inside the body, just like the root is not inside the fruit. Rather, the root and the fruit are joined by branches, and those branches are created by an energy—*prāna*. This *prāna* is the *force* by which the world moves. Modern science studies this *prāna* through mechanical theories where it is described as gravity, electromagnetism, and such. We cannot perceive *prāna* by the senses, quite like we cannot perceive the above noted mechanical forces. We can, however, perceive their *effects* on matter. Since the soul interacts with the body through *prāna*, we also cannot perceive the soul inside the body. The contention of materialists, that if the soul truly existed it must be given a "position" in the body, is false, and their inability to find the soul in the body is not a testimony to the soul's non-existence, as the soul and the *prāna* cannot be perceived in matter. We only know of their existence through their effects, and therefore, just as 'force' is a theoretical construct in science—indirectly confirmed by the confirmation of the theory—similarly *prāna* and the soul are to be confirmed indirectly.

Truly speaking, therefore, the soul never falls into matter in the Greek sense as the combination of substance and form. Rather, the soul is connected to a material body when its *consciousness* is directed into the body through the *prāna*. As this consciousness is directed into the body, the soul considers himself to be that body. That delusion of the soul is termed as *false ego*. The false ego or *ahamkāra* manifests when the soul contacts the *Śakti* called *prāna*. As we know quite well, when a person gets some power, he becomes very proud; he thinks: "I am something". If we take away that power, the ego collapses. Therefore, the false ego or the idea that "I am something" is a material element produced as a consequence of the soul obtaining some of God's power.

The material world is created when God delegates His power to the soul. The moment the soul obtains this power, he is deluded into thinking "I am something" and "I have power". Thereafter, this false ego expands into other specific details creating the soul's mind and body. The expansion of the ego into the body and mind is elaborated in *Sāñkhya* and at every step the expansion proceeds through the application of the soul's *prāna*. This expansion of the ego into the mind and the body represents the gradual delegation of power from God to the soul, by which the ego expands into delusions of self-grandeur. When the material world is to be wound up, God takes that power away from the soul gradually. As the power is withdrawn, the ego begins to shrink, and step-by-step the material expansions of the ego begin to collapse. Thus, the gross body disappears followed by the mind and followed by the ego. The soul is now left powerless, and the sign of that powerlessness is that he is egoless. Nevertheless, when he gets the power again, he again develops ego.

Thus, to test the goodness of a person, one must give them power. Everyone can be a nice person when they don't have power. The real test of goodness is when they can act egoless even with power at their disposal. Even the advanced souls are therefore deluded by power into thinking that they are the doers of great actions, when their action is caused by the delegated power of God. We might now ask: If God knows that the soul will misuse the power, then why does He give it to the soul in the first place? Shouldn't God be benevolent, like a mother who will not give the child dangerous toys in order to keep him safe? The answer to that quandary is that if the power is withdrawn the soul loses his happiness, like a child who would cry because he has no toys to play with.

God delegates His power like a mother will give some toys to the child, fully aware that the child is likely to misuse them and get hurt in the process. Indeed, the child is also likely to blame the mother for giving him a dangerous toy if he gets hurt and blame her for not giving the playthings if she takes them away. The argument against God's benevolence is therefore pointless because regardless of what God does, the soul can respond with a complaint.

The fact is that no toy is dangerous, but every toy can be so if you don't use it appropriately. Spiritual philosophy is not about discarding all material objects. It is rather about accepting those objects and using them without getting hurt. When the energy delegated by God is used in His service, the energy causes no harm to the soul, and even more energy can be delegated. Therefore, the delegation of the energy isn't the problem; the problem is the soul thinking that by possessing this energy temporarily he has become God.

The deity of God or those of demigods don't involve (a) mutation of the soul, (b) falldown into matter, or (c) a universal soul. God, demigods, and the soul have an individuality, but the power or *Śakti* is always with God although He delegates it to others—more and more, if they use it correctly. Thus, through the power of delegation, a soul can become more and more powerful—i.e., demigods—and worshipped as being a great personality. But this is only because the soul is humble and uses the power in God's service. The dawn of pride signals the beginning of the fall whereby the power is withdrawn.

Vedic texts describe that God's *Śakti* has two aspects— *āvaraṇātmikā* and *prakṣepātmikā*. When the power is delegated—called *prakṣepātmikā*—the soul feels empowered and thinks "I can do whatever I like" and manufactures many plans of enjoyment considering himself the master of the world. When this power is withdrawn—*āvaraṇātmikā*—the soul considers himself powerless and falls into depression and sadness, feeling incapable. God is kind so He delegates, but then withdraws, because the soul misbehaves. In this way there are ups and downs in life because the soul is maddened by power.

Shiva is the master of *Śakti* or material power that manifests as *prāna*. *Yogis* who seek mystical powers worship *Shiva*. Some *yogis* worship *Śakti* directly in order to obtain mystical powers. But, ultimately, this power is withdrawn at the end of creation, and as the power is withdrawn, gradually the body collapses into the mind, the mind collapses into the ego, and the ego finally disappears because the soul loses all his power. In that state too, the soul is said to be liberated because he is out of material entanglement, but that liberation is like that of a person who pretends to be humble because he has no power. When the creation ensues again, the lust for power causes the soul to fall again. In that sense, the monist liberation—while real—is not the ultimate state of spirituality. The material world constitutes the misuse of God's power, the monist state is liberation by losing power, and the spiritual world is the domain of the proper use of power—for God's service. Nevertheless, even in the material world there are powerful personalities who have obtained enormous power over others because they know how to use it appropriately. These powerful persons are demigods, and power corrupts them to a lesser extent.

As the saying goes: "power corrupts and absolute power corrupts absolutely", spiritual advancement means that power doesn't corrupt the soul, and power is delegated to the soul in order to test if he is incorruptible.

The study of *prāna* is amenable to scientific inquiry quite like modern science studies forces of nature. However, *prāna* is not a mechanical force because it interacts with the soul, and effects changes according to its desires. When *prāna* is strong, the soul is able to work and enjoy. When *prāna* is weakened, the body is unable to function properly, and the soul is unable to enjoy. Thus, sickness of the body is the result of the weakening of *prāna.* The study of *prāna* as a force involves a science about how the soul is trapped in matter. It is not a science of matter per se. For example, in the material science, we speak about the motion of particles as the cause of change in matter. But in the Vedic description, matter is not changing. Our material body is a possibility—a state—that exists forever but is chosen by *prāna* and the soul is connected to a body. At every instant the soul acquires a new body and discards the old body. The body itself, however, does not disappear; it remains a possibility forever. Therefore, matter is not described as a *thing*. It is described as a possibility. The mind can perceive the possibilities while the senses only perceive the facts. This mental perception involves the soul contacting the mind through *prāna* and seeing the existence of a body that is not yet connected. Through such perception, we realize how we can move our body to a new location or do some work. In that sense, we cannot see the future body by our eyes. But we can develop our mental perception to see what the senses cannot see.

The basis of true religion is a science of matter quite different from modern science. As we noted in the first chapter, it is a science of personalism as opposed to impersonalism. This science doesn't have to be accepted on 'faith'. It can rather be articulated logically and rationally and tested empirically in our own lives. If and when such a science is understood, we will also realize that just as the ideas of modern science are universal—because they are stated logically and rationally, and because they are confirmed through empirical experience—true religion is also universal. That universality is not to be achieved by vehement proselytizing; it is to be confirmed based on reason and experience. The Vedic texts help us *discover* that science; they don't *confirm* their truth to us. The job of confirmation lies with each individual: understand the concepts and test them in your own life. If you find them good explanations of your experience, you have validated a theory of nature.

I am convinced—based on the reasons outlined in this book, and the confirmation of these reasons that I found in my everyday experience—that this ideology can be tested by everyone, and this book invites people to read, understand, and test the ideas. Adopt them if the tests are successful. You don't have to change your 'religion'; you are urged to transform your life. My goal is not to increase the count of people who claim to be followers of 'Hinduism'—as the Vedic religion is spoken of in modern times. I aim not to change your 'faith'—as you may have registered in your country or listed on your passport. I'm aiming for something far more profound, namely, the understanding that each person—regardless of their race, color, nationality, and religion—is ultimately a soul trapped in a different kind of human body because he desires to misuse the power differently. Some give up the power but are unable to give up the desire to misuse it. The greatest soul is one who accepts the power in the service of God, neither misusing it, nor fearing the entrapment.

The Existence of the Soul and God

Many people will object to the above description. They might argue: you have presupposed the existence of the soul and God in order to explain the world. What evidence exists to confirm that they indeed exist?

Obviously, we cannot empirically—i.e., sensually—confirm the existence of the observer to the observer himself. But as Descartes famously noted, *cogito ergo sum*, regardless of what I can doubt, I cannot doubt my own existence, because that self-doubt leaves nothing certain—including the certainty of every other fact obtained through reasoning or empirical experience. By and large, no religion truly denies the existence of the soul. Some religions—e.g., Buddhism—are silent on the matter; they are not opposed to the existence of the soul, nor do they confirm its existence. But, if there is no soul, then there really is no need for God either. Therefore, before we can speak about the reality of God, we have to first speak to the question of the soul's existence. This issue is not pertinent to most religions—especially if they accept the existence of the soul and God. But the issue is nevertheless important because the *reasons* why we accept the existence of the soul and God have a lot to do with their nature.

I have noted earlier that both the soul and God—in Vedic philosophy—have three qualities: *sat* or relation, *chit* or concepts, and *ānanda* or pleasure. Of the three, modern science studies *chit* as particles and *sat* as force. The desire, intention, and pleasure are totally neglected, and the universe is purposeless. Furthermore, even the concepts and forces are described linearly rather than hierarchically, which results in the dissolution of meaning because a symbol is an entity that acquires a meaning in relation to a 'higher' entity. This 'higher' and 'lower' are properties of space, and if space is conceived hierarchically, then objects are also symbols. Current science flattens this space and makes the world meaningless; together with purposelessness, meaninglessness takes away the need for the soul as two of three properties—*ānanda* and *chit*—are made irrelevant. The third property—*sat* or awareness—is now explained only based on material forces, in a complete denial of choice.

The cardinal example of such a force-based description is Einstein's general theory of relativity which collapses the distinction between matter, force, space, and time, describing the world deterministically. There is, however, one problem—that of inelastic collisions—which renders this entire scheme indeterministic. In an *elastic* collision the particle retains its mass; an *inelastic* collision is one in which a particle changes its mass due to collisions. Once a particle's mass is changed in a collision, the entire future of the universe becomes indeterministic. The problem therefore arises due to the distinction between a *particle* and its *mass* or material property, because the particle can change its properties during a collision. A single such change renders the entire theory indeterministic—i.e., incapable of predicting the future. Inelastic collisions are a fact of life, although they can never be modeled in a deterministic theory. As a result, there can never be a deterministic theory of nature. There is also a second-order problem, namely, that gravity is at present inconsistent with atomic theory and their unification remains an unsolved problem. However, even if this problem did not exist, gravity by itself would be incapable of predicting the future due to a separation between particles and masses.

In Vedic philosophy, the soul is the particle and the body and the mind are its properties. The *sat* of the soul results in forces—the *prāna* which is partially studied as gravity. But this *prāna* is a power to cause a change; it is not change by itself unless the soul wills the use of power to make a change. Therefore, the force is not deterministic; rather, it acts under the soul's control. The indeterminism in both gravity and atomic theory attests to these problems; they are fundamentally incapable of predicting the future because the force or energy only acts under the soul's will. Now, if things were totally up to each individual soul, the world would appear to be totally chaotic. The fact that the world is organized—e.g., that planets go around in their orbits periodically—is because some souls (controlling the motion of planets and stars) act in a duty-bound manner, fearing the repercussions of violating their assigned jobs. The perceived order in nature—e.g., as the periodic motion of planets which gravity models as force and particle—is not due to the law of gravitation. It is rather because there are souls who have free will to act differently, but they act in an organized manner due to the moral law of action and consequence.

In that sense, there is no such thing as a 'gravitational law', although there is force that causes things to change under the control of some soul. The law can be violated, and the planets can—in principle—change their course at any time. However, the awareness of the moral consequences of such actions—called *karma*—prevents them from doing such things. For instance, if the sun stopped in its trajectory, a huge number of living entities would be inconvenienced, and that inconvenience constitutes adverse *karma* for the sun: he has to bear the collection of all the individual inconveniences on himself. Such a possibility is known and feared by the soul controlling the sun's motion, and the sun therefore stays in its orbit and we observe the periodicity and assume that it must be due to a mechanical law of gravity when the fact is that the real law that keeps the sun in its orbit is the moral law of consequences.

The existence of the soul, therefore, doesn't have to be empirically confirmed. It can also be used as a *theory* in which the predictions of nature are explained differently than in modern science. The essence of this theory is that reality has three facets—relation, concept, and goal—which makes the universe three-dimensional, although this space now enables meaning, purpose, and consciousness. Pending the empirical confirmation of the soul, therefore, the soul can also be used as a *theoretical construct* and this hypothesis would be confirmed if other things based on this hypothesis are confirmed.

That brings us to the question about the existence of God—perhaps the toughest and the most difficult topic even among the many religions. If we have confirmed the reality of the soul based on the above hypothesis, then we would be faced with the problem of *counting* these souls. Who should we count first? Who should be the leader of all souls? This question seems difficult in an ordinary sense, but the problem is already solved if we induct meaning, purpose, and awareness as a hypothesis: we realize that these three properties construct an *inverted tree* which originates in a *root.* God, in Vedic philosophy, is identified as the root of the world, the origin of space. The God 'hypothesis' is therefore not a separate hypothesis from the soul hypothesis. We cannot separately conceive of the soul and God, although they are separate. Rather, as noted above, when the universe is described as an inverted tree, God is the root of the tree, and the soul is situated on some part of the tree. The confirmation of the soul via the above hypothesis is also God's verification.

That brings me to the crux of the issue vis-à-vis the universality of religion. The issue is simply that we are arguing for changing our definition of *space*; we are saying that space is not three physical dimensions; it is rather three distinct properties created from the three modes of nature. We are also saying that these three modes of nature originate in the properties of the soul, so each person has a direct access to its confirmation. God is then the Supreme Soul, which means that He has the same properties of cognition, emotion, and relation as the soul. His *position* in nature is however different; unlike the other souls who might be situated as branches and leaves of the cosmic cognition, emotion, and relation, the Supreme Soul is the root of this tree. The origin of the universe is therefore fixed but the soul's position is not. Nevertheless, the soul and God—the most problematic and contentious ideas in religions—can be defined scientifically through the definition of space and time.

Just as the ideas of space and time can be confirmed empirically as part of a theory that predicts and explains phenomena—even though we can never perceive space and time directly through senses—similarly, a different notion of space and time, and thence the notions of soul and God can be empirically confirmed in science, even though we cannot perceive them directly.

This is then the basis on which I claim the universality of religion: there is a scientific theory of space and time which can be empirically confirmed individually and collectively. The individual confirmation will prove that we are souls. The collective confirmation will prove that there are other souls, and to distinguish and identify them we need to *count* them. Counting needs a beginning—in space, time, and individual. Only a person who is the origin of space and time is also God. Truthfully, nobody believes that they created this fascinating universe. Therefore, God is a scientific hypothesis on par with the existence of the soul, and it is necessary to explain the existence of the world. God will, therefore, have a location *in* space and time—and the location will be their *origin*. This origin is the highest point in space and time, because these are inverted trees, and the highest point of all existence is the tree's root. We don't have to disagree on what God is, and where He lives. We have to just find the origin of space and time scientifically. In so far as the theory of space and time is universal, the understanding of the soul and God is also universal.

The Question of Science-Religion Synthesis

I am therefore proposing a non-sectarian view of religiosity in which we end the debate of whose God is better or worse, whose scripture is true or not, and whose morality is superior or inferior. My proposal is that the soul and God can be known scientifically—by studying the nature of space and time. The conclusions of this study—namely that God is the origin of the world, that the soul has free will and can change his position, and that God has given the soul avenues to exercise his free will by changing his location on the tree—are consistent with most known religions. I doubt that people debate the existence of the soul, God, free will, and matter, and still claim to be religious. What they debate about is all the rest—i.e., the nature of the soul's bondage, the consequences of our free will—how good or bad will be determined, and how one can transcend the material existence of choice and consequences. But I will argue that these are not questions of 'faith'. When the question of the existence of the soul and God can be settled scientifically, these are truly second order and relatively easier questions to answer—based on the same theory.

In that sense, all of religion is amenable to scientific inquiry. Not everything in every religion may turn out to be true. And many things in many religions may only be true in a given context of goal, place, and role. As a tree diversifies, it creates many branches, twigs, and leaves. The description of one leaf may be different from that of another, but both leaves have emerged from the same root. As long as the root remains invisible, the branches appear disparate, and the debate about the truth of the religions will continue. To resolve this debate, and to find the truth that transcends the contradicting viewpoints, we seek the root from which the branches and leaves have emerged.

I'm aware that most religions and their practitioners will find this proposal inacceptable. But many rational and non-dogmatic people may find it useful. There is a price to be paid in the process—not all religions will turn out to be *absolute truths*. But we can show how the core principles of religion—e.g., the soul, God, and free will—are absolutely true, while other factors such as the proper use of free will for a time, place, and person are only *contextually true* to that time, place, and person. Some of the ideas about moralities that were applicable in the past may not apply now. Some of the moralities that were unique to the place and the people of the past may not apply now. In that way, we can change *dharma* or duty and morality, without changing the core principles of the soul, God, free will, the nature of the soul's entanglement in matter, and the various ways in which the soul can escape this bondage.

If we remain caught in the differences across religions, we inevitably fail to focus upon the things that we commonly agree upon. The ideas of the soul, God, free will, and morality—as the laws of God—are themselves under attack today. Nobody seems to have an answer to these attacks, although the attackers themselves have no *evidence* against them. The attackers might simply argue: I cannot give you evidence for something that doesn't exist.

But I will argue that if you had a sufficiently robust theory of nature you could prove the non-existence *theoretically*. These are called proofs by way of contradiction or *reduction ad absurdum*. If a consistent and complete explanation of the material world can be built without the ideas of the soul, God, free will, and morality, then the mere confirmation of the theory would *theoretically* confirm the non-existence of the soul, God, and morality. Conversely, if such a theory cannot be found due to the problems of indeterminism outlined above, and a consistent and complete theory of nature can be found based on the ideas of the soul, God, and morality, then by the mere confirmation of such a natural theory, the notions of the soul, God, and morality would be automatically confirmed. Therefore, my proposal is not merely about understanding the religious diversity while operating within the bounds of some specific religious assumptions. The proposal is even broader—i.e., it is not afraid to take on the atheistic critique on its home turf—theory and experiment.

The project of religious unification—that cuts across diverse religions—is no different than the project of scientific unification. There is one religion because there is one science—the universal theory of reality. If religion is true, then it can and should provide an explanation of the world. The challenge is therefore singular—and offered to both science and religion: Who has a better explanation of our experience, and our most fundamental questions? I think religion must accept that challenge and not hide behind the facades of revelation, faith, morals, mind-body dualism, and scriptural priorities. It is alright to bring all those ideas on the table, but the final test for an ordinary person is not which book the idea came from, but whether it is indeed true.

As time passes, the forward march of materialism will undermine people's faith in any religion. Or, even if they maintain their faith, their understanding of the soul and God, free will and morality, bondage and freedom, will become inconsistent with science and practical experience. They may then continue to follow a faith in namesake but will practically not adhere to most of its teachings because of the numerous contradictions between the advancing materialism and the tenets of their religion. In that sense, religion has no future unless it takes on the path of reason and experience, the process of understanding the self in relation to the universe and answer fundamental questions about the nature of body and mind, that which constitutes right and good, apart from what we consider to be true by reason and experiment.

In a simple sense, we need a unified theory of truth, right, and good. The good will make us happy, but that good must be right to make others happy too, and that collective happiness can last only if based on the nature of truth. We cannot pretend to build a science that gives us a truth, and a religion that deals with right and good. Any science that doesn't answer questions of right and good is incomplete. And any religion whose claim of right and good is not based on the truth given by scientific inquiry is fundamentally flawed. In that sense, there has to be a 'marriage' of religion and science, but in another sense, they were never truly divorced to begin with. The divorce was conceived when the philosophical understanding of material nature became separated from the understanding of the soul. In short, we stopped asking questions like: Why am I here? How did I get here? What can I do to get out of this place? Does my life have meaning? What constitutes the ultimate meaning? When the study of material truths is divorced from the questions that every person asks, then the quest for such truth will also fail to satisfy the inner needs in a person. The divorce between religion and science is artificial and relatively recent. We have to ask the same questions that have been asked for millennia. And we have to change the science of nature to become suitable to answer them.

It has been said that "science without religion is lame, and religion without science is blind"[5], but the analogy assumes two separate individuals—a lame and a blind—joining hands together in some curious inexplicable way so far not properly explained. My contention is that attempts at "synthesis" are not taking anyone anywhere. There is, instead, a single science of truth, right, and good; it has been artificially separated in modern times: science taking on the mantle of truth, and religion that of right and good. The understanding of the soul unifies these three judgments because the quest for truth is the *chit*, the quest for right is *sat*, and the quest for good is *ānanda*. Just as we cannot separate the three aspects of the soul, or find a method by which they are joined, similarly, we cannot perform a "synthesis" of religion and science presuming that they were different to begin with. The terms 'religion' and 'science' should rather be redeemed more precisely as "the rational and empirical inquiry to answer the most fundamental questions of human existence."

A considerable amount of sincerity is required to even accept these questions. On the part of religions, the 'faith'-based approach turns out to be a non-starter because the method of inquiry is not "rational and empirical". On the part of science, the rational and empirical approach still proves insufficient because we are not even trying to deal with the "most fundamental questions". I therefore believe that both science and religion—in their present form—will cease to be relevant over time. This trend is visible all over the world as fewer students pursue pure sciences because technology, pharmaceuticals, law, marketing, politics, music, acting, and fashion seem more rewarding. Similarly, fewer people take religion seriously or even consider it true. They may continue support for both science and religion, primarily because supporting science is equated to modernity and accepting religion is necessary to remain culturally connected to the past. But the statistics on such support are the smokescreen that hide the underlying truth—namely that fewer people care either about religion or about science, relative to everything else possible.

If religion doesn't adopt a rational and empirical approach, and if science doesn't turn toward the most fundamental questions of human inquiry, then they will rapidly become irrelevant to the large majority of people.

Moving Forward or Moving Backward?

A dominant cultural argument against the dialogue between religion and science, and indeed giving religious ideas like the soul and God importance in the modern world, is that these are things of the 'past'. That we must look to the future rather than to the past, a journey that the West began during the Renaissance and Enlightenment ages, when the domains of religion and science were separated by Cartesian metaphysics: science was to deal with questions of *truth*, while religion was allocated questions of *right* and *good*.

Before we answer if this approach is viable, let's take a brief walk down memory lane. The philosophical separation between science and religion wasn't the end of Enlightenment. During the same period, and very soon after the proposed separation, much of the task of deciding the right and the good attributed to religion was taken away by the separation of religion from politics; it was primarily the goal of politicians to decide what is right and good for society—based on democratic and majoritarian principles. Religion was reduced to providing some overall moral guidelines, but not required or allowed to intervene in the actual social structure influence or even law formation. That power rested solely in the hands of the state and the ruler. Shortly afterwards, even the political system lost much of its power because the main purpose of the state was to provide economic prosperity to the people; the principles of morality and jurisprudence were then subordinated to that of economic well-being. Then, this economic well-being came to be defined as the well-being of the businesses which created the jobs for the common people; if the businesses were not doing well, then the common man would surely suffer. Eventually, even the well-being of the businesses came to be seen as the successes of those who create, manage, and own these businesses—a fraction of society.

Modernists assert the truth, rightness, and goodness of every major step in this journey, but obviously, the outcome of this journey is hardly satisfactory for the majority of the population. Statistics coming from diverse sources now show that 82% of the profits of economic activity performed by the entire population now go to a mere 1% of the population[6]. In other words, the quest for the liberation from the oppression of religion has reinvented slavery. If society continues on the same path and direction that it has pursued over the last few centuries, then it will certainly lead toward revolution and anarchy, where the wealth aggregated by the rich would be redistributed to the poor. This, of course, is not new; it has happened in the recent memorable past during the French, Russian, Chinese, and other socio-cultural revolutions. The cause of these disruptions wasn't a particular political ideology; the cause was extreme poverty and hopelessness suffered by the majority of the population.

The question, however, is: Given that this scenario is inevitable if we stay the modernist course, what would we like to replace it with? I will propose that the project of modernism—beginning with the separation of the questions of truth from those of right and good—has been a bad experiment, because there is no basis on which such a separation can be made. The soul's *chit* is truth, his *sat* is rightness, and his *ānanda* is goodness. We cannot separate these questions without dividing the soul itself into three parts, but the soul is indivisible. You and I don't judge truth independent of right and good. We first seek our happiness—i.e., goodness—and then find the ways to achieve it—i.e., truth. But, since we also live in a society, our desires for happiness must be subordinated to the well-being of others, and therefore, goodness must be subordinated to rightness. There is hence a clear hierarchy of the judgments: the right is at the top, the good is below the right, and the truth is below the good.

This doesn't mean that I will choose the good according to my whims and fancies. It rather means that of all the things that exist as truth, I will pick those few which make me happy. That choice of picking a subset of truth is enabled by my desire for happiness. However, I cannot seek my happiness in disregard of the rightness of my actions and desires. Therefore, I must foremost understand the nature of rightness—which is defined by my duties or *dharma*.

The question is thus not one of moving forward or backward as defined by the modernist project. The question is of finding the happiness under the dictates of morality. That question is identical to the religion of *Brahma* which outlines the duties and responsibilities of each person, empowers them to perform their duties, but holds them responsible for their dereliction. If one considers this religion insufficient, and the process of working and enjoying, an endless repetition, then there is the religion of *Shiva*—namely, living by oneself outside the material world. If one is further dissatisfied by this proposal, then there is the religion of *Viṣṇu*—living with others who have similarly realized their individuality and yet decided to subordinate it to that of God.

If you reject all these alternatives, then you have the dogma of modernism and materialism—euphemisms for the reinvention of slavery in which a small percentage of people will lead lavish lives at the expense of everyone else. Your hope, under the materialist project, is that you will be one who controls slaves, instead of being someone's slave. But this hope is going to rapidly decline as modernism moves forward. For example, when most of the society is impoverished, who can the rich take wealth from? Their focus will now shift to other wealthy people, until most of the wealth with the currently wealthy is further concentrated in even fewer numbers of wealthy people. This process has to repeat continuously, until it is reversed. Which means that if it is not reversed, your prospect of being wealthy and powerful diminish every day.

Society is commonly envisioned as a Bell curve with the large majority of the population being in the center, and a few at the edges. A relatively flatter Bell curve means a more even distribution of resources and much greater opportunity for everyone. A steeper bell curve means a high concentration of resources with a few, and declining opportunities for everyone else.

Under modernism, the Bell curve is steepening. Modernism came out of the rejection of nobility and religion, and for a time it seemed to flatten society. But by rejecting the principles of morality that were previously upheld—to a greater extent than they are held today—the Bell curve has steepened even further. We must note that the steepening of the Bell curve is directly attributable to the morality of the top rungs of society. If the leaders are immoral, the Bell curve steepens because they steal from the poor in order to make themselves richer and more powerful. The morality of today's elite is even lower than that of the elite in the past. Therefore, what led to their overthrow in the past is true today as well. But overthrowing doesn't solve the problem if the higher echelons of the new society remain immoral; the Bell curve may flatten for a short period of time, but it will steepen again even faster.

The real answer is developing a good understanding of truth, right, and good, and how immoral action leads to suffering. In other words, the rich and immoral today will be reborn as poor and destitute in their next lives and complain against the very class to which they once belonged. It doesn't matter what religion you belong to, and whether or not you believe in morality. The point of natural law is that it is upheld whether or not you know about it, or believe in its existence. The only way to institute morality in society is to inform the people about the moral laws of action and consequence. If such laws are unknown, then the social Bell curves will rise faster, and collapse more suddenly. More and more societies will be created and destroyed, and more people will suffer out of ignorance of the consequences of their own actions.

The urgent need for interreligious and science-religion dialogues arises in order to prevent such catastrophes. The goal is singular—we have to at least understand the religion of *Brahma* and institute morality in society. This understanding is scientific, rational, and empirical, rather than sectarian or based on faith. The consequences of not accepting this religion of morality—and continuing on the path that we call 'modernism'—are also amply clear. With that clarity, the path of going backwards in time can also be the path of moving forward in terms of a healthier, happier, saner, and a more stable society.

Problems of Cultural Dissent

Many people are still likely not going to be convinced due to historical, cultural, and racial reasons. They have grown in different parts of the world, belong to different races, have different cultures, speak different languages, and practice different religions, which attribute them different histories.

People are emotionally rooted in their civilization, nationality, language, religion, and culture and identify with it. This identification is the *ego*—the sense of *I* and *mine*; from it desires and pleasures are created, and from the ego stem our aspirations and goals. But there is a more fundamental reason for the existence of the ego: we identify with things and circumstances around us because it helps us feel secure. The soul is lonely in this world and afflicted by fear. Identifying with things other than the self helps the soul feel less lonely and insecure. If this identity were weakened, the soul's fear would return, and that fear would in turn result in anger and conflict. Thus, people are naturally more comfortable in the surroundings they identify with. A person living in a foreign country, for example, tends to be more careful about his words and deeds than in his native place. Similarly, people feel more comfortable with others who speak the same language, who share the same religion, or who follow the same culture. When the soul's fear is set to rest due to identification with the surroundings, his innate arrogance again becomes more prominent. One takes pride in their culture, language, religion, and culture, and considers it superior to other things; this is because the fear has been put to rest.

Thus, due to the ego, one identifies with one's natural history, feels afraid when that is potentially at any risk, and feels confident, proud, fulfilled, and superior to the others when present in comforting circumstances.

This ego is a natural hurdle in any kind of dialogue because the two parties involved in a discussion are emotionally invested in their opinions;

those opinions make them feel safe and comfortable, confident and fulfilled. The ego hence prevents a genuine understanding of which of the two positions might indeed be superior. As we have seen many times earlier, difference always means a hierarchy. You count from 1 to N, and the counting begins at the top—i.e., by identifying the first, highest, topmost, and best. Since nobody identifies with something inferior—if they truly knew it was inferior—the ego ensures that the thing that one identifies with is always prioritized at the top. Even if one becomes aware of the fallacies and faults in their position, the resulting loss in confidence and pride naturally results in a decline in the sense of security and an increase in fear. Under this fear, one refuses to accept the truth. This natural human psychology plays an important role in any discussion of culture and history, because everyone is emotionally invested in it.

But we must also understand that the soul is different from its nationality, race, religion, society, family, and culture. If these identifications become a hurdle in accepting the truth, then one has to be strong to embrace the fear. The pursuit of knowledge is frightening, because it brings our assumptions—which made us comfortable and secure—into question. For this pursuit to be successful, one has to be brave to accept the truth; many people cannot face their fear, and therefore they cannot learn new things because this novelty makes them insecure; they seek comfort in the false although the well-known.

The problem of race, nationality, and culture interfering in the quest for truth is very real and pertinent, but very few people talk about such things because the conversation is itself highly disconcerting. The primary method of overcoming the fear of the unknown is to increase one's familiarity with it. But there are secondary methods, such as building better cultural, historical, ideological, and linguistic bridges. Vedic knowledge, for instance, has been locked for ages behind linguistic barriers, a problem that is now being addressed through books published in English and many other languages. In this section, I will attempt to describe a completely different kind of bridge—one of shared ancestry for all of mankind, and common origins for all kinds of cultures. Nothing can work better for interreligious dialogue than knowing we are descendants of a common lineage. Just as the children who leave the home of their parents to live far from their place of birth become strangers to those who stayed back, similarly, humanity has become a stranger to itself due to migration from one part of the world to many others. While historical lineages are not directly relevant to philosophical topics, they have been noted in nearly all religious texts just in order to bring that shared sense of history and culture.

All religions describe their lineage and history. But this lineage takes two forms—biological and spiritual. The biological lineage concerns the generations of kings and queens, rulers and their descendants. The spiritual lineage concerns the succession of teachers and disciples. In many cases, the biological lineage is also the spiritual lineage, when spiritual knowledge is passed down from parent to child. As a result, the rulers become philosopher kings or queens who inculcate the spiritual understanding in the country or place of their ruling. However, in other cases, the spiritual lineage is different from the biological one because the spiritual leader is not the progenitor of his followers. In the Vedic tradition, for example, the disciples consider themselves 'sons' and 'daughters' of their *guru* and regard them as benevolent instructors. The relationship between *guru* and disciple is so deep that it often supersedes the biological relationships, and one refers only to the spiritual lineage, ignoring their biological heritage. Ultimately, in a religious context, the biological heritage is unimportant, and the spiritual heritage is all-important.

I'm making this point because often when we read about lineages in religious texts, it is entirely possible that they refer to spiritual teacher-disciple relationships, not merely the biological heritage. Maintaining an unbroken succession of teachers has been considered extremely important in the Vedic tradition, even when the tradition migrated from oral to written. Of course, in the oral tradition, it was indispensable. But even in the written tradition, the master-disciple relationship is essential for the disciple to understand the true meaning of a religious text by placing himself in the context of the time, place, situation, and person in which those texts were uttered, but the context itself was not noted in the text. The true understanding of the text depends on understanding the context, and that's primarily what the teacher brings. He has immersed himself in the context and inherited it from his own teacher. In that sense, religion cannot be understood except through an unbroken lineage of teachers and disciples, and therefore religious texts cannot be translated or explained by those who haven't themselves immersed themselves in the subject by accepting a teacher who in turn accepted tutelage in the past.

Many academics translating or commenting on spiritual texts miss this point. They fail to recognize that one doesn't become a doctor, lawyer, engineer, or scientist simply by reading books at home. Such reading is not forbidden, but that reading doesn't qualify one to teach the subject or practice it in the real world. Academic scholars who study religious texts without committing themselves to the tutelage of an expert master are like the surgeons who learned surgery at home by reading books and want to operate on patients without being certified as qualified surgeons by other surgeons. Even modern academia disallows such practices; you have to pass an exam, obtain a certificate, and often recertify yourself to continue teaching or practicing.

The point is that a lineage is essential, and it must always be spiritual, although it can sometimes also be biological if the spiritual knowledge is being transmitted to one's offspring. Thus, the biological lineages must also be considered spiritual, and all lineages may not be biological, because everyone is not inclined toward a religious life and the disinclined would naturally be averse to passing something which they did not themselves accept. The lineage thus terminates at the point where one rejects the religious principles, and only those lineages which continue the tradition need be considered important. In light of this fact, we can conclude that not all lineages are mentioned; the important ones—from a spiritual standpoint—are noted because they continue to have a noteworthy spiritual influence on later generations. Therefore, when we speak about the lineage, we are not necessarily talking about the biological parent and child inheritances. That list is obviously too long and complex, and irrelevant to our spiritual understanding. The important fact is to see how *knowledge* was transmitted through generations.

Religious History in Vedic Texts

Vedic texts describe a lineage beginning in *Brahma* as the provider of religious principles or *dharma* in this world. The lifetime of *Brahma* is over 311 trillion years, and a single day of his life is 4,320,000,000 years. Within this day 14 *Manu* appear —the creators of human civilization and its moral laws; each *Manu* lives for 306,720,000 years. At the end of *Manu*'s life, there are intervening periods of partial destruction of the universe, including the end of all human life. After that intervening period—which lasts 1,728,000 years, a new *Manu* recreates human life again, imparting the laws of *dharma* for humanity once again. According to Vedic descriptions, the current age of the universe is over 155 trillion years—we are past the halfway mark, and the present human civilization was originated by *Vaivaśvata Manu* about 120,533,116 years ago. This is how hold the human race is at the present moment. In other words, all modern theories of recent evolution of man from apes are rejected, and a detailed counter explanation of the humanity's past and present is provided, along with specifics on times, places, situations, and persons.

When a *Manu* creates the human civilization, he imparts the rules for their living in a text called *Manu Smṛti.* We might note here that *Manu Smṛti* is not an eternally true text, because the *Manu* themselves change in 306,720,000 years. Contrary to much other Vedic knowledge, which is considered timeless, the *dharma* prescribed by *Manu Smṛti* is codified rules applicable for the duration of the reign of a particular *Manu.* At the end of the current *Manu*'s reign, the human civilization will again be annihilated and recreated by the next *Manu* who will then impart the new rules encoded again in a (different) *Manu Smṛti* applicable for the next 306,720,000 years. With this background, we can understand why *Manu* is given this importance in the Vedic system: his rules are not eternal, but he is still the originator of this particular iteration of the human civilization. He has been empowered by *Brahma* to define the rules of *dharma* for this age, and therefore the text authored by him—although not the word of God directly—is still the rulebook for humanity for this age.

The *Manu Samhita* notes that this iteration of human civilization was created in a place called *Brahmavarta* in between two rivers—*Sarasvati* and *Drishadvati*—which is identified with the ancient Indus Valley and Harappa civilization. *Manu Smṛti* describes a section of India, lying between the Himalayan and the *Vindhya* mountains to be secondary to *Brahmavarta* and the land of the *Aryan* peoples. The other places are designated as *mleccha.* This term has come to have derogatory meanings over time, but it wasn't meant as a derogatory word at that time; it meant all those who don't follow the social system called *Varṇāśrama* prescribed by *Manu* as part of the *Manu Samhita.*

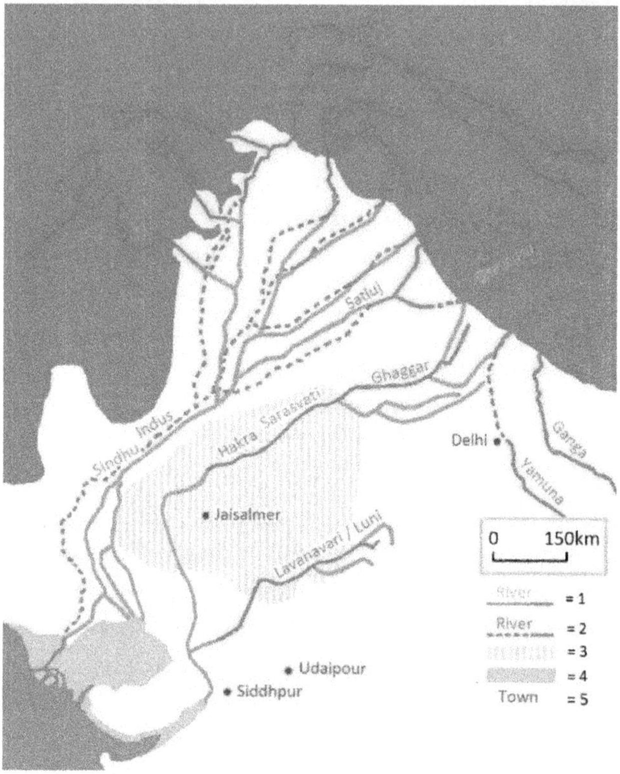

Figure-22 Indus-Sarasvati Civilization

Manu Samhita 2.17[7]. *That land, created by the gods, which lies between the two divine rivers Sarasvati and Drishadvati, the (sages) call Brahmavarta.*

MS 2.18. The custom handed down in regular succession (since time immemorial) among the (four chief) classes (varṇa) and the mixed (races) of that country, is called the conduct of virtuous men.

MS 2.19. The plain of the Kurus, the (country of the) Matsyas, Pankalas, and Surasenakas, these (form), indeed, the country of the Brahmarshis (Brahmanical sages, which ranks) immediately after Brahmavarta.

MS 2.20. From a Brahmana, born in that country (Brahmavarta), let all men on earth learn their several usages.

MS 2.21. That (country) which (lies) between the Himavat and the Vindhya (mountains) to the east of Prayaga (the meeting of Ganga and Yamuna rivers) and to the west of Vinasana (the place where the river Sarasvati disappears) is called Madhyadesa (the central region).

MS 2.22. But (the tract) between those two mountains (just mentioned), which (extends) as far as the eastern and the western oceans, the wise call Aryavarta (the country of the Aryans).

MS 2.23. That land where the black antelope naturally roams, one must know to be fit for the performance of sacrifices; (the tract) different from that (is) the country of the Mlekkhas (barbarians).

MS 2.24. Let twice-born men seek to dwell in those (above-mentioned countries); but a Sudra, distressed for subsistence, may reside anywhere.

The term *Brahmavarta* specifically means the land in which the religion of *Brahma* is followed. This religion illustrates the division of society into four classes, called *Brahmana*, *Kshatriya*, *Vaisya*, and *Sudra*, and prescribes specific duties and responsibilities for them. We might note yet again that *dharma* means duties; you can define duties only after you define the roles. In that sense, the prescription of religion begins by defining the roles—the social classes—followed by their responsibilities or what they are supposed to do. The meaning of *Brahmavarta* is simply that in this place the society is divided into 4 classes, and each class has a specific duty defined in *Manu Smṛti*.

MS 1.31[8]*. For the sake of the prosperity of the worlds He (God) caused the Brahmana, the Kshatriya, the Vaisya, and the Sudra to proceed from his mouth, his arms, his thighs, and his feet.*

MS 1.87[9]*. In order to protect this universe He, the most resplendent one, assigned separate (duties and) occupations to those who sprang from his mouth, arms, thighs, and feet.*

MS 1.88. To Brahmana he assigned teaching and studying (the Veda), sacrificing for their own benefit and for others, giving and accepting (of alms).

MS 1.89. The Kshatriya he commanded to protect the people, to bestow gifts, to offer sacrifices, to study (the Veda), and to abstain from attaching himself to sensual pleasures;

MS 1.90. The Vaisya to tend cattle, to bestow gifts, to offer sacrifices, to study (the Veda), to trade, to lend money, and to cultivate land.

MS 1.91. One occupation only the lord prescribed to the Sudra, to serve meekly even these (other) three castes.

MS 1.92. Man is stated to be purer above the navel (than below); hence the Self-existent has declared the purest (part) of him (to be) his mouth.

MS 1.93. As the Brahmana sprang from mouth, as he was the first-born, and as he possesses the Veda, he is by right the lord of this whole creation.

This definition of *dharma*—which we commonly call 'religion' at present—had little to do with transcendence; its substance was social organization and duties of the four classes, and how people of different qualities and activities must lead their lives. Of course, the ulterior purpose of this description was to transcend the material world, but *dharma* did not mean only the description of the transcendent reality. Instead, as outlined in the *Manu Smṛti*, it proceeded to define the conception of a child, marriage laws, the sacrifices to be performed by different classes, the laws of land and taxation, the rites of passage through different phases of life, the duties to be performed at these stages, the rites at the time of death, and so forth. We might also note—as we have in the past—that this religion of *Manu Smṛti* is different, although not contradictory, to the religions of *Shiva* and *Viṣṇu.* The religion of *Brahma* involves the performance of rituals for the demigods, strict social stratification, and obedience to the laws of *Manu.* But the religions of *Shiva* and *Viṣṇu* deemphasize these principles in the pursuit of transcendence and God's love.

For example, a person who renounces social life in order to perform meditation and penance is outside the social system. He or she might live in a forest, eat fruits, leaves, and roots, subsist on whatever nature provides, and he is not required to perform the daily rituals prevalent in *Brahma*'s religion. Similarly, one who dedicates himself to the worship of *Viṣṇu* can neglect many of the prescriptions of *Brahma*'s religion, as long as they don't disturb others who live in the same society and therefore share the social order with others. The key point is that *Brahmavarta* represents the starting of *Brahma*'s religion, and the cradle of civilization for humankind. But it doesn't represent the only type of religion, even within the Vedic system. Some religions can step outside this system—because they are practiced away from society e.g., the worship of *Shiva*. Others may stay within society but practice a more advanced system of religion—e.g., the worship of *Viṣṇu*. This simultaneous existence of the multitude of religions is one prominent reason why Indians have been comfortable with religious diversity for ages. But this diversity is not arbitrary. The rules of *Manu Samhita* constitute the lowest common denominator considered prudent by the father of humankind—*Vaivaśvata Manu*. One is welcome to follow higher forms of religion as propounded by *Shiva* and *Viṣṇu*, but one is not expected to fall below these criteria and still be designated 'human'.

In that sense, the societies that evolved into other social systems—e.g., less than four classes, with incompatible roles and responsibilities, or they did not perform all the prescribed functions as defined by *Manu*—were designated *mleccha*. Inherent in this designation is the idea that not everyone is qualified, inclined, or capable of practicing all the rules of *Manu's* religion. The standards for his system are very high, and not every human was meeting those standards even at that time—which is why even then they were identified as *mleccha*. That doesn't mean that they did not have a religion or social system of rules and regulations. It rather means that their system was different and did not meet the highest standards outlined in the *Manu Samhita*. In that sense, they were considered 'inferior', although they were societies and religions, too. It is noteworthy, therefore, that the Vedic system doesn't advocate a single religion, and everyone else a 'heretic'. It rather prescribes the highest system, and then recognizes that others may not necessarily follow this system. They have the freedom to form separate societies and practices and live by the rules that they can agree to follow—in a society of similar agreements.

They are, however, not permitted to mix with each other, because such mixing will cause the others—who wish to live by a higher standard—to feel discomfort. For instance, certain societies may not wish to encourage the killing of animals and the consumption of meat. Others may consider alcohol and intoxicants detrimental to spiritual advancement. Such a society will encourage those who desire to kill animals or consume intoxicants to leave their land and join another land where others have similar proclivities. The birds of the same feather flock together; living with like-minded people is convenient and prudent: you can follow a common set of rules and expectations.

Such an approach to religion (where you set the highest standards, but allow people to follow whatever they can, and disallow indiscriminate mixing of different ideologies) naturally leads to the stratification of society. It is not that the Vedic system is the original system of religion and every other religion was *derived* from it. Quite to the contrary, the Vedic system set the highest standard for itself, and designated a place for its practice. Everyone else was allowed to do whatever they wanted but go to a different place to live if they did not agree with the Vedic principles. Therefore, Vedic philosophy is not the origin of diverse religions; rather, diverse religions emerged because they could not practice, or did not want to practice the Vedic standards of civilization. Because they did not conform to the Vedic rules, they were considered *mleccha*—uncivilized or inferior. Again, this isn't a *racial identification* as most people think today. It is rather based on a set of rules governing a society; if you follow those rules, you are *Aryan*. If you don't follow the rules you are *mleccha*. There is simply no concept of race, or other such distinctions.

Most Indians, for example, don't follow the *Varṇāśrama* system today. The so-called *Brahmana* don't spend time performing the Vedic rites, or studying the Vedic texts. They don't want to live by begging alms; instead, they prefer to have a job—like the *Sudra* of the Vedic system—serving some other person. They are not renounced; often they may be attached to the consumption of meat and intoxicants. Similarly, the *Kshatriya* are not warriors; they are simply politicians who crave the power of a political position, not the risks of protecting the *Brahmana*. The *Vaisya* similarly don't contribute earnings to the *Brahmana* in charity; they may in fact be involved in tax evasion and other forms of illegal activities. By the standard of *Manu Samhita*, they are *mleccha*.

The Emergence of Diverse Religions

It should therefore be understood that the different cultures, societies, and religions have a common *biological* origin in *Vaivaśvata Manu*, but they don't have the same spiritual lineage. Each society that split from the rules of *Manu*, formed their own social order and its classes, designated different rules for these classes, and practiced different kinds of religious systems. They split from the system of *Manu* because they did not, or could not, practice the standards set by *Manu*. As the societies diversified, they spread to different parts of the world, creating their own culture and social orders. People born in these societies thereafter mostly carried on the traditions of their ancestors because they were already split from the *Brahmavarta* society, and no society wanted to mix the different types of rules and religions with each other.

It is therefore appropriate for each religion to trace their lineage to a different preceptor because, for that society and social order, there was indeed a different preceptor who set the rules for that kind of living. What is inappropriate, however, is that each such social order consider itself the best order. If the religion recognizes the highest standard as ensconced in *Manu Samhita* and tries to imbibe the principles as far as it can, it will also realize its own standard relative to the standard defined by the father of mankind—*Manu*. But, as we noted earlier, this generally doesn't happen because the ego in the soul propels it to seek solace in their surroundings, and then the pride—as fear is mitigated by such a support system—makes them feel superior to all others. The problem of religious conflict is caused by the ego making the person consider himself superior, when then might actually be inferior.

All societies, religions, and cultures therefore have their origin in the principles of *Brahmavarta*, but as they moved away from that place in order to lead a different kind of life, they also abandoned many of its principles. Nevertheless, because these societies originated in *Brahmavarta*, they also carried forward many of its ideas, principles, and moralities. The important thing in the study of cultural evolution is to look at the similarities that point toward the common origin, rather than the differences wrought over a period of time. The differences are naturally expected because those who moved away from *Brahmavarta* didn't do it because of a short supply of food, water, or a place to live. They moved away because they could not or did not want to conform to the standards of living outlined in *Manu Samhita*. It doesn't mean they rejected everything in the Vedic system; it does mean they rejected some of it.

The tract of land called *Brahmavarta* lost its population nearly 5000 years ago. The place of *Aryans*—to the east of *Brahmavarta*—continued its worship of *Shiva* and *Viṣṇu*, but due to the decline of *dharma* in *Brahmavarta*, the rest of the world was dissociated from the religion existing in India. When the Indus-Sarasvati civilization perished, the social system, its divisions and laws, and much of the day-to-day life described as *dharma* ceased to exist and was replaced by many other kinds of religions. However, the Vedic system that dealt with other topics—not covered by *Brahma* and *Manu*—namely, the description of God, the nature of transcendence, and details about the nature of the soul, and its relation to God, how the soul is trapped in the material energy, and how the material energy evolves over time, etc. survived in India.

Today, we know this for a fact—the books on rituals, and their actual practitioners have ceased to exist in any meaningful form. However, the philosophical principles of transcendence still exist. India, or the land of *Aryans*, never developed an alternative social, economic, and political system, but they failed to continue the older system due to the decline of the Indus-Sarasvati civilization. As a result, India has continually declined culturally, socially, and politically—the practical aspects of day-to-day life—while maintaining an advanced philosophical understanding of the nature of reality and transcendence. India therefore presents today a contradiction. It is poor in the practical exigencies of—e.g., in the rule of laws, trade and business, wealth and prosperity, cleanliness and organization, military power and education—but still rich in the study of ancient books, temple worship, yoga, meditation, etc.

Meanwhile, other lands, which evolved their own social systems, rules of law, economic, social and political systems became economically, politically, and socially strong, although devoid of a superior understanding of transcendence, or even of material nature. The contrast that we see between India and the rest of the world—primarily the Western world—has to do with this discrepancy: India failed to follow the legal, social, economic, and political system of *Brahmavarta* as it declined, but maintained other things much better. Ultimately, you cannot sustain a higher philosophy on an empty stomach, in a disorganized society, under war and strife, and under declining rule of law. But the question is: what is the right social, economic, and political system of *dharma* compatible with the higher philosophical principles? This question is important because every other society that invented a new social order did not carry forward the superior philosophical understanding in the Vedas. They instead chose egalitarian, democratic, and materialistic principles to organize society viewing the world as a *flat* structure devoid of hierarchy instead of viewing it as a body in which the head is more important than the feet.

The diversity of religions seen at present should be viewed in the light of this question. They are organized on the principles of equality, liberty, and democracy, rather on the principle of hierarchy. When society is flattened, then the scientific understanding of the world is also flattened, leading to the rejection of demigods as higher controllers of the material world. We derive our understanding of nature from the type of experience we get from society. It is therefore not surprising that while scientific theories about nature were being invented in Europe, it was on the wave of sweeping social-cultural transformation. As society is flattened, space and time are also flattened. We stop thinking in terms of higher and lower, better or worse, objectively. The many forms of God, and how the world emanates from an original person, are also rejected. One still maintains in religion a transcendent person, or simply an impersonal reality, or perhaps a void, but the relation between that transcendence and the material world ceases to be understood. Society gradually drifts toward more hedonism and materialism, because the higher principles of organizing the world—i.e., the transcendence of matter—are lost.

The decline of the Indus-Sarasvati civilization therefore should be viewed not merely as the death of a particular social order, but as the dissociation of diverse social orders governed by different religious ideologies, and their varying successes in bringing happiness to the people living in them. If this watershed moment in history—and its true significance—is not understood, then everything else seems to be a chaotic and disconnected set of events taking the world in different directions. But if the decline of the Indus-Sarasvati civilization is properly understood, then the rise of diverse religions, their relation to the prior existing social order, and the invention of new social, political, and economic orders—which were previously called *dharma*, governed by the principles outlined in *Manu Smṛti* by *Manu* as the father of mankind—are easily comprehended. Today, it is hard to see the connection between the ancient civilization in India and the newer cultures, religions, and civilizations in the rest of the world because the link between the two—which lay at India's doorstep, and in between India and the rest of the world—was severed.

How the decline in the cradle of civilization led to the emergence of new civilizations, and how the death of the principles of *dharma* led to diverse other religions becomes incomprehensible without keeping their link in mind. I would therefore argue that the history of world religions can be easily understood not as transfer of information from India to the rest of the world, but as transmission from a civilization that doesn't exist anymore to both India and the rest of the world. The worship of the sun, the moon, planets, and stars, the practice of rituals as worshiping these deities, the construction of temples and other such places of worshipping God, the forming of deities, the use of fire as a method of worship, the sacrifice of animals in rituals, and the chanting of incantations during such rituals are so pervasive across diverse religions that we have come to think of them as a 'collective unconscious' about the nature of religion itself rather than seeking their origin in the Vedic culture.

When we emphasize the differences and neglect the commonalities, we fail to see how religion was meant as a social order, in which the *Brahmana* priests cultivated knowledge and performed rituals for the benefit of society. They led an austere and simple life out of begging alms, and yet were regarded as the beacons of light for everyone else—including those far richer or more powerful. The ideals of this *Brahmana* culture pervade across all religions even today where the priest is expected to lead a simple and austere life, cultivate the understanding of material reality and transcendence, and provide the education to the rest of the masses. What is the origin of this commonality? Religions the world over are equated with humanitarian deeds—such as education and caring for the destitute. Why should this caring be the job of the religion rather than the work of the ruler of the state, of businessmen, when they obviously have a greater number of resources and power at their disposal?

Numerous commonalities between diverse religions become apparent simply by studying the Indus-Sarasvati civilization. Indeed, all attempts at interreligious dialogue are also conducted on the basis of these commonalities, underemphasizing their differences. The supposition is that the leaders of religions are *Brahmana*—austere, renounced, kind, knowledgeable, and charitable. They are meant to guide society at large, not merely practice their own advancement. They are superior to the *Kshatriya* who rule the land, or *Vaisya* who own the businesses and much of the nation's wealth. Every time these principles are violated, the religious leader loses his or her respect. But we must ask: on what basis do we see the universality in the religious ideals? Why are truthfulness, kindness, cleanliness, and austerity defining properties of religion, when there can been so many other potential definitions?

My answer to these questions is that the world religions came out of the Indus-Sarasvati civilization. It was the most sophisticated and advanced in terms of social organization and the morality of the people, and that example became the guiding principle for everyone else in the world; although they discarded many of the philosophical and practical details of the *Brahmana*, they tried to imbibe the same examples in their newly created religions.

Scientific Analysis of Religious Systems

We noted in the previous chapter that *Brahma* has four heads through which he speaks about four moral principles which have to be ideally applied to four kinds of relationships. The four moral principles are truthfulness, austerity, charity, and cleanliness. The principle of *austerity* entails hard work and sacrificing one's desires for a higher cause. This principle primarily appears in the master-servant relation in which the servant serves the master selflessly, undertaking pain and difficulties in order to satisfy the master. However, austerity also means detachment and there is a natural detachment between the master and the servant—the master can choose a different servant, and the servant can choose a different master. There is hence no 'commitment' in the relationship, as compared to others which are relatively more committed. This principle of religion primarily applies to the *Sudra* class in society, which serve the other classes, but can choose to serve a different master. Their choice is not whether to serve, but whom to serve. As they are free to change their master, the master also considers them a replaceable resource.

The principle of *charity* appears in the friendly relation; a friend can borrow or take money, land, animals, etc. from their friends. Charity is based on the principle of kindness toward others and applied in the relationship of equality. A servant serving his master, for instance, is not considered charity, because the servant offers his hard work to the master in return for compensation. If the compensation disappears, the servant will leave for another master. Thus, the master-servant relation is not one of equality because there is no charity involved in it. There is a fair price for the work, and equal opportunity in choosing other masters or servants. The friendly relation is different; one doesn't seek charity from strangers; one seeks it from friends because the assets of a friend are considered shared property due to their equality.

The principle of *truthfulness* applies to the paternal relation. The relation between master and servant is one of diplomacy; of course, the servant is not expected to cheat, but the master doesn't expect knowledge from the servant, nor does the servant want to know the nature of reality from the master. The servant is there to do what the master desires to be done. Likewise, the friendly relation is about sharing time and resources, not about one person becoming another's teacher. Indeed, if a friend gives honest truth, the receiver will generally consider it an affront on their friendship because the friends are considered equal and not expected to give each other knowledge. The function of imparting truth is those of the parents and teachers. There is a natural relation in which the *guru* imparts knowledge to the disciple, and the ideal relation for learning from someone is to treat them like a parent or *guru*. If someone wants to learn, but treats the teacher as their friend, the process is never successful because there is a natural and healthy contempt between friends: neither party considers the other party superior in order to accept their guidance and advice. A friend is there to share and help on a platform of equality, not meant to advise. Accordingly, if someone truly wants to learn the truth, they must accept the other person as their parent or teacher, rather than as a friend.

The principle of *cleanliness* applies to the marital relationship. The house has to be clean and orderly, life has to be lived in a systematic manner through a routine, the earning of wealth for the family has to be through legitimate methods, and one should not have a conjugal relationship outside marriage. The principle of cleanliness appears through systematic or process-oriented working. It is dominantly highlighted through a *routine* in life. For example, there has to be a fixed time when everyone rises, does their work, eats and prays together. Routine means that everyone gets to fulfill their desires but there is a time, place, and quantity for it, because there are other pressing things that have to be done due to routine. It means, for instance, regulated eating, sleeping, sex, and work. To perform this routine of life, things have to be systematically organized; you cannot have clutter around in the house and expect to lead a routine; you cannot expect a happy married life if everyone has a different time of eating, sleeping, and working. You cannot expect stability if the man is in and out of jobs, or the woman is disorganized.

There are hence, in this universe, four types of recognized relations, and four types of moral principles. We are not expected to mix these relations or compromise the duties involved in them. For instance, one is not expected to have a sexual relationship at the workplace, with a friend's spouse, with a person at the level of one's parents, or with one's teacher's wife. The reason is that the married partners can maintain a routine, but you cannot maintain routine and systematic life if you are not married to the partner. Commitment is the hallmark of routine, and that commitment is marriage. Similarly, the parents are not expected to pay their children to do work at home; the children are not servants or employees who work for a return in payment. Doing so will mean that the children will stop listening to the parents for advice; they will treat them like employers who are allowed to request tasks in return for money, but they are not expected to 'interfere' in their lives with good counsel.

There is hence an ideal expectation for each kind of relation, and that ideality defines the perfect *dharma* for each role. This ideal is called the material element *mahattattva* which denotes moral principles or the ideal enactment of a role. The body of *Brahma* is said to be comprised of *mahattattva* which means he is the embodiment of ideal social conduct. His religion accordingly is one that prescribes the ideal behavior for each role in society. If a role involves shades of two or more relationship types, then one has to apply the principles of *dharma* and identify the ideal action. One should, however, never mix the duties of one relation into another. As we noted earlier, it is possible for someone to act like a child in a marriage, or act like a friend with their parents. One may become a servant in conjugal relation, or act as a friend to one's employees. The misapplication of the principles of charity, truthfulness, austerity, and cleanliness is not considered *dharma*. But in modern times—and indeed in different religions—these principles have been repeatedly misapplied.

Modern egalitarian notions of society, for example, apply the ideal of equality in friendships to every relation. Thus, parents are not allowed to discipline their children because the child perceives the parent as an equal. The women compete with men because they consider each other equals. Similarly, there are norms about how employees should be treated as equals to employers. The morality of egalitarian equality is not a bad idea per se, but it is an idea that is limited to friendships. When it is extended to every relationship, then it violates the principle of *dharma*. The four principles are therefore not universal ideals; they are rather contextual to the four types of relations.

When a particular moral value is universalized, then it is inappropriately applied to all relationships. The universalization of these values ultimately means the undermining of other values. For example, if the children are friends of the parents, then the children will treat the parent's or teacher's advice as yet another friendly 'opinion' no better or worse than their own (uninformed) opinion. The children who treat their parents as equals fail to respect their guidance. As the child grows up, he leaves the parents to fend for himself, quite like they left their friends in order to pursue a career, marriage, etc. As this trend takes hold in society, the older generation realizes that it has to fend for itself later so it makes fewer sacrifices for their children. Most parents resign to the fact the children don't listen to them and leave them to their fate. Similarly, as men and women become equals, their relationship of mutuality begins to deteriorate, resulting in competition rather than complementarity in the marriage. Over time both partners are unhappy and often separate. The key point is that the idea of equality is not bad *per se*. But it is not a *universal* value. There is a certain context and relation in which it has to be applied. But if one applies this value universally, then all other relations are destroyed.

Mahattattva signifies these moral principles, and their ideal applications. *Brahma* is the very form of morality—and he has four heads through which he speaks about the four principles of *dharma* and their application. *Manu* then translates those general principles into very specific commandments about social order. Different cultures and societies embody this morality in different ways. If a society is more hierarchical—e.g., some of the Eastern cultures—then the principle of equality is not applied to subordinates and children. Similarly, if the society is flattened—e.g., in most Western cultures—then equality is applied everywhere. *Dharma* means not just the specification of moral values such as austerity, truthfulness, charity, and cleanliness. It is also about deciding when we should be charitable and when we should punish. It is the application of a particular principle in a very specific contextual relation.

Similarly, there are questions about the prioritization of rights and duties. When is the correct time to demand our rights? And what is the appropriate time for fulfilling our duties? When a mother aborts a baby, for instance, is her right to lead a carefree life of greater importance, or is the child's right to be born into this world to be given higher priority, which means the mother's right has to be subordinated to her duty in relationship to the child? When should we prioritize rights, and when should we emphasize the duties?

The Vedic prescription is that there are no rights; there are only duties. What we call our 'right' is actually *karma.* If we deserve it, we will get it. If we don't deserve it, we will not get it, and that failure to fulfill our 'rights' is a consequence of our own previous actions. Our 'rights' are actually 'duties' of the other person. Therefore, the Vedic system never speaks of 'rights'; it only speaks of 'duties'. The system never says that it is the *right* of a parent to punish their children; it says that it is the *duty* of the parent to discipline the children—when they need to be disciplined. The *dharma* based on rights—as practically all modern legal and social systems talk about the right to education, right to happiness, right to a decent life—are all flawed. We cannot fulfill these rights if we don't have the requisite *karma* and blame still rests on the person who fails to fulfill his or her rights. We can, however, still fulfill our duties based on our abilities and opportunities, provided we desire so.

The *Varṇāśrama* system of *dharma* is not therefore yet another socio-cultural system. It is the perfect system of *dharma* which is based on the understanding of *karma*; it defines one's duties, and doesn't define any rights. Over time, this religious system—which originated in *Brahmavarta*, or the place of *Brahma*, the giver of moral values—has declined for two reasons. First, people stopped following the four moral principles. Second, people universalized rather than contextualized the moral values to specific kinds of relationships. The rejection of morality, or its universalization are both flawed religions. Accordingly, when one applies a moral principle to a relationship where it is not expected to be applied, one doesn't follow *Brahma*'s religion, and as a consequence one automatically creates *karma*, which forces one to suffer. One is not rewarded for following the principle of equality everywhere. One is rather punished for applying this principle into inappropriate relationships.

In this way, we can scientifically analyze religions as to which moral value is applied in which relationship, and whether that application is appropriate. If we look around the world, the traditional values of servants, friends, parents, and couples, are espoused in nearly all religions. Even Abrahamic religions, for instance, hold up these values in the right context. There are hence prescriptions of how a married couple must behave, how parents must deal with their children, how the elders and teachers have to be respected, and how servants are free to serve different masters. However, many of these principles declined rapidly over time. For instance, the principle of a servant being allowed to choose his master was rejected with the advent of slavery where a servant is bought and sold in order to work for a particular master without adequate remuneration, and often under forced labor and torture. This is a violation of the principle of *dharma* for the *Sudra*, who are meant to serve others, but not bound to a particular master; both master and servant can choose each other, and the master has to provide adequate remuneration. The advent of slavery—and its justification, often based on scriptures—constitutes irreligion.

We must understand that if a religion produces such caricatures of *dharma* it is not ideal religion. It might have other admirable values, but due to the neglect of some such values, adverse *karma* is continually created, which causes the person to suffer endlessly, and under that suffering they tend to seek rights and forego their duties, creating even more adverse *karma*.

Materialist Accounts of Cultural Diversity

Historians study the evolution of human culture across the world, and they could help in tracing the origins of the culture if they investigated the numerous commonalities between these cultures. But instead, they have focused on the human differences, seeing the commonalities with apes and primates. The history of the spread of human culture and civilization is at present mired in the evolutionism in which man originated in Africa, migrated to the Middle East, and from there emigrated to Europe and Asia, eventually reaching China, Russia, and Australia, and from there to the North and South Americas.

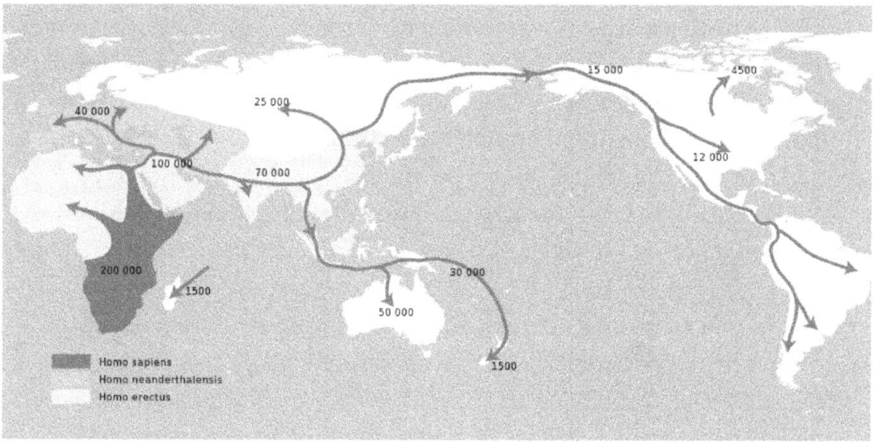

Figure-23 Evolutionary Migration of Humans

The path of the spreading of the culture can remain invariant, but what tells us about the direction of arrows in this spreading? The guiding light for these arrows is evolutionism rather than culturalism. Culturalism is the idea that individuals are products of their culture, and they must live and realize themselves in their culture. Culturalism, however, doesn't answer the question of why a person is born in a specific culture and none else. A culture embodies a particular type of *guna* or the things people enjoy and abhor. A soul is born into a culture depending on their *karma*. If they have good *karma* and they have very similar *guna* as that of the culture, then the soul would like to enjoy his life among similar people. If, however, the person has bad *karma* then their *guna* would typically be opposed to the culture in which they are born, or they may have the same *guna* but they will face the wrong end of a culture's problems. They will either suffer because they cannot find like-minded people, or because they indeed find like-minded people who cause them to suffer.

For instance, if one despises intoxication, then being forced to consume intoxicants—because everyone in the society and culture has a drinking habit—is going to create much misery for the person. On the other hand, the same consumption of intoxicants would be considered pleasure for a person who enjoys intoxication. Therefore, *karma* simply indicates good or bad outcome based on right or wrong action. But the definition of good and bad is relative to a person's *desires*. A person can be born in a society of alcoholics due to bad *karma* (if they despise alcohol) or due to their good *karma* (if they enjoy alcohol). Thus, the same *karma* can lead to radically different outcomes. A soul is born in a particular society due to their *guna* and *karma*; the *guna* is the person's desires, and the *karma* is the nurture they will receive in society.

So, culture denotes a certain type of desire or pleasure enjoyed by the soul. Each culture has some good and some bad attributes which means some will enjoy and others will suffer. If a person has the desire to enjoy intoxicants, but the religion forbids such pleasure, then the person will suffer in that religion. Therefore, people tend to modify the rules of religion to suit their desires. Thus, intoxication, animal killing, extra marital affairs, abortions, gambling etc. have been legalized in modern societies, and a person is not expected to be punished or reprimanded for such actions in modern time. These new forms of 'religion' are not religious because they are so far from the moral values of *Brahma*. Nevertheless, since they exist, and people follow them, they are allowed to enjoy their *karma* relative to their desires. Such enjoyment, however, limits the future potential for happiness. This limited potential then manifests in terms of social decline, unfulfilled desires, and even sick bodies.

The *guna* represent the *ānanda* of the soul, which leads to different desires for pleasure. The evolutionist neglects the desires in living beings and considers the world to be driven by chance mutation rather than purpose. Similarly, in studying genetics, the evolutionist ignores the *karma* of the soul, which represents the *sat* of the soul, and it places the person in different situations. The fact that some people are born in Africa while others are born in Europe has to do with their *karma* where they face certain types of situations because those events are primarily occurring in those parts. For example, in recent times, extreme poverty, famine, civil wars, and systemic rapes and murders have been prominent far more in Africa than in Europe. Those events are inevitable, but the person born in that event is not inevitable. In particular, *you* can avoid being born in such situations by performing your *dharma*.

When the *sat* and *ānanda* of the soul are ignored, only *chit* is left—which constitutes the hierarchy of the body, senses, mind, intellect, ego, and morality. The evolutionist flattens this hierarchy too, and only considers the body—neglecting the senses, mind, intellect, ego, and morality. Thus, the moral values embodied in the *mahattattva* are not even a natural principle in evolution. Evolutionism will always fail to explain why a person is born in a particular land and society, instead of another place and time. Similarly, it will fail to explain why certain types of societies even exist, when they come into being and why they disappear over time—i.e., the cultural evolution of the world.

The true cultural origin of mankind lies in *Brahmavarta* from where it went eastward to India and the rest of Asia through a tract called the land of *Aryans*, and then Westward to the Middle East, and toward Europe. In other words, the direction of human migration is very likely consistent with the modern picture as far as the paths are concerned. They are inconsistent with the directions on the Westward movement. To fathom the true path, we have to discard biological evolution as the cause of mental, cultural, and social differences. We have to rather view *guna*, *karma*, and the hierarchy of the body, senses, mind, intellect, ego, and morality, and how it manifests in culture and society—as the cause of biological variations. Thus, everyone with African genes is not born in a land of strife and disease; some are also born in peaceful and prosperous lands. This birth denotes their *karma* or the *sat*. Their desires for enjoyment are generally consistent with the society in which they are born—provided they have good *karma*. Their body type, however, denotes their *abilities*—acquired as a combination of *guna* and *karma*. Evolution is not the explanation of cultural diversities. The real explanation is that the soul desires diverse pleasures, follows or disobeys the laws laid out by *Brahma*, thus creating good or bad *karma*, which forces it to migrate away from the land where strict rules are followed, to create a new place where the rules are relaxed for enjoyment. The soul thinks that by relaxing the rules of *dharma* he will be able to enjoy unlimitedly according to his desires, but his life is mired into natural disasters, social unrest, pestilence, wars, and disease.

The sum and substance of history is that the ideal principles of living were imparted by *Brahma* through *Manu* but while some people followed, others did not or could not follow these strictures. They left the land of *Brahmavarta* to find other lands, empires, cultures, civilizations, and religions, which often carried forward many of the principles practiced in *Brahmavarta*, but some of these principles were discarded and compromised over time. As these principles were violated, and the souls born in such societies had a history of such violation, they also suffered through natural disasters, war, and diseases, often wiping out large swaths of society in a very short period of time. Biological evolution has very little to do with this evolution. If we understand how the soul is forced to move by his *guna* and *karma*, which are either consistent or inconsistent with the principles of *dharma*, then we can explain the human history as the consequence of deviation from the principles of *dharma*.

The Problem of Civilizational Contact

One major factor commonly employed in order to divide different religions is their *geographical proximity*. It is supposed that if two civilizations and cultures emanated in different parts of the world, then they must indeed be disconnected. After all, the world has become well-connected on the last few hundred years with the advent of ships, aircraft, telecommunications, etc. How could people exchange ideas without such means? In fact, how could a religious uniformity exist in the world without such advanced communication? Would the different segments of society not become disconnected without it?

Geographical proximity is used as a *methodological tool* in understanding religions: if two places were physically far away, they must be disconnected ideologically. Ideological similarities must therefore be pure accidents. Historians of religion have failed to ask a very fundamental question: If God and demigods cannot be seen with our eyes, then what was the need to postulate the existence of such entities in so universal a manner the world over? How could every civilization and culture make the same mistake again and again? This question becomes especially ponderable if we postulate that these civilizations were disconnected from each other due to geographical distances.

In modern times, the similarity between Judaism, Christianity, and Islam is accepted because they originated in the same geographical region.

Similarly, the similarities between Hinduism, Buddhism, Jainism, and Sikhism are understood because they originated in the same country—India. Likewise, Zen and Tao, Confucianism and Buddhism, are correlated because of the physical proximity. Shamanism and Animism are related in the Americas due to the postulate of physical connectedness. But due to continental and geographical divides there are vast swaths of land that appear to be physically inaccessible without the recent advent of communication and transportation technologies. In lieu of such mechanisms, we suppose that the religions originating in diverse lands could not have a common origin, or to postulate a common origin, we must first provide explanation of physical contact among different cultures.

This ideology and method of explanation assumes a particular theory of space, which is flawed. Space in modern science—and indeed in the last several centuries—has been viewed as a container with three physical dimensions. Every object in this space is independent of each other, and to interact, some object must *travel* to another place. The ideology of such interaction is now formalized in science with the notion of traveling force particles.

Space in Vedic philosophy is an inverted tree, which has higher and lower nodes; the lower nodes are logically derived from the higher nodes, like a detailed concept is derived from the abstract concept. Thus, objects don't have to travel in space in order to be connected to each other. The very fact that a location in space *exists* entails that it is connected to a conceptually higher location. The different points in space are connected by *prāna* which modern science calls "force"; therefore, the locations in space are held together by force between higher and lower locations. An object changes its properties if its connection to other objects is altered—even if an object itself did not change its properties. This force or *prāna* remains invisible to the eyes because it is the very structure of space; we don't perceive *prāna* quite like we don't perceive space itself. However, if we were to construct a theory of space, then we will need a theory of force, and these two theories will not be separate.

To an extent, this idea is already present in modern scientific theories such as gravity where matter or mass is the structure of the space, and we cannot distinguish mass, and the force it exerts, from space itself. However, because we treat matter physically, we still cannot understand that the thing we call 'curved' space in modern science appears curved because it is a tree. Light in this curved space goes not in straight lines but up and down the branches of the tree. Since it goes up and down, we attribute change in the path of light to the 'curvature' of space, when it is in fact caused by a tree topology. Indeed, when a theory of light is formed in this space, we will realize that light never 'travels' in space; light is always a causal interaction occurring *non-locally*—i.e., without a travel. The higher location *causally changes* the lower location and you cannot ever attribute that change to a traveling particle. In that sense, you don't need a 'messenger' to travel from one place to another in order to create an effect. Just changes in the properties of the higher location will automatically cause changes to occur in the lower locations connected to it.

In the context of religious history, this model of space entails that when religion rises in the higher location, it will automatically cause a rise in religion in all other locations connected to it—without a visible particle going from one place to another. Conversely, when the religion in the higher place declines, nobody has to go from one place to another to cause the religion to decline. Religion will decline automatically everywhere as the higher place declines. Hence, traveling particles, or messengers of cultural contact are not needed to propagate specific ideas. These ideas will emerge automatically in a new place—that we suppose lies far away from the higher location. This, of course, doesn't preempt or forbid a physical and cultural contact between civilizations. It does, however, mean that such contact is not necessary to assert the similarity between religious doctrines or practices across the world. All it takes to bring a global change is to identify the higher location in space on earth and bring a change on that place, in order to effect a universal change.

The thesis of geographical distances preventing cultural contact resulting in the relative isolation of individual societies and their religions—which is then inferred as the mutual independence of religions—is founded on a flawed theory of space. People don't have to cross continents, navigate the seas, or fly in space to bring about a change in the other place. We can also bring a global change by changing the higher location in space—if we knew what that place is. But knowing that place requires a scientific theory and an advanced subtle perception. In lieu of these factors I will venture that the location of the Indus-Sarasvaṭi civilization was indeed such a higher location. When religion was dominant in this place, it automatically prevailed everywhere else. As religion in this place declined, it naturally led to decline in all other places.

In Vedic civilization, certain places such as *Prabhāsa*, *Naimisāranya*, *Kurukśhetra*, and *Badrikāśrama* were considered 'holy' places for the performance of Vedic rites. *Brahmana* and *Kshatriya* used these places to perform meritorious deeds. The kings also changed their capital cities in order to spread their influence naturally to the rest of the land they ruled. These ideas are not accidents; they are all part of the same understanding of space in which actions performed in one place have an automatic effect in other places. Certain places were designated 'holy' because they were 'higher' in space—i.e., the effect of activities in these places would naturally spread in other places.

Once the hierarchical understanding of space was lost, all places became equal. Even if meritorious deeds were performed elsewhere, they had limited effects, and a small amount of demerit in the holy place would exert a greater detrimental effect everywhere else. Therefore, the uplift of the holy places is of far greater importance than the uplift of all other places. This sophisticated understanding rapidly declines in *Kali Yuga*. The first prime minister of independent India—Jawaharlal Nehru—for instance, considered the places of industrialization the new 'temples' of India, neglecting the holy places. All holy places in India today lie in a dilapidated state due to the dominant materialism, which sees advancement through mechanization rather than religion.

The decline of religion in India is not because of growing mechanization; it is because people have neglected the holy places and stopped the performance of *dharma* in these places. They don't know that a small amount of piety in the holy place brings far greater results to the whole world. We don't have to clean the whole country at once; if we can clean the holiest of all places first, then cleanliness will automatically propagate to the rest of the world. Great *Āchāryas* therefore have established certain places of learning and spiritual advancement. *Śrīla Prabhupāda* for instance envisioned that the cult of *Sri Chaitanya* will spread globally from the land of *Mayapur*. The spreading of this cult is an automatic and unperceivable effect, caused by the nature of space itself. Even if nobody travels from such holy places to every other part of the world, the spiritual advancement of a higher place will automatically cause spiritual ideas to manifest in the other places. Conversely, if the higher place is neglected, the lower places will also continue to languish spiritually.

The commonalities among cultures, languages, religions, and societies have been a major area of study for the social sciences. Psychologists such as Carl Jung attributed this commonality to a 'collective unconscious', indicating that we are born with common ideas because they seem to manifest all over the world in repeating patterns. Structural linguistics and its proponents such as Noam Chomsky have attributed the commonalities across languages to a 'deep structure' in all languages from which a 'surface structure' manifests. Structuralism in cultural studies, similarly, argues for the universalities in human culture in order to explain cultural similarities. And anthropologists following such ideas explain the commonalities to human nature itself.

All these explanations barely scratch the surface of the true nature of space. We see common patterns in language, culture, symbolism, and societies because the world is structured like a tree, which causes similar ideas to appear simultaneously in different parts. The language, culture, civilization, and social order in the higher place is the 'deep structure', from which many 'surface structures' are manifest like leaves from a root. This similarity between 'deep' and 'surface' is not necessarily caused by cultural exchange through traveling messengers. It can also be caused imperceptibly. We cannot explain this emergence if we don't know how the cause manifests an effect due to the nature of space, and in that sense speculations about linguistic structuralism and the collective unconscious are loose approximations of reality. Still, even these descriptions are better than those which aim to explain religious similarities based on actual physical contact among the different individuals.

The objections raised by historians and religionists in trying to explain religious commonalities are at best loose approximations of reality in modern cultural and linguistic studies. At worst, they are completely false. The true explanation is space itself, and hence it has a much wider applicability than cultural universalism. If we get past the materialist explanations of how similarities appear, we can stop spending time in discussing the events of traveling individuals. We can, in fact, completely disregard physical contacts as the primary vehicles of cultural exchange. We can now rely on exploring the commonalities and neglect the *mechanisms* by which they are emerging.

6

The Diversity of Religious Views

If religion has given birth to all that is essential to society, it is because the idea of society is the soul of religion.
— *Émile Durkheim*

The Worship of the Sun, the Moon, and the Stars

We noted earlier that the worship of *Viṣṇu* as the creator of the material world spread all over the world through sun worship because the form of *Viṣṇu* represents the *chit* of the soul from which all knowledge and action springs. While the form of *Viṣṇu* is not perceivable through the senses, the sun can be. In fact, we can say that we see everything else due to the sun. Naturally, in order to believe in the existence of *Viṣṇu*, one would have to form an image of His persona. The sun is such a natural image. In Vedic texts, the sun is therefore considered a natural expansion and deity of *Viṣṇu*—since we cannot perceive *Viṣṇu* by our senses, He appears to everyone in the form of the sun.

We similarly noted previously that the worship of *Shiva* as the creator of all the pleasures spread over the world as the worship of the moon as the form of *Shiva* represents the *ānanda* of the soul from which desire, purpose, and pleasure emanate. *Shiva* is not perceivable through the senses, but the moon can be perceived. The moon is, culturally, a symbol of desire and pleasure. The moon also appears in darkness, and it is hence identified with the deepest desires which are invisible to other people because the inner world is 'dark' to the outsiders. The moon is that image or deity, visible to everyone, which represents our deeper desires.

The moon is regarded as a representation and expansion of *Shiva*—the symbol by which we can understand *Shiva*.

The worship of *Viṣṇu* and *Shiva* continues in the Vedic system, through their deities. Since people question the veracity of these deities, those who have a problem in such deity worship—because they cannot understand how a person is expressed symbolically through a deity—are encouraged to worship the sun and the moon. The Vedic texts hence describe that the most important and powerful rulers in the world came from only two lineages. These are called the dynasties of the sun and the moon—*Suryavansha* and *Chandravansha*. The descendants of these lineages spread all over the world, taking with them their heritage of sun and moon worship. The people ruled by these kings inherited the system followed by their rulers and so the system of sun and moon worship was popularized from the rulers to the general population. Hence, we can view the diversities of religion in terms of the descent of rulers and the histories about the sun and the moon dynasties are useful materials in deciphering the evolution of respective religions over the ages.

Vedic texts indeed delineate such a history in the ages gone by, quite like the other religious texts. But as we have noted earlier, this history is sometimes biological and at other times cultural. Even in the case of biological descent, the important thing—from the standpoint of religion—is not the inheritance of land, property, or wealth, which comes through biological descent. The important thing is the dissemination of ideas, principles, and rules through generations. If this cultural history of master-disciple relation is deemphasized in order to emphasize a biological heritance, then the history loses significance from a cultural, philosophical, ideological, and religious standpoint. Similarly, it is also important to understand the lineage going back to the father of mankind—*Manu*—whose religious principles are ordained by *Brahma*, but in many cases these principles were distorted over time to suit different desires and to fit into the context of a specific society. Unfortunately, when such modifications were made, the cultural legacy dating back to *Manu* was deemphasized in order to highlight a new beginning, a cultural renewal, and a break from the past. Such renewals might indeed be progressions from the past, but only if they bring the society closer to the *dharma* of *Manu*. When the lineage is deemphasized, the biological history is known, but the ideological connection to the past is unknown. Now, one sees the parent-child descent, but how one religion partially approximated the original religion is not mentioned. In other words, the branches of the single religion are presented as religions in their own right, instead of looking at their philosophical roots.

I will not therefore rely on the chain of biological descent, even though such descent is described at length in both Vedic texts and other religious texts. Discriminating the biological lineage from the teacher-disciple lineage is often difficult, and in many cases, it is hard to connect these lineages because the Vedic texts continued to outline—for the most part—the succession of generations who followed the Vedic principles, while other religions relied on portraying their arrival as a new beginning. There are very few incontrovertible connections that can actually help us understand the genealogy of religious evolution. But this genealogy is not important, because the real evolution is based on ideas and not on biological heritance. Therefore, it is sufficient to suppose that these ideas were widely prevalent and propagated through the rulers who conquered a land or uplifted a place by religious principles to cause the ideas to naturally spread to different parts under his control.

We might note here that *Brahma* is not explicitly worshipped in the Vedic system, although he is regarded as one of the trinity. *Brahma* is, in fact, not even regarded as a Supreme Being, unlike *Viṣṇu* and *Shiva* who are said to transcend the material world. More precisely, *Brahma* is a *role*, occupied by a person, for the duration of the universe. However, as the universe in Vedic description is created and annihilated, a different person occupies the role of *Brahma* in each iteration. Thus, the role and the person are not identical. In contrast, for *Viṣṇu* and *Shiva*, the role and the person are identical. Hence, *Brahma* is not directly worshipped in the Vedic tradition although he is the founder of all religious principles in the Vedic system. Vedic texts describe how both solar and lunar dynasties have descended from *Vaivaśvata Manu*—who is the son of *Brahma* and the creator of humanity, and yet he doesn't prescribe *Brahma*'s worship through his lineage. While *Vaivaśvata Manu* is the son of *Brahma*, his children are the originators of the solar and lunar dynasties.

Vaivaśvata Manu is said to be initially without any children, but by the grace of sage *Vaśiśtha* he got a daughter named *Ilā*. *Manu* wanted a son, so sage *Vaśiśtha* transformed *Ilā* into a man called *Sudyumna* by the benediction of *Viṣṇu*. Once, while roaming in the place called *Ilāvṛta-varṣa*,

Sudyumna was again transformed into a woman, and married *Budhā*, the son of the moon, and gave birth to a son name *Purūravā*. By prayers to *Shiva*, *Sudyumna* got the benediction that he would become a man every alternate month. In this male form, *Sudyumna* continued to rule his kingdom and had 3 sons—*Utkala*, *Gaya*, and *Vimala*. Nevertheless, eventually *Sudyumna* gave away his entire kingdom to *Purūravā*, who was begot through the lunar lineage, thus leading to the birth of the lunar dynasty. *Vaivasvata Manu* had 9 other sons—*Vena*, *Dhrishnu*, *Narishyan*, *Nābhāga*, *Ikshvāku*, *Karusha*, *Saryati*, *Prishadhru*, and *Nābhāgarishta*. Among these, *Ikshvāku* became the progenitor of the solar dynasty.

It's noteworthy how both solar and lunar dynasties emanate from *Vaivaśvata Manu* who is the sun's child[1]. But because one of his sons is transformed into a woman, her child—begot through the moon's son—becomes the father of the lunar dynasty. The import is that these were patriarchal dynasties and they continued the lineage from their father's side. Furthermore, since *Sudyumna* was blessed by *Shiva* to continue ruling his kingdom as a man every alternate month, it appears that the rulers of kingdoms also had to be men. Through this blessing, *Sudyumna* felt obliged to *Shiva* and gave away his entire kingdom to his son *Purūravā*—to whom he was a mother—instead of the children to whom he was a father. Thus, even though *Sudyumna* hailed from the solar dynasty, his son from the lunar lineage led to the lunar dynasty. We can thus trace the two dynasties to a single person—*Vaivaśvata Manu*.

Thereafter, only the solar and lunar dynasties are considered the primary dynasties for humanity, in this particular age of *Vaivaśvata Manu*. Since *Manu* is in the solar lineage, by default the solar dynasty is considered the most important. All further sages under the supervision of *Manu* continue to follow his lead. And therefore, the importance of the lunar system is deemphasized in this age of *Manu*. As a result, in most cultures we can find sun worship being given greater importance than moon worship. Furthermore, we can also see why *Brahma* is himself not worshiped directly even though he creates humanity and delegates the authority of moral principles to *Vaivaśvata Manu*[2].

Philosophically, *Brahma* who ordains the moral principles of society is not, in fact, in the Vedic understanding, truly God. This might seem interesting to people who believe—for example, through Christianity, that God delivered the Ten Commandments to Moses—because God in the Vedic understanding is one who completely transcends the material world, and hence moral principles as well. The moral principles are always defined by *Brahma* and his sons. *Viṣṇu* and *Shiva* don't deliver commandments of morality; they ask to be directly worshiped and that worship is the only and the final commandment. Therefore, ideally speaking, the 'God' who delivers commandments is to be understood as *Brahma* as he prescribes rules for time, place, and peoples.

Vedic texts describe two kinds of creators of the universe—primary and secondary. *Viṣṇu* and *Shiva* are the primary creators as the origins of material energy and that of the material desires for this energy. *Brahma* is then the secondary creator who organizes these elements into society, providing the essence of moral principles, and then delegates the delineation of those principles for different societies to different individuals. The systems of *Viṣṇu* and *Shiva* emphasize their own worship. There is no morality to be followed other than surrendering oneself to *Viṣṇu* and *Shiva*—remembering and singing their glories. All philosophy is subordinated to this surrender. Since *Viṣṇu* and *Shiva* demand such surrender, they are God, as opposed to *Brahma* who presents the 'commandments' of human life. Thus, when a religion views God as one who ordains commandments, it is considering *Brahma* as the God of the moral rules. Since *Brahma* is never worshipped directly, His form remains relatively unimportant, which is the most likely reason why religions based on moral commandments have underemphasized the form of God although they do view Him as a person. We might say that *Brahma*'s form is that of *dharma* or moral principles, so by following those principles one worships His form.

Relative to the worship of *Viṣṇu* and *Shiva*, therefore, *Brahma*'s worship is impersonalized, even in the Vedic system. This doesn't entail that *Brahma* himself doesn't emphasize the worship of *Shiva* or *Viṣṇu*. It only means that when the focus shifts from a personal form to obedience to a moral code, then the specific form of God is relatively deemphasized. For this reason, we can see that many modern religions speak about a personal God, but say very little about His appearance, qualities, activities, and relationships. Even though God is depicted as a person, the things that we associate with such persons are not described. In the previous chapter we discussed four kinds of relations, which exist in the material world; we also discussed the ideal forms of relations as conjugal, paternal, fraternal, and servitor. When *dharma* is emphasized over the form of God, then the focus is on the ideal dealings among the humans, with primarily one relationship—that of a servant—in relation to God. We must understand that this is because we are following a relatively impersonalized system of duties and moralities ordained by *Brahma* instead of the personalized worship of *Viṣṇu* and *Shiva*. The form of God, His activities and relationships, also remain abstract for the same reason, although God is a person.

However, *Brahma* is still understood as the 4 faces which propound 4 moral values, and the 7 sages are considered his 'children' who expand these moral values through the 7 layers of conscious experience—moral principles in the *mahattattva*, intentions in the ego, axioms of knowledge in the intellect, diverse ideas in the mind, different kinds of abilities and crafts in the senses, the different kinds of sensations, and finally, the objects of the senses. Each moral principle manifests in these 7 ways, and therefore, their combination is described as 28 stars or *Nakṣatra* in the zodiac. They are sometimes called *lunar mansions* because the moon denotes desire and the mansion for the moon denotes the boundaries in which this desire has to be fulfilled. Morality therefore is higher than desire, because desire has to be fulfilled within the constraints of morality. The moon or desire passes through different mansions, which mean various desires—denoted by the moon's changing phases—are also governed by different moral constraints of the *Nakṣatra*.

To worship a particular star sign or *Nakṣatra* is to worship a particular type of morality in a specific type of relationship. Thus, those born under different *Nakṣatra* are dominated by different types of morality influencing their desire: they are prepared to subordinate their desires to that moral principle because they consider it higher than their desire itself. The *Nakṣatra* of birth also means that a person may not accept other kinds of morals, in other kinds of relations; for example, one might consider it bad to do certain types of deeds but may not consider it wrong to think or desire such things. Conversely, others may consider it bad to think and desire but may be unable to stop themselves from doing the deeds anyway and be inflicted by moral guilt. Their guilt represents that they are moral beings, just as one who doesn't cross the bounds of actions but has such thoughts are moral in a limited sense.

While *Brahma* is not directly worshipped in the Vedic system, the texts describe the existence of four demigods—*Yama*, *Indra*, *Soma*, and

Varuna—who have their places in the four directions[3]. Each of these demigods is associated with water, fluidity, drink, and flow. *Soma* for instance is associated with a type of beverage which enables one to enjoy sex for very long periods of time. *Indra* is said to be the demigod of rain. *Varuna* rules all kinds of water bodies such as rivers, lakes, and ponds. And *Yama* is the master of the *Vaitarani* river which appears as very sweet to the pious and hellish to the sinful; it is said to purify the soul of its sins. As we have seen earlier, the suffering and enjoyment of the soul is created by his desires; for the same situation, the pious enjoy and the sinful suffer. The river thus represents the transformation of desire.

These four demigods should be understood as the representations of the four kinds of pleasures and pains obtained through four kinds of relationships. Thus, *Yama* is the pleasure and pain obtained through the master-servant relation; he subjugates the desire like a master forces the servant. But for those who are already pious, his influence is like a supporter. *Soma* represents the pleasure and pain in the husband-wife or lover relationship; the pleasure is the enjoyment of sex, but the pain is its exclusivity and commitment. *Varuna* is like a friend; in Vedic texts he is spoken of as *Mitra*, the deity of contracts and negotiations, deals and meetings. He surrounds, restrains, covers, and checks; that can be pleasurable if it acts as a protection, but it can get painful if the person is bound by rules. *Indra* is described as a protector as long as he is not threatened by another person's advancement; he acts like a protector, but he must remain the superior authority; he demands surrender and authority; he represents the parent who protects the children in the time of need, but also demands obedience and submission to what they have to dictate.

Brahma thus represents controlled enjoyment, and every form of *dharma* means the fulfillment of desires, but within boundaries. *Shiva* and *Viṣṇu* on the other hand represent the liberation of freedom from the constraints. *Shiva* denotes freedom by way of rejecting enjoyment and being with oneself. *Viṣṇu* similarly denotes the liberation of enjoying through serving others.

The seven sages or *saptarishi*—are not directly worshipped, but they have their lineages, which can be considered the lineage of *Brahma*. They appear in Vedic society through the 7 *gotra* or genealogies propagated by the 7 sages. In modern time, these *gotra* are said to be the following: *Vishvāmitra*, *Jamadagni*, *Bharadvāja*, *Gautama*, *Atri*, *Vashista*, and

Kashyapa. The *gotra* identifies the ancestors—all the way to the sages who are considered progenitors. Thus, the system of *Brahma* appears through the worship of demigods and forefathers, and rituals were prescribed to make offerings to these personalities.

The Worship of Male-Female Deities

We have seen how the soul and God have three aspects—relation, cognition, and emotion. We have also seen how the soul acts through the delegated power of God—called His *Śakti*—which we also identified as *prāna.* Vedic texts also describe how this *Śakti* divides into three parts—based on relation, cognition, and emotion—to create three *Śakti.* The *Śakti* of relation is called *bhūti-Śakti* or the power of being; through this power, the soul—or *I*—becomes "I am", which then expands into many subordinate roles such as "I am a teacher", "I am Indian", "I am male", etc. The *Śakti* of cognition is called *kriya-Śakti* and is more directly identified as *prāna*; through this power, the soul—or *I*—becomes "I have" which then expands into many subordinate parts such as "I have a body", "the body has hands", "the hand has fingers" etc.; this *Śakti* creates the whole-part relation in which the soul is the whole with many body parts. The *Śakti* of emotion is called *māyā-Śakti*; through this power the soul—or *I*—becomes "I want" which then expands into many subordinate desires such as "I want happiness", "I want food", "I want to look good", etc.

As we saw earlier, when the soul obtains some power, he develops an ego—or the sense of *I.* This *I*—as noted above—divides into three parts of the ego— "I am", "I have", and "I want"—in accordance with the three aspects of the soul. Each of these three aspects is hierarchical; it exists as a tree. The total material existence of the soul is thus comprised of three trees. These trees overlap and intersect with each other. Wherever they intersect, we can observe the world in a third-person manner. Whenever they don't intersect, the branches of these trees merely exist as a possibility, which can be known in the first-person manner, but cannot be known in the third-person manner.

The *kriya-Śakti* creates the many parts of the body; the *bhūti-Śakti* creates different functions of these body parts; and *māyā-Śakti* gives each part and function a purpose. It is notable that the same part can perform many functions, and each function can be used for different purposes. Therefore, the body has three kinds of descriptions—part, function, and purpose. In the Vedic system of medicine, these are also called *pitta*, *vāta*, and *kaphā*. The energy called *pitta* is responsible for creating the body parts. But these parts don't function by themselves; the energy that causes them to function is called *vāta*. Then each function has a purpose called *kaphā*. A diseased body is one in which either some parts are missing, or the parts are not functioning, or they are functioning but not as they were designed or supposed to function. Modern medicine doesn't have any science for *function* and *purpose*; therefore, it only studies the parts, and even these are flattened, which means that the role of the senses, mind, intellect, ego, and morality are neglected in the body.

The description in terms of parts, functions, and purposes is both necessary and sufficient to explain all aspects of the world, because (a) the soul has these three aspects, (b) God has the same three aspects, and (c) God delegates His *Śakti* to the soul in order to create his body, control its working, and then enjoy through it. The term *vāta* and *prāna* are often confused. *Prāna* is the force that causes things to be created, modified, and destroyed. This creation, modification, and destruction applies to parts, functions, and purposes. *Vāta* just denotes the function—produced by the *bhūti-Śakti* or power of being. *Prāna*, however, indicates (in some contexts) only that which creates, modifies, and destroys the body, and (in other contexts) all three types of energies.

Thus, in *yoga* philosophy, the bodily exercises called *āsana* and the breathing exercises called *prānayāma* pertain to the *kriya-Śakti* or the body parts. There are two other things—the *sat* and *ānanda*—which correspond to our *karma* and *guna*, respectively, which are outside this control. Thus, we might do *yoga* and *prānayāma* quite well, and that will help us avoid the problems arising from our body and mind—which is called *ādiatmika*, or the suffering (or pleasure) given by our own body. However, it cannot prevent the suffering from the contact or relation to other living entities—which is called *ādibhautika*—or even natural causes which are called *ādidaivika*. Finally, such exercises don't free one from material desire, fear, or pride. They do quieten the mind, and placate the body, but the desire for happiness remains. In fact, most people practice *yoga* only to enjoy their lives more, rather than to become free of these desires—which is the key purpose of *yoga* practice. Vedic texts describe that the freedom from desire comes through the surrender to *Viṣṇu*: *Shiva* can end the enjoyment of material desire, and thereby the journey of birth and death caused by such desires, but He is the master of that desire and therefore His worship still constitutes the realm of material desire.

As we have seen earlier, material desire is simply a place of duality; which means that "I want this" automatically implies "I don't want *not*-this". In the material world, we cannot choose *neither*—we have to choose something. We also cannot choose *both*—we are allowed to only pick one of the alternatives. By material desire thus we simply mean the domain of dualistic logic.

Each of the three deities in the trinity—*Brahma*, *Shiva*, and *Viṣṇu*—have the same three aspects of *sat*, *chit*, and *ānanda*, and therefore each of these personalities are associated with a *Śakti* as a feminine "consort". Owing to this, the Vedic system has a *Shakta* school of worship along with the *Vaishnava*, and *Shaiva* schools, different from *Brahma*'s *karma-kānda* system. We might note that *Śakti* is ultimately transcendental—She belongs to *Viṣṇu*, who first delegates the power to *Shiva*, who then delegates it to *Brahma*, who in turn delegates it to the different demigods, who then delegate it to other living beings. Since the power is delegated many times, we are successively under the control of demigods, *Brahma*, *Shiva*, and *Viṣṇu*, and each one is venerated. As the soul rises to higher planetary systems in the material world, he becomes free of the power delegated through the demigods but still remains under the control of the power delegated by *Brahma*. As he transcends the material existence, he is freed from *Brahma*'s control, but remains under the delegated power of *Shiva*. When the soul transcends the realm of *Shiva*, he remains only under the delegated power of *Viṣṇu*. Since the soul never becomes equal to God, he is always under some power—originally the power of *Viṣṇu*.

Each time the power is delegated to a lower authority, the person becomes powerful. The delegated power is then called his *Śakti*, and manifests as a female deity. The male is the powerful, and the female is his power. Clearly, you cannot have a powerful person without the power. Similarly, there is no impersonal power—i.e., without the control of a person. In that sense, the power and the powerful are inseparable. And yet, the powerful is slightly superior to the power: the power acts under the control of the powerful. The power is called the 'servant' of the powerful in many places. Then again, the power and powerful are described as female-male couples, in which the female never violates the desire of the male, and the male never transgresses beyond the limits of the power. You cannot achieve something that is outside your power, and in that sense the power limits you. However, you can still do things within the limits of that power, which is an option of your choosing.

This is then the origin of the male-female philosophy that pervades Vedic texts and was traditionally implemented in Vedic society where the male is the powerful and female is his power. The female constrains or sets the bounds for the male's choices, but the male choses whatever he wants within those bounds. The female is independent to set those constraints and the male simply has to accept the female's boundaries. In that sense, the female is said to be superior—the male lives under the female's limits. But, since the male chooses within the bounds of the female, the female is said to be executing the order of the male; hence, the male is said to be superior. Now, the bounds set by the female are in turn defined by a higher-level male—indicating the amount of power delegated to the lower-level male. Therefore, the bounds set by the female are ultimately a choice of the male—but a higher male.

In the case of the material creation, for example, the higher-level male is *Saṅkarṣaṇa* who is also called *Param-Śiva*. This deity delegates the power to a lower level male—who is called *Shiva* in the material world. The delegated power is called *Durga*—the term "*durg*" indicating a fortress within which the male—*Shiva*—is confined. *Shiva* can therefore choose what happens within the material universe, and that universe becomes His 'playground'. The *Śakti* follows the choices of *Shiva* in the material world, but the *Śakti* sets the bounds on what *Shiva* can choose—He cannot choose something outside the material universe. In that sense, *Shiva* is bound by *Śakti*, but *Śakti* acts according to *Shiva*'s will. Hence, both *Shiva* and *Śakti* are said to be supreme for different reasons. *Śakti* is superior to *Shiva* because She confines *Shiva* in the material playground. *Shiva* is superior to *Śakti* because He chooses from among the alternatives. Both *Saṅkarṣaṇa* outside the universe and *Shiva* inside the universe are represented as *time*. This time—or the sense of changing and passing—is produced due to desire, which means that without desire (and the presence of the soul) there cannot be any change. The material world exists as a possibility which is converted into reality by the choice exercised by *Shiva*.

The descriptions of male and female superiority are not contradictory ideas as modern notions of male-female conflict portrayal. Instead, they define ideal male-female relations in which the domains of male and female choice are separated—the female defines the bounds of the male's choices, by making a 'house' and creating a place for the male, from which the male can choose. But what happens in the house is constrained by the male's desire. Similarly, the bounds on the female are chosen by a higher-level male. Therefore, there are two males—one higher and the other lower—and similarly two females. The higher female is called *taṭasthā-śakti*, which is also identified as *Brahman*. Within the *Brahman* or the realm of souls, the material world is created—as the realm of material desire of which *Saṅkarṣaṇa* is the master. Then *Saṅkarṣaṇa* delegates this power to create numerous individual universes, in which *Shiva* (also sometimes called *Saṅkarṣaṇa*) becomes the controller. Ultimately, however, even *taṭasthā-śakti* or *Brahman* is a *śakti* which means that the soul is female rather than male. In the material world, male and female are simply roles with their different duties—prescribed by *Manu Samhita.* But in a spiritual sense, underlying both male and female roles is a female.

The higher male creates the house by delegating a certain number of options as *Śakti* to the lower male. This house constitutes the limits on the female's freedom—She cannot exceed these limits. However, the lower male is also within that house, and hence bound by the limits of the female. This is then the rationale underlying the idea—prevalent in almost all traditional societies and religions—that the 'place' of the woman is inside the house, although the man is allowed to go out to build other houses or to bring the energy—such food and firewood—inside the house. The male has the twin roles of higher and lower—which go outside the house to bring additional energy and live inside the house to enjoy it. The female, however, only lives inside.

There is no conflict between male and female as long as these roles are respected. Unfortunately, however, modern society considers male and female as equals, which is now the primary reason for unhappy alliances and divorces. Modernists claim that these gender roles are the creations of a patriarchal society whose main goal was to oppress the woman. The fact, however, is that this has little to do with materialistic notions; it is based on a spiritual philosophy. Many places in Vedic texts thus define the female to be superior to the male—inside the house. In some cases, for instance, *Kali*—a consort of *Shiva*—is shown as standing with her foot on *Shiva*'s chest. In other places, the *Śakti* is described as enjoying sex with *Shiva*. And in yet other places She is described as the servant of *Shiva*. To a naïve onlooker, all this appears contradictory, but these are all consistent descriptions. The *Śakti* standing on *Shiva*'s chest is the outside-in perspective from which *Śakti* is the power who limits the fulfillment of *Shiva's* desires; He cannot fulfill what His power cannot achieve. The description of *Śakti* serving *Shiva* is one of *Śakti* doing the bidding of *Shiva*. And their union is the combination of desire and the power to fulfill it.

Thus, *Shiva* is the desire, and *Śakti* is the power. The power exists as a possibility of being used for different purposes. The desire creates the purpose. Their union hence produces an effect—a "child" of *Shiva* and *Śakti*. The living beings in this material world also have desire, and they are delegated the power by *Shiva*. That power is the limit of what desire they can fulfill, and hence the power binds their desire. But once they have the power, they can still choose how to use that power—in order to create 'child' effects.

This existence of *Śakti* in the material world (and beyond) is the primary reason why deities have both male and female forms, and they are 'married' to each other; this 'marriage' is not merely a social custom like in the human society. Rather, they are bound in an alliance because the desires of the male are congruous to the powers of the female. Note that if the female was powerless and the male had innumerable desires, then the male would be dissatisfied with the female. Conversely, if the female had enormous power, but the male had no desire, then she would feel unwanted. In either case the couple would be unhappy together. For them to be happy, the power in the female has to match the desire in the male—which becomes the basis of their alliance. Thus, a happy alliance means that the female will not do what the male doesn't want, and the male will not demand something that is outside the female's ability. The alliances between male and female forms are made on this basis.

When you hear about the female being the power, you might wonder: if the female is power, then why does she appear weaker than the male? This is where philosophy is needed again. The 'power' in question is one of *expansion*. The Sanskrit term for woman is *stri*—the phoneme *str* has the same meaning as in English words like strap, strip, stream, street, etc.: each of them signify something elongated. The power of the woman is to elongate the tree of material creation in which a parent node produces many child nodes. The man cannot bear children, but the process of expanding into children is also the process by which the material world expands. For example, as we have seen previously, the *prāna* expands *manas* or idea into *vāk* or sentence. Similarly, the male denotes the idea, and the female denotes the power. She expands the idea into her children, because the male doesn't possess that power. The female's body is suitable for material expansion; but she can expand only if there is an idea. The male and female are complementary, not competitors. When these ideas are put into perspective, then modern false notions about the roles of men and women, patriarchy and matriarchy, are easily solved.

Once we understand the nature of *Śakti*, then we can see why each of the three deities—*Brahma*, *Shiva*, and *Viṣṇu*—have female consorts, who are in one sense their master, and in another sense their servant. As the master, the female restricts the male's desires—She tells Him what *not* to do, because it is outside Her capacity. In essence, the female tells the male to not desire any other female and remain loyal to her. But if the male is loyal to the female, the female does everything in her capacity to make the male happy. The essence of the female desire is that she wants the male to yearn for every part of her existence—Her existence being all that She can do. When the male yearns for every part of the female, she is able to realize herself fully. The essence of the male desire is that he yearns for every part of the female. By doing so, the male is able to fulfill every conceivable desire that can potentially be fulfilled in the union. Their yearning and combination lead to their sexuality. Hence, in the Vedic texts, sensuality and sexuality are not considered obscene. Rather, God and His *Śakti* are said to be embraced in a sexual union, but this sexuality must be understood as a different type of desire than mundane desires.

The ultimate yearning of the soul (as God's *taṭasthā-Śakti*) is that God—the Supreme Male—will lust for her. The lust or love is therefore between God and the soul, not between the souls. The practice of spiritual life is for the soul to become desirable and beautiful to be attractive to God's lust. This constitutes the most esoteric aspect of Vedic philosophy, which is often paraphrased in common parlance as "God's love" or that "God wants the soul".

Similarities in Vedic and Christian Doctrines

We find some amazing coincidences in descriptions across diverse religions. One such similarity has been the great flood narrative of *Vaivaśvata Manu* and a nearly identical story narrated in the Bible, where *Noah* is described as a pre-flood patriarch who was entrusted the responsibility of gathering herbs, seeds and animals into a great boat when the world is destroyed—and returned to its pre-creation state through a partial destruction.

Śrīmad Bhāgavatam, 8th Canto, 24th chapter describes the story of how Lord *Viṣṇu* incarnated as a fish to save a king *Satyavrata* during the reign of *Cākṣuṣa Manu*. The king is—at the end of the story—appointed as *Vaivaśvata Manu*, and the present *manvantara* is named after him as the *Vaivaśvata Manvantara*. The story goes as follows. Lord *Viṣṇu* appears as a small fish while *Satyavrata* is offering the water of the river *Kṛtamālā* into the river itself and asks the king to save him from the bigger fish in the river. As the king puts the fish into a water jug, the fish quickly outgrows the jug. He then puts the fish successively into bigger and bigger water bodies, but the fish outgrows each one of them rapidly. On inquiry from *Satyavrata*, Lord *Viṣṇu* reveals Himself and tells *Satyavrata* of the great impending flood a week from then. He asks him to collect all the seeds and herbs to travel in a boat along with the 7 sages, for the duration of *Brahma's* night (the flood occurs during the night).

In the Christian story, after the flood God blesses *Noah* and his sons to repopulate the earth, but their life span declines from thousands of years to just over a hundred years. In the Biblical genealogy, we can find certain rulers reigning over lands and populations for several hundreds of years. But if we add up these durations, the time elapsed from *Noah* to *Moses*—the patriarch of the *Abrahamic* religions—cannot be more than 5,000 years, the age of the Earth as per the Bible. The human life span in this duration hasn't changed that much, besides, the Earth hasn't been flooded in so massive a manner to cause universal destruction followed by reestablishment of all species.

In one sense, the Biblical story is not literally accurate. But in another sense, it is true because these events indeed occurred, just not at the time claimed for them. The story of *Vaivaśvata Manu* for instance is several million years old. To describe a story with such antecedents, the religion would have to fill many gaps in the intervening period, including, for example, the description of various ages called *yuga*, the cyclic nature of time by which the same events occur again and again, the longer lifetimes of demigods, and previous incarnations of God. As we elongate the narrative, we need increasing sophistication to explain it. If a religion wants to simplify the message—because it appears either too complex to teach, or because the narrative has too many alternatives which are potentially confusing to the audience—then some salient features of different stories may be melded together to produce a narrative that is not entirely false, and yet without the attendant complexities.

We might note that even in Vedic texts many stories are melded in this manner. For example, King Parīkṣit asks *Śukadeva Gosvāmī* about the *Śrīmad Bhāgavatam*, who then narrates the description between *Sūta Gosvāmī* and the sages at *Naimiśāranya*, in which there are other conversations between *Janmejaya* and *Vaiśampāyana*. Due to the cyclic nature of time, the same story occurs in different ages with minor variations. Due to melding, the story of an older age may be narrated after the story of the later age, because it did indeed occur in the later age, but some of the differences in the story might be incorporated from a previous age. The need for historical accuracy is sometimes disregarded in such texts, because the message is more important than the time, place, situation, or person. What they say is far more valuable than when they said it, where they said it, to whom they spoke, and the conditions of that speaking, because the text is not meant for historical analysis; it is rather meant for transforming a person's life. This doesn't mean the content is necessarily false, but that the irrelevant details may be simplified.

Another remarkable similarity between Vedic and Biblical descriptions concerns what the Bible calls the Garden of Eden as the heavenly place, and what Vedic texts called Mount *Meru* as the hill on which the demigods live. The idea of demigods living on a hill was prevalent in Greek times too—this hill was called Mount Olympus. But the idea that the world is ruled from a higher place—designated as a hill—is common to many cultures. In this case, the heavenly place is said to have four rivers and a land of gold in both cases.

Genesis 2:10-14[4]*. A river watering the garden flowed from Eden; from there it was separated into four headwaters. The name of the first* *is the Pishon; it winds through the entire land of Havilah, where there is gold. (The gold of that land is good; aromatic resin[a] and onyx are also there.) The name of the second river is the Gihon; it winds through the entire land of Cush. The name of the third river is the Tigris; it runs along the east side of Ashur. And the fourth river is the Euphrates.*

Viṣṇu Purāna, Book II, Chapter 8. Falling from on high, as she issues from the moon; she (Ganga) alights on the summit of Meru, and thence flows to the four quarters of the earth, for its purification. The Śītā, Alakanandā, Cakṣu, and Bhadrā are four branches of but one river, divided according to the regions towards which it proceeds.

Śrimad Bhāgavatam, 5.16.20-21. The mud on both banks of the River Jambū-nadī, being moistened by the flowing juice (of the falling Jambu fruits) and then dried by the air and the sunshine, produces huge quantities of gold called Jāmbū-nada. The denizens of heaven use this gold for various kinds of ornaments. Therefore, all the inhabitants of the heavenly planets and their youthful wives are fully decorated with golden helmets, bangles and belts, and thus they enjoy life.

We can see some remarkable similarities here—(1) the four rivers, (2) the land of gold, (3) the gold being an aromatic resin as it is created by the drying of the *jāmbu* fruit juice. A similarly kind of remarkable similarity exists between the descriptions of God surrounded by 24 elders in Genesis 4.

Genesis 4:1 After this I looked, and there before me was a door standing open in heaven. And the voice I had first heard speaking to me like a trumpet said, "Come up here, and I will show you what must take place after this."

Genesis 4:2 At once I was in the Spirit, and there before me was a throne in heaven with someone sitting on it.

Genesis 4:3 And the one who sat there had the appearance of jasper and ruby. A rainbow that shone like an emerald encircled the throne.

Genesis 4:4 Surrounding the throne were twenty-four other thrones, and seated on them were twenty-four elders. They were dressed in white and had crowns of gold on their heads.

Genesis 4:5 From the throne came flashes of lightning, rumblings and peals of thunder. In front of the throne, seven lamps were blazing. These are the seven spirits of God.

Readers will recall the earlier descriptions in Vedic texts where *Kṛṣṇa* has 24 incarnations, organized at 6 levels in groups of 4, and together with *Kṛṣṇa* this constitutes the 7 levels of consciousness with self-consciousness being the 8th. These 7 types of awareness are called the 7 spirits of God in the Bible.

Similarly, the Christmas tree, since pre-Christian European beliefs represents the *axis mundi* of the entire universe[5], an idea that readers would have seen several times in the Vedic context in this book. In addition, the Bible speaks about the origin of the world from sound or 'word', and, in a nearly identical description in the Vedic texts, the origin is from *śabda-brahmān*.

The cosmology we discussed in the previous chapters comprises of 6 successive steps of creation, with the soul being the 7th and eternal step.

- The soul represents one
- The soul is conditioned by duality or oppositions
- The soul enters the material space of three modes of nature
- At the point of entry, the soul is given four kinds of duties
- Within these four duties, the soul can enjoy five pleasures
- The pleasures are fulfilled by getting six kinds of qualities

The universe is thus created in 6 steps, which is probably the basis of the legend in the Biblical Genesis that the universe was created in 6 days, each 'day' reserved for completing a single step. The soul is eternal, so it is never created or destroyed. In Vedic cosmology, the universe is also said to be covered by 7 layers—each 10 times bigger than the previous layer. The implication is that the material world is 'built upon' the soul as successive layers of covering that divide and subdivide the previous layers to create the soul's experience. The universe is therefore nothing other than experience. However, it is called *material experience* because it begins in duality, or the realm of opposites.

The 7 layers of the universe can be compared to the 7 levels of experience. There is hence a life in which the soul is satisfied by moral principles themselves, but has no goals, beliefs, thoughts, senses, sensations, and objects. Successive life forms acquire more and more levels of experience. The universe is a shell of 7 coverings in which the soul within the 7 shells has all the 7 levels of experience from morality to objects. However, this is not necessarily the only kind of experience possible. We can also imagine a life of dreams in which the other 6 experiences from sensations to morality exist, but the objects don't. There are hence life forms even in the 7 coverings of the universe, but their experience is successively limited to fewer tiers, but as a result of focusing on a fewer tiers of experience they naturally will enjoy and master those tiers much better than those whose attention is divided in many tiers.

I've been careful to avoid commonalities which could be perceived as generalities in human society—such as the idea of the soul and a personal God, such as God being omniscient and omnipotent, or the notions of heaven and hell. I'm talking about very specific and highly unintuitive ideas about creation and cosmology which have practically no relevance to the religious beliefs; at least, one could hold the eternity of the soul and God, without saying that heaven was a mountain from which four rivers flowed in four directions and that mountain could also be understood as a tree about which the world rotated. Or that the world emerged from sound as the first representation of God. Or, that the world is annihilated by extensive rains but the person who survives this flood becomes the patriarch of the new life created afterward. These specific similarities attest to the fact that we cannot view such ideas as being independent of each other. Of course, we would also be very hard pressed to explain the specific sources from which they were borrowed, which leads to the problem of explaining the ideological similarity through physical contact. As we have seen earlier, we don't have to find a physical contact in order to explain ideological similarities; the mechanism for that is quite different.

There are also some similarities in the genealogy. For instance, *Abraham* the common patriarch of the Abrahamic religion has a name very similar to *Brahma*. Somewhat more surprising is the fact that his wife is named *Sarai* or *Sarah* quite like *Sarasvati* is the consort and wife of *Brahma*, who is the provider of religious principles. The difference, however, is that *Abraham* is 10 generations from *Noah*, whereas *Brahma* is much older than *Vaivaśvata Manu*. Should we consider this narrative entirely a coincidence? Or should we give credence to the fact that *Brahma* is indeed the giver of religious doctrines, although in this age, the doctrine arrives to humans through the *Manu*?

The story of Adam and Eve, who live in heaven, but fall down from there due to disobeying the order of God by eating the fruit of the forbidden tree is nearly identical to the descriptions of falldown given in *Vaishnavism* where the soul falls down into the material world, tempted by the desire to enjoy the pleasure of the material world—which is described as a tree with the sensual pleasures afforded by the fruits of this material tree. The theme of Jesus taking the sins of his disciples is also very similar to that in *Vaishnavism* where the *guru* accepts the sins of his disciples and returns to retrieve the fallen soul from the material existence. Similarly, the surrender and acceptance of the word of God as the only requirement for liberation from the material existence is a recurring theme in the *Bhakti* traditions where a deep insight into the nature of reality is not necessary if one only surrenders and takes the name of God as the final truth. The rejection of demigods in favor of the worship of the Supreme Lord is also a recurring theme in the personalist schools of Vedic philosophy where demigods are considered posts and roles occupied temporarily by souls due to good deeds, and though they have the power to grant material boons, they cannot liberate the soul from material existence itself.

Finally, we have the oft ignored fact that both Vedic and Christian theologies note the importance of the trinity. In Vedic texts, as we have already noted, the trinity is *Brahma*, *Viṣṇu*, and *Shiva*. Christianity has the Father, the Son, and the Holy Ghost. If we were to draw a parallel, *Viṣṇu* is the Father, from whose navel the son *Brahma* is born, from whose anger *Shiva* is manifest. *Shiva* is the representation of *tamo-guna* and He lives like a ghost—covered in ashes, with matted hair, and dons the moon on his head (the symbol of night). He drinks intoxicants, dances a fearsome *tāndava*, and is the destroyer of the world. The essence of this trinity is that the soul is given a material body by *Viṣṇu*. That body is then situated into material roles with their duties. But the soul has its desires by which it sometimes fulfills these duties and at other times abuses the authority of the role. The three aspects of the soul—*sat*, *chit*, and *ānanda*—and their manifestation into deities, amply bear out this trinity, and practically everything in Vedic philosophy can be summarized in terms of this trinity—both within the material world as well as in the realms beyond matter.

In essence, there is a considerable similarity between Christianity and Vedic religion if we look at the schools of *Vaishnavism*. The differences in these two appear prominent when we consider the system of *dharma* emphasized by *Brahma*, which led to the worship of demigods and the performance of rituals. The difference is also prominent when we consider the *Shaiva* and *Shakta* systems because both these systems involve considerable levels of mystical practices, besides, of course, the delineation of the feminine aspect of the divine, including the description of the material world as the conjugal intercourse between a male *puruṣa* and a female *prakriti*. Then there is the conflict with impersonal monism which is not exactly personal monotheism.

Factually, when the Europeans started translating the Vedic texts into English and other European languages during the colonial era, they were deeply attracted to the ritualistic, mystical, masculine-feminine divine interplay, along with the pervasion of numerous demigods which reminded them of the erstwhile pagan religions that prevailed in Europe prior to Christianity. Having already rejected paganism, they considered Vedic philosophy less advanced to their religion and went on to describe it as a primitive worldview of an unsophisticated population believing themselves to be far more advanced. They did not look at the similarities, or neglected them, and they overemphasized the differences. The Vedic worldview became known to the rest of the world largely through the colonial enterprise to subjugate and deride the ruled population, by asserting the European cultural superiority, which morally entitled them to rule over the primitives in order to save them from hell.

Europeans also never understood why the Vedic system never believes in religious conversion or in designating a person with a religious denomination. They found in this system a relative lack of organization of the kind that they saw in the Church and Papacy and found the diverse teachers—who lived a simple life, often in poverty—as a sign that their religion did not empower them. Of utmost apprehension to the Europeans was the 'caste system' which had indeed become a caste system from its original meritorious 'class system'. They found it contrary to the purported

Christian ideas of the equality of all humans, the freedom of speech and self-determination as moral rights, although the extent to which they themselves practiced it during the colonial era is now known to be questionable. There was, hence, a natural disdain for the Vedic system, which they carried in their translations of the Vedic texts, which then formed the mainstay of how the Vedic texts came to be seen in the West for two centuries and had a lasting impact on the West's view of India.

Meanwhile, most of the Vedic spiritual leaders themselves were callous about what the West thought about their religion. They were more interested in their spiritual advancement, rather than convincing the non-believer. Remember that according to the Vedic system, one reaps the results of one's activities. Therefore, fixing someone else's problems—if they don't want them to be fixed—is not the problem of the religious practitioner; nature's laws are already there to reward and punish the person according to their deeds. Hence, the religious leaders themselves made few attempts to counter the Western narrative. They saw the West as murderous, materialistic, and engrossed in sense pleasures—all the disqualifications for true spiritual advancement.

Very little was done by way of the similarities, and much has been done to exacerbate the differences. Of course, this is not to imply that there are no differences. Philosophically, the dominant area of difference is *karma* and reincarnation in the Vedic system by which a soul on Earth can become a demigod in heaven, or fall into hell, from which they are resurrected once their demerit for sins or merit for good deeds are exhausted. Heaven and hell are thus not eternal. Indeed, the idea of such eternity in Vedic philosophy would constitute a violation of free will—i.e., you could not mend your bad ways at a time in the future, or not fall from your superior position at a later time. I will discuss such differences in doctrines in the later part of this chapter.

The Three Semitic Goddesses

In Northern Arabia, prior to the dawn of Islam, three goddesses were widely worshipped: *Al-Uzza*, *Allat* and *Mannat*, and all three of them were very popular goddesses in Mecca at the time of the prophet Muhammad. The God—*Allah*—was associated primarily with *Allat*, the Mother, whose name means simply "The Goddess", just as *Allah* simply means "The God". They are described in two ways—sometimes as three wives of *Allah* and at other times, *Allat* and *Mannat* are seen as daughters of *Al-Uzza*. The deities of these forms were destroyed in 630 AD when Muhammad and Muslims conquered Mecca[6]. Nevertheless, the Quran mentions the existence of the three feminine forms as goddesses as the revelation by God himself in the *Shūra 53*. The initial verses in the *Shūra* 53 (5-18) describe the descent of God as "soundness".

Taught to him by one intense in strength -
One of soundness. And he rose to [his] true form
While he was in the higher [part of the] horizon.
Then he approached and descended
And was at a distance of two bow lengths or nearer.
And he revealed to His Servant what he revealed.
The heart did not lie [about] what it saw.
So will you dispute with him over what he saw?
And he certainly saw him in another descent
At the Lote Tree of the Utmost Boundary -
Near it is the Garden of Refuge -
When there covered the Lote Tree that which covered [it].
The sight [of the Prophet] did not swerve, nor did it transgress [its limit].
He certainly saw of the greatest signs of his Lord.

Now, the first words spoken by God after His descent are:

Have ye thought upon al-Lat and al-Uzza (53:19)[7]
And Manat, the third, the other? (Koran 53:20)[8]

Until this point, the descriptions are unambiguous. The ambiguity begins hereafter when, according to some accounts[9], these two verses were originally followed by two additional verses that asked for surrender to these deities. These two verses are now called the *Satanic Verses* because Mohammed subsequently retracted their existence as we will see subsequently.

These are the exalted cranes (intermediaries)

Whose intercession is to be hoped for.

The intermediaries whose mediation was required by God were of course the three deities describe above. The Quran today, however, according to the descriptions, replaces the above two verses with the following two verses:

Are yours the males and His the females?
That indeed were an unfair division! (Koran 53:21-22)

The import is that if Arabs prefer sons to daughters, then why would God prefer the feminine? Note that in this description, the three feminine forms are considered God's daughters. On the basis of this purported replacement of verses, the contemporary designation of the "Satanic Verses" arises. The claim is that originally God asked Muhammad to surrender to three deities—*Al-Uzza*, *Allat* and *Mannat*—but a verse that asked him to surrender to the three deities was replaced deriding their feminine gender as being inacceptable.

The reason for the existence of the "intercession" verse and its subsequent retraction is said to be the fact that Muhammad's religion grew very slowly, and he was estranged from his tribe. According to the biographical accounts of Muhammad, authored by Muslim scholars (at-Tabari and Ibn Sa'd), Muhammad longed for reconciliation with his tribe and God revealed *Surah 53* to Muhammad as guidance on how such reconciliation might be achieved. The above accounts indicate that after this revelation was completed, reconciliation was attained, and everyone seemed to have been delighted. However, it would have also meant the continuation of "pagan" worship, and (apparent) contradictions with essential premises like "there is no God but God" implying that divinity could be pluralistic, rejecting the need for a new religion.

Therefore, claim the advocates of the *Satanic Verses*, it was retracted, and the retraction was justified as *Jibril (Gabriel)*, the angel of revelation, informing Muhammad that Satan had used Muhammad's desire for reconciliation with the pagan leaders to insert into God's revelation the verses about the interceding cranes, which then came to be known as the *Satanic Verses*. The attempt at reconciliation and its subsequent rejection are noted as follows.

And they indeed strove to beguile thee (Muhammad)
Away from that wherewith We (God) have inspired thee,
That thou shouldst invent other than it against Us;
And then would they have accepted thee as a friend.
And if We had not made thee wholly firm
Thou mightest almost have inclined unto them a little.
Then had We made thee taste a double (punishment)
Of living and a double (punishment) of dying,
Then hadst thou found no helper against Us. (17:73-75)

Never sent We a messenger or a prophet before thee
But when He recited (the message) Satan proposed (opposition)
In respect of that which he recited thereof.
But Allah abolisheth that which Satan proposeth.
Then Allah establisheth His revelations. Allah is Knower, Wise;
That He may make that which the devil proposeth
A temptation for those in whose hearts is a disease,
And those whose hearts are hardened –
Lo! the evil-doers are in open schism. (22:52-53)

The "Satanic Verse" contention rests on the claim that the satanic verses were originally insinuated into God's message, but they had to be later abrogated. Nevertheless, the abrogation is not explicitly mentioned, although the circumstances under which it might have arisen are described. Since that time, there have been debates about the role of Satan in Islam. For instance, if Satan could have insinuated himself to Muhammad on this particular occasion, what else might he have whispered, and what else should be abrogated? But my intent here is not to get into those debates or question the veracity of the Islamic religion. I'm rather intent on exploring the nature of the Semitic goddesses, which preceded Islam, and whose abrogation Islam prescribes.

There is considerable similarity between the three Semitic goddesses and the description of *Shiva* and His consorts—*Sati*, *Pārvati*, and *Kali*. *Pārvati* is the powerful one; she rides a tiger. *Parvata* is a Sanskrit word that denotes "mountain"; hence, *Pārvati* means someone born of the mountain. Indeed, she is described as the daughter of king *Himavāna* (also called *Himavat*) who represents the *Himalayan* mountains. The

Semitic deity resembling *Parvati* is *Al-Uzza*. Both are depicted as riding big cats; both are associated with mountains. She is shown on the left in Figure-24. The difference is that *Al-Uzza* is associated with a star, but *Pārvati* is not associated in this manner in Vedic texts.

Mannat derives Her name from Arabic *maniya*, which means destruction, doom, and death. She has a dark complexion and was worshipped through a black stone at *Quidaid*, near Mecca. The Vedic deity identical in all these respects is *Kāli*. She is the consort of *Shiva* and brings death. She drinks intoxicants from a chalice and has a dark complexion. The gown of *Mannat* spells Her name in *Sabaic* (which does not use vowels and is written right to left), M-n-t., and in the *Tantra* texts *Kali* wears a garland of 50 skulls each signifying a letter of the Sanskrit language. *Mannat* is shown on the right in Figure-24. Both *Kāli* and *Mannat* are signifiers of time, which causes death and destruction.

Figure-24 The Goddesses Al-Uzza, Allat, and Mannat

In the middle of Figure-24 we can see *Allat* who is often identified with *Aphrodite*. She is a Goddess of Springtime and Fertility and holds in her hand a lump of frankincense. The Vedic deity of *Sati* is *Shiva*'s consort due to which *Shiva* is sometimes depicted in a half-man, half-woman form, because *Sati* is the erotic principle that joins the male and female as parts of the same Divinity. Vedic texts describe that when *Sati* self-immolates Herself because *Shiva* is disrespected by Her father, *Shiva* carries Her body feeling intense separation. It is interesting that the three goddesses are associated with the moon in different ways. *Al-Uzza* is associated with a star, *Mannat* with a waning moon, and *Allat* with a crescent moon (at times the sun resting in the crescent moon). There is hence an ideology about the sun, moon, and stars in the three deities.

Greek, Roman, and Egyptian Goddesses

We previously discussed the three consorts of *Shiva* which constitute three kinds of *Śakti*—as the divisions of material desire. *Sati* is the aggression in material desire, and by Her influence we feel powerful, and capable of conquering the world; She constitutes what we generally call self-confidence in our ability to fulfill our desires; She gives us hope, courage, and optimism in life. *Durga* creates fear in us; by Her influence we become afraid and strike fear in others. Fear acts as a counterbalance to unbridled optimism; as the saying goes: "fools rush in where angels fear to tread", fear forces us to reexamine our assumptions and plans rather than simply rely on our self-confidence. Finally, *Kāli* creates the power of rationalizing the frustration and telling ourselves that we are correct in our approach and the problem lies with someone else. If this rationalization is missing, then we fall into depression, guilt overtakes the person, and paralyzes them. However, if this energy is very strong, then one rationalizes every problem into someone else's fault, and refuses to take responsibility; the person now blames 'fate' and 'destiny' for their suffering.

The Greeks, Romans, and Egyptian civilizations worshiped many deities which had remarkable similarities with those described in Vedic texts. For instance, *Aphrodite* is a Greek goddess who represents love, beauty, passion, and sexuality. She represents desire and confidence and after her numerous stimulants are now called *aphrodisiacs.* She is represented by roses, doves, and swans, all indicators of peaceful pleasure and happiness. In Roman culture she was also known as Venus, owing to which Venus has now come to represent feminine sexuality as opposed to Mars which denotes masculinity. A very similar deity in Egyptian times was Isis who was worshipped as a mother.

Greeks also worshipped the complete opposite of Aphrodite as Nemesis. If Aphrodite represented desire, pleasure, confidence, and passion, then Nemesis was the very opposite of it. She is in fact said to bring retribution to those who become arrogant and proud. She is described as a dark-faced goddess, the 'daughter of Justice', remorseless, and vengeful. The Romans called Nemesis by the name Invidia, which meant "indignation at unmerited advantage". In some Greek carvings, Nemesis is shown as standing on the head of a man, which is nearly identical to deities of *Kāli* who is shown as standing on the chest of *Shiva* and sometimes with a chopped off head in her hand. Given these negative images associated with this deity, the word 'nemesis' itself has come to presently denote an adversary, rival, opponent, and antagonist. Indeed, if desire and happiness is the protagonist then sadness and depression is the antagonist. This sadness comes onto those who have been overconfident and began attributing their success to their own powers and abilities. In that sense, Nemesis destroys the pride and ego—crushing the 'head' of a proud person below her 'feet', chopping off their 'head', or standing on their 'chest'—which are all adequate and visceral metaphors for the destruction of pride.

Similarly, there is Artemis the Greek goddess of war, victory, and identified as the mother of nature. She bears arms such as bow, arrows, and a quiver, or sometimes a hunting spear. She is often identified as the moon goddess, and then the patron goddess of many animals such as deer and bears. Artemis sometimes took another goddess—Nike—as a charioteer when going on wars; she is a deity identified as the giver of victory, especially to Olympic athletes, probably the reason why the name is used as a popular sports brand. Her Roman equivalent is Diana, another goddess identified with hunting, nature, animals, moon, and woodlands. She is also said to wear a crown of the crescent moon, a symbol generally identified with *Shiva* in Vedic description. These deities have a remarkable similarity to the Vedic person named *Durga*.

Other than Vedic texts, there are no cohesive and clear associations between deities and the philosophy of nature. There are in some cases closer links between these deities and human psychology, but there is so much overlap in the descriptions of other systems that we can approximately point to an association but very hard to know accurately. As these associations weaken, the understanding of the deity also declines in the population. At which point even the deity's form may be modified, interpolated, or combined with other forms, and it is not clear what the erstwhile worshippers were really talking about. In that sense, I personally don't see how delving into all the details of the surviving information about the various gods from Roman, Greek, and Egyptian civilizations today can factually aid in their understanding. Such an understanding is possible when we ground these deities into some natural principle that we can see in our own lives, or some philosophical thesis that is widely useful and its principles are then personified as deities. Therefore, I will not dwell much more on the topic, except to note that there are numerous similarities between these deities but because there isn't a philosophy surrounding it, probably the understanding is lost in folklore and guesswork.

The Worship of Animals

We have seen how the sun, the moon, and the stars divide into many parts, which are individually identified with different deities. Each of these deities is associated with a different kind of animal which acts as their transportation *vehicle*. Thus, *Indra* has an elephant as his vehicle, *Brahma* has a swan as his vehicle, *Shiva* rides a bull, *Viṣṇu* flies atop an eagle-like bird, the sun rides in a chariot driven by horses, *Yama* mounts a buffalo, *Ganesha* rides on a mouse, *Sarasvati* flies on a peacock, *Varuna* moves on a crocodile, *Durga* has a tiger as Her transport, the moon rides on an antelope, *Lakshmi* rides an owl, and humans are vehicles for *Kubera*—the god of wealth, gold and property. Collectively, they are all called *Vāhana* or carriers of the deity by which a type of cognition, emotion, or relation 'reaches' their respective destination.

Therefore, if you wanted to acquire material prosperity, happiness, or good relationships, you would primarily worship the above said deities but also the above mentioned 'vehicles' that can bring those things into your life. We might note that these 'vehicles' are not literally the animals that we see in our day-to-day life; however, in the same sense that the demigods have a body with a form—hands, legs, belly, face, etc.—which are all conceptual, similarly, the 'animals' quoted above are also conceptual bodies. Furthermore, just as there is a specific individual person who has the form of a demigod, similarly, there is an individual person who has the form of the above said animal. For instance, the elephant of *Indra* is named *Airāvata*, the eagle of *Viṣṇu* is named *Garuda*, the mouse of *Ganesha* is named *Dinka*, the bull of *Shiva* is called *Nandi*, and so forth. Therefore, the animals in question are not the generic species, but individuals with a form resembling those of the species we perceive.

The vehicles of God and the demigods are emblematic of certain qualities. For instance, the bull of *Shiva* symbolizes virility and strength, and as a result the bull has come to symbolize sexual prowess. Similarly, the swan of *Sarasvati* symbolizes peace and grace, and her quality of learning is acquired by those who possess these qualities. The mouse of *Ganesha* symbolizes agility, busywork, and alertness, and the luck granted by the deity comes through the qualities of his vehicle. The tiger of *Durga* symbolizes the stealth, speed, and the skill to fight, and the conquest of inner fear and the ability to conquer others symbolized by Her comes through the possession of these qualities. In this way, we can view the demigods as providing certain outcomes, and their vehicles as symbolizing the preparation required to receive those results. The demigod 'rides on the back' of the said animal, which means that if you possess the qualities of the animal, the demigod can come riding to you on that quality.

It also means that the demigods cannot simply provide an outcome to a person who is unqualified to bear that quality. Thus, for instance, learning will not come by the grace of *Sarasvati* to one who is not gentle, peaceful, and gracious. Similarly, luck given by *Ganesha* will not come to a lazy person who just wishes their luck to improve; it will come to one who is busy as a mouse. Sexual pleasure from *Shiva* will not come to one who is sickly; it will come to one who is healthy and virile as a bull. Therefore, if you want the grace of a demigod, then you have to first have the grace of their carriers or acquire the qualities which can then become the containers in which the results can be held. Otherwise, even if we obtain those results, we won't be able to hold them, like sand falling through the gaps between the fingers. It is an important fact that we often miss that this worship doesn't constitute begging without effort. Every boon has a vehicle through which one receives the demigod's grace.

This doesn't mean that everyone who is gentle and peaceful will automatically be learned. But it does mean that everyone who is learned by the grace of *Sarasvati* must have become gentle and peaceful. Similarly, everyone lucky by the grace of *Ganesha* must be busy like a mouse looking for various opportunities, analyzing and testing them for their suitability, and running hither and tither trying to find that one thing that might answer their needs. In short, success meets preparation. Just preparation is not enough to guarantee success, but the demigods will generally not grant the success to an unprepared person. In that sense, the worship of demigods is not a substitute for actual hard work, character development, seeking opportunities, and using one's intellect to analyze and test the difference between the available alternatives. It is only meant to ensure that our preparedness actually meets with success. In rare cases, when the demigods grant the boons to the unprepared person—because the person has performed many austerities to please them—the results of these grants are short lived. Thus, one might gain a lot of wealth but will lose much of it because of his carelessness. Similarly, one might become learned but if he is not gentle and peaceful, the learning will become futile.

The regard given to animals in traditional systems of religion should be understood as the path on which a person acquires the qualities inherent in the animal as a preparation to receive the demigod's grace. We might say that to reach the qualities of the demigod, one must first acquire subordinate qualities. The 'road' to the destination involves preparation, and as we acquire these qualities we move closer to the demigod although we don't necessarily reach the destination, because there might be other qualities required to complete the journey. In that sense, these 'vehicles' to the demigods are paths of human perfection which one follows in order to reach a higher place.

Paradoxically, in some cases, instead of 'worshipping' the animals in order to acquire their qualities, the animals were 'sacrificed' to the demigods in an act of sending a pick-up vehicle to them so that they can come to the worshipper—i.e., grant the qualities they represent, embody, and control. This sacrifice of animals required not just killing the animal, but actually sending the soul to the demigod for a better life than they were leading at present. The person who sacrificed the animal also had to give up their *karma* in order to arrange a contact between the animal qualities and the demigod (recall that *karma* is the agency that creates a contact between two entities). Thus, by killing the animal and giving it a better life, the sacrifice took away the *karma* of the person who made the sacrifice, gave that *karma* to the animal, and thereby created a 'path' between the demigod and the worshipper through which the demigod's qualities were received by the worshipper. It is as if the demigod received a transportation vehicle by which he can come to the worshipper. Note that even in this process, the worshipper sacrifices his *karma* in order to get something from the demigod, and the sacrifice has to be performed in a way that the animal soul actually reaches the demigod to be born in the same form, enjoying similar pleasures, although the life is now significantly improved.

Such a sacrifice constitutes the win-win-win scenario in which the demigod gains a new asset (his vehicle), the animal gains a better life (to be the vehicle of the demigod instead of an ordinary animal), and the worshipper obtains the qualities embodied by the demigod. Such a sacrifice is not merely animal killing, because everyone is benefited in the process. However, since *karma* is temporary, upon its expiry the animal will die, the results obtained from such worship will be lost, and even the demigod will leave his body to be reborn. And yet, there is a process by which such sacrifices could be performed, and became the basis of incessant animal killing by greedy worshippers even when they did not have the understanding of how to impart one's *karma* to the animal so that it can become the vehicle of demigod's travel. When this understanding is lost, instead of giving away one's *karma* to enjoy a better life, the person sacrificing the animal incurs adverse *karma* and suffers in the future. Such sacrifices were prevalent formerly when the process by which one can take one's *karma* and give it to someone else in order to obtain a benefit in return was well-known. The process is akin to a business transaction, although it involves a profound understanding of the laws of *karma*.

Animal worship and animal sacrifice are therefore two sides of the same coin. By the worship, the worshipper acquires the qualities of the animal, and therefore becomes the vehicle on whose back the demigod travels. Similarly, by sacrificing the animal, the demigod travels on the animal's back. In both cases, there is mutual benefit to each of three parties—the animal, the demigod, and the human worshipper. For instance, if the animal is worshiped, it will receive a good life to enjoy in the present body. If the animal is sacrificed, it will still receive an even better life to enjoy in a new body, if the process is performed properly. If, however, the science underlying the process is unknown, then the animal will suffer, the demigod gets nothing, and the human worshipper simply incurs bad *karma* for nothing in return. Hence, animal sacrifices are forbidden because the science of ritual sacrifices is lost.

Land, River, Ocean, and Mountain Worship

Quite separate from the worship of animals is that of nature; it manifests in considering your land of birth your 'mother' or 'father'. Different kinds of living beings are born to live in different kinds of natural habitats; these include land, water, air, etc. Within these habitats are specific places such as flat plains, mountains, rivers, oceans, deserts, hot, wet, and dry climates, etc. From our physical vision, we don't necessarily see a boundary that demarcates one place from another; boundaries such as countries appear to be entirely man-made and seem to have no relevance to the construction of the natural habitat. But, if we look closer, there are boundaries in nature that identify a *closed* system within which we find a homeostasis or equilibrium which if disturbed will cause the destruction of many life forms until a new equilibrium is attained. The equilibrium exists because there is a cycle of exchange which runs at some steady pace, and any increase or decrease in the pace—a *deviation* from the equilibrium—will force the system to return to its original state.

For example, within a forest, the deer eat the grass, and the tigers eat the deer. If tigers ate more deer, then they will run out of deer, compete with each other for food, until only a fewer tigers remain, and the deer population will then grow again, allowing the tiger population to grow back into its erstwhile state, provided the tiger don't eat more deer again. Similarly, if the tiger ate less deer, then the deer population will increase and they will then run out of grass and the deer population will then decline rapidly, until it reaches the optimal level where there are fewer deer, the consumption of grass is back to its original levels, and there are enough deer so that the tigers can survive, and there are enough tigers to keep the deer population in check.

The key point here is that a certain finite number of variables determine the equilibrium state. If you change any of these variables, the entire system will undergo a disruption until it settles down into a new equilibrium. For example, if suddenly there was an expansion in the grassy lands, then the deer could expand into the new grasslands, and multiply their population without running out of the food. The tigers will now have more deer to feed on, and even their population can increase, until there is enough grass for enough deer for enough tigers. In other words, the system will settle into a new equilibrium. These are not new ideas; they are frequently studied in the evolution of biospheres, the effect of ecological changes on the population of species, the growth or extinction of a particular species from a given biosphere, etc. The new idea is simply this: What determines when a new variable will be added into or removed from the equilibrium system to take it to a new equilibrium? Clearly, the addition and removal of such variables—once the system is already in equilibrium—must involve a breach in the system's *boundaries* by which some new variables enter the system or exit from it. Alternately, some variables—such as a flowing river—which were previously entering and exiting the system might change their flow and result in a disruption.

Inherent in any kind of equilibrium is the idea of a *boundary*. This boundary may be a physical object (such as a wall) that separates the outside from the inside. It may also be some kind of tacit agreement by which variables in a system simply don't interact with other variables; for example, there are unwritten boundaries of cultural, racial, and economic strata that separate people from getting closely entangled with the people of the other strata. So, the boundaries are not always visible to everyone if you only look at physical objects, but they can be seen at deeper levels of existence such as cultural differences, ideological differences, differences in goals, or moral values. Regardless of how we perceive these boundaries they can be perceived if we are sufficiently perceptive and the evidence of that boundary is that variable changes in one system don't affect the other systems if they are separated.

In classical physics, science conceives that every object affects every other object in the universe. But in atomic physics, we know that an object interacts with only one object at a time, because their interaction involves the emission and absorption of some energy, and that energy is *quantized*—i.e., it is discretely emitted by a source at a particular time, and discretely absorbed by a particular sink in a particular place. Thus, all objects are not always interacting. Rather, a certain object will only interact with a particular object at a certain time and place. How the time and place of the interacting object is to be determined remains an unsolved problem in atomic theory. In a loose sense, we cannot say which tiger will eat which deer at which place and which time, although we can say that each tiger has a certain probability of eating once every few days, and each deer has a certain probability of living to a certain age. These probabilities are strictly a function of the boundaries (in atomic theory they are called *ensembles*). If you stretch or contract the boundary, the probabilities within the system—e.g., how long a species will live, and how often it gets to eat—will also change until a new equilibrium is established again.

The key question now is: Given the fact that we can observe the existence of such equilibria in nature, and given the fact that these equilibria can be produced only when there is a boundary, how do we determine what the boundaries are, and what causes the boundaries to change? These boundaries are analogues of the 'skin' on a living being which demarcates it from others. The interactions within the boundary constitute a homeostasis, and then the interactions between these boundaries constitute a different homeostasis. The observed patterns of behavior would automatically change if the boundaries were shrunk or expanded, or if two boundaries dissolved to form a larger boundary. There is hence empirical evidence for such boundaries, but there is no theoretical explanation of why such boundaries exist in nature.

It is in light of these facts that we can think of ecosystems as living entities. When they come into existence, a boundary is created followed by the establishment of equilibrium within that boundary. A single variable change inside the boundary causes a temporary disruption, but the system will always return to its equilibrium as long as the system boundary is not breached. Similarly, such ecosystems are also embedded inside a larger boundary, and the ecosystems are therefore also interacting with each other like living entities constituting another equilibrium within the larger ecosystem boundary. The larger ecosystem is therefore also a living entity, which creates an equilibrium simply by asserting a boundary. Thus, mountains, rivers, forests, oceans, deserts, and plains are all ecosystems, within a larger earth ecosystem.

The earth is a living entity that creates an equilibrium within itself, but this ecosystem interacts with those of the other places—the sun, the moon, the stars, etc. Likewise, the sun, the moon, and the stars are also in equilibrium within themselves, and in interaction with other parts of the universe. The world is thus organized hierarchically as ecosystems. And in the very sense that we consider the sun, the moon, and the stars as personalities, similarly, the earth as a whole is a personality, and it has delegated smaller regions, constituting relatively self-contained ecosystems, to other personalities. The boundaries of these ecosystems are not visible to us most of the time. But these boundaries are the *bodies* of the living entities. We cannot see them with our sense perception, but we can perceive the *evidence* of their existence—namely, that the existence of the boundary creates a state of equilibrium. The boundary therefore cannot be sensually perceived, but it can be known as a conceptual entity. Hence to perceive such living beings too one has to employ mental perception. Thus, the *form* of the living entity has a shape, size, color, smell, sound, etc. provided we can raise our perception to experience mentally.

The existence of these living entities determines the dynamics within and between ecosystems. Their forms are not fixed, because the ecosystems can change their form. Similarly, these living entities are not eternal, because ecosystems can be created and destroyed. In fact, one such living entity can consume another one when one ecosystem absorbs the other. To the extent that the ecosystem circulates goods and materials within and without other ecosystems, it is said to be living. In fact, the rate of this circulation constitutes the 'breath' that circulates in and out. Then each ecosystem plays a type of role in relation to others, which constitutes its duty; therefore, society or the ecosystem as a whole has a duty, the controller of that society is responsible for ensuring that the duty is being performed. Finally, in each such society a certain type of happiness can be enjoyed, which is the happiness of being together and part of that society, identifying with each other culturally and socially. Thus, every aspect of the soul—namely, relations, cognitions, and emotions—can be associated even with a society or an ecosystem, and these too are living.

In the case of humans, we call ecosystems 'civilizations'. They are born, then expand and become more powerful, and then they dwindle and die. All of history—as the study of cultures, societies, languages—is one part of studying the evolution of civilizations. Thus, the Greek, Roman, Mesopotamian, and Egyptian cultures were also living entities; they just lived longer than individuals in that civilization. Each such civilization defined its rules and laws for internal interaction, and then the attitudes toward the outsiders. Some cultures thought they had a preeminent position in society, and they could control the other societies. Others felt controlled and compelled by the others but worked hard as a society to maintain their cultural and social integrity from being invaded from the outside. Depending on the relation to other civilizations, each culture has a certain role and responsibility—which we can call their collective *dharma*. If the society follows that *dharma* then it will produce good *karma*, which will ensure longevity and prosperity for that society. But if the society neglects its *dharma* then it will create adverse *karma* and ensure its suffering. In this way, *dharma* is not restricted to just humans. Rather, societies, cultures, countries, and civilizations themselves are duty bound to *dharma* and that is not because of an impersonal system of laws; it is because there is an individual person responsible for ensuring that such duties are followed.

Society, culture, civilization, ecosystems, and biospheres are therefore not impersonal entities because they have a duty and responsibility and that duty and role can be asserted only when there is a person controlling it. Indeed, society in the Vedic culture is described as a body whose head is the *Brahmana*, hands are the *Kshatriya*, the belly is the *Vaisya*, and the legs are the *Sudra*. This is not a metaphorical description if society is a body controlled by a living entity. There are living entities whom we cannot observe by our senses, but we can perceive the *effects* of their existence. They control the destiny of a society and culture, so that the civilization is also 'living' as a person. It 'sees' and 'hears' other civilizations, and it 'knows' about others and the self.

Such ecosystems and civilizations are also worthy of worship when they follow their *dharma*. In that sense, rivers, mountains, forests, oceans, deserts, and plains could be worshiped provided they were following their collective duty. Recognizing their existence, and understanding how one is controlled by their environment, society, rules and regulations, how one owes a debt to this society for giving one a dutiful life of enjoyment is itself an advancement from the gross materialistic perception in which we think that cultures and civilizations are simply man-made entities that exist only in our 'minds'. Post-modernism for example treats laws and cultures as *social constructs*. In other words, it can be whatever we like it to be because there is no ideal behavior expected out of society as a whole. Alternately, society as a whole has no purpose. Yes, we can create civilizations and separate one civilization from another using artificial boundaries, but these are all man-made. The modern world is influenced by such materialism because they cannot perceive the existence of boundaries, and although they can see their effects, they don't recognize them as real physical entities and consider them imaginary.

The modern world is also ruled by invisible personalities, who don't follow *dharma*; they are powerful but not to be worshipped. Worshiping them—e.g., through considering one's nations, laws, cultural norms, economic behaviors, or societal practices itself as *dharma*—is not going to uplift the person in their life. Instead, by following all these civilizational constructs which are widely touted as 'modernity' one will degrade oneself. The invisible personalities ruling the world at present are more like demoniac living beings, under the influence of this age of quarrels called *Kali Yuga* ruled by the person named *Kali* (not to be confused with the goddess *Kāli* referenced earlier). Under his influence, there is progressive decline of *dharma* and artificial new boundaries (e.g., between countries) are created while natural boundaries (e.g., between genders) are broken. There is constant tussle about which boundaries to maintain and which ones to destroy but no matter what boundary is created, nobody is interested in defining and following their respective *dharma.*

In that sense, we can say that the world is ruled by 'evil'; that 'evil' is also a person, who operates by dividing the world along lines that produce natural clashes rather than cooperation and co-existence. The breaking of traditional rules to flatten the society via equality, for example, is like asking both lion and deer to eat grass. Naturally, if both eat grass, they are going to compete with each other. But you can create such a system in which there is a boundary between lion and deer, but no boundary between lion and grass. Social organization cannot be achieved by whimsically breaking boundaries and creating new ones or destroying all boundaries. For a stable equilibrium to exist, there must be boundaries. Furthermore, these boundaries must be created such that each ecosystem can perform its role vis-à-vis other ecosystems. So, ethical and evil societies can simply be distinguished by good or bad organization. When evil predominates, automatically bad organization is dominant. When morality is powerful, good organization is naturally manifest. When morality prevails in society, then one's culture, civilization, country, and society can itself be deified and worshipped through obedience to a higher personality. In that sense, we can personify nations. But when immorality prevails, then deifying nations, civilizations, or cultures can only constitute the path of degradation.

The Rise of Impersonal Philosophy

Impersonalism is a legitimate philosophy when applied to an individual self; it says: I exist, and in this preoccupation with the existence of the self, I'm not concerned about the existence of others. My awareness of the self, therefore, leads to ignorance of the other. It is better than trying to know others while remaining ignorant about the self which is the path of modern science, in which one studies the external world and its objects but doesn't look within to understand the nature of the senses, mind, intellect, ego, morality, and the soul beyond all of this. The materialist dogma teaches people that the world outside is all that exists, and the human body is also reducible to the same matter that we discover through sense perception. Clearly, through sense perception we can see objects but not the senses themselves. Similarly, other deeper levels of reality beyond the senses remain unknown. In this preoccupation with the external world, materialism fosters ignorance of the self. However, as one becomes frustrated with trying to know the world and remaining ignorant about the self, one turns inward, and realizes that the objects in the external world are not the causes of my happiness. Instead, to be happy, one must understand the self and at least restore one's *self-confidence.*

Self-confidence frees the mind from anxiety and depression. Anxiety is the fear of the future—what is going to happen in the external world. And when one is tired of that anxiety, he loses the energy to even battle the fear—which is then experienced as depression. Anxiety and depression are therefore often associated, although they are experienced as different emotions.

The onset of depression leads to unhappiness, and the person oscillates from engaging with fear and withdrawing with depression. Self-confidence is freedom from anxiety and depression; under its influence, a person becomes self-satisfied, which means that the mind is naturally withdrawn from the anxiety caused by the worldly events, and then freedom from depression that one is unable to influence the world through their effort. The philosophy of impersonalism is about restoring self-confidence which leads to fearlessness, and once the fear is gone, depression ensuing from the inability to handle that fear also disappears. Under self-confidence, the mind is pervaded with peace, satisfaction, quietude, fulfilment, and one feels self-sufficient. You don't mind engaging with the world, and don't care if you cannot engage, because the primary relationship is not with the world; it is rather with the self.

We have seen above that *Sati* is the goddess of self-confidence. The term *sat* denotes awareness, eternity, and relationship. When these are combined, one becomes aware of the self and establishes a relationship with the self. This relationship is also eternal, because the self will never leave oneself. Being satisfied in the self, one becomes detached from the relationships of the world which are continually changing. As a result, one no longer seeks happiness from the external relations; one is happy through relation to the self. This state of detachment, self-confidence, and being situated in the self is called *Brahman*. It is the rejection of the material world and its trappings, and selection of the self. Nothing else is asserted or denied, because nothing else matters.

Unfortunately, impersonalism has been distorted in recent times to mean several additional things that are not properly part of it. First, instead of *rejecting* the world—i.e., detaching oneself from its trappings, even though such trappings exist—the impersonalist denies the *existence* of the world itself. Now, it might seem philosophically convenient to deny that the world exists in order to be able to withdraw one's attention away from it; it is a trick one can play with the mind and tell it that the world doesn't exist, or that it is an illusion, so that the mind is no longer attracted to the world. Anything that helps us advance in self-realization is a valuable idea, and in that sense, the denial of the existence of the world—in so far it helps the detachment—is a legitimate trick. But it is not ultimately true, because if the world doesn't exist, then our attraction and experiences of the world must be illusions. If they are illusions, then we are stuck with the problem of explaining how this illusion is created. The illusion is *something* rather than *nothing*. But how did something come about from nothing—given that the material world doesn't exist?

I will not dwell on this problem, as it has no answers. The world exists, and we have to still withdraw from it. The trick of telling the mind to withdraw because the world doesn't exist has a value—it is easier to tell a child that the toys don't exist to prevent him from playing with those toys, rather than tell him that the toys exist but one must desist from playing. Some lies therefore are valuable in the sense that they help one progress. But that lie cannot be the basis of a philosophical rejection of the external world. Nevertheless, *Shankarāchārya*—who formulated this rejection in *Advaita* philosophy—played this trick in order to tell the ritual practitioners to desist from trying to enjoy the material world through demigod worship. He urged them to withdraw inward, because the self is eternal, and the worldly pleasures are temporary. If you want a child to focus on doing their homework, you tell them that all their friends have left and there is no one left to play with, so that the child's mind will now focus on doing the homework rather than be distracted by play. This lie has a value, and that value is to end the mental distraction[10].

Second, when one focuses on the self rather than the external play, the self is realized to the exclusion of the rest. That exclusion includes the existence of the other souls, their desires and destinies. But the ability to focus on the self doesn't truly mean that the others have ceased to exist. Such a stance would be like burying one's head in the sand to conclude that nothing else exists. The focus on the self, therefore, means that we become unaware of other individuals. Again, this is a lie you can tell yourself in order to focus on the self. This latter lie leads to the idea of monism and impersonalism that there is only one self; that there is no individual other than the self so there is no point in trying to find an external reality—the existence of other souls—outside the self. Awareness of the self to the exclusion of all others is partial ignorance, but that ignorance is not an illusion, because the self truly exists. Hence, there is a difference between *ignorance* and *illusion*: the ignorance is that other souls exist but I'm not aware of them, but the illusion is that others don't exist.

The entire *Advaita* is based on treating the ignorance as an illusion. Under this treatment, both the external world and the other souls become illusions, and when this illusion is discarded, the one reality—the self—is discovered. Since there is nothing other than this self, one can also identify this self with God, which leads to the false idea that we are all God. Now, remember, thinking oneself as God is helpful in restoring one's self-confidence, obtaining freedom from anxiety and depression, so long as it is used to trick the mind into detaching itself from the occurrences in the external world. The idea is false, but it is useful in fighting the mental tendency toward anxiety and unhappiness and finding happiness in the self through detachment. One who is trying to free oneself from unhappiness can still use this idea—if it is understood as a trick to fool the mind—rather than as a philosophical truth.

A direct fallout of the thesis of illusion is the rejection of the existence of demigods, of the *dharma* and *karma* entailed by their existence, of the individuality of the different souls, and of the distinction between demigods and God. The dogma of illusion is exceptionally exclusivist and therefore it leads to numerous philosophical problems. For instance, if there is only one soul then even if he hurts others, he has only hurt oneself. That can help a person desist from hurting others, but it also entails that if only the self is being hurt, then there cannot be a moral consequence of this action—and hence *karma*. If there is no moral consequence, then there is no basis for rebirth. This now leads to inner contradictions within the Vedic philosophy where the doctrine of *Advaita* becomes inconsistent with the doctrine of *karma* and rebirth. Nevertheless, for those who have been baffled by the enormity of countless gods and goddesses, this can easily become the path of religious simplification—you can reject all these gods and goddesses as illusions or 'mythology'.

Through such rejection we come to see monism as an ideology that contradicts monotheism and polytheism, when, truly speaking, monism lies between the polytheism of demigod worship and the monotheism of a single God. The monist philosophy simply says: I exist, and I don't care about anything else. It is not a denial of the existence of the world or those of the other souls. It is rather a *choice* to focus the attention on the self instead of others. There is hence a difference between the truth of *Brahman* and the illusory thesis employed in *Advaita* which has now also come to be known as *Māyāvāda*. To the extent that monism can be used to detach the mind from the world, it has value: it tricks the mind into detachment. However, even the child eventually figures out that he has been tricked, and the trick then stops working. Therefore, if the trick has to be successful, it has to be asserted as the truth, but that assertion creates inner contradictions. Therefore, the spiritualist should ideally be treated as an adult—capable of handling the full truth—rather than as a child who has to be tricked in order to convince them to act appropriately.

Renouncing Desire and Finding Emptiness

There is a subtle but important difference between *Advaita* and other voidistic religions such as Buddhism. The difference is that in *Advaita* the soul is considered eternal, although not an individual; it still has the properties of *sat* or awareness, *chit* or cognition, and *ānanda* or pleasure; however, the awareness if focused on the self in order to know the self and enjoy with the self. You can still desire the self, love the self, and seek pleasure in the self. In Buddhism, the existence of the soul is not acknowledged. As a result, there is nothing you can seek, love, or enjoy, as an alternative to the pleasure of the external world. When you withdraw from the external world, you don't necessarily go to seek the self. Instead you recognize the existence of the world but reject the existence of the self. Since there is no self, there is no *enjoyer*. What would the anxiety be about if there is no one suffering or enjoying? When "I" do not exist, then how can "I" suffer or enjoy? There is something that exists—i.e., the world—but the existence of the self is ultimately an illusion.

Quite like Descartes said, "I think therefore I exist", you can invert the proposition and claim that if I stopped thinking and emptied the mind, I would cease to exist. Now there is no difference between body and soul, because there is no soul. The experience of the self is created by the body when there is thought because through thinking a simultaneous distinction between the *thinker* and the *thought* is produced. The idea of a 'thinker' or self is therefore a byproduct of the process of thinking. If we stop thinking, then the thinker will disappear along with the thought. Central to Buddhism is therefore the notion of *co-dependent arising* also called *Pratītyasamutpāda* namely that two imaginary things (*pratīta*) are co-created (*samutpāda*). In this case, the two imaginary things are the thought and the thinker. You cannot keep one and reject the other. Instead, you have to reject both of them at once. This rejection of thought it sometimes called 'emptying the mind' and if the mind has thus been emptied of thought, then the false notion of the self also disappears.

Pratītyasamutpāda has some similarities with the Vedic notion of *duality*. For instance, hot and cold, white and black, east and west are opposites, and yet they are complementary because they describe opposite faces of the same reality. However, in the Vedic system, there is also a reality *higher* than the two opposite faces, which reconciles their opposition. For instance, the two opposite faces of a coin—head and tail—are indeed mutually opposite and yet complementary. But 'coin' is separate from the two opposite faces, and it reconciles their opposition. In fact, the 'coin' is not reducible to the two faces. It is rather like a higher node in the tree which branches into head and tail. Furthermore, when the branches are created, the head will be created ahead of the tail, which is why you can say that the 'head' is higher than 'tail' although they are opposites. This means that there are three things—the whole coin, the head face, and the tail face. They follow one by one, such that even if the opposites (head and tail) are removed, the whole coin still exists, although we cannot perceive it by the senses. The 'coin'—without the faces—is a pure concept; it can be seen as a symbol of value by the mind, its value judged by the intellect, it can be desired by the ego, and it can be considered righteous by the morality. And yet, you cannot perceive it by the senses without the above opposites.

The Vedic view is similar to the Hegelian thesis, antithesis, and synthesis triad except that in Hegel's view antithesis follows thesis and synthesis follows the antithesis whereas in the Vedic view the synthesis precedes the thesis and the antithesis follows the thesis. In other words, even if you remove the thesis and antithesis, the synthesis exists because it is logically prior. Thus, the synthesis is logically the highest, the thesis follows the synthesis, and the antithesis is created from the thesis. If we were to think in terms of colors, then white is the synthesis of all colors; the thesis is an individual color—which further divides into other colors such as red, blue, and yellow—and black is the antithesis. So, white is at the top and black is at the bottom, and they appear as opposites, but white is the synthesis or 'everything' while black is the antithesis or 'nothing'—i.e., the opposite of 'everything'. In between 'everything' and 'nothing' exist the individual things—we can call them 'something'. Hence, 'nothing' is the opposite of 'something', but also of 'everything'. The question is: When we talk about the opposite of 'nothing' do we mean 'something' or 'everything'? The difference is caused because there are three distinct categories instead of just two, although those three are modeled as opposites.

When the soul experiences, it creates a distinction between the knower and the known which constitutes the cognitive notion of the self as different from the other because the soul has an experience different from the thing being experienced. For instance, if you see the color red, then the perception of red is the 'self', and the thing being perceived as red is the 'other'. Through perception, the soul knows itself as the 'knower of red color'. However, the soul is not identical to that experience of being the knower. Even if the soul doesn't perceive the self as the knower and the world as the known, it still exists as the *potentiality* of becoming the knower of some known in the future. In that sense, even if we remove the thinker and the thought, the soul still exists. Indeed, the 'knower' is produced from the soul, like 'something' is created from 'everything'. The 'known' is then defined as not-self and becomes 'nothing'. The soul is therefore higher than both 'knower' and 'known'; the latter are co-created, but the soul exists as potentiality even when both of them do not exist.

Without an experience, you exist as the potentiality of having an experience, but you cannot realize this potential without the experience itself. Therefore, by emptying the mind, the thinker and the thought are gone, and hence the cognitive notion of the 'knower' is dissolved. However, the potentiality of creating the 'knower' still exists. The thinker and the thought may indeed be called phenomenal (*pratīta*) co-creations (*samutpāda*) but by dissolving the thought the cognitive *perception* of the self as a thinker is gone but the thinker is not gone. This is evidenced in the fact that thought can return.

In Vedic descriptions, the soul enters the material world by first adopting a realm of duality called the *karanodaka*; it is a vast 'ocean' of thinker and thought possibilities. When the soul enters this realm, he forgets that he is not the experience of a thinker, nor is he any of the thoughts. The transcendent nature of the soul goes beyond these thinker-thought dualities. But in the realm of duality, the soul doesn't see how he is beyond that duality. Buddhism takes us to the limit of that thinker-thought duality asserting that if you reject this duality you will simply exist as a potentiality of being something, but you cannot realize that potentiality because in the process of realizing or being something, you actually become imbued with the thinker-thought dualism. So, you can empty the mind, and remove the duality, and just exist as a possibility, without even knowing that the possibility—the soul—is in fact eternal.

The salvation of Buddhism is lower than that of *Brahman* because in *Brahman* this potentiality is converted into self-awareness. As awareness, the soul is the thinker, and as the object of that thinking he is the thought. There is hence a duality in *Brahman* but due to self-awareness, the thinker and the thought are the same. Through self-awareness, you realize that the potentiality to experience is eternal because the self is never lost to itself. Therefore, one doesn't have to reject the thinker-thought dualism and empty the mind; we can also convert it into self-awareness and thereby know the self. This is a subtle but important difference between Buddhism and *Advaita*: Buddhism speaks about freedom from material thought, and *Advaita* speaks about self-awareness. They seem very close to each other, and from the current perspective, they are indeed very close. The difference is that in voidism there is no realization of the *sat-chit-ānanda* nature of the soul, but in *Advaita* there is. Thus, *Advaita* speaks about self-existence, and Buddhism about emptiness. The soul is real in *Advaita* but in Buddhism the soul is the thinker—an illusion.

Again, quite like *Advaita*, if one is stuck in the current material dualities of thinker vs. thought, then just emptying the mind is also progress toward realizing the eternity of the soul because the soul can come back to thinker-thought duality eternally. In that sense, whether you regard the soul eternal or not makes little difference because practical experience demonstrates that eternity. On the other hand, realizing that the thinker and the thought are co-created is helpful in freeing the mind from pride, greed, and lust, because you realize that our pride or the sense of self is caused together with the object of experience; if tomorrow that object changes, the pride may be gone. Thus, you shift the focus from enjoying the co-created self as the co-creations are fleeting. You instead observe the fleeting thoughts and the imagined sense of the self, created from these thoughts and don't become attached to the co-created identity. Such detachment from the world takes you toward salvation. It is not the realization of the eternal self, nor is it the realization of other selves in relation to the Supreme Self or God. But it is better than temporary identities.

Buddha is regarded as a form of *Viṣṇu* in Vedic texts; His advent was predicted nearly 3000 years in advance[11] when the Vedic texts were recorded. But His religion also isn't about *Vaishnavism*. It rather pertains to a place called *Kāranodaka* which lies between the material universes and *Brahman* and is produced by two forms of *Viṣṇu* called *Kāraṇodakaśāyī Viṣṇu* and *Saṅkarṣaṇa*; the former creates the space of all material possibilities and the latter converts those possibilities into reality as time; each such reality becomes a universe which is miniscule and insignificant from the standpoint of the two deities, but it becomes very significant for the living entities. *Kāranodaka* is also sometimes called *pradhāna* or the primordial state of the soul before he enters the material energy; in one sense it is spiritual, and yet it not fully spiritual. In some places, this place is also identified with the term 'deep sleep' in which there is complete rest and relaxation marked by emptiness and devoid of self-awareness. So, what is this place truly? *Kāranodaka* represents the state where the soul has forgotten his self because he is out of *Brahman* and is yet not into any of the material universes where he can experience the thinker-thought distinction. It is as if the soul turned away from the self but hasn't yet turned toward the world. It is truly a state devoid of any experience, just like deep sleep is the state in which the soul has no experience (waking and dreaming are the experienced states). Of course, the soul hasn't lost its ability to experience; and yet, it is in the twilight zone between knowing the self and knowing the world, in which one knows neither. It is outside the material universe, and hence in that sense it is transcendent. And yet, it does not constitute self-realization because the self is itself not realized—i.e., one doesn't know of one's eternity.

The Progressive Path of Religious Understanding

The worship of demigods takes one to higher planetary systems within the material universe. But Buddhism can take the soul beyond the universe, and in that sense, Buddha correctly rejected ritualism or *karma-kānda* which involved the worship of demigods and sacrifice of animals to articulate a process by which one can go into the realm called *Kāranodaka*, which is superior to that of the demigods. Not only is it free of the cycle of birth and death, but the restfulness creates a sense of satisfaction superior to material enjoyment. The Buddhist rejection of ritualism is therefore not a simple-minded rejection of *Brahma*'s *dharma* which was prevalent during Buddha's time, but the description of a realm that is better and beyond the material world.

If one watches the historical evolution of thought in India, they can see how the religion of monotheistic God *Kṛṣṇa* declined 5,000 years ago and was then almost completely forgotten. What was left in the aftermath was mindless rituals, which could not be performed correctly because the scientific understanding of nature's working had been lost. The succession of preceptors, from Buddha, to *Shankarāchārya*, to *Ramānujachārya*, to *Chaitanya* has successively outlined a place beyond the material realm. Buddha identifies a place in which the soul is in deep sleep, *Shankarāchārya* a place in which the soul is awake and self-aware but knows nothing else, *Ramānujachārya* a place in which the soul is aware of the self and other souls including the Supreme Soul, but sees God as being free of all contradictions, and *Chaitanya* a place in which the soul is aware of self and others, but sees God as the composite of opposites.

In that sense, those who have no awareness of *dharma* are better off with the religion of *Brahma*; those who have practiced the religion of *Brahma* are better off with the religion of Buddha; those who have perfected the religion of Buddha are better off with the religion of *Advaita*; those who have realized the eternal nature of the self in *Advaita* are better off with the religion of *Viṣṇu* who is devoid of contradictions, and those who have realized the person of *Viṣṇu* are better off with the realization of *Kṛṣṇa* who is the composite of all opposites. Different emotional attitudes are needed to pursue each of these paths; the religion of *Brahma* is based on the desire to enjoy dutifully; the religion of *Buddha* upon the desire to go into deep sleep; the religion of *Advaita* on the desire to be awake and relish the self; the religion of *Viṣṇu* on the desire to know the absolute reality beyond the self; the religion of *Kṛṣṇa* on the desire to know that reality which is composed of conflicting opposites.

If this progressive path of religious emancipation is understood, one would not see a conflict between the different doctrines, even though they are different. For most people in this world, any kind of religion—even that of demigods—would be a significant advancement from the current state. So, fighting over whose religion is better is like two poor and homeless men arguing about which among the four or five richest men in the world has a better lifestyle. Indeed, there is an objective answer to that question, but from the standpoint of homeless people it is nearly impossible to understand the differences between the pleasures of the richest people. We can still rely on philosophy, as we have done in this book, to answer the question—not to simply say that one's religion is better than others—but to outline the progressive path one has to take to reach the higher destination. In this progressive path, the destination that is higher includes the results of the previous destination but goes beyond. However, it also means that one must have all the realization of the previous destination in order to cross over into a new destination.

The higher destinations are progressively harder to attain. The Vedic texts describe that when the soul leaves the body, he is taken by *prāna* to a new destination. If the soul is advanced, he progressively passes through higher and higher realms of existence. This journey ends when the soul is attracted to the happiness of a particular realm. To go beyond, the soul must give up the attraction of that realm and become attracted to a higher realm. Thus, it is not simply a question of asserting the superiority of one's religion; it is rather the question of whether the soul will accept a particular type of pleasure if offered. For most people the suffering of the mind and body is so great that emptying the mind or being situated in the self would be an extremely relieving state. Most people practice meditation today just to relax their mind or improve their concentration for a few moments in a day. Imagine the level of pleasure if one was able to continue that state unmitigated and uninterrupted forever! Similarly, the place of demigods offers much better food, sex, security, and health than available on earth, and just finding that could be highly desirable. In that sense, regardless of whichever ultimate destination we aim for philosophically, practically speaking most people would settle for much lesser. Whatever they settle for is the current level of their religious advancement.

The test of advancement is if a person can forego the pleasure of sex to aim for the pleasure of emptiness, the pleasure of emptiness to the pleasure of the self, the pleasure of the self for the pleasure of God, and then the pleasure of God for the pleasure of His devotees. Philosophy is not a substitute for practical realization, and the practical realization is the type of happiness one is prepared to give up, because he has found a higher form of happiness.

Many people imagine that science is progressive while religion is static or regressive as they don't realize how much progression exists in religion primarily because each religion portrays itself as the ultimate destination, and comparative religious dialogue is largely a non-starter because if you actually did a comparison then the conclusion would be a higher or lower placement which would be an unacceptable outcome to both sides because the exclusivist likes to believe that theirs is the only path, so even being placed above others in that hierarchy would not satisfy them unless other paths are removed.

Interreligious dialogue is not a necessity because the soul has a choice to go after the type of pleasure he desires. And if one has risen in life to find a higher pleasure, he would generally aspire for even higher pleasure, which leads to the path of progression. But for such a possibility to exist, people have to allow each other to practice their respective religions—*and* one has to distinguish their path from *irreligion*. Mind you, not everything that goes in the name of religion is necessary religious. For example, animal sacrifices without the necessary qualification to send the soul to a demigod invite adverse *karma*. They might have been prescribed at one time, but they don't have qualified practitioners who either know how to do such things nor can they teach others on how the process works. If they don't understand it themselves, what could be the test of the quality of their worship? Therefore, there are many religious paths of progression, but not every path is actually progressive. Philosophy can help us distinguish between progressive and regressive paths, and that is probably the main value we can expect from interreligious dialogues.

Free Will, Falldown, and Resurrection

One of the themes in many religions is that of a 'falldown' from heaven, spiritual world, or grace, into a life of sin and suffering. The original story in most religions is how the soul fell—Abrahamic religions for instance narrate this story through the life of Adam and Eve. Once you have fallen, you must be saved, emancipated, liberated from the sin and suffering of the world. But hardly anyone asks: If the soul could fall previously, can it fall again after salvation? Similarly, can the soul who has deviated into the path of sin, and rejected the path of religion in the process, be emancipated from this in the future? Both are inconvenient questions. If, for example, you ask if the soul could fall again, then you seem to imply that the outcome of practicing religion could itself be temporary because the soul may fall again. Similarly, if you ask if the soul could be ultimately liberated in the future, then you undermine the sense of urgency in the practice of religion—I could do this in the future!

The question of 'falldown' and 'resurrection' are the cornerstone of every religious doctrine because the alternative—where we never fell into the material world, and have always been here, or were simply born into a body and will die eventually—entails materialism and hence denial of religion.

However, once you accept the doctrine of falldown and emancipation, you still need to ask the above two questions to truly understand the doctrine in its full context: (1) can the soul fall again after emancipation? and (2) can the soul be emancipated in the future even if rejects religion right now? As noted above, an affirmative answer takes away the finality of religion, and the urgency in practicing it. How can you convince a person about religion if you actually accept the possibility of falldown or resurrection in the future?

In Vedic philosophy, this conviction is provided through the idea that there are 8,400,000 species of life, and the human life is just one of them. Some species are short lived, while others have very long lives. The birth, death, and struggle of these lives are not very pleasant. So, if you miss the human form of life, it is very likely that you would have to pass through many—if not all—of these species of life before you return to the human form. Religion, in the Vedic description, can only be practiced in the human form. The animals cannot understand the concept of duty and transcendence. Even if they are suffering, they cannot imagine that life outside all these bodies is possible. The animals cannot inquire into the nature of the soul and God, nor can they accept a teacher who can impart them sophisticated knowledge via language. In that sense, if you lose the human form of life, you will take a long time to get back to it, and the process of emancipation is itself very long and tiresome, and most souls find trouble just walking the path of liberation. As a result, you need a succession of human lives. Hence, you not only cannot practice religion in animal life, you most often cannot attain liberation in a single lifetime. If the commitment to religion is weak, and you postpone it to later, it is very likely that the total time taken in this journey would be exceptionally long, because you walk one step forward and probably two or more steps backward.

This description of religious emancipation also allows the possibility of falldown in the future, if the soul so desires to leave the association of God. Thus 'falldown' is not something that occurred just once; it can also occur in the future, if the soul so wants. Religion and God therefore don't provide an insurance policy that cannot be revoked anytime in the future. They rather tell you the proper use of choice, and the consequences upon a misuse. The soul is thereafter free to use or misuse the free will any way he likes. Possible misuses can be delaying the journey of proper use to later or finishing the journey and reaching the destination but deciding to return to material life.

In essence, there isn't eternal heaven or hell for a soul; the heaven and hell are themselves eternal, but you are not eternally guaranteed to live there, and the simple reason for that is *free will*. If you are eternally bound in heaven or hell, you have been denied the possibility of misuse of free will to fall from heaven, or the possibility of correct use of free will to be emancipated from hell. In essence, the soul is eternally free to make choices, and as a consequence of that eternity it is allowed the possibility of falling down or being liberated. If we enforce a permanent hell or heaven, we effectively deny free will.

Now, all religions acknowledge free will, but they have a problem with saying that since you could be liberated in the future, the practice of religion is a *choice* that you can make now or later; they will rather push you to practice it now, or forever be damned. Similarly, religions have a problem in saying that even if you got to heaven you could still fall down, or that even if you went to hell you could still be resurrected. This kind of idea further muddies the waters because now it seems that there isn't any finality in the results. These are serious theological issues, but given the problems associated with giving the soul so much free will that it could fall or resurrect in the future, religions prefer to curtail the freedom: you have to choose now, because the choice is not available later, and if you choose religion now the reward will be eternal. This artificial constraint imposed by eternal heaven and hell is similar in its persuasive intent with the 'the world is an illusion' trick mentioned earlier.

It appears therefore that the doctrine of eternal heaven and hell was formulated to emphasize the urgency of practicing religion right now, and to convince the practitioner the result had to be final and exclusive—even though it meant contravening the doctrine of free will as an innate feature of the soul eternally. The alternative was too complex: namely, you had to acknowledge that all life forms have souls, that there can be many types of religions that may take you some steps forward but may not liberate you, that time is cyclic and it causes the process of repeated birth and death, and the soul has to make choices at every moment of his life and be responsible for their results. Each element of the alternative brings many further problems. For instance, if other religious paths can also take you forward—although may not lead to the final destination—then you have a harder path of explaining what the final destination looks like, how the intermediate steps (that don't attain the destination) are incrementally further from the goal, and how the difference between the process of religion and its consequences arises. The latter, in fact, now requires a cause-effect theory of action and result, which then leads to the questions of causality from choice to outcomes. If some religion doesn't take you all the way to the destination, then this cause-effect theory includes material changes. For instance, you had to *materially* explain rebirth and reincarnation.

In essence, the alternative to eternal heaven and hell is too complicated. It overreaches into a theory of space, time, and causality, but this time the theory of causality pertains to the motion of the soul through different life forms, which could be theoretically explained but would be hard to observe empirically. If you tried to explain the idea of rebirth based on one's innate tendencies and differences in the place, time, and situation of birth, you would now be mired in even more complexity pertaining to human psychology. You will also have to formulate some theory about the situations of birth—e.g., society, culture, civilization, and ideology—into the religious doctrine itself. You now appear to be the victim of the proverbial "for want of a nail" problem, where trying to address one issue leads to another, and yet another, apparently endless chain of things to be known before religion can be made convincing.

It therefore seems quite prudent to cut the chain of an ever-expanding sequence of questions and answers using the eternal heaven and hell doctrine. It serves a purpose—it convinces the practitioner to take the matter urgently and gives him assurance that its results are irreversible. In that respect, the outcomes seem better than other material acts where the results are eventually destroyed, even though you seem to enjoy them temporarily. But since the sequence of questions and answers is terminated so prematurely, most of the questions that humans ask naturally—e.g., about the nature of space, time, causality, other life forms, the theory of motion and change, and the moral problems of why some people are born with a silver spoon and others take birth among bullets, the nature of human psychology, why there are choices and then laws of moralities which restrict those choices—are never answered satisfactorily. The questions that are left unanswered create room for other explanations, which now gives rise to secular philosophy, science, social science, psychology, jurisprudence, and many other areas of human inquiry that operated unfettered by the constrains imposed by the religious doctrine.

To practice these sciences, they must be detached from religion (e.g., as body and mind) because religion did not answer the scientific questions anyway. They must further be detached from politics (separation of church and state) because religion did not address the questions of economic and social organization. Such independent thought systems compete for power and sway the population in different directions—depending on the questions you prioritize. If the question of emancipation is foremost in your mind, then religion is most important. But if practical necessities of life are of greater importance then you will naturally give priority to the theories that deal with such questions. In other words, by terminating the chain of questions and answers prematurely, religion created room for its own ideological competitors.

Most people at present believe that the contradictions between modern ideologies—e.g., between religion and science, or between politics and religion—cannot be resolved, because they don't understand its origins in the problem of free will, and how the problem was oversimplified as eternal hell and heaven. Through such oversimplification, religion undermined its roots by allowing room for other conflicting ideologies. Most people who continue to practice religion simply accept it on 'faith' because a rational explanation would be very long and probably exhausting for most people. However, if the problems in understanding the big picture lead to oversimplification of the picture through a religious doctrine, a self-contradiction is produced. The contradiction within religion is that free will exists now, but not in the future. The incompleteness in religion is that religious doctrines don't answer numerous pressing questions about the nature of the world we live in; in fact, they sometimes appear to state things contrary to what we can observe and confirm rationally. So, how could we consider them the complete truth of reality?

For this reason, you can find Vedic texts such as the *Śrīmad Bhāgavatam* deal so extensively on seemingly irrelevant topics like the nature of matter, the structure of the universe, the tiers of human psychology, the different forms of human life, the nature of the atom, and its relation to space and time, the description of various types of religious practices for emancipation. The picture is so complex because the question of free will is incredibly complicated. The idea of free will leads to laws of right and wrong, but that right and wrong can be applied only if you choose based on your desires, which then involves the question of what you like, or good and bad. What you can choose must truly exist or your choice or desire will never be fulfilled. As a result, the question of good and bad must be subjected to the facts—i.e., the decision of true and false.

The question of true and false can only be answered if there is meaning because only meanings can be judged to be true or false; material particles simply exist, but they don't mean anything; so, these particles cannot be *propositions* unless they are treated as *symbols*. To treat some particle as a symbol, you have to talk about relations with other particles, and you need contextuality, because meanings are always given in relations and contexts. Now, you need to construe a hierarchy of wholes and parts, ideas and their instances, goals and plans, and you must have a science that explains their respective laws.

Some religions get tired of trying to explain all this attendant complexity and reject the idea of moral consequences. They postulate that the soul is actually God, or that the soul and God are non-different. If there is no separate God, then He cannot judge the soul. In fact, the choices made by individual souls are actually choices made by the universal all-pervasive consciousness. And this universal consciousness cannot be held responsible by anyone else, because there is no one else other than this universal consciousness. Hence, moral judgment is not a serious philosophical problem. If you are not judging actions as right and wrong, then you can advance the idea that nothing is right and wrong, it just seems like that to us because it is an illusion of the mind. If all these judgments are illusions, then there is no basis for making choices or thinking that something is good or bad for me—after all, there is no 'me'. But when you don't have to make a choice, then why do you need to know the nature of truth? It is what it is, and your attempt to call it true or false is also wasteful, just like the other judgments of right or wrong, and good or bad are pointless. Now, you are left with the self, without God, and the world is illusory.

But the problem is that nobody is going to take you seriously. You cannot cure your diseases by calling them illusory. You cannot stop birth and death by considering it an illusion. If you drop a heavy rock on your foot, it will still hurt regardless of whether you think the idea of good or bad is relative. In other words, life goes on independent of such claims, but the claims of illusion help make the unbearable heaviness of a real philosophy seem much lighter.

Simplified religious doctrines have a purpose—they get a practitioner started on a journey of progressive emancipation without a seemingly endless chain of questions and answers to be answered beforehand. But they run the risk that the questions that were left unanswered will be answered by a competing doctrine in ways that conflict with the thesis promulgated by the religion. As time passes, the two (or more) ideologies begin to conflict; the conflict confuses the practitioner, undermining his or her faith, thereby stagnating the path of progressive emancipation—the very purpose of oversimplification. In that sense, oversimplification defeats itself over the longer run, and one has to go back to the point where the chain of questions and answers was terminated through an oversimplified assumption and reopen the question again.

7

Mythology and Psychology

I could not say I believe. I know! I have had the experience of being gripped by something that is stronger than myself, something that people call God.

—*Carl Jung*

The Resurrection of Mythology

The stories you read or heard as a child probably had messages. They were stories about truthfulness, sacrifice, honesty, hard work, love, justice, humility, and how patience always pays in the end. Clearly, many of these stories we read as children were fictitious, but they had a moral. Can we now invert the relation between a story and a moral—the moral coming at the end of the story—to suggest that such stories were originally written to illustrate the morals? The moral—in this inverted picture of the story—lies not at the end of a real-world event; it is rather the root from which the story itself springs. The story's narrative creates a succinct and palatable method of delivering the understanding of morality, quite like mnemonic techniques are used to memorize complex lists, tasks, and other difficult-to-remember things. The mathematical order of operations—Multiply, Divide, Add, and Subtract—for example can be memorized using the mnemonic "My Dear Aunt Sally". You could imagine, therefore, that stories found in religious texts—which personalize the message through colorful personalities of gods—are like mnemonics, which were created in the past to help people memorize moral values.

Many people who are tired of trying to understand or justify the truth of the moral stories found in religious texts take recourse to thinking of them as just stories, which were authored to convey a moral to the population who read them. Under this compromise, the stories in religious texts would not be treated as literally true—as events and personalities that truly existed in the past or at the present. However, they could still be very valuable to us in describing the nature of good and bad, right and wrong, and the ideas that uniquely make us humans. Gods and demons are not 'outside' our mind (in this view). They are rather ideas *in terms of* which we judge and perceive the world.

Those familiar with Western philosophy will recognize this idea to be very *Kantian*. Immanuel Kant—often considered the greatest philosopher after Aristotle—came up with this idea in the attempt to respond to Hume's attack on scientific causality. Hume had argued that the idea of a cause involves two things—(a) succession of events—e.g., that Y follows X, and (b) necessity—i.e., that every time X is present, Y must always be found necessarily. Hume argued that no matter how many times you actually observe the succession of X and Y, you can never perceive the causal necessity itself. Therefore, you could never formulate an *empirical law* that said that Y *necessarily* follows X. This—if you recognize it for what it is—is a deadly attack on the idea of scientific laws. According to Hume, since you cannot observe necessity, you cannot formulate such laws. Hume's attack on metaphysics—as Kant wrote later— "first interrupted my dogmatic slumber"[1]. Kant then came up with the idea that the order we see in the world is not the order in the world itself; the order is the mind trying to make sense of the world. Ideas such as necessity, causality, lawfulness, space, time, objects, force, etc. are all mental constructs that we apply to sensations. Science in this picture is as much about the external world of sensations as it is about the internal method of giving the sensations meaning. This meaning involved attaching concepts to sensations which could not in themselves be perceived. Space, time, causality, necessity, etc. cannot be perceived, although they can be conceived. The conception gives the world meaning.

Kant called these ideas *synthetic a priori*— "synthetic" because they were not "analytic" or reducible to even more fundamental ideas, and "a priori" because they could not be obtained "a posteriori", through observation.

Kant's idea led to a revolution in philosophy and scientific thinking where the scientist was liberated from the necessity to *prove* that his model of reality was indeed the true nature of reality itself—because how could you ever prove the reality of concepts such as particles, waves, mass, momentum, energy, etc. if you could never observe their existence by the senses? They had to remain pure conceptual constructs, although would be considered *useful* in modeling observations. Of course, this leads to the problem that you and I could model nature in different ways, and Kant was acutely aware of this problem; it undermined the very foundations of science as truth discovery, the fear being that there could be many good theories that described nature equally well, and we would not decide between these theories using empirical criteria. Kant's response to this problem was that this was not going to happen because humans had a universal and shared way of looking at the world, and ideas such as causality, space, time, law, necessity, possibility, force, etc. are universal.

Kant was of course wrong on this count. For example, during his time Newton's physics and Euclidean geometry were considered universal ideologies about space and time. When, at the dawn of the 20th century, Einstein invented relativity using a different geometry—Riemannian geometry—the idea that everyone saw the world in the same fundamental ways turned out to be false. Nevertheless, the core idea instituted by Kant—that scientific theories are descriptions of nature created by humans, and they don't have to be true if they make predictions accurately has become the mainstay in science. Now, you don't ask if a theory is true. You ask if it will make correct predictions.

The problem is that the theory might predict correctly today but incorrectly tomorrow, because—as Hume had observed—there is no *necessity* associated with such theories. This idea was formalized by Karl Popper through the thesis of *falsifiability* in which a scientific theory can never be *verified* because future discoveries may in fact disprove the theory. A scientific theory was one that could be empirically tested, and in principle *falsified.*

Psychologist Carl Jung took the Kantian ideas forward in the context of religions. The stories in religious texts are for him not literally true, or perhaps their truth could not be asserted because the empirical evidence for their existence cannot be verified. Nevertheless, just as scientific theories are ways of describing the world, similarly, religious stories can be how *humans* perceive the world based on innate ideas about right and wrong, good and bad. In other words, just as science wants to order the world in terms of space, time, force, and objects, similarly, religious stories are also theories about the same world using morality and goodness. For example, if a man who laid a trap for someone then fell into the same trap, you could describe these events in terms of moral concepts—"Do unto others as you will like to be done to you". If Kantian ideas are applied to such types of descriptions, then the ideas that lead to them are indeed shared by millions of people, across diverse cultures, civilizations, places, and time. You could therefore say that such ideas indeed constitute the structure of our mind—or how we perceive the world.

This is indeed how Jung proposes to understand religious stories and personalities—not as literally true, but as embodiments of the morals and ideas in terms of which we want to organize the world in our experience. He called these morals and ideas *archetypes*, which included things like "good wins over evil" kinds of stories where a "hero" loses everything to "evil" before he fights valiantly to defeat that "evil". Time after time such stories have been used as the basic plots of narrations in literature, movies, and drama. Why should religion be any different? Such stories could be treated as codifying our morality in an easy-to-understand manner, and they are therefore reflections of the human psyche. They don't exist outside the human mind, but that's not a problem because they exist in every mind who thinks of the world morally. The crucial fact that proves this thesis is the universality of such stories, and Jung spent considerable effort in illustrating the universality of the archetypes.

In this narrative about religious stories, the personalities we find in the religious texts are quite like objects—e.g., particles and waves—of scientific theories. The stories associated with them are then quite like trajectories of such objects in scientific theories. Each type of material object is associated with a type of behavior—e.g., Newton's laws of motion for particles, and Maxwell's laws for waves. Similarly, our mind sees personalities in nature—e.g., "hero", "teacher", "devil", "mother", "father", "wizard", "temptress", etc.—who have their predefined behaviors of trajectories. When we see those behaviors, we model our observations in terms of the primitive archetypes, which is no different that describing the world in terms of particles and waves. The crucial thing here is that you have to identify the behavioral patterns correctly and then you will be able to see the appropriate archetype in those events.

There is, hence, no need to think of God or Satan as real beings that truly exist in the world; we can also consider them as primordial ideas that exist in the *collective unconscious* and are used to spiritualize or demonize reality. Science and religion are therefore two different ways of describing the same world: one impersonalizes the reality, whereas the other personalizes it. In so far as you could not assert the reality of a scientific theory (because it is always falsifiable), similarly, you could not say the religious story is inferior. After all, it is always manifest in your thinking; how then could it be false?

Jung's move was really smart. He resurrected the truth of religious texts in a time when they were under attack from scientific rationality—applying the same criteria as that which could be applied to science itself. Both religion and science in this understanding are human fictions. However, since they are so pervasive across human civilizations, you could argue that by modeling the world in this way we reveal the nature of the mind that models it thus. Religion is thus not about God and Satan as real beings; it is rather about the mind which universally comprehends the world in terms of such archetypes. The empirical evidence for the 'truth' of religion then lies in the fact that diverse cultures have adopted and employed these ideas and have been able to inculcate the moral values in their societies based upon such narrations. The battle between God and Satan, for example, represents the conflict between good and evil. These ideas are so pervasive that we see every fight—e.g., between nations or football clubs—as one in which the good guys are fighting the evil guys.

In one fell swoop, Jung resurrected all of mythology as the study of the human psyche. Therefore, if you heard about the fall of Adam and Eve from the Garden of Eden, you must think not in terms of real people who fell from a real garden, but as presenting a recurring story in which the rational side of a person (Adam) is tempted by their emotional side (Eve) when the emotions are stirred by an enticement (the snake) who offers a pleasure (poisonous fruit) which has earlier been forbidden by God (the moral sense). Upon indulging in that forbidden pleasure, you lose the happiness you had (life in a garden). The point of the story then would be to not give in to your temptations and allow better sense to prevail to preserve your happiness in the longer run.

How many times have you seen this story repeat in your life, or around you? How many movies have been made, for example, where a married couple loses their happiness because one of the partners decides to indulge in an extra marital affair, and both partners fall from their platform of happiness?

Jung's point is that such stories are embedded in our psyche as moral narratives. They represent the ideal and exalted behaviors expected of humans, and nobody gets tired of telling these stories again and again. The pattern of the story is the *archetype*, and religion is the sum total of such stories. However, since these stories are already embedded in our deep psyche, in one sense they are unconscious, and when religious texts narrate them, they only state what we can easily relate to, and by bringing them to the surface through a narration, the religious texts only present what is already within. The gods and deities are therefore not real personalities. They are instead part of our psyche and religion shows us the mirror in which we can see what lies deep within as the unconscious. Contrary to Freud—who viewed the unconscious as depraved ego, perversion, and lust—Jung saw human ideals in it.

The Analysis of Dreams

Both Freud and Jung considered the analysis of dreams as essential tools to understand the unconscious. The dream was understood as having a manifest part, which was sensually experienced—e.g., as forms, colors, sounds, etc. But there was also an unmanifest part, which constituted the dream's *meaning*. For example, if you see a dream in which you are sitting in the back seat of a car, driven by a hooded driver, and the front and back seats are separated by a soundproof glass, then a psychoanalyst may interpret this dream as you having no control over your life (inactive on the back seat), that your life is being controlled by some unknown forces (the hooded driver in the front seat), to which you are unable to communicate (the soundproof glass between the two of you). The problem is that the same dream can have many interpretations. For instance, it could also denote your repressed fears in which you see yourself losing control over your life, and that fear makes you avoid relationships in which the other person might be perceived to have more power to control you. That would mean that you don't want to get into the car with another person. Or, it might even be the recurring trauma of an incident where you were kidnapped by a taxi driver, and you fear that the same thing will repeat.

What is the true meaning of a dream? Does it denote our repressed fears, which I have seen in other people's lives and we fear that it might happen to us too? Do they indicate something that I anticipate might happen in the future because such incidents have already occurred to me in the past? Or do they indicate something that I crave for, but I'm unable to realize it in my life? The psychoanalyst hopes to solve the mystery by asking you more questions, performing associations between the incidents of the dream and the meanings that you might attach to such incidents, or even assuming that certain events have a universal significance rather than just individual meaning. But as you can imagine, this is a very tricky and slippery slope. There is no guarantee that the psychoanalyst will figure out the individual's true context, and then be able to give those experiences a meaning that is relevant to the dreamer.

The problem of dream interpretation is common to any kind of interpretation. In linguistic interpretation, for example, the meaning of a word is based on many factors. The meaning depends on the language used in communication; a sound can mean something different in another language. The meaning also depends on the context in which the sound is being uttered; the same word can mean different things in different contexts. Sometimes, to understand the meaning, you have to understand the nuances of a speaker, because different speakers express the same meaning in different ways. You might have to guess their intentions—e.g., is the person talking about facts, saying something sarcastically, or means to deceive the listeners? Finally, you have to also know the history and personality of the person—e.g., has this person always been honest, or is this person a habitual liar, or that he is normally honest, but he might be under compulsion due to adverse situations right now?

The potential permutations and combinations of these factors are so enormous that it is practically impossible to simply interpret the meaning of some sense experiences without knowing a whole lot about the person. That knowledge, of course, takes a long time. And since the situations are constantly changing, what you know from the past may not be applicable right now. Any kind of generalization you make based on the past may be potentially false. This basically means that it is very *hard* to interpret the true meaning, although the difficulty doesn't repudiate the fact that a meaning always exists.

The same problem exists in the case of dreams as well. It is not easy to know the true meaning of a dream, because the events of the dream are just symbols which could be produced from many different types of meanings. However, the methodological difficulty in interpreting the dream correctly doesn't deny the fact that a meaning always exists; you just don't know what it is.

When this realization is applied to the interpretation of religious texts, or to the human psyche, the recurrence of stories across cultures, civilizations, eras, and religions doesn't imply that they have the same meaning. For instance, in the purported battle between good and evil, which side do you think is good, and which side do you consider bad? In sporting events, for example, one is naturally partial to the team which is playing for their country. The people of your country are—in this interpretation—naturally good, while those of the other country are seen as bad. Thus, the audience indeed perceives the game as a match between good vs. bad, but each side considers themselves good, and the other team bad. Clearly, the same sensations are being interpreted as symbols of good in one case, and symbols of bad in another.

The notion of an archetype—e.g., a battle between good and evil—doesn't take us very far, unless we can identify a method of interpreting correctly. Again, remember that this is a *methodological* problem, not a problem of meaning itself. So, I'm not saying that because we cannot find the meaning easily entails that the meaning doesn't exist objectively. I'm only saying that what you consider good might be considered bad by another person. For instance, you might consider charity and bravery an exalted ideal, but someone might consider it foolish and dangerous to sacrifice one's life for someone else. In what sense then can we say that there are universal ideals that we all share? Isn't the presumption that we are all similar, and hence we inherently interpret the same text, dream, or situation in the same way, itself a problem? Isn't the idea that we will share the same ideal contradicted practically every day where we get into conflicts with other people because they have different ideals?

This is then the central problem of embedding the morality into our psyche: everyone's psyche is different. Yes, certain ideals have indeed recurred over civilizations and cultures, but you cannot interpret that recurrence as the *necessity* of the morality of the idea because you may not have looked long and hard across every possible culture and civilization. This problem is no different than the one highlighted by Hume who saw it impossible to assert necessity. Without that necessity, your morals are relative to the group under study. Thus, those who don't agree with the message of the religious texts might disagree with the claimed ideals and might propound a different ideal. Now you have to probably resort to democratic ideals—i.e., claim that those ideals shared by the majority of the people must be considered 'universal'—but now you have the problem of how the majority opinion changes over time. The moralities we share today are for instance not similar to the moralities of the past. The libertarian ideals, for instance, are relatively recent in history. Certainly, they are opposed to the ideals ensconced in the religious texts. That contradiction between the left and right wings in every society itself attests to the fact that moralities of societies have been evolving with time. In what sense can we then claim to participate in a universal and collective unconscious?

Ideas vs. Ideals

All ideas are not ideals. We might have some ideal ideas, and other non-ideal ideas. If we claim that we participate in a collective unconscious, we are presuming a universal definition of morality, and that doesn't exist. The collective unconscious also evolves with time, but the very existence of strife and conflict over the ages indicates that people did not agree on the ideals. If they were participating in the same collective agreement, there could be no battles between good and evil, because both guys must be on the same side. Owing to these problems, we cannot embed the ideal in each individual's psyche. The attempts to claim the universalism of ideals is just contrary to facts. This naturally entails that the truth of the religious texts cannot be attributed to the collective unconscious, because there is no such universalism in reality.

It is quite possible that the instructions, commandments, or events depicted in some religious texts may not have actually occurred, and they might be allegories of things that people thought were good stories for describing a particular type of moral. But the ability to find some moral people who convert those morals into stories for explaining those morals to others doesn't make those morals universal, nor do they imply that all such stories must indeed be allegories, because if they are indeed only resident in our psyche—which is clearly not universal—then we are inevitably faced with moral relativism. Under that relativism, each person is free to decide what is good for them, which means there cannot be an objective judgment of their actions, and you must either defer to majority opinion, or not judge a person's morality.

The human psyche has ideas and some of these ideas may also be ideals. But every such idea cannot be considered ideal. The Freudian position in which the unconscious is always depraved is false because some ideas are indeed ideals. Similarly, the Jungian position in which all the ideals come from the human mind is also false because there is no way to decide which minds were ideals (as there are depraved minds too) unless you have a predetermined notion of the ideals. If we include all the minds in the definition of ideals (since the collective unconscious is shared across all minds) then some depraved ideas must also be included in ideals, and the notion of good vs. bad would cease to exist. Similarly, if all individuals shared the ideals from the collective unconscious, then how could anyone be depraved? And if no one was depraved then what would be the use of religion as the enunciation of ideals over depravation? The study of the unconscious tells us what our ideas are. But it says nothing about whether the ideas are ideals. We cannot infer all ideas as being depraved as Freud did, nor can we infer that a person is inherently good and hence they must always carry the ideals within themselves. We have to allow for the objective assessment of ideas against the ideals, and that is possible only if the ideals lie outside the individual psyche. Now, we are required to postulate the existence of a person who is ideal—whose psyche is the ideal ideas.

Such a person has been called God in all religions, and He ordains morality as His thoughts because His thoughts indeed constitute the ideal. Those ideals are applicable to each individual as the perfection to be attained, and in that sense the ideals are universal. But they are not universal because they already reside in each individual psyche. Such an attempt to resurrect religion as the myths of the human mind begs the question that if each individual already had those ideals then why would they ever have a conflict or be depraved?

The psychoanalytic attempts to explain religion as the creation of the human mind therefore don't stand the simple tests of rationality and empirical observation because they either reject the possibility of ideals or they embed the ideal in the individual minds. Both attempts are ultimately atheistic because they reject the possibility and necessity of an external ideal. The myths we carry in our minds are often just illusions, regardless of how pervasive they might be. Particularly in the material world, which is defined by the existence of oppositions—e.g., hot vs. cold, black vs. white—we cannot hope to find a universal ideal simply by looking into the psyche. We have to transcend this psyche and seek that person who is free of such dualities because only in that psyche will we find consistency—which should be the preliminary requirement for judging the ideal's universality. In essence, the ideas in a person whose experience is not influenced by dualities must be considered ideal.

Freud in one sense correctly analyzed the genesis of psychopathology in the conflict between the id and the superego. The id constitutes the desires of the person—which I have previously called the *ānanda* or the pleasure-seeking tendency. The superego is on the other hand the moralizing tendency in the person—which I have previously called the *sat* or the role and responsibility of the soul. Freud thought that to be happy, a person has to be free of these conflicts, and that meant discarding the morals imposed by the superego. One wonders why he did not think that this conflict could be resolved by bringing the desires of the person caused by the id in line with the superego. After all, if everyone succumbed to their desires and disregarded the moral strictures necessary to organize any kinds of society, then would society not descend into anarchy in which everyone just does whatever they want?

Freud's diagnosis about the inner conflicts is correct, but his prescription about disregarding the strictures of the superego to attain resolution is wrong. The same resolution can also be attained by taming the beast of desire. It may not be easy, but the alternative is a non-starter. The ideal person is simply one whose morality or duty has no conflict with their desires. That is, they relish the performance of their role and duty, and desire nothing else. That proposition is hard to attain in all situations because we are forced into circumstances that may compel us to do things that are against our desires. The conflict between morality and desire is created by such circumstances. But we can also envision circumstances where our desires are identical to our role. In such a situation we desire nothing more than to be in the role, and hence the demands of the role are completely consistent with what we desire. Such compatibility between desire and morality leads to the resolution of the contradiction that leads to psychopathology and should be the resolving prescription.

In such a situation, our ideas (desires) become consistent with the ideals (role). This doesn't entail a *global* consistency such that someone else will not have a role that demands the things that we don't want to do. It means that just as I have the role which I desire, another person will have the role they desire. Our roles can be mutually opposite, but the opposition presents *complementarity* rather than *contradiction.* In a sense, the contradictions are not external—i.e., we don't have to conflict with others who like to do other things as long as they don't infringe on what I am doing. The contradiction and conflict is always internal—I am not able to do the things I want to do because my situation demands something contrary to my desires. The world of ideality can therefore involve mutually opposite roles, executed by mutually opposite desires. But the roles never come in contact with each other to create a conflict.

Thus, one person is making pots and the other person is breaking pots. They are doing opposite things, but they are not *preventing* each other from doing what the other wants to do. The person making pots can therefore enjoy his role of making pots because that is what he desires to do. His enjoyment is not constrained by the fact that someone else breaks pots. Similarly, the person who is breaking pots can enjoy his activity of pot breaking; his enjoyment is not limited by the fact that someone else is making pots. The pot maker and the pot breaker are complementary; they seem to do contradictory things, but because they don't *prevent* the other from doing what he or she wants to do, there is no competition between them, and hence no contradiction.

There is hence a simple definition of ideality—freedom from contradictions: both internal and external. The internal contradiction is resolved when our desires become consistent with our roles, duties, or moralities. The external contradiction is resolved if we are freed of *envy*: the pot maker is not jealous of the pot breaker and is not threatened by their breaking of pots. Both persons enjoy their respective activities; they seem superficially contradictory, but the resolution of fear and envy makes them totally complementary.

Psychoanalysts don't take this path of resolution because they presume that a person can never be free of envy and fear, and that they can never obtain what they truly desire. If they cannot obtain what they truly desire, then they can never be happy due to internal conflicts. And if they cannot be freed of fear and envy, then they cannot be freed of external conflicts. The internal conflict forces an external conflict when the person who is unsure of ever fulfilling their own desires (due to their limiting situation) tries to prevent the other from fulfilling their desires, thus becoming the limiting situation for the other person, causing external conflict. Thus, internal conflict leads to an external conflict, and the external conflict feeds the internal conflict. As long as these conflicts exist, the person can never be happy, and that unhappiness is the psychopathology that psychoanalysts are fond of discussing. But the problem is that they truly don't think that the internal conflict can be resolved. There is hence a sense of hopelessness in this thinking and Freud embodied this hopeless feeling. Conversely, Jung hoped to address the conflict by presuming that everyone will have the same morals and will desire the same thing.

Freud and Jung therefore represent the opposite ends of the spectrum—Freud embodying the ideology of conflict, and Jung the ideology of conflict resolution by discarding the diversity. We can say that Freud saw the world as one of dualities and oppositions, while Jung saw it as universal idealism. But these are not real answers to the problem of conflict. We cannot become identical to the other person and we cannot possess the same morals—i.e., roles—and desire the same things. That universalism is itself monism, and it is attained only when we stop interacting with others and live by oneself. The conflict ceases because as we discard the association of others, we reject all our duties and hence moralities; we live under the morality of self-love; that morality is not bad if we are not infringing on other's self-love; hence a collection of self-lovers, who don't envy other self-lovers can co-exist peacefully. But how long can a person live on self-love, when the self is limited and finite?

The real answer lies in transcending the realm of duality as well as the realm of monism into a third realm where both internal and external contradictions are resolved because the person is situated in the role they desire, and they don't envy the role and desire of others to hinder their lives.

This brings us back to the three realms of *Brahma* (contradiction), *Shiva* (monism), and *Viṣṇu* (complementarity) that we have discussed previously—although this time through the considerations of psychopathology.

Ideals vs. Non-Ideal Ideas

The ideal world of *Viṣṇu* produces the non-ideal world of *Brahma* when the soul looks at others and feels envy. The pot maker for example might think that the pot breaker is destroying the pots that he is making. He stops looking at his own happiness in making pots and starts worrying about the pleasure of the other person who enjoys breaking pots. The pleasure of the pot breaker in destroying the pots that the pot maker has previously created makes the pot maker unhappy. Now, the pot maker wants to stop the pot breaker from breaking the pots—thereby creating an undesirable situation for the pot breaker—which then leads to their conflict. The world of complementarity thus becomes the world of conflict, giving rise to the world of duality, in which everyone looks not at their pleasure and what they want, but what others are doing, and how their actions are hindering their own actions, resulting in the desire to prevent the other person from doing what they enjoy doing. The net result is that two individuals have contradictory desires, and they will clash.

As one person desires to prevent the other, the other now wants to defend himself and his work, with a counterattack on the offender if needed. This entire dynamic is the material world, and it is caused by something very simple: We stop looking at the type of work that will make us happy and become envious of what makes others happy. Then, we either want to do what they are doing—imagining that it would make us happy. Or we want to prevent them from what they are doing—imagining that their actions cause us pain. The recipe for happiness is rather simple: don't look at others, look at yourself. Don't worry about how others are enjoying; focus on what you want to enjoy. Avoid the possibility of conflicts with others or being a threat to them. Pursue that which will satisfy you. Of course, such a thing is not always possible in the material world because even if you were non-envious, others will be envious of your happiness, and they will try to prevent you from being happy.

The philosophy of non-interfering work can be practiced only when one becomes detached from the *results* of their work, without neglecting their *desire* to do a certain type of work, under the control of their *duties*. The pot maker is offended by the pot breaker because those pots are the *results* of his work. He might want to sell these pots in order to get some money for other things—including the process of making more pots. If therefore those pots are broken, the cycle of making and selling pots may itself come to an end. There is hence legitimacy in *defending* one's work, territory, property, life, and limb, even to continue the process of making pots and everyone is thus entitled to the happiness obtained from their work. They are also entitled for a fair price for the pots they make, in order to continue the cycle of pot making.

At this point, the moral law of *karma* becomes necessary to understand the relation between happiness and conflict. Yes, sometimes others will attack the individual and hinder their work in order to become happy, and it is our duty to defend that work. But it doesn't mean that their attacks will be successful, or our defense will produce the desired result; the results are actually governed by *karma*, but we have a duty to perform our actions. In the material world, unpalatable situations are expected due to the results of previous actions, which cause others to hinder our lives. But this hindrance can be minimized if we focus on doing our duties and take action against the person hindering us—if the situation demands—but we must know that such defense may not succeed. However, if we have performed our duties then the effects of *karma* wane over time and the soul is liberated from adverse conditions. That liberation is the ideal through which each person is able to enjoy their work and their happiness is not dependent on the activities of the others.

The fact is that if the pots were eternal, then the pot maker will have no work after a while: everyone will have the pots they need, and since their pots are eternal, the pot maker need not make any more pots. Thus, pretty soon, the pot maker would be out of his job, and hence out of the activity that he wants to enjoy doing. To sustain the activity of pot making, there has to be someone who breaks pots. We can call this thing nature or time that automatically destroys things over time, but pot making cannot be sustained without pot breaking. Similarly, if the pot maker did not make any pots, then the pot breaker could not enjoy the pleasure of breaking pots. In that sense, the maker and the breaker are defined by their mutual opposition, although the opposition lies in between the complementarity of making and breaking, rather than the act of *preventing* the other from making and breaking. As long as the pot breaker doesn't prevent the pot maker from making pots, he can have the delight of breaking pots. But if he indeed stops the pot maker, then he will lose his own pleasure of pot breaking. Likewise, if the pot maker prevents the pot breaker from breaking pots, he will quickly run out of the need for pots and thereby lose the pleasure of making pots. The complementarity of making and breaking means that neither can exist without the other, but if one tries to prevent the opposite, then one also loses the very requirement for one's actions.

Even in the material world, therefore, we are defined by such opposites. The legitimate action for the pot breaker is to buy the pot from the pot maker and then do whatever he likes with it. That way, the pot maker has obtained his due for the effort he put in, and the pot breaker has the pleasure of destroying pots. In this way, the pot breaker doesn't *hinder* the pot maker, although he does precisely the opposite of what the pot maker does. The simultaneous co-existence of the opposites is a hallmark of living with others (monism doesn't have this problem, because one lives by oneself). We should therefore never expect universalism of shared ideals even when life can be ideal through the resolution of internal conflicts between roles and desires. The resolution of that conflict itself entails that other people don't interfere in my role. They are, however, free to perform their role—e.g., of pot breaking—thereby creating the necessity for my pot making to exist. When one realizes that their work depends on the work of others who do just the opposite, so long as their work doesn't stop me from doing mine, the world can be an ideal place.

The world becomes non-ideal if we *universalize* the ideals. This is seen, for example, when one country tries to impose their ideals—e.g., of democracy, capitalism, egalitarianism—on the others in the belief that their ideals are universal. If a sadist meets a masochist, there is no adversity between them. One enjoys torturing and the other, being tortured. In fact, they help the other in fulfilling each other's desires. Adversity is produced when a person who enjoys torture tortures a person who doesn't. This is a subtle difference between the complementarity of opposites and the opposition between the contraries. Under the material influence we believe that opposites must always create a contradiction, which is not true. Opposites can indeed exist in a harmony, and such opposites are needed to mutually sustain each other. In Buddhist philosophy (as previously mentioned), this idea is called *Pratītyasamutpāda* or the co-dependent arising of the opposites[2]. Both the materialist and the monist don't truly understand the nature of this opposition because the materialist tries to destroy the opposite and in the process destroys his own identity, while the monist tries to escape the world of dual oppositions but foregoes pleasure in that process. The transcendentalist is one who understands how the opposites are co-created and necessary for their mutual sustenance, and their co-existence doesn't entail a contradiction if they don't hinder the other.

In Vedic texts, the demigods and the demons co-exist happily as long as one doesn't try to hinder the other in their jobs. They create the *choice* for others who want to follow their ideals. The demigod ideal involves giving each other greater choice and responsibility, while the demonic ideal involves taking away that choice and responsibility. Each side can enjoy their ideal as long as the demigods and the demons don't impose their ideals on the other, and as long as one doesn't get tired of one's own ideals to create an internal contradiction. The fact, however, is that in the material world the soul is always envious of the other person—the grass seems greener on the other side of the fence. Thus, one doesn't know what will make them happy, and there is always an internal contradiction in every person, which makes them unhappy.

A masochist will eventually want to be a sadist, and a sadist will desire masochism. The person who has more choice and responsibility will eventually get tired of the pressure of responsibility and then desire an idyllic life free of such tensions. And a person who has little choice and responsibility will desire the power of greater choices and the concomitant responsibilities. Thus, the rich often envy the poor thinking that a simple life free of many tensions must be ideal, while the poor desire the life of richness and power. Therefore, aside from the external conflicts in which one person fears the others and tries to curtail their choices, there is always an internal contradiction in each person due to which they tend to desire what they don't have and envy the others who seem to be happy enjoying the opposite kind of life. This is then the paradox of life: you hate and fear the opposite, but you desire those opposites. Even if you stopped hating the opposite, you may not be able to stop desiring the opposite. Thus, for instance, a rich man may not hate the poor, but he may still desire the life of simplicity and abhor his duties that produce stress. When the opposite desire is created, then one is naturally envious of the other.

Therefore, even in the world where one has clearly demarcated each one's duties, and realized that these duties don't contradict each other's pleasures, there is always a potential to change one's desire and see life from a completely opposite perspective. The rich, for example, want to go on vacations to destress themselves from the pressures of their responsibilities. And the poor, similarly, take on the pressures of life in order to earn some power and riches.

The soul is incomplete in the sense that he cannot be at many places simultaneously and see life from opposite perspectives at once. And yet, he has the desire for this completeness—not to see everything at once, but at least to experience them one by one. The rich therefore desire to give away their richness, and the poor want to give away their poverty. Life would be nice if the rich and poor could swap their lives and experience the opposites.

Now, a person who indeed enjoys a rich life of responsibility—but sometimes abhors the pressure of duty—doesn't truly want to give up their role and pleasure permanently. He or she may, however, desire a temporary relief from their job where they can hand over the responsibility to someone else temporarily, and then take back the reins of control and power at a later time. Similarly, a person who likes a simple and idyllic life but sometimes abhors the difficulties that come with such simplicity doesn't truly want to reject their life, although they may temporarily desire a relief from their difficulties. Thus, both sides have a dominant position regarding what they want. But they also have a subordinate position with regard to what they might be missing. If one is forever fixed in their role and pleasure, they will sometimes feel the need to move over to the other side, and if such a role swap was impossible, they would then fall into the position of envy—the attempt to grab someone else's position. An ideal world is one in which one can *temporarily* change their position while maintaining the option of going back to their dominant desires.

Thus, the world of *Viṣṇu*, where each person has a fixed position is not perfect, although it is far more perfect than the material world of conflicts, or the world of monism where one lives by oneself. The Vedic texts describe an even better world called *Goloka* (the world of *Kṛṣṇa*) where the souls are generous and compassionate toward each other in giving up their roles if the other person wants them. Yes, they may not desire a role swap, but they are humble and compassionate to prioritize other's desires over theirs. While such a change is very unlikely because one is normally very happy with their work, and the pressures of life—which arise from conflicting situations—don't exist if one is simply situated in their role of choice, there is always a possibility of such a change, and the change reduces the incidence of any envy.

The master thus may sometimes want to be the servant, and the servant may sometimes become the master. The parent might sometimes want to be the child, and the child may sometimes want to be parent. In this process, they don't change their form or body comprised of abilities. However, they indeed change their *roles* and the resulting *pleasures*. Thus, the child can sometimes play the role of a mother—dictating to the mother what she must do and the mother would happily take the position of child. Similarly, the servant may take the role of a master and tell the master what he must be doing, and the master would happily accept the guidance of his servant. Similarly, the husband will take the role of the wife, and the wife that of the husband. Such role reversals are meant for a person to enjoy the opposite type of pleasure.

One such role reversal is described in *Gaudīya Vaishnavism* where *Kṛṣṇa* (the all-attractive person), takes the role of His consort—*Rādha*— and advents in the form of *Sri Chaitanya* in order to experience Her mood and love. Even God is therefore envious, and He desires what He doesn't have. But this envy is considered the highest form of pleasure— because it is, in one sense, a guilty pleasure, when *Kṛṣṇa* renounces His dominant role as the male, and accepts the subordinate role of His lover. Through such a role reversal, *Kṛṣṇa* remains a male, and all His powers and abilities are unchanged. However, by accepting a different role He changes the type of pleasure enjoyed in the process.

Religion as the Pursuit of Idealism

Greek philosophers—especially Plato—were preoccupied with *ideas*. They did not dwell much on the *ideals* because their theories of ideas as incarnations into material substance were flawed, and their prescriptions of ideals were also distorted. Since that time, there has been an irrevocable separation in Western philosophy between epistemology (as the study of ideas) and ethics (as the evaluation of ideals). This separation has then been the bane of understanding the relation between ideas and ideals— resulting in many forms of contrived dualities such as between form and substance, mind and matter, emotion and reason, science and religion, impersonal and personal, knowledge and art, choice and determinism, monotheism and polytheism.

The problem of meaning—as the simultaneous existence of opposites—leads to the problem of logical contradictions as a result of which the West has pursued universalism as the route to reject one side of the contradiction. Similarly, because opposites define each other, and universalism is therefore practically impossible, the West has automatically descended into relativism where everything that anyone does must be equally good and the collective good must be defined by the majoritarian position in deciding the social laws. The West also believes—somewhat arrogantly—that its contrived system of self-contradictory ideas constitutes the ideal for the rest of humanity.

If one is looking for answers then there is hope in Vedic philosophy regarding the nature of the soul and God, how the soul has ideas but they are non-ideal, how our ideals become non-ideal if we clash with others, how ideality is partially attained by separating from the world, and how perfection lies in complementing the roles of different individuals. This perfection ultimately emerges from the humility and compassion by which we can make the sacrifice to give up what we desire in order for someone else to have their way.

The soul has desires—which make it selfish. In the material world, the religion of *Brahma* encourages the soul to remain selfish but subordinate that selfishness to one's duties. The performance of duties creates good *karma* but the selfishness leads to conflicts and bad *karma*. The soul remains stuck in the cycle of birth and death. The religion of *Shiva* encourages liberation from the material world in order to free oneself from this cycle of birth and death because in the material world it is not possible to always avoid bad *karma*. However, this religion also advocates a form of selfishness—i.e., the soul lives for itself and by itself. It results in liberation from the cycle of birth and death, but it bars him from the pleasure of activity and knowledge. The religion of *Viṣṇu* describes a world in which everyone leads a complementary existence in which their roles are fixed, and conflicts are naturally prevented. And yet, the soul is still selfish in the sense that he focuses on his role, and is uncompromising with regard to his own pleasure, although he doesn't interfere with others' pleasure. That's why the religion of *Kṛṣṇa* in *Goloka* urges to go beyond even the selfishness of complementarity and be prepared to sacrifice their happiness for the happiness of others. Alternately, we can say that there is happiness derived in making the other person happy, so it is not truly considered a 'sacrifice'. This constitutes the definitive philosophy of religion as *love*.

The religion of *Shiva* describes a place called *Brahman* which is the place of self-love. The religion of *Viṣṇu* describes a place called *Vaikuṇṭha* which is the place of God-love, but it is not a place of loving other souls. The souls desire to be 'near' God, and hence 'liberation' is understood as proximity to God. Four such types of liberation can be attained—*sālokya* (living on the same planet as God), *sāmipya* (living in proximity and association with God), *sārupya* (having a similar form as that of God), and *sārsti* (having the same powers as God). We must realize that this 'proximity' is *semantic*; as two objects get closer to each other, they also become conceptually similar to each other. Thus, as the soul gets closer to God, he also becomes ever more similar to God. The soul, however, doesn't merge into God, and doesn't become identical to Him.

The state of merger, where the soul is in God's body, is *Brahman*. However, in this state, the soul doesn't enjoy the relationships that God enjoys. He still has a close relationship to God—closer than others—but it is so close that the soul doesn't know the distinction between himself and God. He just thinks he has become God but is devoid of all relations and pleasures. The key point is that a relationship requires some difference. The difference should not be so great that you simply cannot relate to the other person. But the difference should also not be so small that you don't find a difference and without that difference there is no attraction. The attraction is very weak when the distance grows, but it also rapidly drops as the distance becomes very small.

In this regard we might note a problem in modern theories of force where the force decreases with increasing distance, and increases with decreasing distance, by the inverse square law. This means that as the distance becomes zero, the force of attraction must be infinite. Thus, as the particles get closer to each other their mutual attraction will become infinite and they must collapse into each other—which then leads to the idea of 'black holes'. The problem is that inside the black hole, the force of attraction must be infinite. How can you deal with infinity in science? Then there is a second-order problem of atomic theory where each particle has a finite form and they are not point particles. Therefore, the distance between them can never be zero. Thus, on one hand we have a theory of gravitation where the distance between particles can become zero, and on the other, a theory where the distance must remain finite. How can we reconcile the gravitational theory with that of atomism? This is one of the greatest unsolved problems in modern physics and it cannot be solved in a physical theory because we have to conceive of particles where the attraction increases as the distance is reduced but as the particles get too close to each other they will cease to be attracted to each other. If the particles get any closer, they would be repelled apart—as each particle needs its own 'space'. There is hence a neutral distance at which the particles are neither attracted nor repelled, and that lack of push and pull fixes their positions.

Brahman is such a position for the soul and God. The soul gets very close to God—due to initial attraction to God. But as the soul gets closer, the attraction between them ceases. The soul reaches a position of neutrality in which he neither has the distance to build a relationship nor the proximity to become averse to God. This position of the soul is hence alluded to nicely when *Brahman* is described as the 'effulgence' from God's form. This 'effulgence' is actually very close to God, and yet outside His form. In this state, the soul neither has an attraction to God, nor is he averse to God. The relationship of aversion is called the material world, and the relation of attraction is called the spiritual world. The state of aversion is caused when the soul wants to be God, and therefore he tries to take God's position by becoming one with Him. This means wanting to invade the space or position occupied by God by getting too close to Him. Paradoxically, aversion to God is greater proximity to Him because we are talking about distance in a semantic sense in which the soul is trying to replace God and become God himself, or merge into God. Thus, in the material world, we are closest to God in the attempt to *become* God. This leads to intense aversion to God as we are unable to occupy His position. When the soul is liberated into *Brahman,* he moves a little away from God and is situated in the neutral position between attraction and repulsion. Then as he moves further away from God, he develops a relationship under attraction.

As the soul moves away from God, he looks similar to God, and feels similar to Him, although he can see that he is different from God. As the distance increases, the form of the soul changes and the difference increases.

The religion of *Goloka* is one of distance rather than proximity. In this the soul considers himself fallen, and therefore considers others superior to himself. If anyone desires to take his position, the soul is imbued with gratitude and relief because he considers himself unqualified to play the role. Also, since the soul thinks himself fallen, he has no qualms in making someone else happy by relinquishing his position. Instead of wanting to go closer to God, he desires to remain away from God, thinking himself totally unqualified for proximity. The soul is thus described to have a paradoxical feeling—the feeling of distance because he is unqualified, and that of intense separation because of the distance. He doesn't want to go closer because he considers himself fallen, and he cannot live separated because of his intense love. His separation from God—created by his own feeling of being fallen—intensifies his love, and these feelings of separation from God (instead of proximity) are considered the highest form of religion. The religion of *Goloka* is in one sense a progression over the religion of *Vaikuṇṭha* because the soul has gradually increased the distance. And yet, as this distance increases, the nature of religion changes because the soul is totally purified of his selfishness—even the desire to be happy in the association of God, and of course the desire to merge into God's body.

The term *māyā* thus has different meanings. In the material world, it means "I am not God, but I want to be God". It leads to the desire to be the lord and master of the world one purviews. Freedom from *māyā* means "I am not God, and I don't want to be God". As this *māyā* progresses, the soul is again in *māyā* thinking "I am not God, but I want to be in relation to God". Finally, the soul feels that "I am not God, and I'm unqualified to be near God". In each case, there is separation between the soul and God, but the soul's response to that separation is different. In that sense, *māyā* never affects God; it only affects the soul, by changing his relation and distance to God. When the soul manufactures a sense of isolation from God due to his own humility, he considers himself far from God. As a result, there is no envy of God, and the soul is farthest from the possibility of a falldown: falldown would mean that a soul first wants to get closer, then enter the neutral position, and then become God himself.

In the religion of *Goloka*, the soul never seeks God. Rather, God seeks the soul. The soul loves God from a distance but is never confident, proud, or arrogant to actually approach God. God is attracted by the combination of that intense love and humility, which makes the soul extremely "shy" because the intense love is hidden and suppressed due to the feeling of humility. This *shyness* or *coyness* is the most fundamental trait of the soul in *Goloka*, contrary to *Vaikuṇṭha* where the soul is bold and wants to see God face-to-face, considers Him almost an equal—especially with growing proximity. Thus, in the religion of *Vaikuṇṭha* the soul interacts with God. But in the religion of *Goloka* he is just busy thinking of and serving God to the point where God wants to see him. There is an inner contradiction in the soul because he craves for God's love but considers himself unqualified to meet Him. The pleasures felt through such contradictions in the soul are paradoxically considered the highest.

Since psychoanalysts have analyzed such contradictions to be the basis of unhappiness, it is noteworthy that there is also a place where internal contradictions constitute the highest pleasure. The place of such perfection looks remarkably similar to the world we experience presently, but there is a subtle difference. In the material world, there is a contradiction between desire, role, and ability, due to which we abhor and neglect our duties, and desire something that we don't currently possess. In the spiritual world, this contradiction is resolved as a person is attached and happy with their role. However, a new contradiction *within* desire, ability, and roles is produced. The person is conflicted because desire conflicts humility, the duties conflict each other, and they have contradictory abilities simultaneously. One duty requires a person to be serious and strict, and the other one expects them to be playful and forgiving. One ability is to relish the pot making and the other is to relish pot breaking. Regardless of what they choose—desire or humility, one duty or another, one ability vs. its opposite—there is always pleasure, and yet always a contradiction. That contradiction entails that every pleasure is guilty because you could have prioritized exactly the opposite type of experience.

Thus, in the material world we suffer due to contradictions between *sat*, *chit*, and *ānanda*. In *Brahman* one is freed of the contradiction by rejecting all desires, roles, and bodies. In *Vaikuṇṭha*, the contradiction between *sat*, *chit*, and *ānanda* is resolved and there is no contradiction within desires, roles, and abilities. But in *Goloka* the soul is again internally conflicted—this time due to conflicting desires, abilities, and roles—which makes for guilty pleasure.

Religion simply means going from ideas to ideals. There are four distinct stages of this idealism identified in Vedic philosophy, which have existed in different religions the world over. Since three of these religious ideals correspond to different worlds, they cannot be simply equated with the unconscious psyche. We could say that we can become aware of these worlds, but we are presently unaware of them, and hence they are unconscious for us. But the unconscious is not that of Freud or Jung who used these terms to indicate something that manifests in our current life although we are generally unaware of its existence. Similarly, even the demigods are within this world, but they are present at higher levels than our current existence. Their world is part of the material universe and yet higher or superior to our current existence.

As we go higher, we move closer to ideals. Thus, even moving upward to the level of demigods is progression on the path of ideality; liberation from the material existence as an isolated individual, even greater ideality; realizing ourselves in relation to God and resolving inner conflict is more ideal; finally, experiencing the contradictions of opposite desires is the most ideal.

The Nature of the Unconscious

The descriptions of the higher worlds within the material universe, and the worlds beyond the material world, are not "myths", nor are they embedded in the individual psyche or a collective unconscious. To an extent, when the ideals of the higher worlds become our ideas at the present, we become partially aware of their existence. But that awareness doesn't reduce the ideals to the ideas. The ideals remain different from the ideas; they might become our ideas to varying extents. But the ideals may also be mixed with non-ideal ideas, which would mean that we perceive the ideals in different people to varying extents, but everything in their ideas is not necessarily ideal. All the ideals are ideas, but all the ideas are not ideals. In that sense, searching for ideas and then treating them as ideals turns out to be a flawed view of the ideals.

Treating the unconscious as the repository of ideals is such a flawed view. The unconscious is also many non-ideal ideas, as Freud correctly noted. But the existence of such flaws doesn't entail that every idea in the psyche is necessarily non-ideal. In that sense, we can neither reduce the psyche to perfect ideals, nor can we treat every idea to be a non-ideal. Both extremes are false, and by understanding the reason they are false we can see why religion is not entirely embedded in our psyche (because our minds can be non-ideal), nor is religion totally outside the mind (because our minds can have ideal ideas). We have to see the ideas and the ideals as separate, and we have to convert the non-ideal minds into ideals by discarding the non-ideal ideas. That process of personal transformation of the mind constitutes the religious journey.

Psychoanalytic studies identify the many layers within a person, which is far better than viewing the person as just body and soul—as practically all philosophers have done since Greek times. In *Sāṅkhya*, for example, higher than the body are the senses, higher than the senses is the mind, the intellect is higher than the mind, the ego even higher than the intellect, and ultimately our moral sense—comprised of material moralities—is even higher than the ego. All of these are relatively unconscious if we remain focused on the body. They become more conscious as we focus inward into the deeper layers.

The world of objects and their properties—including the body—is called *vaikharī*. This is what modern science studies, but *vaikharī* is only one of the four different levels of reality, and science models *vaikharī* as if none of the deeper levels of reality existed. For instance, if mind is a deeper reality, then the world of objects must be treated as symbols of meaning, rather than as meaningless things. The awareness of a deeper reality automatically alters our conception of even the gross reality. The mind then interacts with the body as not two different types of material substances—as Descartes believed. The mind is rather the meaning and the body is the symbol of that meaning. They interact via a method of instantiating the meaning into a symbol, or dividing an abstract meaning into detailed meanings, or viewing the meaning as a goal and the body as the incremental process by which the goal is realized.

Deeper than the objects is a world of experience, comprised of the senses, mind, intellect, ego, and morality; this is called *madhyamā*, most of which is unconscious for most people. For example, the senses of the observer are naturally attracted or repelled toward objects. This is conscious, but we are unaware of the past habits which cause the senses to be naturally repelled or attracted. Similarly, the mind is naturally active or inactive. We can experience the activity or inactivity, but we don't understand why it is sometimes active and at other times inactive. The mind is thus partially unconscious. The intellect comprises our innate assumptions. We might articulate some of these if called for, but most people remain unaware of their assumptions. They presume them to be 'true' or 'facts' or 'obvious', but why a person believes in certain ideas is not always known to them. The intellect is therefore also partially unconscious. The ego produces our goals, but why do I prefer some goals over others—or why I find them worthy pursuits in life—is not always clear to us. In that sense the ego is largely unconscious. Similarly, our moral sense comprises of our sense of righteousness, but why I define righteousness in a particular manner different from others is not always known to us. We might simply *believe* that hard work is righteous as opposed to laziness, but why I accept hard work as a virtue and laziness as a vice is not necessarily obvious. Without clear answers, the moral sense is also mostly unconscious.

Deeper than this realm of conscious experience—which is partially unconscious—is another realm which is wholly unconscious; it is called *paśyanti* or the reason that I want to be in the material world. Why is death a bad thing as opposed to life? Even though life often gets very difficult, most of us prefer such troublesome life over death. Why? What is it that we achieve through living when everything we accumulate—education, money, fame, power, etc.—would be lost either within this life, or certainly at the point of death? The short answer is that we don't acquire education, money, fame, or power for the sake of those things. They are the means—the goals for which we work—but they are not the ends that act as self-evident justifications. We acquire these things because we want to be happy. We enjoy certain things and we despise other things. You can ask anyone: Why do you like this dress, food, or lifestyle, as opposed to others? And the answer would be: "I don't know; I just like it; it is who I *am*. Our likes and dislikes constitute our deepest *personality*.

This personality is wholly unconscious to us, not in the sense that we cannot know what we like, but *why* we like it. If you eat both boiled vegetables and fried and spicy curries, there is still something you prefer to have, but you cannot explain why you like one type of food as opposed to the others. Now, you may like spicy food, but you may not get it through the opportunities. Or you may like it and get it, but your body may not accept such spicy food. The *ability* to digest spicy food, and the *opportunity* to obtain such food, are different from the *desire* for it. Often times, we suppress our desires either because the ability or the opportunity doesn't exist. So, we are not talking about how my likes are adapted to the situation and our abilities. We are talking about what makes us like certain things and dislike other things—innately, not by force.

The soul is even beyond this personality built out of desires for pleasure. The soul is eternal and spiritual, but the desire for pleasure is a material covering that gives us the illusion of a unique and different personality but because the soul doesn't perceive the desire as a covering, he identifies with that desire as himself. Knowing the *paśyanti* means seeing it as different from the soul or the self. It means that when I desire material pleasure, it is not *me*. That desire is itself produced by a deep—and unconscious—material reality but since we cannot distinguish the self from that desire it is unconscious. The soul is called *para*—or transcendent—and when the soul doesn't know that it is transcendent to the material existence, he is unconscious to himself.

In that sense, so much of what we experience is just a fraction of reality. When the external world is modeled as things rather than symbols, its semantic nature remains unconscious, and therefore *vaikharī* is unknown. When we remain unaware of why I have a certain type of bodily and mental abilities, then the body and the mind are unconscious. When we don't see the difference between the soul and the desire, then the desires are unconscious. And when we don't realize the eternity of the soul—and fear death—then the soul is unconscious to itself. The unconscious is not the exception; the conscious is a small fraction of the whole, and hence an exception to the unconscious.

Freud mostly studied the unconscious parts of the material desire, while Jung considered the relatively more conscious parts of the moral sense. They could universalize these ideas because every soul has desire and morality. However, in another sense, we cannot universalize these things because every soul has a *different* desire and morality. Their desires and morals are like branches of a tree emanating from a root. The root is God, because God is the original desire and morality. The soul accepts a branch emerging from this root as his own desire and morality, but the soul has a *choice* to jump to another branch and thereby change his desires and moralities. Since every branch has emanated from the root, it carries some properties of the root, and hence we can always see similarities between the branch and the root. But the branch is never the root. The similarity doesn't mean that these are not different branches, or that there isn't a root beyond these branches. It would be a mistake, for instance, to think that because the leaves of a tree look the same, therefore there is no need for the root which causes their similarity.

Dreams are indeed interpretable into meanings, but what prevents the psychologist from giving the waking experience a similar meaning? If my dreaming experience has ulterior meanings which might not be obvious to me while dreaming, why can't the waking experience also possess meanings which may not be apparent to me through that waking experience?

Dreams attest to a very important fact in life—namely, that you can experience without any contact with the external world. As a result, the *madhyamā* or conscious experience is also called the "dreaming state" as opposed to the "waking state" where the world of objects is experienced. But experience is not comprised of the same types of objects as the body. Dreaming simply tells us that I can have experiences without the existence of external objects. By implication, the body is not necessary for sensual experience. The *madhyamā* is therefore called the "subtle body" of the soul, different from the "gross body". The gross body is particularly obvious during waking experience, and the subtle body is the only thing we are aware of during the dreaming experience. One can also discard the experience of the subtle body and just experience the personality of desires; this is called the "deep sleep" state. And one can discard all material desires and exist without desire—the "transcendent" state.

The *vaikharī* and *madhyamā*—objects and their experience—are considered the 'inside' of the material universe. Vedic cosmology also describes how the universe is covered by 7 layers—each 10 times larger than the previous one. These layers represent the desires of the soul, only a fraction of which are manifest in our dreams, and a small fraction of such dreams become reality. These 7 layers correspond to the 7 tiers of waking and dreaming experiences—objects, sensations, senses, mind, intellect, ego, and morality. All these 7 layers constitute the *chit* or the *cognition* of the soul. But the desire for such cognition is the deeper need to enjoy, which we never 'see' (as an objective reality) because we consider that desire to be our very personality.

The first covering of the universe is the desire for sense objects; it covers the universe of sense objects, and it is ten times the size of the universe. This means that we can never be satisfied by the universe because the realm of desires for objects is ten times bigger than the sum total of all the objects. Similarly, the second covering of the universe is the desire for sensations; we can experience a finite number of colors, forms, sounds, tastes, and smells, but the desires for such sensation are 100 times bigger than all the possible sensations of this universe. Thus, we can never be satisfied by the sensation of this entire universe because the desire for sensation is 100 times larger. Similarly, the third covering of the universe is the desire for senses; the human senses are different from those of cats, dogs, tigers, eagles, etc. But the desires for having a certain type of sense and ability—through a different species of life—are 1000 times bigger than all possible species in the universe. Thus, we can never be satisfied by this world even if we enjoyed the experience of each and every form of life because the desire for different body types is 1000 times bigger. In this way, the desires expand 10-fold at each successive covering.

Each such covering of the universe is inhabited by a form of *Shiva*—and they are sometimes called *Rudra*—the form of God who is crying out of anger because these coverings are places outside the universe and therefore, they embody all the desires that can't be fulfilled. The universe of conscious experience is only 1 part in 10,000,000, which means that if we roamed the entire universe and experienced everything that could be experienced through every possible life form in the universe, we would have just fulfilled 1 part out of 10,000,000 parts of our desire. The remaining 9,999,999 parts of desire will remain unfulfilled, and we will be therefore crying out of anger.

Every person's deepest level of material unconscious is a realm of frustrated desires, and every person is deeply anguished and angry if you understand them deeply. No matter how accomplished or fulfilled a person seems from external perception, he has billions—if not trillions—more reasons to be unhappy. The universe is designed to keep us unhappy as we are exposed to far greater number of desires than can actually be fulfilled. Of course, if there were simply no fulfillment at all, then we would quickly leave the universe. We stay in this universe—despite unfulfilled desires—because we don't know for sure which desires cannot be fulfilled. Indeed, we hope that if some of our desires are not fulfilled yet, they may be fulfilled in the *future*. This hope is not completely false; we can indeed enjoy more pleasures in the future. However, the sum total of all that we can enjoy over and over still leaves a significantly larger portion of desires that can never be fulfilled. We try to approximate our unfulfilled desires with those that can be fulfilled through much effort.

The unconscious—in the most profound sense—is these unfulfilled desires. They make us angry, aggressive, frustrated, and yet hopeful. Crossing this realm of the unconscious is much harder than giving up experiences. That is, you can repeatedly enjoy the pleasures of this world, and a fraction of your desires would be fulfilled. But since the total number of desires—which were left unfulfilled—is 9,999,999 times bigger, even giving up the desire for all that can be experienced in this world doesn't mean freedom from desire. You are still left with a huge number of desires to be fulfilled. Now you have a choice: realize that these can never be fulfilled and give them up by escaping the realm of desire. Or try to approximate these unfulfilled desires by those that can be fulfilled—by falling back into the realm that you rejected.

The Problem of Immorality in Religion

Those who have made sincere attempts at religious idealism by rejecting the pleasures of this world often discover that as you discard the carnal enjoyments you also come in contact with a significantly larger swell of desires that were previously undiscovered and hence unconscious. The enormous realm of desires that was earlier suppressed by the incidence of sensual, mental, intellectual, and moral pleasures afforded by this world—which roughly approximated and hence kept the other desires from surfacing—rears its head as you start rejecting the satisfaction of the other desires. In essence, as you transcend some desires, you experience a significantly larger realm of desires. Thus, the rejection of sense enjoyment doesn't actually end it quickly. The desires are revectored into other things that we were not aware of earlier.

Thus, *Śrīla Bhaktisiddhānta Sarasvati Thakur* writes in the essay entitled "Organized Religion" that "The church that has the best chance of survival in this damned world is that of atheism under the convenient guise of theism. The churches have always proved the staunchest upholders of the grossest form of worldliness from which even the worst of non-ecclesiastical criminals are found to recoil." This is fairly familiar to anyone who has had intimate experience with organized religion, and most people in fact turn toward atheism because they find the upholders of religion in this world engaged in either the same types of materialistic activities as the other atheists, or in some cases heinous acts that far exceed the monstrosity of the materialistic acts of ordinary people who might not be as committed to the religious principles.

Why and how a person who decided to reject the materialism of this world could fall prey to worse forms of crimes that those which even the committed materialists reject and abhor? The confusion resulting from the depredation of the spiritual leaders makes their followers even less dedicated to religion, and indeed to the purported ideals to be upheld. Indeed, most vocal critics of religion in modern times attribute to religious institutions the occurrences of wars, terrorism, child abuse, politics, and other perversions. Innumerable people—who started out starry-eyed idealists—have left the religion at the beginning of their spiritual quest because they found its practitioners lacking in many ways, joined another religion in the hope that such difficulties will not be encountered there, or rejected religion per se. Some have also thereby come to detest God and any form of religious authority.

The situation is paradoxical because no religiously-inclined person joins a religious institution with the intent to rape, murder, abuse, or combat. They mostly join with noble intentions but at some point, perversion manifests. Nobody is able to accept that this is part of religious progression, although the crimes are not justified, because joining a "church" doesn't make one enlightened. One has to conquer the material desires, and the anger about the fact that they are not fulfilled—after understanding that they can never be fulfilled. If the desires and the associated angers are not conquered, the "church" itself will not help you. The "church" is only to facilitate contact with other like-minded people in order that they can share and learn from each other. However, religions portray the membership of "churches" as salvation. When their claims of salvation are contradicted by the observed behaviors, they fail to use the "church" for providing like-minded association and learning, while undermining the belief and trust in their own ability to make progress.

It is not that the practice of religion makes a person more evil. It is because the desires we know of are only a fraction of all that exist unconsciously. As one controls some of the superficial desires, the pressure of other, deeper desires increases. These fantasies now manifest in perverted ways. As perversions rear their head, the religious practitioner is overwhelmed and loses faith in their ability to conquer desire. He or she becomes more aware of the anger and unhappiness arising from unfulfilled desires, and the pursuit of the ideal henceforth means facing greater internal trial and tribulation than we generally like to acknowledge. The dominant position advocated by most religious institutions is that as you pursue the ideal, you will automatically become peaceful, satisfied, and renounced. In fact, the mere acceptance of an institution is often touted as the solution to all kinds of material miseries. The truth is far from such oversimplification because the fact is that the greater the sincerity shown by the practitioner, the greater is their trial by fire.

This seems self-contradictory to most people because they assume that if they make small steps toward God, the journey will get easier with each passing day. The central problem of religious practice—and why it is generally rejected by many people at present—is that it involves an uphill climb that gets steeper with passing time, until one crosses out of the significantly larger realm of material desire. This realm is so much larger that the rejection of all the material pleasures of this world is much smaller by comparison.

It is here that the psychology of the unconscious becomes most relevant to religion; it helps us see why the entire perceivable universe is just the tip of the iceberg of desire fulfilment. Of course, we cannot perceive much of the perceivable universe because the senses and the mind aren't advanced enough. This fact is recognized today in science by claiming that the part that we can see is only 4% of the total matter that exists; the remaining 96% exists but we cannot perceive it, and hence it is called "dark matter" and "dark energy". However, even beyond the matter that we currently cannot perceive due to underdevelopment of the mind and senses, there is another greater realm of unfulfillable desires. By understanding this realm, we can realize that the material world is built upon desire—which means that it is not a place devoid of purpose. The most primordial reality is not the atoms that we measure by the senses. Even the sensations, senses, mind, intellect, ego, and morality—which are higher than the atoms—are not that primordial, even though they are indeed much more fundamental than the body. However, even when you go past these material elements that comprise our psychophysical existence, there is a much bigger realm of desire that has forever been dissatisfied and frustrated because it could never be fulfilled through the material experiences. The collective unconscious—if we use this term in the above new sense—is the set of increasing realms of desire that one has to cross in order to escape the material realm. The hill to be climbed is steep; by comparison the rejection of all the material pleasures is simply arrival at the foot of the hill to be ascended.

A "pit" or "well" is therefore a familiar analogy for the material world. If you have fallen into a deep well, just getting above the water in the well is not exit from the well itself. There is a far greater distance to cover, compared to the level of water in the well itself. Thus, you might not drown in the water because you are above its surface, but you are still in the danger of falling back.

This fact has lessons both for practitioners of religion and those who criticize religions. The lesson is that our universe has to be viewed as a realm of desire fulfilment. The part that we can experience is the one that fulfills desires. The 'covering' of this fulfilment is those desires that are never fulfilled. Thus, the soul goes 'inward' from the part that remains unfulfilled to the part that can be fulfilled. Religion is about transcending this realm of desires. Those who set out on religion must look inward to the unsatisfied desires and treat them not as things that will automatically disappear, but as the greatest hurdles yet to be conquered. Similarly, those who criticize the pursuit of religious ideals must realize that unless you try to climb the mountain you don't really know how high it is. It is easy to criticize, but even a person who falls from grace—because advancement on the path reveals the unconscious—has only fallen temporarily. The sincere practitioner—who doesn't lose heart in such falls—will keep climbing and would be born more perfect in their next life from where they will continue their journey out of material desire.

The well-intentioned critiques of fall from grace should drive us toward greater perfection, not back into the world of desire fulfilment that we need to escape from. Such critiques only tell us that the journey is harder than we thought, and the unscrupulous critics are unaware that there is an ocean of desire waiting to surge within them, or themselves have no desire for perfection: they would rather remain imperfect and criticize others for trying (and failing) to attain perfection. Neglecting such critics is probably good, as long as it doesn't blind us to the reasons that we fell from grace to begin with.

The Use of Psychology in Religion

Psychology can be a great aide in understanding the structure of the body, senses, mind, intellect, ego, morality and desires of these beyond. Vedic texts thus describe the psychophysical structure at great length, as much as they discuss cosmology: the places of different kinds of pleasures. In one sense, the entire description is about conscious experience; since most of that experience falls under "psychology" one might say that that its study is imperative.

The world is described as three trees of relation, emotion, and cognition intersecting with each other to create conscious experience. These trees constitute the 'universal' space. Within the universal space are many relative spaces, each with their origin at different places on the universal tree. The relative space always begins in morals, and proceeds into ego, intellect, mind, senses, sensations, and sense objects—the 7 tiers of experience. However, the universal tree is only comprised of the 3 modes of nature—*sattva*, *rajas*, and *tamas*. It is just 'sound' without 'meaning'. That is, it exists, but we cannot call it morality, goals, assumptions, thoughts, sensations, senses, or objects. The individual soul gives the 'sound' its meaning by calling some 'sound' morality and another 'sound' sensation. The interpretation is created when the soul moves on the universal tree. As the soul is situated on a particular branch of the tree, he considers that the 'origin' of the world, and the 'sound' there is interpreted as morality. Then branches from that 'original' branch is called ego, and so forth into intellect, mind, senses, sensations, and objects.

Thus, the same location on the universal tree can be interpreted as sensations by one living entity and thoughts or goals by another living entity. This is their *relativism* by which they see the *same* world in a different manner. The relativism, however, is based on the universalism—the universal tree.

This fact has very important implications for mythology. The implication that what you consider ideas are sensations for a higher living entity. What may seem relatively unconscious would not only be more conscious but even perceived as sensations by the higher being. Thus, for instance, we experience colors, tastes, and smells by our senses, but the ideas perceived by the mind are not directly perceived as sensations because they are more abstract.

However, sensual properties are commonly employed as *metaphors* in language: for example, he is acting *obtuse*, this guy is a *blockhead*, his speech is very *rough*, she has a *hot* temperament, he is feeling *bitter* about his separation, she is feeling *blue* after the death, his *cold* words have left me *paralyzed*, his brain is very *sharp*, the boss *cut* him to *size* through reprimand, he is a *smooth* operator, her husband has a *pungent* personality, I have been *burnt* by his lies, his words were going way *above* the audience, he has left the past *behind* him, I am looking *forward* to meeting you, I want to be on the *right* side of the law, you are looking *delicious*, he is a *dense* guy, I have been in the *grips* of his emotions lately, she *holds* the family together, and so on, *ad infinitum*.

We don't realize how essential these metaphors are to our conversations and why ideas are described in terms of sensations. If the mind is grasping meanings and the mind is higher than the senses, then why does the mind employ the terminology normally reserved for the senses? The short answer is that ideas in the mind are no different than sensations and objects. What we call an idea is just a higher object in our *relative* space. For someone else, the same object will be a sense, a sensation, or a sense object. They can clearly taste, smell, hear, touch, and see by their senses what we can only think. Nevertheless, while we cannot touch, see, smell, hear, and taste ideas in the mind, we have an inkling of what it means to sensually perceive the ideas, and the concepts, personalities, emotions, relations, and actions are described *as if* we were perceiving them sensually. Thus, the ideas in our head—e.g., beauty, knowledge, power, fame, detachment, and wealth—also have a form, taste, smell, sound, and touch. Normally, since these ideas are very abstract, we are not able to give them forms, but that only means that they are far deeper and prior to the origin of our relative space. If, however, we raise the location of our relative space on the tree of the absolute space, then the ideas that we can only think of metaphorically at present would be seen sensually. Then we can say that beauty has a taste, smell, sound, form, color, and touch. Knowledge too has a sensually perceivable form, and power can be smelt and heard.

The use of metaphors in language forms the cornerstone of all poetry and literature. If the poet or writer just described the world in terms of objective measurements of the instruments, or even as sense perception, there would be little value in their work. Poetry and literature become valuable due to the metaphors, which means one has to see the same world from a higher vantage point where the ideas will become sensations or from a lower perspective where the sensations would be elaborate far more than normal. In other words, the poet, writer, artist, etc. have the artistic freedom to rise above or descend below on the tree in order to perceive and describe the world differently. However, they don't have the freedom to imagine what is unreal. Through artistic freedom, it rains cats and dogs, the woods call to embrace, the darkness of the night swallows the lonely stranger, and clouds are a blue quilt.

The ideas and ideals in our minds have forms, tastes, smells, sounds, and touches, by which they can be sensed quite like we eat food and smell the roses. However, we don't see their form because of our position in the absolute space. The ideal ideas in our minds are personalities called demigods or different forms of God. Similarly, the evil ideas in our heads are personalities called demons. Each of the ideal or non-ideal ideas has a form, which means that they can be sensually perceived, although *we* might not perceive them as such. These ideas can alter the world around us, so they have hands. They can appear in one place and disappear in another therefore they have legs. We see the world through such ideas, so the ideas have eyes. The ideas speak to us about things that are not directly in the idea but can be indicated by the idea; hence these ideas have a mouth. The ideas include other ideas which were previously 'consumed' inside to build them, so the idea has a stomach. An idea has many meanings in different contexts, so the idea also has a mind that changes. The different meanings of the idea are manifest in different contexts, and those contexts are the intellect of the idea in which that meaning is judged to be true. The idea can be utilized to fulfill some purposes, and is generally mooted with some objectives, so the purpose underlying the idea is its ego. Similarly, the purpose may be righteous or unrighteous, so it also has a moral. Finally, there is a soul who enjoys the different facets of the idea, so these facets constitute his body and mind. The idea in our mind is the body of a personality.

It is not that ideas and ideals are embedded in our psyche. It is rather that the body of a personality can be coextensive with the thoughts in my mind. I can metaphorically capture that form, but that form is sensually perceivable to the demigod, or even to others who raise their relative space upward. What we call 'mythology' is evident in everyday linguistic use, literature, and poetry. In so far as metaphors are not necessarily drawn from religious texts, there is a wider problem of understanding ideas in terms of sensations that we cannot disregard. The solution to the problem of metaphorical thinking addresses the concerns about religious texts embodying 'mythology'. These are called 'mythology' by those whose perception is not advanced, or that their relative space in the universe is situated so low on the absolute space that they cannot understand how ideas are themselves sensations for someone else.

As one uplifts their personal reference frame relative to the absolute reference frame, he first acquires the forms of the higher beings as his morals. Then the same form gradually becomes a goal, then an axiom, then a concept (derived from an even higher axiom), then a sense, then a sensation, and finally an object. Meanwhile, the soul has crossed into the realms of higher desires, which means that he also enjoys and relishes such experiences and abhors the previous experiences that were based on lower desires. The moral values embodied in religious texts as the worship of demigods and the different forms of God are similarly personalities that can be perceived by the senses as color, form, taste, smell, sound, and touch, simply by changing our desire. Such a change involves a rising within the realm of desire, which means that lower-level desires—and their associated pleasures—have to become distasteful. If the soul has acquired a new taste, then his relative space has moved in relation to the absolute space, and now new experiences are obtained.

Religion is therefore contiguous with psychology, if the structure of the psyche is understood as being constituted of numerous higher levels of experience, produced by higher levels of desire for pleasure. Going higher in that realm of desire constitutes religion and falling lower in that realm of desire is atheism. These are not absolute and logical opposites, but relative grades of advancement in which as the soul rises upward, he naturally discards the lower pleasures. Accepting God is hence also a matter of sense experience and the soul can see God like we presently see tables and chairs. The question is: Does the soul desire to see God, and has he rejected the lower desires?

The Reality of God

In the *Brahma-Samhita* it is stated that the advanced soul continuously perceives God through the eyes anointed with love. That 'love' is a desire which moves the soul's relative space upward, and the soul's 'eyes' are automatically uplifted in order to see what was invisible earlier. The vision of God is produced by the soul's motion in space, but it is not the physical movement of hands and legs while our mind continues to think the same thoughts, the intellect continues to carry the same assumptions, the ego continues to maintain the same goals, and the moral sense continues to see morality in the same mundane duties. The 'motion' in question here lifts the soul's perceptual reference frame by changing his desires, which then results in changes to the senses, mind, intellect, ego, and morality. Thus, by change of desires, the soul acquires a new body and mind, and hence perception. With such a body and mind, the soul directly perceives God like we see tables and chairs at present.

It is a misconception that the scientific study of motion can be studied rationally and empirically while religion is entirely based on faith. There is, instead, a more generic science that includes the motion of hands and legs, but goes beyond to cover the change of sensations, senses, thoughts, beliefs, goals, and morals. It is only because the idea of 'motion' in modern science is treated as the physical motion of hands and legs, while the other kinds of changes in the senses, mind, intellect, ego, and morality are neglected that we have contrived the non-existence of the soul and God, and advanced forms of perception accompanied by the change in our perceptual apparatus. If and when this understanding of 'motion' is *generalized*, we will realize that religion is also a theory of motion. However, it is a theory of motion that deals with the changes wrought at the deepest level of desire in order to effect a new morality, ego, intellect, mind, senses, sensations, and finally a body. The modern theories of motion, on the other hand, are simply bodily changes while keeping all other deeper levels of reality unchanged—and at a very low level.

God has the same three properties as the soul—cognition, relation, and emotion. As relation, He is the original and the ideal paramour, parent, child, friend, master, and hero, who has His counterpart lovers, children, parents, friends, servants, and admirers. The relation represents awareness, and it involves the distinction between two parties—the knower and the known. Through God's energy known as *bhūti-śakti* or "I am", God divides Himself into the Self and the other—thereby creating the soul. The soul is hereafter a knower and known, just as God. However, since the soul is created by the power of relationships—*bhūti-śakti* or "I am"—the result of this expansion depends on the nature of the relation that causes the expansion. Originally, the relationship is a neutral one—both God and soul *respect* each other as individuals, but they also maintain a convenient distance from each other. The soul doesn't get very close to God to infringe His privacy, nor does God get very close to the soul to infringe his position. Both exist as independent individuals; since they are not in a relationship, they are not aware of each other. This state of the soul is also called *taṭasthā-śakti* because from this neutral distance to God, the soul can increase the distance and create a loving relationship (called *antaranga-śakti*) or attempt to move closer to God in the attempt to overtake His position in an enterprise of competition and envy (called *bahiranga-śakti*). The latter constitutes the soul's falldown into matter as we have seen.

The term *bahiranga-śakti* is translated as 'external' energy. It is actually closer to God, but that proximity causes a competition or revulsion. The externality is emotional, namely that one tries to compete with God and pretends to be like God. The term *antaranga-śakti* is translated as 'internal' energy. It is actually farther from God, but that distance creates a fondness. The internality is the emotional attachment caused by increasing distance. Finally, *taṭasthā-śakti* is translated as 'marginal' energy; it is in between the external and internal attitudes, and thus constitutes the emotionally neutral stance.

The important point is that the soul is created by God through His power of relationship and therefore there is never a time when the soul is not in a relationship with God. The relationships, however, can be either competitive, neutral, or loving. The journey from matter to *Brahman* to *Vaikunṭha* and *Goloka* simply involve moving away from God—i.e., from trying to compete with God and take His role, to be situated in a neutral role where one becomes a non-competitive individual, to a distance where one seems very similar to God in mutual acknowledgement of each other, to a distance where the attraction between them grows proportionately with their increasing distance.

This concept of 'distance' is known to us through every day phrases like "familiarity breeds contempt" and "absence makes the heart grow fonder". If you go too close to someone you infringe on their privacy and the proximity results in competition for space. Similarly, if you go far away from them, there is natural attraction which makes you desire them intensely. Such a concept of distance is perceived in a relation between persons and is contrary to the physical notions of relation where "out of sight" entails "out of mind" because the relation is weakened by distance. Physical theories of force are based on the weakening of relation with distance, and its strengthening with proximity. But the semantic notion of relation is based on the strengthening of the relation with distance and its weakening with proximity. Therefore, in the physical relation, as the objects move away, their mutual attraction declines. However, in the semantic relation, the objects are mutually defined as opposites; as their mutual distance grows, their mutual attraction grows proportionately.

In this way, the soul is an *expansion* from God, which primordially exists as *Brahman* or the effulgence of God emanating from His form. As mentioned before this effulgence is neither too close to God, nor too far from Him. It is at a convenient distance in which the effulgence is separate, and yet it is God's effulgence. Hence, the *Brahman* is equated to 'light' and the soul is that 'light' which 'illuminates' God in that the soul is in a silent and neutral relation.

As emotion, God is the original feeling of detachment in relation to the soul—i.e., God doesn't bother the soul, so long as the soul doesn't bother Him. However, as the distance between the soul and God increases, there is growing fondness and attraction between them. The feeling of detachment is then converted into more intense feelings of a master, friend, parent, and lover. If instead the distance between the soul and God decreases, the soul gets into competition with God, trying to overtake His position and become God.

Once such relationships are established, and their associated feelings are created, then both the soul and God are involved in exchanging things with each other, and their body, mind, intellect, ego, and morality, together with the byproducts of these senses created through the energy of exchanges called *kriya-śakti*. To experience the full range of exchange, both the soul and God have senses, mind, intellect, ego, and morality, which act as the senses by which the soul and God perceive each other, give and take from each other. In the material world too, God gives the soul material things, and God takes from the soul those material things. When God gives those things lovingly, the soul ignores the love and imagines that these things are obtained due to his own effort. However, when God takes away those things, the soul blames God for making him unhappy, when that parting could also be construed as a gift to God. The essential difference thus is never in the acts of giving or taking. It is only in terms of how these exchanges are interpreted—enjoyed or suffered.

Thus, our lives—which involve gain and loss—can also be studied as exchanges in relation to God where God is giving and taking, but the soul due to its competitive nature doesn't see life that way. Instead, he views the exchanges as transactions occurring with other such souls trapped in a body.

If we understand the tree structure of space, then we can see that energy doesn't move directly between the leaves of the tree. Rather, this energy goes up and down the tree, and therefore an exchange between two souls is actually two exchanges between soul and God. Therefore, even when I'm giving some food to another person, God is taking food from me, and God is giving food to the other soul. If God doesn't mediate this transaction, the food cannot be transferred between the souls. Therefore, I'm not giving to the other person, nor is the other person taking from me. Rather, God is giving, and God is taking in two separate transactions. When we forget the existence of God, then these two separate transactions are connected as a single transaction, which then leads to the false notions about exchanges between material bodies. The idea of such exchanges is then generalized into the idea of 'force' and 'motion', and from such false ideas we produce deterministic theories of nature.

Materialism and atheism are simply the act of seeing the combination of two exchanges involving the soul and God, removing God from the picture and imagining them as direct exchanges between two souls. Then when God is removed from the picture, the soul is also removed, and only the mind is accepted. Then, since the soul has been removed, even the mind is removed, and only the body is recognized. Then even the body as a whole is not perceived, we just think that the exchange is occurring between two hands—one giving and the other taking. Then one further imagines that the actual contact is not between the hands, but only between the parts that come into contact—e.g., the palms that transfer the object. In this way, modern science continues to *reduce* the exchange, ultimately viewing it as a force between atoms.

This atheistic construction of an interaction between two individuals is however false because we are unable to predict when exactly which events will occur, or when an individual will give to whom, and when he will take from whom. The inability to make such predictions manifests in the incompleteness and indeterminism of scientific theories. In short, if you reject God, and collapse two separate interactions into one, and then you successively reduce the interactions from the whole to the parts, you will also fail to predict when and how things will happen: you will be baffled by randomness in nature.

The notion of God is hence a scientific construct, which can be stated very simply as the idea that space is a tree, whose root is God, the soul is a branch originally produced by the energy of relation with God. But the soul is never separated from God because his very existence is through that relation. The so-called rejection of God is not true break in the relation; it is only a change in relation from loving to competition. Matter is simply that energy which constitutes a competition with God with growing proximity, and spirit is that energy which constitutes cooperation with God with increasing distance. *Brahman* which lies in between material and spiritual worlds is the neutral distance. Thus, all of existence—material and spiritual—is a continuum described in relation to God. The soul changes his relation to God and thereby obtains different kinds of experiences. This motion of the soul in relation to God constitutes his *free will*. In all cases, this free will comes with a *responsibility*. That is, if you determine your relationship with God, you are also obliged to fulfill it. Thus, if you decide to compete with God, then you must compete fairly—according to the rules of the game. You are not allowed to compete unfairly, because such unfair competition has penalties. Similarly, if you decide to love God, you must love Him according to the rules of the game of love—i.e., without envy. Breaking the rules of love means moving from loving into competition.

Everything that modern science describes as interaction between two objects, can also be described as interactions between the soul and the Supreme Soul. These interactions are governed by rules and laws, but they are different kinds of laws—of competing, or remaining neutrally apart, of being close in a relationship but respectfully, and intensely craving the other person. These are different kinds of 'games' of life created by God (called *lila*). The soul can choose the game he wants, but he has to play by the rules of the game. The soul cannot create a new game, destroy the existing games, nor can he change the rules of the game. In scientific parlance, we can state this simply as the fact that energy is not created or destroyed, the laws of nature cannot be changed by our whims. Our free will is therefore not about creating and destroying the games of life, nor is it about changing the rules of the game. The choice is simply to pick the game we like to play and then play by the game's rules.

The Reality of Religion

God too has choices, and out of that choice He *prefers* to play some games more than others. Thus, He prefers the game of individuality over the game of competition, the game of respectful and mutual cordiality over the game of individuality, and the game of intimacy and love over that of respectful cordiality. However, God is not a brute who forces His choices over others. Therefore, even though He prefers certain games over other games, He still allows the soul to play the games that He doesn't personally prefer to play. Thus, in some of the games God is a reluctant participant while in others He is an eager member. God is like a kind parent who might not desire to play the games that children play, but He still acquiesces to play with the children. However, God is not a kind parent in the sense that if you decide to play a particular type of game, you cannot then bend, change, disobey, or fault the rules themselves. You are supposed to know the rules of the game before you choose the game. You cannot start playing the game and then decide that its rules are not to your liking. Knowing the rules and playing by the rules is respectively called *jnana-yoga* and *karma-yoga* in this world. If you desire to stop playing the game with God, and want to play only by yourself, the rules are called *aśtānga-yoga*. If, instead, you want to play the game of love, the rules are *bhakti-yoga*.

Every type of game can be played, and each type of game has its rules. Because each game has it rules, the knowledge and obedience to the rules constitutes *religion*. But since there are many games, there are also many types of rules, and hence many different types of religions. The game of the material world is refereed by *Brahma* and he determines the rules of the game. These rules are then described as the principles of *dharma* by *Manu* and transmitted to others through a multigenerational chain of disciples. The game of self-love is refereed by *Shiva* and He then describes a process of conquering one's desires and transcending the world of desire, to just live by oneself. The game of love with God is refereed by *Viṣṇu* and He tells us the rule of *bhakti-yoga* by which the soul and God can be mutually respectful and affectionate. Finally, the game of intimate love is refereed by *Kṛṣṇa* who also describes a different process of *bhakti-yoga* in which God and the soul intensely desire each other.

The game of *Brahma* is identical to material science, although different from *modern* science. Similarly, other games have well-defined rules, and they can be described rationally and logically, and if one agrees to play by the rules, then one can also verify that such a game can be played through practical experience. In that sense, we can conclude a few things. First, there are many religions, because ultimately all games are described in relation to God. The idea of a single religion that applies to everyone is hence false. Second, each type of religion has a different set of rules, and to play the game, we must follow the rules; there is no permanence in any game because you could break the rules, and thereby have to bear the consequences or play another game. Third, all the games are not the same from God's perspective, although the soul has the choice to play whichever game he likes. Fourth and finally, each such game can be described rationally and experienced practically; there is a practice by which you become a good, better, and best player, and you don't begin playing the game at the highest level until you become a very good player.

Everything that exists is organized like a tree, so there are innumerable types of games within the four types of games highlighted above. Each such game has different rules and nuances, so in that sense there are infinite games associated with their own rules. Each such game brings a different experience and pleasure. If you bend the rules of the game—because you don't like the rules of the game that you are currently playing—then you will be automatically transported into a different game where you can enjoy the rules of the new game. The experience of the new game is however different, and the transfer from one game to another game is called *transmigration* of the soul. If you have broken the rules of the game, then you have to pay a *penalty*. That penalty includes the transfer into a different game plus other things that you might not necessarily like, but it is a consequence of breaking the game's rules.

When you are learning the game, you have to be under the supervision of a coach—also called a *guru*—who can teach you the rules and how to improve your play. Not everyone necessarily knows the rules of the game they want to play, and not everyone necessarily has the best play to begin with. A coach can tell you about your strengths and weaknesses; you preserve the strengths and you overcome the weaknesses. In that sense, a *guru* is essential to any type of game because he enlightens you about the rules and improves your play. However, if you don't know the rules, and decide to play independently, then you will turn out to be a bad player who often breaks the rules or plays the game imperfectly, and then you will be transported into a different game.

Such *gurus*, preceptors, teachers, and sages are to be revered because they teach us about the rules of the game and help us perfect our plays. They are not God, because they did not invent the game, and they did not create its rules. In that sense, nobody can suddenly become a *guru* unless trained and ordained by a previous *guru*. The *guru* is revered like God because he assists the soul in perfecting his play and teaching him how not to break the rules. But the *guru* is not God Himself, and anyone who pretends to be one is faking it. The teachings of such teachers constitute the religious texts and they are the rules of the game to be followed. Since many games can exist, there can be many religions and texts. They correspond to the different kinds of games in existence. Not every game is the most perfect game—not from the perspective of the soul who can desire to play a different game—but from God's perspective Who has a preferential hierarchy of games. In that sense, choosing the religion and following its rules is ultimately the soul's choice. It is possible to objectively describe the hierarchy of religions and even outline if some of the rules in those games were modified erroneously, because ultimately all these games are subject to scientific—i.e., rational and empirical—scrutiny. But that hierarchy is the *space* in which the soul is free to roam according to his free will.

There is hence value in describing the hierarchy so that one can choose the better game. But there is no value in universalizing the idea of religion because that universalization constitutes the denial of free will. Interreligious studies have a value—they can be used to understand the hierarchy of games. But the choice of a religion is not to be determined by such hierarchy, because it ultimately depends on free will. The rational understanding of religion involves knowing the different games and their respective rules. But do you like a particular game and its rules—which entail a corresponding responsibility? In that sense, the soul is free to choose whichever religion he likes provided he understands its rules and consequences of disobeying them. The hierarchy of religions can also be used to understand the different games and their respective effects, and a choice should ideally be made after such understanding.

Interreligious studies are generally prevented because there is no clarity on their hierarchy and because the ego identifies with a particular religion it is unprepared to accept that their game may be inferior to other games. In fact, there is a tendency to believe that one's game is the only possible game in the universe, due to which anyone else who is not playing the same game is supposed to be doomed to hell and eternal punishment—in essence denying the choice of games. Overcoming such misconceptions is the primary goal of interreligious dialogue which reinstates free will and the choices thereby are made after understanding their consequences, plus one must know the rules of the game which cannot be disobeyed according to the chosen game.

Epilogue

Monotheism is the highest form of religion, but this religion includes, rather than precludes, the other two forms of religiosity—monism and polytheism. The religion of monism arises when the soul can experience his own existence but cannot perceive the existence of the other souls, because God is not perceived. This religion transcends the material world and involves the freedom from the cycle of actions and reactions—called *karma*. However, there is also a religion in the material world that involves the cycle of actions and reactions that involves the performance of one's duties in order to obtain freedom from *karma*. The religions called polytheistic deal with the effects of actions and their reactions, delivered through the demigods. *Karma* acts in three ways—called *ādidaivika*, *ādibhautika*, and *ādiatmika*—and creates the suffering or pleasure from one's own body and mind (*ādiatmika*), from other living entities (*ādibhautika*), and from natural phenomena under the control of demigods such as floods, droughts, earthquakes, etc. (*ādidaivika*). *Karma* is under the control of demigods who create the pairwise contacts within the body, between bodies, and between the body and other natural phenomena. In that sense, demigods are worshipped to provide favorable natural conditions such as ample rain and sunshine, fertile soil and other natural resources.

The demigods cannot change one's *karma*, however, they are still involved in delivering the results of one's *karma*. In the Vedic system, the demigods were worshipped so as to keep the natural conditions for living favorable and so the general population never has to suffer. The rulers of the land then ensured that the principles of *dharma* were upheld so that no living entity suffers due to other living beings. Once the *ādidaivika* and *ādibhautika* suffering is eliminated, one is still left with *ādiatmika* suffering—from one's own body and mind—for which the person cannot blame anyone else. Adverse *karma*, in a well-organized religious society, would therefore only manifest through one's mental and bodily diseases; moreover, such diseases cannot be cured, because the more we find cures for diseases, the more diseases will expand.

In such a situation, one is compelled to see the cause of one's suffering and this cause cannot be attributed to bad natural conditions or other living entities. Hence, you cannot pass the blame of your suffering onto others. You have to rather ask: Why am I suffering due to my own body and mind? This focuses the attention from outwardly causes and that shift in focus necessitates a person to realize that the suffering is due to their *karma* because they cannot blame anything else for their suffering. If the *ādidaivika* and *ādibhautika* sufferings are not addressed, we have a natural tendency to blame others for problems—e.g., that I am suffering because I was born in a bad situation, or because there have been droughts, earthquakes, floods, and famines. The purpose of the *dharma* in the Vedic system is for the *Brahmana* to satisfy the demigods to eliminate the suffering from natural causes, and for the *Kshatriya* to eliminate the suffering due to other living entities—e.g., criminals. If a person has adverse *karma* but is born in a law-abiding society which itself lives under the protection of demigods, then their good *karma* is spent in creating such favorable conditions, and the remaining suffering is due to body and mind. This suffering has to now be countered by healthy living and mind control.

The Vedic system thus pushes a person toward self-realization and God-realization. The self-realization takes one out of the cycle of birth and death to experience an eternal existence. God-realization further makes the person see other such liberated souls—all living in relation to God. However, if the basic principles of social organization and favorable natural conditions are not available, then the practices of self and God realization are very hard. People would remain busy fighting for survival due to natural calamities or struggling to battle the society in which they are born into. The prescription of *dharma* in society, and how disobedience to this *dharma* creates *karma* constitutes a natural law. Religion or transcendence can be practiced only in conformance with this law, not by violating it. Therefore, when we reject the existence of demigods, we neither attain salvation from material bondage, nor happiness in this life. This is indeed the situation in modern times—people are neither becoming liberated and spiritually advanced by following a religion, nor are they able to lead a comfortable life. Most people are just struggling for survival.

Therefore, while the ultimate goal of religion is monotheism, the understanding of demigods (or 'pagan gods') is essential because one cannot transcend the world without understanding *dharma* and *karma*. The personalization of nature constitutes such an understanding; it is an inferior understanding to the transcendent nature of a single God, but it is the pillar on which the soul gets liberated from the cycle of birth and death and becomes capable of seeing other spiritual beings including God. At present time, because the understanding of *dharma* and *karma* is very weak, people are simply acting without this knowledge, which means that they are continually implicated in the laws of action and reaction, which will bind them repeatedly to rebirth.

In that sense, the personalization of nature, and how nature is governed by empowered personalities is the most urgent precursor to spiritual advancement. This worship was deemphasized—and should be deemphasized—only when the understanding of *karma* is used to further the cycle of desire fulfillment, which also keeps the soul in the cycle of birth and death. There are hence legitimate reasons for both rejecting this system and for accepting it. Since this system is not the ultimate truth, it is neither eternal nor the final goal. And yet, without it one cannot lead a peaceful life, get liberated, or perceive God's existence. When religion is broadened to include polytheism, monism, and monotheism, and they are structured into a hierarchy from polytheism to monism to monotheism, then we obtain the full understanding of religion. In that state, the contradictions among various religions—so prominently seen today—disappear. At that point, many flawed concepts in religions—which arise because they reject aspects of reality in order to focus on a goal—are also nullified.

Notes and References

PREFACE

1. Kuhn, Thomas (1962). "The Structure of Scientific Revolutions". Chicago: University of Chicago Press

2. Meyer, Stephen C. (2013). "Darwin's Doubt". New York: HarperOne

3. Christensen, Clayton M. (2015). "The Innovator's Dilemma: When New Technologies Cause Great Firms to Fail". Harvard Business Review Press.

4. Odekon, Mehmet (2010). "Booms and Busts: An Encyclopedia of Economic History from the First Stock Market Crash of 1792 to the Current Global Economic Crisis". Routledge; 3rd edition.

5. Rossides, Daniel (1998). "Social Theory: Its Origins, History, and Contemporary Relevane". Rowman & Littlefield.

6. Turchin, P. (2003). "Historical Dynamics: Why States Rise and Fall". Princeton, NJ: Princeton University Press.

7. The Ontological Argument states that we can conceive of a being who is greater than everything else. Even an atheist can conceive of such a thing. Since it can be conceived, it must also exist in reality. The problem here is that if you think that everything emerged from a mathematical formula, then by the same argument such a formula must exist. The goal of an explanation must be to produce a hierarchy in which our minds are byproducts of an origin; everything that exists in my mind is not necessarily outside—e.g., my thought 'sky is purple' is only in my mind. All things in the mind aren't real; but reality includes things in my mind.

8. Pickover, Clifford (2005). "The Möbius Strip: Dr. August Mobius's Marvelous Band in Mathematics, Games, Literature, Art, Technology, and Cosmology". Thunder's Mouth Press.

9. The definition of demigods here is not the same as that used in Greek mythology, where a demigod denotes a child of gods like Zeus, which would be themselves considered demigods in the Vedic system. The literal meaning of demigod is half-god, but when demigods like Zeus are treated as gods, then their children become half-gods, and the definition is somewhat mixed with humans. Furthermore, the term 'demigod' is not a single appellation because the universe is hierarchical and there are many such demigods organized in a hierarchy like a government which has higher- and lower-level bureaucrats. All this administrative bureaucracy is called 'demigods', although some of these are indeed lower 'children' of higher administrators. Overall, the entire bureaucracy is a representation of the ruler—God.

1: INTRODUCTORY BACKGROUND

1. Harari, Yuval Noah (2014). "Sapiens". New York: Vintage.

2. This is well-known as the 'measurement problem' in atomic theory where reality exists as a possibility of being many things, but only one of those things becomes real at the point of observation. In classical physics, we could reduce the probabilities to the dynamics of a flipping coin, but in atomic theory there isn't another fundamental theory—i.e., classical mechanics which describes the flipping of the coin. As a result, we have no explanation of how the coins flip, although we can see them flipping at the point of measurement. Now, this isn't a very hard problem if we recognize that change comes from two things—possibility and purpose. The knife in your hand can be used to cut vegetables or saw through wood, and the actual use depends on the purpose you are trying to fulfill. That purpose cannot be reduced to things we can observe, because the purpose lies in the *future*. In effect, the measurement problem involves a choice of converting possibilities into reality, choice requires a purpose, and that purpose lies in the future. The problem now is that we are trying to describe how the future influences the present. Is that such a hard problem? It is, if one has accepted the dogma that the present is sufficient to describe the future. In a broadened sense of causality, the actions in the past create consequences in the future, through the judgment of right and wrong. Similarly,

we have personal ambitions about the future through the judgment of good and bad. Truth alone is inadequate for scientific predictions; we also need to induct and integrate the judgments of right and good into our scientific thinking.

3. I will revise this point later and show that we see the roles and goals *indirectly.* For example, if you are talking to an aristocrat, his body language reflects his role. Similarly, if you are talking to a happy person, their body language, tone, pitch, and so forth indicate their emotional state. Our role and goal are reflected in matter as the *style* of expression, separate from its *content.* The style is also cognitively accessible, but there is room for interpretation because the content can sometimes be interpreted as style, or vice versa. Hence, the role and goal are accessible cognitively, but it requires a more nuanced perceptual model.

4. The life story of Srinivas Ramanujan is rather illustrative in this regard. He is believed to have seen abstract ideas and theorems and used to write down those conjectures without proof. In a sense, while other mathematicians were toiling to convince themselves of the truth through paper and pencil proofs, he could directly see those objects, like we see colors and forms through our eyes. You don't feel the necessity for a 'proof' of color if you are seeing it directly. Similarly, Ramanujan did not feel the necessity for a proof for his conjectures.

5. Kuhn, Thomas S. (1996). "The Structure of Scientific Revolutions" (3rd ed.). Chicago, IL: University of Chicago Press.

6. Jung, Carl G. (1981). "The Archetypes and The Collective Unconscious, Collected Works" (2nd ed.). Princeton: Bollingen.

7. Pagans literally meant 'villagers' who worshipped the pre-Christian demigods, as opposed to the city-dwellers who first adopted Christianity. The term had a derogatory connotation built within it from the start because the villagers were considered uneducated and uncivilized relative to the sophisticated city-dwellers. Their religion was also accordingly considered inferior by the Christians. Similarly, the term 'propaganda' meant the city-dwellers spreading Christianity from the cities to the villages where the villagers (pagans) worshipped pre-Christian gods. As a result, 'pagan gods' literally means the gods of the (uncivilized) villagers.

2: OVERVIEW OF THEOGONY

1. In a tree topology, the relation of consciousness to things is the path from the soul to the individual thing—the path goes top-down and bottom-up. Similarly, the relation between things is also a path, however, this path—following the connections on the tree—ascends to the closest location of mutual attachment and then descends to the destination. The process of this ascent and descent is the same as that between the soul's connections to the world. Therefore, the relation between things and the relation to those things involve a similar process.

2. The sense of being is what "I am". Common example of such ideas of being include the roles of father, mother, child, employee, citizen, etc. All these roles are prefixed by "I am" creating our sense of being in relation to the world. We will see later that this connection between things and to things is *prāna,* which makes us aware of the world, and is the energy that enables us to act in the world. Therefore, *sat* is also called consciousness as it connects the soul to the world. It is also the force that helps the body make changes to other things. Finally, since *sat* acts in relation to the world, the activity is governed by the normative rules of morality and therefore *sat* is also the basis of all the laws of nature. The role, the force, the cause of consciousness, the cause of change, and the laws of nature are all different descriptions of the same thing, easily understood in the tree topology.

3. The universe is created in Vedic cosmology by a form called *Garbhodakśāyī Viṣṇu.* Though He is the highest, He resides at the bottom of the universe! The reason is that He represent the *chit* from which all material ingredients are created, and *chit* (representing the truth) is the lowest in the material world relative to *sat* and *ānanda.* From the navel of *Garbhodakśāyī Viṣṇu* emerges *Brahma.* Though He is subordinated to *Garbhodakśāyī Viṣṇu,* He sits at the topmost position in the universe because *sat* (consciousness, morality, laws of nature) are highest in the material world. Once *Brahma* has been created, *Rudra* who represent the material emotions is manifest. Thus, from the viewpoint of manifestation, *chit* is highest, *sat* is second, and *ānanda* is third. However, in the material world, morality subordinates desires, and desires subordinate the truth. Therefore, *sat* is highest, *ānanda* is second, and *chit* is third. If we understand this distinction we can overcome the confusion that often stems from the varied descriptions in the Vedic texts.

4. "Śrīmad-Bhāgavatam; Canto 3, Chapter 7, Verse 7". Vedabase website. Retrieved from: http://www.vedabase.com/en/sb/3/6/7.

5. This idea is called 'social constructivism' in modern sociology, and it claims that our identities—e.g., gender, race, nationalities—are socially influenced and to be a certain type of identity (e.g., male vs. female) we have to transform the social fabric. Social constructivism is often a key component of left-wing ideologies, where the fact that society is always in flux entails that we have no permanent identity. There is a corresponding spiritual version of social construction in which society is not in flux because every soul is defined in relation to an original and eternal Being. The problem is not 'social construction' but whether this construction is in relation to an absolute origin or relativized to each individual itself.

6. The father and mother of God are not the origins of God, so the relationship is not biological or material. Father and mother of God are also souls—parts of God's identity—which means God has a part of Himself which acts as His father, another part which acts as His mother, and so forth. In the present world, when a person's relationships to others are disturbed, there are two prominent ways of recovering from the problem. First, one has to revive their relationship to God. Second, one has to care for oneself as their own father, mother, child, or lover.

7. Herbert Spencer (1864), "Principles of Biology". He writes: "This survival of the fittest, which I have here sought to express in mechanical terms, is that which Mr. Darwin has called "natural selection", or the preservation of favored races in the struggle for life."

8. See Dalela, Ashish (2016). "Mystic Universe". Bangalore: Shabda Press.

9. The term 'narcissistic' generally has negative connotations because a person loves himself or herself, not anyone else. However, such a person cannot live without the other, because we still need to eat, live, work, learn, and play—which involve something other than the self. Narcissism in such cases is merely exploitation of the others for selfish ends, and it is not true narcissism in which a person is completely self-absorbed without needing or depending on anyone else. *Kṛṣṇa*'s narcissism is different because He is independent of everyone else and doesn't need to use any-one for His pleasure. The term 'narcissistic' should therefore be viewed in this con-text, not in the conventional context of exploitation.

10. Historically, in the Vedic religion the impersonal philosophers have always been worshipping *Shiva*. The reasons for this are not always made fully clear. One

reason cited by the impersonal philosophers is that the material world is *māyā* or the consort of *Shiva*. Therefore, giving up this *māyā* means entering the body of *Shiva*. Another reason for identification is that the material world is temporary, but *Brahman* is eternal. Since they are also described as *Shakti* and *Shiva*, the eternity of *Brahman* becomes *Shiva*. However, there is an even more profound reason, which manifests when we study the *Vaishnava* literature in which *Shiva* is described as *Saṅkarṣaṇa* or the embodiment of time. Then we can see more clearly why the consciousness of the soul is said to be eternal, why *sat* is identified with eternity, how eternity means time itself, and why time is personified as *kāla* which is then said to be another form of *Shiva*. Thus, when we study the different descriptions closely, we see how they are describing the same fact although in different ways as eternity vs. temporariness, *Shiva* vs. *Shakti*, *māyā* vs. *Brahman*. A closer look at the history of impersonal philosophy also affirms that the *Brahman* in question is actually not impersonalism; it is actually the body of *Shiva* but this body is different from that of *Narayana*. These two bodies are compared to milk and yogurt in the *Brahma-Samhita*. The milk is smooth and you cannot see separated particles in milk, but yogurt is granular, especially if you make yogurt at home. Thus, the meaning of granularity is that the souls who are part of *Shiva* view themselves as separate individuals whereas the soul part of *Narayana* think they are truly part of God. Therefore, *Brahman* realization is not true realization of oneness. It is oneness like the *yogurt* which remains granular; *Narayana* oneness is better oneness.

11. "Chaitanya Charitāmrita, Part 1, Chapter 5, Verse 40". Vedabase website. Retrieved from: https://www.vedabase.com/en/cc/adi/5/40.

12. There is sometimes a confusion between the 'activity' component of *chit* and the power represented by *sat* which causes this activity. We can compare these two as *change* and the *force* that causes that change. In modern science, the change is called 'motion' and the cause of that change is a mechanical 'force'. In Vedic philosophy, the changes are described conceptually—eating, sleeping, mating, defending, running, talking, writing, etc.—while the cause of that change (which acts as the force) is called *prāna*. *Prāna* is the manifestation of *sat* and it creates the role in which activities are performed. The 'force' causing changes in science is therefore replaced by the role which compels us into duty-bound activities.

13. For the reader interested in a detailed discussion of this topic, I will refer to you

my book *Gödel's Mistake* which describes how the confusion between *name* and *concept* leads to *Gödel's Incompleteness.*

14. *Turing's Halting Problem* is in essence the inability to check the semantic correctness of a program. There are two forms of semantic correctness. First, the program must finish a job. Second, it must finish the intended job. The second form of correctness follows the first. Turing's Halting Problem states that the first form of semantic correctness cannot be checked by an automated procedure or a program. As a result, the second form of semantic correctness is also impossible. The first form of correctness—namely, whether a program will finish a job—is tantamount to the program coming to a halt. It may not have done the right job, but it should at least have finished the job. The Halting Problem states that we cannot know if the program will come to a halt. This is generally made possible due to infinite loops in a program; once the program enters such a loop it never terminates, and therefore never finishes the program. Loops can be created due to *recursion* which means a function in the program calls itself, or when a function X calls another function Y which in turn calls the previous function X. Recursion represents a fractal geometry in the program by which one descends down the tree. The issue of recursion is simply that one doesn't know if the tree ever ends, or the space in which that tree has been constructed is bounded with a limit. This bound will be knowable if the root of the program represented the whole—i.e., the *meaning* of the program which is subdivided by the descent down the tree. In programming languages, this root is called the "main" function of the program but there is no way to give the "main" a meaning of what the program is truly about. As a result, there is no way to know if the tree emanating from the root is finite.

15. "Śrīmad-Bhāgavatam; Canto 3, Chapter 26, Verse 34". Vedabase website. Retrieved from: http://www.vedabase.com/en/sb/3/26/34.

16. The change in location is not a physical movement of the soul. It is the *perceived* location, or the fact that the soul believes that it is moving in space. Factually both matter and soul are stationary. However, the soul attaches itself observationally to a part of the tree and considers that to be his own body and mind. That attachment to the tree is the soul's consciousness created by *prāna.*

17. This system is sometimes called *Varṇāśrama* where *varṇa* represents the division of labor in society by identifying four classes and *āśrama* represents the

concept of guided living under the instruction of a teacher, who takes the person through different stages of life of childhood, youth, retirement, and renunciation. The social classes are called *Brahmana* the intellectuals, *Kshatriya* the warriors and administrators, *Vaisya* the businessmen, and *Sudra* or the laborers who work for the previous three classes. The *āśrama* are *Brahmacharya* or the celibate student life, *Grihastha* or the married working life, *Vānaprastha* or the retired married life, and *Saṃnyāsa* the renounced life away from family and attachments.

18. Everett, Hugh; Wheeler, J. A.; DeWitt, B. S.; Cooper, L. N.; Van Vechten, D.; Graham, N. (1973). "The Many-Worlds Interpretation in Quantum Mechanics". Princetion Series in Physics. Princeton University Press.

19. Deussen, Paul (1897). "Sixty Upanishads of the Veda". Delhi: Motilal Banarsidass.

3: THE RELIGION OF THE SUN

1. The term *prāna* is sometimes used instead of *vāyu*. These exist within the body and constitute our *choice* of what accept or reject in experience. For example, our body naturally comes into contact with different people and things in the world. However, we pay attention to some things, and we ignore other things. We are also expected to attend and ignore things based on our moral duty. *Prāna* or *vāyu* represents the awareness by which we attend or ignore to different things coming in contact with our body and mind; things that are ignored may still exist but we would not be conscious of them. Similarly, there is a distinction between doing things consciously and unconsciously. Therefore, when we speak of a 'relation', we refer not to the contact between material objects but to the choice of which contacts we pay our attention to while neglecting the others.

2. Although I use the term "motion", the bodies are not moving in the conventional sense of changing their position. Instead, the soul *changes* bodies, such that the older body becomes invisible and the newer body becomes visible. This principle of change applies equally well to our motion as to the planetary motion. In Vedic cosmology, the different positions of the planets are not the same planet in a different position but a different body—that is more appropriately called a 'state'—which becomes manifest and unmanifest. Matter is state, and soul is the object. The soul accepts different states, the states are fixed, and depending on

association with the soul the state is either manifest or unmanifest.

3. "Śrīmad-Bhāgavatam; Canto 12, Chapter 11, Verses 29-44". Vedabase website. Retrieved from: http://www.vedabase.com/en/sb/12/11/33.

4. "Śrīmad-Bhāgavatam; Canto 12, Chapter 11, Verses 45-50". Vedabase website. Retrieved from: http://www.vedabase.com/en/sb/12/11/45.

5. "Bhagavad-Gita As It Is, Chapter 8, Verses 24-25". Vedabase website. Retrieved from: https://www.vedabase.com/en/bg/8/24.

6. "Śrīmad-Bhāgavatam; Canto 7, Chapter 14, Verses 20-23". Vedabase website. Retrieved from: http://www.vedabase.com/en/sb/7/14/20.

7. The Śrimad Bhāgavatam compares this to an ant moving on a potter's wheel; the potter's wheel of the zodiac moves clockwise while the sun is the ant on the potter's wheel who moves counterclockwise. The sun's counterclockwise motion is slower than the zodiac's clockwise motion. Therefore, when the two motions are combined, the net effect is a clockwise motion and thus the sun appears to go clockwise even though its own (slower) motion is counterclockwise. There is hence a theory of the sun's 'dragging' different from the observation of celestial positions. This theory is discussed at length in my earlier book titled *Mystic Universe.*

8. At various points in this book I have spoken of material reality symbolically. Every symbol has a meaning. Therefore, when we say that the sun is a representation of *Viṣṇu* we mean that the meaning of this symbol is *Viṣṇu.* We can also say that the sun is a deity or form of *Viṣṇu* which expresses His qualities.

9. In Vedic texts, some demonic planets are inhabited by snakes. A snake is well-recognized as an ungrateful creature such that it converts milk into poison, and doesn't hesitate from biting the person who feeds and protects it.

10. These are respectively the basis of capitalistic and socialistic economics theories. In the capitalistic ideology, the government's role is minimized and the producers and consumers are allowed to freely determine the value of a commodity and whether they desire to consume it. In the socialistic ideology, the government's role is maximized—initially to control the exploitation of the deprived consumers

who are at the mercy of the producers—but eventually taking control over the economic system determining what is produced and consumed.

11. Modern science is pursued not for the sake of knowledge itself, viewing it as the source and the cause of the world. It is rather pursued for greater power of the nations, and their economic well-being. Most scientific research today has become the instrument of the military-industrial complex which doesn't have knowledge and objectivity as its primary focus. Most people publishing papers in journals employ sophisticated and complex terms although there is hardly any new content, or the meaning of that content is depraved although the presentation is embellished. The goal of the academics publishing such papers is to generate name and fame for themselves, and even if the need for fame doesn't result in outright lies, there is so much speculation mixed with facts that it is hard to separate the truth from imagination. Incessant publishing of papers—even when there are no new novel and confirmed ideas—constitutes the pursuit of fame which is used to establish the value of an academic within the system; if you aren't famous due to numerous papers you lose your job. All these are symptoms of the priority inversion in which knowledge and objectivity are subordinated to power, wealth, fame, and beauty. The culture of *Brahmans* of seeking knowledge and objectivity by keeping oneself separated from wealth, power, fame, and beauty has been gradually lost, and the net result of that change is that all the six qualities must gradually decline. This means that power will be divided into many universities pursuing diverse agendas, knowledge will be divided into innumerable scientific disciplines and journals, people will enviously refute each other's ideas by hair-splitting the trivialities in order to establish their own superiority, and the ignorance of the teachers will be masked by sophistry and complicated terminology.

12. By Basavarajtalwar (Own work) [CC BY-SA 3.0 (https://creativecommons.org/licenses/by-sa/3.0) or GFDL (http://www.gnu.org/copyleft/fdl.html)], via Wikimedia Commons. Wikipedia website. Retrieved from: https://upload.wikimedia.org/wikipedia/commons/0/0e/Melakarta.katapayadi.sankhya.72.png.

13. Sarma, Sreeramamula Rajeswara (2012). "The Katyapadi System of Numerical Notation and Its Spread Outside Kerala". Revue D'Histoire de Mathematique.

14. The middle finger is called in Vedic palmistry the finger of Saturn (which is

described as a malefic planet in the original Vedic astrology texts) and the index finger the finger of Jupiter (which is described as a benefic planet).

15. At present, 8 forms of classical dance are well-recognized. These are *Bharatanatyam*, *Kathak*, *Kuchipudi*, *Odissi*, *Kathakali*, *Sattriya*, *Manipuri* and *Mohiniyattam*. However, this diversity of dance is similar to the diversities in music and philosophy; the existence of different schools of music and philosophy doesn't necessarily indicate that they are independent, although in most cases work is needed to establish their unity and continuity from a single tradition.

16. "Hasta Mudra Gallery". Retrieved at: https://web.archive.org/web/20121219192551/http://blog.indianartz.com/gallery/hastas/

17. Carroll, Cain (2013). "Mudras of Yoga: 72 Hand Gestures for Healing and Spiritual Growth Cards". Singing Dragon.

18. Our consciousness is distinct from the senses of perception. The senses indeed 'go out' to perceive as they 'attach' to the objects being perceived. Thus Bhagavad-Gita 2.58 states: "One who is able to withdraw his senses from sense objects, as the tortoise draws his limbs within the shell, is to be understood as truly situated in knowledge." From here, we can note that the senses can go inward or outward, and to the extent that consciousness pays attention to this inward or outward movement it appears to go in or out, but factually *prāna* only controls our body and senses, and therefore it causes the inward or outward movement but it is not itself not in contact with the external world. Thus, even if we control the external world, it is through the senses being activated by *prāna*.

19. "Bhagavad-Gita; Chapter 2 Verse 62". Vedabase website. Retrieved from: https://www.vedabase.com/en/bg/2/62.

20. "Bhagavad-Gita; Chapter 7, Verse 11". Vedabase website. Retrieved from: http://www.vedabase.com/en/bg/7/11.

21. Many people will recognize this issue in modern time through the prevalence of lesbian and gay relationships in which people with similar bodies are attracted to each other because despite being in the male or female body, they experience the opposite *rasa*. However, the irony is that a lesbian feels emotionally male, and gets

attracted to another lesbian who is also feeling emotionally male. Thus, their bodies are both feminine, and their emotions are both masculine. How can a person derive true satisfaction in an emotional relationship when both partners consider themselves to be male, even though they just *appear* to be female? Factually, such relationships only help a female body to feel like a male emotionally, but they are neither physically nor emotionally compatible.

22. Arindam, Chakrabarti (2016). "The Bloomsbury Research Handbook of Indian Aesthetics and the Philosophy of Art". Bloomsbury Academic.

23. I refer to this system because the *Hindustani* classical music system was significantly influenced by modified by the *Moghul* rulers in North India. The systems have some overlap but also numerous differences in understanding.

24. Pragyabati, Singha (2006). Ph.D. Dissertation. "The Rigveda Pratisakhya: Its Phonetic and Morphological Expositions. Chapter 5." Shodhaganga Website. Retrieved from: http://hdl.handle.net/10603/92918.

4: MOON AND STAR RELIGIONS

1. "Śrīmad-Bhāgavatam; Canto 10, Chapter 1, Verse 42". Vedabase website. Retrieved from: http://www.vedabase.com/en/sb/10/1/42.

2. "Śrīmad-Bhāgavatam; Canto 10, Chapter 1, Verse 32". Vedabase website. Retrieved from: http://www.vedabase.com/en/sb/10/1/32.

3. Beck, J.S. (2011). "Cognitive Behavior Therapy: Basics and Beyond". The Guilford Press.

4. Experiments on free will by Benjamin Libet and others subsequently have reinforced this understanding of free will whereby the desires are automatically created and the observer only has the choice to reject these automatically produced desires. Libet, owing to this observation, described free will as free won't—namely our ability to discard the desire *after* they have been created. This notion of free will is consistent with the *yoga* system of philosophy where the meditative practices are used to take the mind away from such desires. They are also necessitated by morality—just because you have evil desires doesn't mean you can enact them because

there are moral strictures that prevent such actions.

5. There is a subtle but important difference between role and opportunity. For instance, I might have the opportunity to steal someone else's property, but that is not my role or duty. *Karma* enables the opportunities, but by *guna* we make the choices, and these choices are subject to the moral duties. Violation of these duties again leads to *karma* which create the new opportunities.

6. "Śrīmad-Bhāgavatam; Canto 5, Chapter 22, Verses 8-10". Vedabase website. Retrieved from: http://www.vedabase.com/en/sb/5/22/8

7. Gosvāmī, Dānavīr (2007). "Commentaries on the 5th Canto Bhāgavatam Cosmology". Rupanuga Vedic College.

8. The idea that material objects have 'desire' might sound unintuitive to many people, so we must ask: What is desire? Desire is a sense of incompleteness within us; we all feel incomplete without the other things, and desire is simply the attempt to overcome that incompleteness. Material objects too are incomplete, and they need to combine with other material objects to overcome that incompleteness. This is one of the causes of chemical reactions when we treat these reactions semantically; the other cause is *consistency.* Due to inconsistency, the molecules break apart, and due to incompleteness they combine into more complex structures. In that sense, the truth of the material symbol (caused by inconsistency) and the purpose of the object (caused by incompleteness) have physical effects and therefore the 'desire' for objects is an objective fact even within objects.

9. "Bhagavad-Gītā As It Is. Chapter 3, Verses 38-43". Vedabase website. Retrieved from: https://www.vedabase.com/en/bg/3/38.

10. "Śrīmad-Bhāgavatam; Canto 12, Chapter 2, Verses 27-28". Vedabase website. Retrieved from: https://www.vedabase.com/en/sb/12/2/27-28.

11. For an extensive discussion see my book *Mystic Universe.*

12. Wilson, H. H. (1864), "Visnu Purāna – A System of Hindu Mythology and Tradition". London: Trübner & Co.

13. As mentioned before, the 28th *Nakṣatra* is the combination of all *Nakṣatra.*

14. The law states that while the total energy is conserved, the 'work' performed by the energy must be lesser than the total energy applied. For example, when you run a motor to pump water, some amount of energy is spent usefully in pumping the water, but the pump also heats up in the process which is wasted energy. Similarly, when an electrical substation sends power to your home to drive a fan or a light bulb, some amount of energy is lost in the transmission equipment. In most cases, energy efficiency—i.e., the actual work you obtain from energy—is 80%. The remaining 20% of the energy is wasted in the process of using it.

15. As a result, in the Vedic system, there is no emphasis on mechanization and industrialization. The comfort you obtain by industrialization is always lesser than the energy you put in. Economists don't understand this problem, because it is a physics problem, not an economics problem. It is a fact of history that all modern prosperous societies were built on the hard work of slaves, by looting wealth from others, and through exploitation of the powerless, rather than industrialization. The stolen wealth and manpower were used to fuel industrialization and what was lost in the process was discounted (because it was stolen) and what was gained through the process was eulogized. Over time this wealth has been destroyed, and modern society has invented a new way of creating wealth—printing money. Anyone who understands the second law of thermodynamics understands that you will always get less than what you put in, because someone is going to take your wealth as profit or taxes. The legitimate process is only one in which what has been taken can be returned fairly. For instance, when a government charges taxes but uses the money on people's welfare, then the money is well-spent. But because economics is in the throes of industrialization, the ideology of legitimized theft still prevails. Now the governments don't return the money to the citizens; they spend it on useless activities championed by the rich and powerful, who are depicted as the leaders of economic growth as they suck the people dry.

16. The division by 3 is very standard in all places due to the modes of nature. There are two such divisions commonly prevalent. First is the division by the three aspects of cognition comprising *ādibhautika*, *ādidaivika*, and ādiatmika. The second is the division by *manas*, *prāna*, and *vāk*. If these three are combined, we obtain a division by 9. The former would mean that there is an effect of the sun on the other planets which constitutes the *ādibhautika*; the effect of such interaction

on the sun constitutes the ādiatmika; and the sun prior to such interaction is *ādidaivika*. Similarly, the cognition represented by the sun comprises of concepts, activities, and symbols that represent the concepts produced through the activity.

17. SB 11.16.27 Translation: "Among the vigilant cycles of time I am the year, and among seasons I am spring. Among months I am *Mārgaśīrṣa*, and among lunar houses I am the auspicious *Abhijit*."

18. This can explain why the *Nakṣatra* are called the lunar houses—the house of each of the wives of the moon represent the time he spends with each wife.

19. Traditionally, the prayer rosary contains 108 beads. There are also 108 Upanishads. Some people identify 108 *marma* points, or meridians in the body which—through pressure—are used to cure diseases in the body.

5: PRINCIPLES OF RELIGIOUS UNIVERSALISM

1. There can still be system of morality—called choice and responsibility—among the individuals. The demons for instance don't love God, but they have a morality of individual choice and accountability. In the modern society, we call this type of 'religion' secularism in which you work hard, pay your taxes, buy and sell things from other individuals and lead an honest life built on government laws. As long as you are comfortable and happy doing this, you don't need God. Secularism is therefore a demonic ideology. It propagates the advancement of science, democracy, liberalism—giving each person a freedom to do whatever they like—as long as they don't hurt others. However, there is simply no concept of loving God, and as a result there is also no basis on which people can love each other. Each person becomes an island onto oneself—leaning on others through economic transactions of give and take—but without a genuine stake in anyone else's life.

2. I preclude from this list the 'religion' of humanism and secularism, because the ultimate purpose of religion is transcendence from material existence, and a 'religion' that espouses morality without emphasizing transcendence can be precluded from the list of true religions. Humanism celebrates the individuality of the person with their right to self-determination and the pursuit of happiness independent of the happiness of God, although the humanist depends on the facilities provided by God, which he describes as the laws of nature. These laws are the rules of choice

and responsibility, whose violation leads one into a life of hell. However, even those who obey these laws and escape hellish life are not necessarily religious even though they might indeed be pursuing a morality of selfish pursuits in the 7 lower planetary systems. The universe is divided into two halves—of this the top half follows the religions of *Brahma* and *Shiva* compatible with the existence of *Viṣṇu* and counts as religious life. The lower half pursues the religions of *Brahma* and *Shiva* without the acceptance of *Viṣṇu*. These are irreligious lives, not just by where they exist, but by the *ideology* that they represent. Therefore, even though humanism and secularism are found in the present world—which is part of the upper half of the universe—I will not include them in the religious ideologies because they are represented in the lives of the persons in the lower half.

3. Forbidding the worship of statues, so called idolatry, comes into Christianity through Judaism and is one of the Ten Commandments. The Catholics have Jesus's sculpture on the walls of Churches and Orthodox Christians have icons depicting God Himself as well as Jesus. Therefore, even with the Abrahamic religions, there are varying degrees to which iconography is rejected. Some religions, even outside the Abrahamic religions, for instance, worship the books on God as good as God. In Sikhism for instance, only the book is worshipped. If a religion were to reject iconography completely, it would also have to reject the scripture because what is scripture if not the use of the symbols and sounds of meaning?

4. For a detailed discussion of how the soul is sometimes 'male' and at other times 'female', I refer the reader to my book Emotion. Dalela, Ashish (2018). "Emotion". Shabda Press.

5. Einstein, Albert (1949). "The World as I See It". New York: Philosophical Library.

6. "Richest 1 percent bagged 82 percent of wealth created last year - poorest half of humanity got nothing" (2018). Published on Oxfam International website. Retrieved from: https://www.oxfam.org/en/pressroom/pressreleases/2018-01-22/richest-1-percent-bagged-82-percent-wealth-created-last-year.

7. "The Laws of Manu, Chapter 1, Verses 87-93". Sacred Texts website. Retrieved from: http://www.sacred-texts.com/hin/manu/manu02.htm.

8. "The Laws of Manu, Chapter 1, Verse 31". Sacred Texts website. Retrieved from: http://www.sacred-texts.com/hin/manu/manu01.htm.

9. "The Laws of Manu, Chapter 1, Verses 87-93". Sacred Texts website. Retrieved from: http://www.sacred-texts.com/hin/manu/manu01.htm.

6: THE DIVERSITY OF RELIGIOUS VIEWS

1. There are two kinds of lineages generally employed—genealogical and philosophical. *Vaivasvata Manu* is the genealogical child of the presiding deity of the sun. However, he follows the philosophical and moral tradition of *Brahma*. In the sense that a disciple is called the "son" of his *guru*, even though the *guru* is not the biological father, similarly, *Vaivasvata Manu* is the son of his *guru Brahma*.

2. "Man". Online Etymology Dictionary. Retrieved from: https://www.etymonline.com/word/man

3. There is similarity between these 4 demigods and the 4 gods in Greek religion: Zeus (ruler of Olympian gods) has similarities to *Indra* as both wield the thunderbolt. Hades (ruler of the underworld) has similarities to *Yama* because both are rulers of hell, Poseidon (god of waters) has similarities to *Varuna* who is also the god of water, and Aphrodite (goddess of love) has similarities to *Soma* who is the god of pleasures. In Greek religion, these 4 gods were also considered siblings; although they are not siblings in Vedic descriptions, they are situated in the 4 directions and hence at the same 'level'.

4. New International Version (NIV)

5. See, for instance, in Norse mythology, the Mythical Tree Yggdrasil connecting the nine worlds: Lindow, John (2001). "Norse Mythology: A Guide to the Gods, Heroes, Rituals, and Beliefs". Oxford University Press.

6. Three expeditions mark the demolitions of the three deities:

(1) al-Uzza demolition carried out by Khalid ibn al-Walid. Reference:
Abu Khalil, Shawqi (2004). "Atlas of the Prophet's Biography: Places, Nations, Landmarks". Dar-us-Salam.

(2) al-Lat demolition carried out by Abu Sufyan ibn Harb. Reference:
Rahman al-Mubharakpuri, Saifur (2003). "Tafsir Ibn Kathir (Volume 9)". Dar-us-Salam.

(3) Manat demotion carried out by Sa'd ibn Zaid al-Ashhali. Reference:
Abu Khalil, Shawqi (2004). "Atlas of the Prophet's Biography: Places, Nations, Landmarks". Dar-us-Salam.

7. "Qur'an, Chapter 53, Verse 19". Corpus website. Retrieved from: http://corpus.quran.com/translation.jsp?chapter=53&verse=19.

8. "Qur'an, Chapter 53, Verse 20". Corpus website. Retrieved from: http://corpus.quran.com/translation.jsp?chapter=53&verse=20.

9. Rosenthal, Franz (translator) (1989). "The History of al-Ţabarī". Albany: State University of New York Press.

10. Shankarāchārya is an incarnation of *Shiva*, who rules the mode of *tamas* and the Vedic texts state that he appears to spread the illusion of impersonalism.

11. "Śrimad Bhāgavatam Canto 1, Chapter 3, Verse 24". Vedabase website. Retrieved from: https://www.vedabase.com/en/sb/1/3/24.

7: MYTHOLOGY AND PSYCHOLOGY

1. "Kant and Hume on Causality". Stanford Encyclopedia of Philosophy. Retrieved from https://plato.stanford.edu/entries/kant-hume-causality/.

2. Harvey, Peter (2001). "Buddhism". Bloomsbury Academic.

IMAGES

Cover background image: "AdobeStock_477" (image ID: #47730035) by DavidMSchrader, AdobeStock Extended License by CS Begu, order number ADB035214020BE

Figure-4: "Biological classification" by Peter "Pengo" Halasz (released by the author into the public domain). Retrieved from:

https://en.wikipedia.org/wiki/File:Biological_classification_L_Pengo_vflip.svg

Figure-12: "Nervous system diagram" by Persian Poet Gal (released by the author into the public domain. Retrieved from:

https://commons.wikimedia.org/wiki/File:Nervous_system_diagram.png

Figure-22: "Sarasvati Ancient River" by Io Herodotus is licensed under Creative Commons BY-SA 4.0. Retrieved from:

https://commons.wikimedia.org/wiki/File:Sarasvati-ancient-river.jpg

Figure-23: "NordNordWest - Spreading homo sapiens ru" by Urutseg (released by the author into the public domain). Retrieved from:

https://commons.wikimedia.org/wiki/File:Spreading_homo_sapiens_la.svg

Figure-24: "Al-Uzza Allat Manate colorate" by Djahuti (released by the author into the public domain). Retrieved from:

https://commons.wikimedia.org/wiki/File:Al-Uzza_Allat_Manat_colorate.jpg

Index

www.ingramcontent.com/pod-product-compliance
Lightning Source LLC
Chambersburg PA
CBHW031943090426
42739CB00006B/62
* 9 7 8 9 3 8 5 3 8 4 1 1 0 *